DEDICATION

I dedicate this book to the Holy Spirit of Jesus. For without Him, I would not have known that I needed a Savior. But because of His faithfulness concerning the things of Jesus, I am a child of the Son of the living God. Without His guidance and instructions, I would not know which way to go or what decisions to make that line up best with the word of the Lord, for His purpose and will for my life.

His counsel always is steadfast and true. His teachings are without flaw. The depth of His knowledge brings me comfort in knowing that He knows what is best for my family and me. He never has lied to me and never will because He cannot lie, as He is the Spirit of truth.

Jesus living in me today is more real and more alive than He has ever been because of the workings of His Holy Spirit within my life. His gifts are miraculous and never grievous, as I see them operating through myself and through other believers in such a way that is undeniably God the Father and Jesus the Son doing the works through His Holy Spirit that dwells in us.

His faithfulness to Jesus's children is without equal by any standard of protection and provision. He is, without a doubt, in my mind and heart, the best comforter, helper, teacher, and counselor that I have ever had in my entire sixty-three years of living on His earth. Without Jesus baptizing me in His Holy Ghost (Spirit), with the evidence of speaking in tongues, I am sure where I would be—lost and undone, without God or His Son.

He brings Jesus to me in ways that only one could wish for. His presence and power sustain me at every turn and are as necessary as the air that I breathe. He fills me with His presence and power for the work of God. I highly recommend that you throw out all your previous prejudices and preferences when it comes to the Holy Spirit.

The Bible's subject on the Holy Spirit of Jesus, concerning Him baptizing His believers who asked Him for the promised gift of His power and authority, may be controversial, but according to the Bible, the Holy Spirit is just as real and needful today as He was then.

ACKNOWLEDGMENTS

Rosalyn A. Hamrick	Proofreader
James J. Hamrick	Cover Graphics
Author	Foreword
Cimperman & Co. Photography	Author's Portrait
33 Vine Avenue, Sharon, PA 16146	
724-342-6131	

Written in Bedford County, Virginia, on God's thirty acres of land with the most beautiful view of the Peaks of Otter in the Blue Ridge Mountains that we see daily.
Began writing: 3-1-2015 Date Completed: 7-31-2015

CONTENTS

Foreword 9
Introduction 13

Chapter 1   Baptism of the Holy Spirit 17
Chapter 2 25
Chapter 3 29
Chapter 4 36
Chapter 5 45
Chapter 6 53
Chapter 7 64
Chapter 8 74
Chapter 9 83
Chapter 10 96
Chapter 11 107
Chapter 12 117
Chapter 13   Gifts Jesus Gives to Men Part 1 134

Chapter 14	Gifts Jesus Gives to Men—Part 2	149
Chapter 15	Gifts of the Holy Spirit—Part 1	162
Chapter 16	My Personal Experience	179
Chapter 17	Origins of Demons	186
Chapter 18	Gifts of the Holy Spirit—Part 2	201
Chapter 19	Gifts of the Holy Spirit—Part 3	217
Chapter 20	Fruit of the Holy Spirit—LOVE	235
Chapter 21	Fruit of the Holy Spirit—JOY	249
Chapter 22	Fruit of the Holy Spirit—PEACE	264
Chapter 23	Fruit of the Holy Spirit—LONG-SUFFERING	286
Chapter 24	Fruit of the Holy Spirit—KINDNESS	295
Chapter 25	Fruit of the Holy Spirit—GOODNESS	306
Chapter 26	Fruit of the Spirit —Rightly Dividing the Word of Truth	321
Chapter 27	Fruit of the Holy Spirit—FAITH	344
Chapter 28	Fruit of the Holy Spirit—GENTLENESS	362
Chapter 29	Fruit of the Holy Spirit—SELF-CONTROL Part 1	377
Chapter 30	Fruit of the Holy Spirit—SELF-CONTROL Part 2	394

Closing Thoughts and Summary 405
What Must I Do to Be Saved? 431

FOREWORD

As I sat at my computer one day reading various post on Facebook, I notice that there was only a few that mentioned the Holy Spirit. When they did mention Him, it mostly was when the Father, Son and Holy Ghost, was in a statement or prayer.

I searched even further for a deeper image of Him, even to asking questions about Him on the various posts that were presented. What I found, was nothing short of amazing to me. Many Christians did not know a great deal about Him, and I would say that many fell under the category of Job, in the 42nd Chapter verse 5 which reads. *"I have heard of You by the hearing of the ear, But now my eyes sees You. Therefore I abhor myself, And repent in dust and ashes." NKJV.*

This of course we know, was before Job had gone through his greatest trials of losing everything, including his family, he had only heard of God and believed in Him. Like Job, this is where many of the Church is today, not only with God the Father, but with Jesus His Son and His Holy Spirit.

While faith comes by hearing and hearing by the word of God, once faith comes to a believer and they call upon Jesus to be saved, then we are to grow in the grace and knowledge of our Lord and Savior Jesus Christ. This growth process is all too often stunted when a believer does not take full advantage of the promised gift of the Father, which is Jesus and His Spirit.

Once Job had experienced God in all his lose and pain, he cried out to God and repented for not knowing Him better prior to his trial. Where once he only heard about God, his own eyes seen Him at work in his own life, and because of this, everything was turned around for Job. We need a turn-around moment in the Church today!

After realizing that many believers did not have a close relationship with Jesus's Spirit, I started posting information from God's word about Him, pertaining to the Baptism of the Holy Spirit according to the scriptures, His gifts, and His fruit. With each post, I tried to limit them to as short as possible, but the information can be overwhelming if you present your case properly.

After noticing I was on Part 22, and each of these Part's was anywhere from 3 to sometimes 9 or 10 pages long, the thought came to me that this would make a great book, with each part being a Chapter. I had the peace of God in the matter, so I immediately stopped posting and began editing each Part with an informative book in mind.

Half way through I realized that the Holy Spirit of Jesus Christ our Savior was the one that is in control of all operations of not only the Church, but the World as well. A truth I have known for 37 years, but compiling all this information together in one place, brought life to it in a way that I have not experienced.

The Holy Spirit, the One who "letteth", will let, until he be taken out of the way. KJV 2 Thess. 2:7. The NKJV reads *"For the mystery of lawlessness is already at work, only He who now restrains will do so until He is taken out of the way."* We know this is the taking away of the Church when the rapture is activated and all believers unite with Jesus to receive their glorified bodies.

Thus, "The Operative" was created for the believers in Christ to obtain the relationship with the Holy Spirit as Jesus and the Father initially intended. This, I believe is the great awakening of these last days that will usher in an unprecedented true Holy Ghost Revival within the Church, and the World will see who they are in the light of who Jesus is, in each believer, and they too will repent, because of the goodness and the love of God!

THE OPERATIVE

Like Job, many will cry out, *"I have only heard of you Lord with the hearing of my ears, but now I see you with my own eyes!"* It is my prayer that "The Operative" will take each reader there, as the Church catches the vision of who Jesus's Holy Spirit truly is.

INTRODUCTION

Have you ever struggled with a topic in the Bible that you just knew had more to it than what you were being taught or have learned on your own? I believe that being baptized with the Holy Spirit, with the evidence of speaking in tongues, is one of those topics. Many believers struggle with this topic in their walk of faith with Jesus Christ, while others just pass it off like a fleeting thought.

Much of this has to do with a lack of knowledge of the truth about this second baptism that the Bible is very clear on. Fear is another reason why many believers sidestep this topic and do not fellowship with those who are baptized in the Holy Ghost. Yet it was Jesus Himself who said that He would send another comforter, because while He was in the flesh during His earthly ministry, the Holy Spirit was in Him in fullness, and Jesus, in the flesh, was the comforter at that time during His three-and-a-half years of ministry on earth.

It was not until He was crucified and raised from the dead and seated at the right hand of the Father that the plan and design of God enabled Him to return to His Church during this dispensation via His Holy Ghost, which, according to the scriptures, He was faithful to do so by sending the other comforter. And through studying the word of God, we know that the other comforter is His Holy Spirit of promise.

If you were the enemy of the Church, and you wanted to remove the power that it began with, wouldn't you tell lies to those who would listen and repeat these same lies throughout their lives, knowing that many family members and friends would continue with these lies from one generation to the next—that is, until somebody within that lineage heard and accepted the truth and changed the course of their destiny by speaking words of truth about the Church's power?

This is what our adversary, the devil, has done when it comes to people talking about the baptism of the Holy Spirit within many churches throughout the world. Traditions of this lie were passed down from generation to generation until several denominations were formed that continue to speak evil lies concerning the baptism of the Holy Spirit.

But God is arming believers in these last days with His truth concerning this topic, and many are hearing what the Spirit of the Lord is saying and are experiencing the results for themselves. The benefits of being baptized with the Holy Spirit by Jesus Christ, who is the baptizer, are eternal gifts of power and substance of God the Father and Jesus, His Son.

Come with me on a spiritual journey, probably like none other you have taken. Find out the who, what, when, and where of this miraculous gift given to all believers who ask Jesus for this gift during these last days that we are living in.

Discover just how connected we all are in the body of Christ and why. Explore the hows and the whys through which the gifts of the Holy Spirit operate, through the believers who are baptized in the Holy Spirit. Search the scriptures with me to learn why God chose "tongues" as the evidence of the believer's baptism or being filled with His Son's Holy Spirit and whether or not they have ceased to exist, like some still believe.

Learn the purpose the Lord has in allowing His Holy Spirit's fruit to grow within us and why we need His Holy Spirit dwelling within us in this capacity to ensure that His fruit grows not only properly but also strong within each believer in the power of His might.

THE OPERATIVE

Many questions will be answered by the word of God as the final authority regarding this topic. As you learn to rightly divide (understand) the word of God, you will acknowledge that by doing so correctly, your spiritual growth will be as planned by God. Not learning how to rightly divide the word of truth could very well be detrimental to your spiritual well-being.

If you, as a believer in Christ, want to really know the truth about the baptism of the Holy Spirit, then *The Operative* is the book that you need to read. You need to know that Jesus makes Himself available to all who ask Him for His Holy Spirit of promise. God's word and it alone will be the guide and the light that will bring us out of darkness pertaining to this topic while shining His marvelous and glorious light upon the baptism of the Holy Spirit with the evidence of speaking in tongues, revealing the truth about His Holy Spirit's relevance for today, while Jesus remains seated at the right hand of the Father.

Enjoy!

Serving people Christ,
James J. Hamrick
President and Founder of
Catch the Vision Ministries

CHAPTER 1

Baptism of the Holy Spirit

"And it happened, while Apollos was at Corinth, that Paul, having passed through the upper regions, came to Ephesus. And finding some disciples, he said to them, 'Did you receive the Holy Spirit when you believed?' So they said to him, 'We have not so much as heard whether there is a Holy Spirit.' And he said to them, 'Into what then were you baptized?' So they said, 'Into John's baptism.' Then Paul said, 'John indeed baptized with a baptism of repentance, saying to the people that they should believe on Him who would come after him, that is, on Christ Jesus.' When they heard this, they were baptized in the name of the Lord Jesus. And when Paul had laid hands on them, the Holy Spirit came upon them, and they spoke with tongues and prophesied. Now the men were about twelve in all." (Acts 19:1–7)

Being a born-again believer for thirty-seven years and a minister for over thirty, I have often been asked about the baptism in the Holy Spirit. There have been several different questions such as, "Is there such an event found in the Bible?" and "Is this baptism still for today?" and "Is it even necessary for Christians today to be filled with the Holy Spirit with the evidence of speaking in tongues to make it to heaven?"

The answers to each of these questions and more will be given throughout this book referencing scriptures in the Bible. My personal opinion will never be given. While on occasion I may give a personal experience or two, in the end it must be the total sum of all references that the Lord has given to us that will lead you to the right conclusions.

After acquiring that which the Bible teaches, then and only then will you have enough information to make up your own mind about the subject of the Holy Spirit and His relevance for today!

(No matter what you have been taught or have accepted as truth, I suggest that we take a new scriptural journey together and learn why we need the Holy Spirit's power for <u>our</u> Christian walk today!)

By taking the time to look into the eternal words of God and knowing what "thus saith the Lord" concerning a matter, you will find that it will make all the difference in the world to you. These truths alone do not apply pressure to your situation or circumstance. You must apply the truth you know to them, to create pressure to change them.

I do not believe that the baptism in the Holy Spirit is a "heaven or hell" issue—meaning that one will not make it into heaven if they are not filled with the Holy Spirit. To the contrary, it is God's grace that is sufficient to get all believers into heaven. However, you will find that being filled with the Holy Spirit, according to the scriptures, gives the believer powerful benefits needed during this life on earth to enjoy His abundant life, which is more than just money, I might add.

You may ask, <u>"Why receive it, then?"</u> I am convinced that because of this attitude, a large majority within the body of Christ does not seek after this promise. During the time it takes to read this book, my prayer is that you will be able to see and understand for yourself not only what the Bible has to say about this wonderful gift from God but also its operation and purpose. After reading and studying these scriptures with an open mind, I am quite positive that you will decide this gift *is* from the Father and given to believers through the works of Jesus and is relevant for today. There is no better place to start than with the <u>prophecy of this gift.</u>

"And it shall come to pass afterward that I will pour out My Spirit on all flesh; your sons and Your daughters shall prophesy, Your old men

THE OPERATIVE

shall dream dreams, Your young men shall see visions. And also on My menservants and on My maidservants I will pour out My Spirit in those days." (Joel 2:28–29)

Hundreds of years before John the Baptist was born, God revealed to man through the prophet Joel that the day would come when the operative in this world, and His Church today, would be His Holy Spirit.

God planned to pour out His Spirit upon all who would believe and receive the promise of this great gift before the foundations of the world. It would be John who first mentioned this gift in the New Testament when he said, *"I indeed baptize you with water unto repentance, but He who is coming after me is mightier than I, whose sandals I am not worthy to carry. He will baptize you with the Holy Spirit and fire" (Matthew 3:11). (See also Mark 1:8.)*

The *He* John was talking about was his cousin, Jesus of Nazareth. This first mention of another baptism from the person chosen by God who was baptizing in water for the remission of sins was significant. John the Baptist was now telling us about another baptism other than his water baptism. John distinctly separated the two baptisms—one in water for the remission of sins and the other in fire wherein Jesus baptized with the Holy Spirit. This could not be clearer.

God's use of John the Baptist to change the dispensation that men were living under was from the *law*, which governed Israel and strangers (Gentiles) who would adhere to the statutes and regulations of God, unto the next dispensation of *grace*. Under the *law*, the high priest, once a year, made sacrifices for each person, placing their offerings on the altar, thus covering their sins for another year. For those who believed and practiced this, upon their death, their spirit and soul went into paradise, and their bodies were buried. (There will be more on paradise in later chapters.)

<u>This dispensation changed with the ministry of John the Baptist.</u> All those who believed John's preaching were submerged in water, symbolizing that their sins had been washed away; thus, God would *not* hold their sins against them any longer in judgment.

Today, the Church still practices water baptism as one of the sacraments. This short-lived dispensation changed once again as God accepted the blood of Jesus shed at Calvary's cross, <u>once and for all</u>. No other way or sacrifice would ever be needed to cleanse men from their sin than *Jesus's* shed blood and its acceptance by God the Father.

John <u>paved the way</u> for Jesus to come on the scene to start His ministry. Water baptism <u>paved the way</u> for the blood of Jesus to wash our sins away, for all of us who believe that God sent Jesus as His only Son, who died in our stead. Those who believe will call upon Jesus's name to be saved as God's new and final way to deal with men and sin in their lives.

Water remains symbolic of this powerful act today, as Christians are baptized in water as a testimony, believing that God sent His only Son, Jesus, to die for them. It symbolizes the old man (dead to the things of God) dying as he is going under the water, and the new man (now alive to the things of God) is washed clean coming out of the water, representing the removal of his sin.

This practice of water baptism, although symbolic in nature, *does not* cleanse our sin away *today*, as only the blood of Jesus can do that. Obedience to water baptism is, however, a first step in testifying to men what the Lord has done for them. It is a powerful witnessing tool, and water baptism joins the rank of other symbols of the acceptance of Jesus Christ as one's Savior, such as the receiving of communion, another sacrament of the Church. Wine symbolizes the blood, and bread symbolizes the body of Jesus. These we partake of as we remember all that Jesus has done for us at Calvary.

During John's ministry, he spoke of one coming after him who would baptize in something other than water. This now introduces us to the other baptism wherein only Jesus Himself baptizes all men (inclusive) who believe in Him and ask Him for this baptism.

"I indeed baptize you with water unto repentance, but He who is coming after me is mightier than I, whose sandals I am not worthy to carry. He will baptize you with the Holy Spirit and fire." Matthew 3:11.

You see, there are two separate baptisms that John preached and taught. One is being submerged in actual $H2O$ (water) for the remission of sins, but only for a brief dispensation of grace acceptable by God until the time Jesus is raised from the dead. After Jesus provided His eternal blood, once and for all, for those that believe in Him, His blood and His blood alone is the current agent that washes sin away, not water. Once God sees the blood of Jesus applied by faith, He never remembers our sins again.

Today, we are still living in this dispensation of God's grace. However, the change that is made by the Lord is from <u>whosoever will come and be baptized in water</u> for the remission of sins to <u>whosoever shall call upon the name of Jesus shall be saved</u>, having their sins washed away with the eternal life-giving blood of Jesus.

In other words, that which was originally written against us in the law was washed clean with no record of sin for all that applied the blood of Jesus to their lives <u>through faith</u>.

As per John's own words, Jesus Himself "baptizes with the Holy Spirit and fire." The scriptures are very clear that during His three-and-a-half years of ministry on earth, Jesus baptized no man: *"Therefore, when the Lord knew that the Pharisees had heard that Jesus made and baptized more disciples than John (though Jesus Himself did not baptize, but His disciples) He left Judea and departed again to Galilee" (John 4:1–3).*

Once Jesus knew that the Pharisees were trying to give Him credit for the baptisms that were being done by the disciples, He left the area to show this to be false, as John and his disciples continued the practice, along with the twelve disciples of Jesus.

Many believe that once a person is born again, they are automatically filled with the Holy Spirit. When we correctly divide or understand what the scriptures teach, we realize that there is no automatic association with being baptized with the Holy Spirit. Since we are not automatically filled with the Holy Spirit, then how do believers become baptized or filled with the Holy Spirit and fire by Jesus?

First, as a foundation, let's establish a few fundamental truths, beginning with the fact that no person can be born again without the Holy Spirit drawing him/her unto Jesus:

"Jesus answered and said to him, 'Most assuredly, I say to you, unless one is born again, he cannot see the kingdom of God.'" (John 3:3)

"No one can come to Me unless the Father who sent Me draws him; and I will raise him up at the last day." (John 6:44)

"And when He has come, He will convict the world of sin, and of righteousness, and of judgment: of sin, because they do not believe in Me; of righteousness, because I go to My Father and you see Me no more; of judgment, because the ruler of this world is judged." (John 16:8–11)

The Holy Spirit is whom Jesus is talking about that God uses to draw men to His Son, Jesus. Upon experiencing being born again, each believer obtains a new spirit as his or her sins are forgiven and washed clean with the blood of Jesus. This happens upon acceptance of Jesus Christ as your Lord and Savior. In order to receive this forgiveness and new life, man's part is to call upon Him to be saved.

"Therefore, if anyone is in Christ, he is a new creation; old things have passed away; behold, all things have become new." (2 Cor. 5:17)

This "2 Corinthians 5:17" experience makes the born-again believer's spirit man compatible with that of Jesus so that He now can live His life in our bodies while abiding in our spirit.

"I am crucified with Christ: nevertheless I live; yet not I, but Christ liveth in me: and the life which I now live in the flesh I live by the faith of the Son of God, who loved me, and gave himself for me." (Gal. 2:20, KJV)

That is the work of the Holy Spirit, pertaining to the born-again experience. He draws us to Jesus by convincing us of sin, righteousness, and judgment. Once we call upon His name to be saved, the Holy Spirit exchanges our old spirit with a new spirit, and all things become new—except the physical body, that is.

Our <u>new spirit,</u> along with our soul, remains within the body given to us at birth, and the life we live in it has begun a process of changing or transforming into the likeness of Jesus Christ our Savior.

Do you notice in any of these scriptures anything about us being filled with the Holy Spirit when we are born again? Even John 3:16 reads, "For God so loved the world that He gave His only begotten Son, that whoever believes in Him should not perish but have everlasting life."

In John 6:28–29 Jesus's disciples said to Him, *"What shall we do, that we may work the works of God?" Jesus's answer to them was, "This is the work of God, that you believe in Him whom He sent."*

Believing in Jesus is actually considered part of working the works of God. Once we believe in Him (Jesus) whom He (God) sent, we are considered by God to have begun working His works in our lives. <u>This is the born-again experience!</u>

As we read God's word further, we will find that all those who are born again become qualified to receive the baptism of the Holy Spirit with the evidence of speaking in tongues. This will become clearer as we continue our journey of searching out the truth of what the Bible says about this baptism of the Holy Spirit and the benefits we receive from this early Church experience.

We know that Joel, the prophet, foretold this event sometime during the eighth or ninth century BC. I think we can agree that was a very long time ago. But nonetheless, God revealed to Joel that the day would come when He would make His Spirit available to all flesh, both young and old.

John the Baptist confirmed this when he said, "There is one coming after me, baptizing with the *Holy Spirit* and *fire*." According to the scriptures, Jesus never baptized anyone with water. He delegated this responsibility to His disciples to administer the baptisms. With this truth in mind, what was John talking about, then, that Jesus would baptize with the Holy Spirit and fire? Let's dig deeper into the scriptures to find the answers.

Before continuing, *now* is an excellent time for you to read John's Gospel—chapters 14–17—all in one sitting, then read Acts 2. Once you finish reading these scriptures, return and we'll proceed.

* * *

Thanks for taking the time to read the above mentioned chapters. In John 14:17, Jesus says that the Holy Spirit is called the Spirit of truth. He also calls Him the comforter and teacher, as He, the Holy Spirit, takes the things of Jesus instructing us with these truths. You see, the Holy Spirit is *not* an *it* as some believe. On the contrary, He is always to be referred to as *He*, in the masculine gender. We too must always refer to Him as such when addressing Him or talking to others about Him.

The Holy Spirit is the third character or personage of God. God the Father (He), God the Son (He), and God the Holy Spirit (He)—these make up what we know as the Holy Trinity. There is one God with each personage or character, having His own responsibilities, each doing their part in the creation and redemption of man, including the judgment of man, along with the judgment of the devil and all his followers.

Learning more about the event that seemingly so many Christians deny the existence of in the Church today will prove very beneficial to your personal walk with the Lord.

Each believer needs to realize that the main character involved with creation before mankind, the creation of mankind, and through Calvary and throughout all eternity is the *Holy Spirit* (the Holy Spirit of God the Father and Jesus the Son.)

He, the Holy Spirit, has been and is the operative of not only the world but the Church as well. To believe Him to be lesser than He is would be a travesty. Like with most things, a lack of knowledge breeds fear of that person or thing. In this case, a lack of knowledge of who He is and how He operates in our lives would allow a degree of the spirit of fear into a believer's life.

We can safely say that acquired knowledge of the Holy Spirit will dispel any spirit of fear that the devil tries to use to short-circuit the power of the Holy Spirit in our lives.

Since we know that the spirit of fear does not come from God, gaining as much knowledge and understanding about the Holy Spirit as possible will work to our benefit greatly. The Bible contains a wealth of knowledge about all that we need to know about God the Father; Jesus, His Son; and their Holy Spirit.

This is why it is so important for a believer in Christ to always go to the word of God, concerning every matter in their life. We should treat this information as if it were instrumental to our health and well-being, because it is.

Before we look deeper into this subject in the book of Acts and other areas of the Bible, the next chapter begins the process of acquiring further knowledge of the Holy Spirit. It is He that takes the things of Jesus and teaches them to each of us so that we can know the truth, and the truth that we will know and apply will set us free.

CHAPTER 2

Taking time to read about the Holy Spirit—which many believers only know *of* by the hearing instead of *knowing* by seeing Him in operation in their lives—is wise. Learning gives experiences that will allow you to become more acquainted with the one who called you unto salvation. These are two different and distinct ways to believe in God.

"I have heard of You by the hearing of the ear, But now my eye sees You." (Job 42:5)

All Job's life, he heard of God. But when he went through his personal trials and tests, with God bringing him through each of them, he *saw* or experienced God's intervention firsthand in his life. I challenge you to see God instead of just hearing about Him, allowing Him to empower your Christian experience by His Holy Spirit.

Scriptures interpret scriptures, and they conclude that being filled with the Holy Spirit, according to the scriptures, is actually a gift given to us by God the Father and Jesus, His Son. They show us that this baptism of the Holy Spirit and fire is a separate experience from that of being born again and water baptized.

"Why is it a different experience?" you may ask. "Did I not receive the filling of the Holy Spirit when I was born again?" I will not try to reinvent the wheel here, so I will quote the writings of C. I. Scofield, DD, and his footnotes on the Holy Spirit from *The New Scofield Study Bible*. Pay very special attention to footnote number 3. Enjoy!

C. I. Scofield, DD, footnotes on the Holy Spirit.
The Holy Spirit, N.T., Summary:

1. *The Holy Spirit is revealed as a divine Person. This is expressly declared (e.g. Jn. 14:16–17, 26; 15:26; 16:7–15; cp. Mt. 28:19), and everywhere implied.*
2. *The revelation concerning Him is progressive: (a) In the O.T. (see Zach. 12:10) He comes upon whom He will, apparently without reference to conditions in them. (b) During His earth-life, Christ taught His disciples (Lk. 11:13) that they might receive the Spirit through prayer to the Father, (c) At the close of His ministry He promised that He would Himself pray to the Father, and that in answer to His prayer the Comforter would come to abide (Jn 14:16–17). (d) On the evening of His resurrection, He came to the disciples in the upper room and breathed on them saying, "Receive ye the Holy Spirit" (Jn. 20:22), but He instructed them to wait before beginning their ministry until the Spirit should come upon them (Lk. 24:49; Acts 1:8), (e) On the day of Pentecost the Spirit came upon the whole body of believers (Acts 2:1–4). (f) After Pentecost the Spirit was imparted to such as believed, in some cases by the laying on of hands (Acts 8:17; 9:17). And (g) with Peter's experience in the conversion of Cornelius (Acts 10) it became clear that the norm for this age was that Jew and Gentile were to be saved on precisely the same conditions, and the Holy Spirit was to be given without delay to those who met the one essential condition to trust in Christ (Acts 10:44; 11:15, 18). This is the permanent fact for the entire Church Age. Every believer is born of the Spirit (Jn. 3:3–6; 1 Jn. 5:1); indwelt by the Spirit, whose presence makes the believer's body a temple (1Cor. 6:19; cp. Rom. 8:9–15; Gal. 4:6; 1 Jn. 2:27); and baptized with the Spirit (1Cor. 12:12–13; 1 Jn. 2:20,27), thus sealing him for God (Eph. 1:13; 4:30).*
3. *The New Testament distinguishes between having the Spirit, which is true of all believers, and being filled with the Spirit, which is the Christian's privilege and duty. (cp. Acts 2:4 with*

4:29–31; Ephesians 1:13–14 with 5:18). *There is one baptism with the Spirit, but many fillings with the Spirit.*

4. *The Holy Spirit is related to Christ in His conception (Mt. 1:18–20; Lk. 1:35), baptism (Mt.3:16; Mk. 1:10; Lk. 3:22; Jn. 1:32–33), walk and service (Lk. 4:1, 14), resurrection (Rom. 8:11), and as His witness throughout this age (Jn. 15:26; 16:8–11, 13–14).*

5. *The Spirit forms the Church (Mt. 16:18; Heb. 12:23) by baptizing all believers into the body of Christ (1Cor. 12:12–13: cp. The universal address, 1Cor. 1:1–2); imparts gifts for service to every member of that body (1Cor. 12:7–11, 27-30); guides the members in their service (Acts 16:6–7); and is Himself the power of that service. (Acts 1:8; 2:4; 1Cor.2:4).*

6. *The Spirit abides in a company of believers, making of them, corporately, a temple (1Cor. 3:16–17).*

7. *The N. T. indicates a threefold personal relationship of the Spirit to the believer: "with", "in", "upon" (Jn. 14:16–17; 1Cor. 6:19; Acts 1:8). "With" indicates the approach of God to the soul, convicting of sin (Jn. 16:9), presenting Christ as the object of faith (Jn 16:14, imparting faith (Eph. 2:8), and regenerating (Mk. 1:8; Jn 1:33). "In" describes the abiding presence of the Spirit in the Christians body (1Cor. 6:19) to give victory over the flesh (Rom. 8:2–4; Gal. 5:16–17), create the Christian character (Gal. 5:22–23), help infirmities (Rom. 8:26), inspire prayer (Eph. 6:18) give conscience access to God (Eph. 2:18), actualize to the Christian his sonship (Gal. 4:6), apply the Scriptures in cleansing and sanctification (Eph. 5:26;2 Th. 2:13; 1 Pet. 1:2), comfort and intercede (Acts 9:31; Rom. 8:26), and reveal Christ (Jn. 16:14). "Upon" is used of the relationship of the Holy Spirit to the Lord Jesus Christ (Mt. 3:16; Mk. 1:10; Lk. 4:18; Jn. 1:32–33), to the Virgin Mary in connection with the incarnation and birth of our Lord (Lk. 1:35), to certain designated disciples (Lk. 2:25 [Simeon]; Acts 10:44–45; 11:15 [household of Cornelius]; Acts 19:6 [disciples at Ephesus]), and to believers generally (Lk 24:49; Acts 1:8; 2:17; 1 Pet. 4:14). Based on*

Lk. 4:18, some understand that the expression has to do with anointing for special service for God, as well as with the original coming and indwelling of the Holy Spirit to and in the individual Christian.

8. *Sins against the Spirit, committed by unbelievers, are: to blaspheme (Mt. 12:31), resist (Acts 7:51), and insult (Heb. 10:29, "hath done spite"), Christians' sins against the Spirit are: (1Th. 5:19). The right attitude toward the Spirit is yieldedness to His way in life and service, and constant willingness for Him to "put away" whatever grieves Him or hinders His power (Eph. 4:31)*

9. *The symbols of the Spirit are: (a) oil (Jn. 3:34; Heb. 1:9); (b) water (Jn. 7:38–39); (c) wind (Jn. 3:8; Acts 2:2); (d) fire (Acts 2:3); (e) a dove (Me. 3:16); (f) a seal (Eph. 1:13; 4:30); and (g) an earnest, or pledge (Eph. 1:14)*

CHAPTER 3

From the scriptures in the Bible, we know that all believers—that is, Jesus's twelve disciples—and all others who *believe* that God sent His only Son, Jesus, to die for all our sins and rise from the dead to give us eternal life believed the same things during the early Church age.

According to scriptures, the early Church believers knew these truths given to them from Jesus Himself (during His three-and-one-half years of ministry plus the forty days He spent with them periodically after His resurrection).

There appears to be two prerequisites before receiving *eternal life*, according to the scriptures. If you do not believe these two truths, you cannot and will not be born again.

1. "Then they said to Him, *'What shall we do, that we may work the works of God?' Jesus answered and said to them, 'This is the work of God, that you believe in Him whom He sent.'" (John 6:28–29)* (A person must believe that God sent His Son.)
2. *"For God so loved the world that He gave His only begotten Son, that whoever believes in Him should not perish but have everlasting life." (John 3:16)* (A person must believe that Jesus was the only Son of God sent by God Himself.)

Based on these two prerequisites, we know that, eventually, the disciples and all those who believed these truths, then and today, became born again (a change of mind and change of course).

During the time Jesus walked with the disciples (Jewish men coming out of the *Law* of Moses), none of them, to that point, had this *grace* to believe. Their thinking was from the viewpoint of the law, which no man could ever keep. The *law* revealed that "all have sinned and fallen short of God's glory." Their thinking was, when was Jesus going to set up His new kingdom here on earth?

However, once Jesus came, His message of believing that God had sent Him for the salvation of the world was all that was needed to change their minds and hearts when they truly heard it and believed.

With this in mind, it is safe to say that all the followers of Jesus during His life, death, burial, and resurrection were considered by God to be born again. They were walking in the light of God's word and truths, given to them by the teachings of Jesus. His words changed their hearts and minds and all others who heard them, for His words are spirit and life.

"It is the Spirit who gives life; the flesh profits nothing. The words that I speak to you are spirit, and they are life." (John 6:63) So then, it was the Holy Spirit of Jesus that was actually taking the words He spoke and giving them life and understanding to the listeners. Isn't this amazing? He is still doing the same thing today.

Believers were not called Christians until the eleventh chapter of the book of Acts (also known as the Acts of the Holy Spirit). When you read the book of Acts, you will quickly begin to understand why this is so.

"Then Barnabas departed for Tarsus to seek Saul. And when he had found him, he brought him to Antioch. So it was that for a whole year they assembled with the church and taught a great many people. And the disciples were first called Christians in Antioch." (Acts 11:25–26)

Jesus spoke these words to them that were recorded in the Gospel of Luke:

"'These are the words which I spoke to you while I was still with you, that all things must be fulfilled which were written in the Law of Moses and the Prophets and the Psalms concerning Me.' And He opened

their understanding, that they might comprehend the Scriptures. (He still uses His same Holy Spirit to give us understanding today.)

Then He said to them, Thus it is written, and thus it was necessary for the Christ to suffer and to rise from the dead the third day, and that repentance and remission of sins should be preached in His name to all nations, beginning at Jerusalem. And you are witnesses of these things. Behold, I send the Promise of My Father upon you; but tarry in the city of Jerusalem until you are endued with power from on high." (Luke 24:44–49)

"Tarry [or wait] in the city of Jerusalem until you are endued with the power from on high"—this was the promise of His Father God that whoever believed could receive the gift of this *promise*. Each of them were already believers and had eternal life, being born again with a new spirit.

If being born again is the same event as being baptized with the Holy Spirit, why would Jesus tell them to wait in Jerusalem for the *promise* of His Father? It is because these are two separate events in a believer's life that are connected by the living word of God (Jesus).

Being born again is given to whosoever calls upon the name of the Lord to be saved. Both are promises from the Father, but its being filled with the Holy Spirit with tongues as proof—that is the *gift* given by Jesus, beginning at an appointed time, a time set by God the Father to move His will forward in mankind's history.

The day of Pentecost (also called Feast of Weeks, Feast of Harvest, or Day of Firstfruits) was that appointed time. Many were already saved or born again prior to this feast of Pentecost that Jesus sent back His Spirit to the believers as the other helper, comforter, counselor, and teacher. This was what He taught during His ministry with them. He promised to send another comforter to take His place, and He was His Holy Spirit.

(Here is something that I do not believe the Church gives much thought to, if any at all.) When Jesus was raised from the dead, He went to heaven, then He returned and *was with them* off and on *for forty (40) days*, speaking of the things pertaining to the kingdom of God. Not many sermons about these forty days, are there?

Imagine this, a month and a half with the <u>glorified</u> Jesus teaching kingdom principles to everyone following Him and believing in His message that He was sent by God as His only Son. During this precious time frame it's possible that much of the information we have today in the Epistles came from these teachings.

Paul, on the other hand, was given many revelations of these same truths that are in his Epistles. Some of his teachings are said to be hard to understand because they were revealed to him by the Holy Spirit as he spent time with Him in fellowshipping with Jesus and His Holy Spirit of truth, whom he met on the road to Damascus. Understanding the spiritual contents of the Bible requires the Holy Spirit of God, who inspired it. He gives understanding of the content and meaning, just as Jesus did when He gave them understanding of what He said, like explaining the parables.

Isn't this what is supposed to happen with us when we read the Bible today? Of course, it is! Never read the Bible without asking the Holy Spirit of Jesus to give you understanding of what you are reading, for He is always faithful to do so.

After Jesus went back to heaven, they continued to tarry or wait in Jerusalem as instructed. They had *no* clue when this promise was coming to them. They only knew to tarry in Jerusalem until it came.

As they waited, the feast of Pentecost was upon them. Out of five hundred people who were following Jesus and witnessed Him taken up into heaven, only one hundred and twenty remained in the upper room, praying as they prepared to celebrate the feast of Pentecost. The other three hundred and eighty believers were those that did not tarry, possibly because they did not believe in the promise of the Father that Jesus spoke to them about. They represent the many believers in Christ today who do not partake of this baptism because they do not believe in the promise of the Holy Spirit and fire from the Father.

"And being assembled together with them, He commanded them not to depart from Jerusalem, but to wait for the Promise of the Father, 'which,' He said, 'you have heard from Me; for John truly baptized with water, but you shall be baptized with the Holy Spirit not many days from now.' Therefore, when they had come together, they asked Him, saying,

THE OPERATIVE

'Lord, will You at this time restore the kingdom to Israel?' And He said to them, 'It is not for you to know times or seasons which the Father has put in His own authority. But you shall receive power when the Holy Spirit has come upon you; and you shall be witnesses to Me in Jerusalem, and in all Judea and Samaria, and to the end of the earth.'" (Acts 1:4–8)

I am sure it was disheartening to the one hundred and twenty, as they remained waiting and praying, as some folks who did not believe in this promise left their company. Faith will wait upon the promises for whatever time the Lord has chosen to manifest that which we are asking Him for. I know this is not always easy, but this is a benefit of the fruit of the Holy Spirit.

It is sad, however, for those that don't believe in this wonderful and miraculous promise of the Father. Even many today in the Church do not believe in this promised gift. It is my belief that this is the revival that is needed most in the world today—a true Holy Ghost revival and outpouring of the Spirit of God within all His believers. When the unbelievers see this event, they will say truly God is among us, because we each will believe the same things and will speak about the same things.

"And we desire that each one of you show the same diligence to the full assurance of hope until the end, that you do not become sluggish, but imitate those who through faith and patience inherit the promises." (Heb. 6:11–12)

Before going any further, let me point out again one very important point found in Acts 1:4–8: If being born again and being filled with the Holy Spirit happen at the same time, then why did Jesus say, "<u>For John truly baptized with water, but you shall be baptized with the Holy Spirit not many days from now</u>"?

Again, it is because being born again and being filled with the Holy Spirit are two different events in a believer's life. These words should do it, with no further proof needed. But alas, I believe that more proof is needed, so I will continue.

Jesus instructed that out of the mouths of two or more witnesses a truth is established. If you cannot take the witness of John the Baptist and Jesus our Savior, then I have my work cut out for me to change your minds with further proof and witnesses on this subject. You will find out, there is no lack of further proof in the Bible, confirming this truth that these are two separate events in a believer's life.

I hope that me as the third witness, along with all the others in the Bible, including the help of the Holy Spirit, will eliminate any doubt and unbelief you may have regarding this topic. Hang on to your hats; here we go!

And they (the remaining disciples) were in one accord in one place. I am sure they were all talking about the same things that they had seen and heard—the teachings from the resurrected Christ and fellowshipping with Him day in and day out until the time came when He left them once again.

<u>However, this time was a little different.</u> Solidifying the truths He taught for the past three-and-a-half years, His assurance was just as real to them as the air they breathed. Even though they did not know what, they knew <u>something good</u> was about to happen to them, because of the reassuring words and promises Jesus conveyed to them.

Still not connecting all the dots in their minds, they remained faithful, trusting Jesus through the promise of the Holy Spirit to be their guide. While praising God and thanking Jesus for all they had experienced to date, they waited with anticipation.

Their minds and hearts were still giddy with joy, unspeakable and full of glory because of Jesus's resurrection. I can see them now talking to each other, making statements like, "Isn't it wonderful what Jesus has done?" "It would be hard to believe if we did not see it with our own eyes and hear with our own ears," and "I did not know He was talking about His resurrected body, I thought He meant He would destroy then rebuild the temple."

Thomas might have been heard saying, "I even touched and handled his resurrected body. I know that He is alive!"

Each of them allowing their experiences to speak for them and as the others would hear, faith came again and again to all those listening. Suddenly, the very atmosphere of the room began to be transformed before their very eyes.

THE OPERATIVE

To that point, they had seen the sick healed, the dead raised, demons cast out, and many hearts and minds changed from the Law of Moses to the law of grace. Still hiding from those who, some fifty days earlier, crucified Jesus, their apprehension was growing, with no further instructions than to "tarry in Jerusalem till you receive the promise of the Holy Ghost."

The result of their obedience would bring change into each of their lives and the lives of thousands of others coming out of the world, even unto millions of souls in this very day we live in!

What power, what event could possibly allow men and women, who feared for their lives as Jesus was being nailed to the cross, to remain in the midst of what then seemed like their enemies too?

A charged earthly atmosphere with heavenly substance of the familiar wind experienced by all those that Jesus had previously breathed upon before His ascension when He said, *"'Peace to you! As the Father has sent Me, I also send you.' And when He had said this, He breathed on them, and said to them, 'Receive the Holy Spirit'"* (John 20:21–22).

Everything changed at that moment. The promise of the Father was set into motion to be released. The fulfillment of the prophecy long ago mentioned was now being received by those chosen to be the first in a long line of believers throughout centuries to receive God's presence and power, through Jesus Christ and His Spirit.

The world, as they knew it, would never be the same. The dispensation of grace was now taken to a whole new level by the outpouring of the third person of the Trinity, the Holy Spirit. His presence and power poured not only upon them but also now within their new spirits and unto as many who called upon the name of Jesus to be saved. Jesus waits to give you His Father's promised gift.

Will you receive His gift today? Or will you be one of those who do not believe in the promise from the Father that Jesus said would come? The choice is yours, and the amount of information to confirm its validity is found practically in every book of the Bible, especially in the New Testament.

Take the time to search for these golden nuggets that will prosper your soul and make you established with the knowledge of the Spirit of truth.

CHAPTER 4

We know that Joel foretold of that day and event. John the Baptist was pointing to the one who would baptize with the Holy Spirit and fire being Jesus. Jesus Himself spoke of the time when the Holy Spirit would come after He was gone, and that those who received Him will receive power (authority) to go into the entire world and preach the gospel or good news of Jesus Christ. Grace was taken to another level through the outpouring of the Holy Spirit of Jesus.

Jesus walked with His disciples for forty days before ascending to heaven until His next return for His bride, the Church. They must have had many unanswered questions, theories, and for some, probably doubts and unbelieving thoughts. His resurrection began the countdown to the day of Pentecost that would begin to turn the known world upside down.

Gathered together in an upper room, the one hundred and twenty continued in one accord. Their spirits filled with joy and excitement as the atmosphere became charged with the heavenly substance of a mighty rushing wind (the actual presence of the Holy Spirit of Jesus).

Fear did not enter into the equation on that day, as they were familiar with the breath of Jesus. This wind was the same breath previously given by Jesus as He blew on them. But this time it was without His physical presence.

THE OPERATIVE

In the upper room, each remembered Jesus's earthly ministry, along with His resurrected fellowship during the forty days He was with them. They were singing and praising God in His name as instructed. Who wouldn't be happy having experienced all these events and having the knowledge of the actual promise from Jesus Himself?

The mighty rushing wind swirled around each of them, like mini tornadoes accompanied by the consuming fire of God. This particular feast of Pentecost would be different than previous feasts of Pentecost, as it would be the one that changed the world. Promised by the Father and placed into motion by Jesus, His Son, there was no stopping it now.

Like the crucifixion, His outpouring of the Holy Spirit of Jesus was not done in some dark corner where others could not see. To the contrary, like all things of God, this too would be experienced before others as witnesses of God's goodness and faithfulness to His promise.

The initial outpouring of the Holy Spirit would be accomplished while Jerusalem was filled with devout men from every region. His plan all along was for all to see and partake of the wonderful works of God. Like a fine-tuned instrument, Jesus sang His heavenly language through His born-again believers for all to hear and believe.

"When the Day of Pentecost had fully come, they were all with one accord in one place. And suddenly there came a sound from heaven, as of a rushing mighty wind, and it filled the whole house where they were sitting. Then there appeared to them divided tongues, as of fire, and one sat upon each of them. And they were all filled with the Holy Spirit and began to speak with other tongues, as the Spirit gave them utterance." (Acts 2:4)

With the breath of Jesus swirling around each of them, they realized this as the promise of the Father, the gift of Jesus's Holy Spirit. "Receive ye the Holy Spirit" ran through their thoughts. One disciple began to speak words not known or understood by the others. (The word *cloven* here means "to partition thoroughly, literally in distribution, figuratively in dissension.")

The first person yielded to the Holy Spirit's presence, and then another, and another until they all were baptized with the Holy Spirit and were speaking in tongues. As the Holy Spirit distributed the tongues (the heavenly language only God Himself via the Holy Spirit understands), this event set His plan into motion.

This introduced not only His Holy Spirit to everyone but also His gift of "tongues", which paved the way for the gift of "interpretation of tongues", or the understanding of what was being said directly to God the Father.

This language was not something learned or made up by the disciples. Nor was it a known language from any earthly languages or combinations thereof or of any time to come. No! This language of tongues is given to the receiver and spoken as the Holy Spirit gives the utterance (words to speak).

Some believers were standing, while others remained seated. They all were speaking (praying in the Holy Spirit) in tongues. Echoing into the streets, this language of tongues was heard by the devout men from many regions. Several languages were representative in Jerusalem that day as it always was during the feast of Pentecost. However, this particular Pentecost brought a language that nobody had ever heard before.

These devout men in the streets heard what was spoken through the disciples, as the Holy Spirit gave them the words to say. (At this time let me share a revelation that I received a couple of decades ago. Many stumble with the truth here because of the tongue issue. Some say that if you do not speak another known language, then you are not legitimately being baptized or filled with the Holy Spirit. I would like to further address this issue.)

To acquire the truth, we must look to the directives of the gifts of the Holy Spirit to find out the revelation of what actually took place on the day of Pentecost and how they each heard (understood) them in their own language.

Let's first look at the twelfth chapter of First Corinthians, verses 1 to 11, and fourteenth chapter, verses 1 to 5:

"Now concerning spiritual gifts, brethren, I do not want you to be ignorant: You know that you were Gentiles, carried away to these dumb

idols, however you were led. Therefore, I make known to you that no one speaking by the Spirit of God calls Jesus accursed, and no one can say that Jesus is Lord except by the Holy Spirit. (He is the one who revealed this truth to men).

There are diversities of gifts, but the same Spirit. There are differences of ministries, but the same Lord. And there are diversities of activities, but it is the same God who works all in all.

But the manifestation of the Spirit is given to each one for the profit of all: for to one is given the word of wisdom through the Spirit; to another, the word of knowledge through the same Spirit; to another, faith by the same Spirit; to another, gifts of healings by the same Spirit; to another, the working of miracles; to another, prophecy; to another, discerning of spirits; to another, different kinds of tongues; to another, the interpretation of tongues. But one and the same Spirit works all these things, distributing to each one individually as He wills." (1 Cor. 12:1–11)

"*Pursue love, and desire spiritual gifts, but especially that you may prophesy. For he who speaks in a tongue does not speak to men but to God, for no one understands him; however, in the spirit he speaks mysteries. But he who prophesies speaks edification and exhortation and comfort to men. He who speaks in a tongue edifies himself, but he who prophesies edifies the church. I wish you all spoke with tongues, but even more that you prophesied; for he who prophesies is greater than he who speaks with tongues, unless indeed he interprets, that the church may receive edification." (1 Cor. 14:1–5)*

Let me point out a couple of things to place this into perspective:

1. First Corinthians 14:1–5 tells us that when someone speaks in tongues, they talk directly to God. Nobody else understands (including the devil) <u>unless</u> someone is given the interpretation.
2. We find another directive in First Corinthians 12:11. This shows us two of the nine (9) gifts that the Holy Spirit bestowed upon men (inclusive) that are filled with the Holy Spirit, which are "tongues" and the "interpretation of tongues." According to verse 5 in the fourteenth chapter of First Corinthians, it says that <u>tongues</u> with the <u>interpre-</u>

tation of tongues become equal to prophecy when tongues is interpreted (spoken in a language that is understandable by all those hearing and understanding that language).

The Bible is clear that as a result of being filled with the Holy Spirit, the recipient of this baptism has the evidence of speaking in tongues. If it's the Holy Spirit's intention to have tongues understood, then He gives an interpretation in the known language so that everyone will understand and become edified or built up in the Church and/or individually.

Thus, I submit unto you that based upon these scriptures, those devout men from every nation under heaven who heard them speak in tongues actually heard the interpretation of the tongues spoken in their own language (which made it appear to those receiving the understanding of the message that these men were speaking in their known languages). Instead of them literally hearing them speak in their own language, they understood in their own language what was being spoken to God in tongues, because the Holy Spirit gave the interpretation in their own understanding, using one of His gifts, called the interpretation of tongues.

The original Greek word used for *hearing* in Acts 2:8 is "*akouo* (ak-oo'-o); a primary verb; to hear (in various senses): KJV—give (in the) audience (of), come (to the ears), ([shall]) hear (-er, -ken), be noised, be reported, understand" (NT:191).

The disciples were speaking in tongues directly to God the Father. Then to accomplish His will in this event (Acts 2:11), "we do hear [understand] them speak in our tongues the wonderful works of God." The same word, *akouo*, is used in verse 11 (for *hear*) as was used in verse 6 (for *heard*). This understanding, I believe, was the interpretation of tongues given to them all, telling them about the death, burial, and resurrection of Jesus Christ, which were the wonderful works of God.

According to scripture, when one speaks in tongues to God, they can ask the Holy Spirit to give the interpretation, and it's up to Him to choose to give one or not. I do not know about you, but I do not speak any other language except English and one of the tongues of the Holy Spirit to God. There are various kinds of tongues because the Holy Spirit uses each of our personalities; thus, no two tongues sound identical.

We experience this when we are given an interpretation of tongues. Here in America, the interpretation of tongues is given during the meetings in English. This is because, generally, the language understood here in America is English. So the interpretation is given in English so that all attending understands the interpretation and are exhorted, edified, or comforted.

Is this making sense? Let me explain it this way: I have spoken in several other countries and have had to use an interpreter. For example, while in Brazil, I preached in English, and most listening to me did not understand English. I had to have my interpreter tell them in Portuguese what I said. Those who understood Portuguese now knew what was said in English; thus, they were exhorted, edified, or comforted.

However, when a Portuguese-speaking person gave a message in tongues and the interpretation of tongues was given in Portuguese, I did not understand the Portuguese version of the interpretation of tongues, so I was not edified. It was not until my interpreter had translated the Portuguese interpretation of tongues into English that I had understanding, so after the interpretation was given to me in English, I was exhorted, edified, and/or comforted by the message. See how easy it is to understand?

The same thing happens when the gift of tongues with the interpretation of tongues is used. The Holy Spirit gives the message in tongues to a person, then if the interpretation of tongues is given to either the same person or another, the Holy Spirit becomes the interpreter by giving us each understanding to the message given in tongues.

Once the interpretation is given in the understood common language, all at that meeting will understand, and all will be exhorted, edified, or comforted.

Remember, verse 11 in First Corinthians says, "But all these [gifts given by Him—that is, tongues and interpretation of tongues] worketh that one and the very same Spirit, dividing to EVERY MAN SEVERALY as He [the Holy Spirit] will."

Thus, the Holy Spirit gives the message and then becomes the interpreter by giving understanding to a person, who, in turn, speaks in a known language so others can understand too. The interpreted messages will always line up with the scriptures in either word or principle. This is how to gauge whether or not they are from God.

Another gauge is, after hearing the message, are you built up? Are you exhorted, edified, and/or comforted? Did the interpretation give you hope or, perhaps, divine direction? Beware of messages that tear down instead of build up. If it is the latter, perhaps the person giving the interpretation is allowing their own thoughts and beliefs to get mixed with the message, instead of keeping it pure by containing what the Holy Spirit has to say. (In later chapters, you will see the difference between today's prophetic messages as opposed to the Old Testament prophetic messages.)

I experienced a very similar and powerful thing in Cuba on one of my four mission trips to that country. I had met, through our ministry, a brother in California, who is an American, from Cuba, named Joseph Fernandez. I asked him if he wanted to go on this trip with me and be my interpreter. He was all too happy to oblige.

Arriving in Ciego de Ávila, the church meeting had already begun, and the pastor introduced Joseph and me to the congregation. I began preaching, and Joseph began his interpreting. Halfway through the message, I noticed that Joseph stopped interpreting and walked off the platform and went up to the back balcony.

There was no urgency to stop preaching, so I continued ministering in English without hesitation. I remember mentioning to the Holy Spirit that I prayed that He was giving them understanding of what was being spoken. The response from the congregation was lively and responsive to the words spoken.

After the meeting, Joseph came down into the crowed of excited and happy people and was talking to many of them, asking them if they understood what I was saying. Each of them said they understood perfectly and responded accordingly to the message given. He then asked them if they spoke and understood English, and each of them said no; they did not speak or understand English. But they trusted God would give them understanding, and He was faithful to do so!

THE OPERATIVE

You see, if we do not place God in a box and limit Him, there is no limit as to what God can do with or for each of us who believe. The gifts of the Holy Spirit are such powerful communication tools and weapons of God, operating in our lives.

Have you seen the movie *Windtalkers*? The Navajo Indians became radio operators transmitting and receiving messages during WWII. They used the Navajo language so that the enemy was confounded regarding the information being sent or received. The enemy could never break the code, and the gift of tongues with the interpretation of tongues is identical. Our enemy, the devil, can never break the code.

This is what happens while speaking to God using the gift of tongues. God does the speaking back to us with the interpretation of tongues that His Holy Spirit operates through His believers.

Unfortunately, the devil has convinced people, including many believers of Jesus, that these gifts, this power, and these weapons are not for today. Wouldn't you do the same if you were the devil?

By convincing believers of Christ of his lies about these gifts, he simply keeps them from using these powerful weapons against him, thus giving them a less victorious life here on earth. Sounds like he has used this tactic once before. We must not be ignorant of his devices.

"Lest satan should take advantage of us; for we are not ignorant of his devices." (2 Cor. 2:10-11) Or are we?

Yet this is exactly what he has done. By convincing people that the baptism of the Holy Spirit is not truth and neither is it relevant for today, this power can never be used against him where they are concerned, telling them that it has passed away and been done away with and that God does not operate like this any longer.

The lies just keep coming and coming, and people who do not know the truth will be deceived by them, and they will miss out on what is available from God as a free gift <u>in addition to their salvation.</u>

Being filled with the Holy Spirit is so much more than speaking in tongues and interpreting messages, as you will see as the information unfolds in later chapters of this book. Revelation knowledge—

necessary for today's Church, the body of Christ—will be given this power once again to gain victory over the devil's devices.

We will see that Christ Himself operated in these gifts during His ministry time here on earth as well as others in the early Church. It only stands to reason that the Lord would want His body of believers to operate in the same power that He started with. I believe that He does!

In Ephesians 5:18–21, it says, *"And be not drunk with wine, in which is excess, but be filled with the Spirit, speaking to yourselves in psalms and hymns and spiritual songs, singing and making melody in your heart to the Lord. Giving thanks always for all things unto God and the Father in the name of our Lord Jesus Christ, Submitting yourselves one to another in the fear of God."*

So you may ask, is being filled with the Holy Spirit with the evidence of speaking in tongues a onetime event or experience? In chapter 5 and beyond, I will answer this question and many others, as we continue with the topic of <u>the baptism of the Holy Spirit.</u>

CHAPTER 5

We now know that in the upper room Jesus filled the believers with power and fire of His Holy Spirit. That power was the same power that gave life back into the dead body of Christ as He was raised from the dead. The same Holy Spirit that God used to raise Jesus from the dead permeates each believer when they are baptized or filled with the Holy Spirit and fire. This gives us power or authority to operate the wonderful works of God, in Jesus's name, with boldness.

On the day of Pentecost, the devout men understanding the wonderful works of God heard those in the upper room, as they were speaking by the gift of tongues given to them by the Holy Spirit, as they were being baptized or filled.

You cannot have the power of God without fire, for our God is a consuming fire. Once filled, the Holy Spirit begins working on burning out of us all that is not like Christ. This is where the fiery trails appear in our transformation. But *why* the use of cloven tongues as of fire?

As mentioned, *fire* is a consuming agent that symbolizes the holiness of God. It consumes sin, which is something that cannot abide in His presence.

"For our God is a consuming fire." (Heb. 12:29)

Fire also symbolizes the purification process of the believer by the tests we endure in our lives.

"But who can endure the day of His coming? And who can stand when He appears? For He is like a refiner's fire and like launderers' soap." (Mal. 3:2)

Fire is also one of the many symbols used for the Holy Spirit. Other symbols of the Holy Spirit are water, wind, and dove.

The eyes of our risen Lord Jesus are as fire, penetrating into the very depths of our spirit and soul, knowing the secrets of our hearts, taking vengeance upon those who do not know God or disobey the gospel!

"And to the angel of the church in Thyatira write, 'These things says the Son of God, who has eyes like a flame of fire, and His feet like fine brass.'" (Rev. 2:18)

"I will kill her children with death, and all the churches shall know that I am He who searches the minds and hearts. And I will give to each one of you according to your works." (Rev. 2:23)

Fire begins to manifest the sanctification done by the Holy Spirit within our lives. While sanctification is given to us by Jesus through propitiation *, it is the Holy Spirit that makes it a reality in our lives through the changes we yield to, as we work out our own salvation with Him in fear and trembling.

> *"hilasterion* (hil-as-tay'-ree-on); neuter of a derivative of NT:2433; an expiatory (place or thing), i.e. (concretely) an atoning victim, or (specially) the lid of the Ark (in the Temple): KJV—mercy seat, propitiation" (NT:2435).
>
> "*hilaskomai* (hil-as'-kom-ahee); middle voice from the same as NT:2436; to conciliate, i.e. (transitively) to atone for (sin), or (intransitively) be propitious: KJV—be merciful, make reconciliation for" (NT:2433).
>
> "*hileos* (hil'-eh-oce); cheerful (as attractive), i.e. propitious; adverbially (by Hebraism) God be gracious!, i.e. (in averting some calamity) far be it: KJV—be it far, merciful" (NT:2436).
>
> "*hilasmos* (hil-as-mos'); atonement, i.e. (concretely) an expiator: KJV—propitiation" (NT:2434).

THE OPERATIVE

"Therefore, my beloved, as you have always obeyed, not as in my presence only, but now much more in my absence, work out your own salvation with fear and trembling; for it is God who works in you both to will and to do for His good pleasure." (Phil. 2:12–13)

Since our spirit man becomes new when we are born again, the fleshly old man remains to start his or her transformation from this world into the heavenly realm. This is the period that we grow in the grace and knowledge of our Lord Jesus Christ, which, by the way, continues for the rest of our lives while here on earth.

"But grow in the grace and knowledge of our Lord and Savior Jesus Christ." (2 Peter 3:18)

The process of putting off the old man and his fleshly ways and putting on the new man with his transformed ways by the Holy Spirit remains with us until we either die or are taken up in the rapture. Either way, we do this with the help of the Holy Spirit and His gentlemanly ways, as He leads us through this glorious changing process from what we are to what He is.

Remember the cartoon of the devil on one shoulder and an angel on the other? The devil is always telling lies, wanting us to do wrong, while the angel encourages the character to always do that which is right. This is the internal battle that continues throughout our lives, which takes place within the mind, where we find out that all spiritual battles actually take place.

"And do not be conformed to this world, but be transformed by the renewing of your mind, that you may prove what is that good and acceptable and perfect will of God." (Rom. 12:2)

The devout men understood in their own language, hearing the good news of Jesus Christ, giving His life for all and making the way, for <u>whosoever</u> will call upon His name shall be saved. Yes, the wonderful works of God, heard and understood by thousands that day, led to thousands of salvations as well.

Those who do not believe that God sent His only Son, Jesus, will not call upon His name simply because they do not believe. This can change at any given moment, as the Holy Spirit is actually the one who convinces men (inclusive) of sin, righteousness, and judgment.

"Nevertheless I tell you the truth. It is to your advantage that I go away; for if I do not go away, the Helper will not come to you; but if I depart, I will send Him to you. And when He has come, He will convict the world of sin, and of righteousness, and of judgment: of sin, because they do not believe in Me; of righteousness, because I go to My Father and you see Me no more; of judgment, because the ruler of this world is judged." (John 16:7–11)

That is a whole sermon right there. Meditate on these scriptures with your spiritual understanding of *grace* (grace is obtaining what we do not deserve and *not* getting what we deserve). For all of you who have loved ones, friends, and enemies who are not saved, do not give up, but pray that the Holy Spirit convicts or convinces them of the seriousness of sin (*not* their *acts* of sins, but because they do not believe in Jesus). Their belief or unbelief actually determines their eternal destinations, either into heaven or into hell, which, ultimately, leads them to the lake of fire after the judgment.

Now back on topic. The disciples found themselves operating in a way and manner that were foreign to them. However, they knew it was from God. Nothing like this had ever been heard of, except in Joel's prophecy, and it bore witness to this truth.

This is why Paul wrote in First Thessalonians 4:5: *"For our gospel did not come to you in word only, but also in power, and in the Holy Spirit and in much assurance, as you know what kind of men we were among you for your sake."* I submit to you that in this scripture, we are told that there are two ways the word of God is experienced:

1. By word *only*—which is where a large percentage of the Church is today. Now I am not belittling this because "faith comes by the hearing, and hearing by the Word of God" (Rom. 10:17).

    This is how an individual's faith is activated and matured, by hearing the word of God over and over. There is yet another level of experiencing the word of God. It is by the power of the Holy Spirit, which brings much assurance of the truth.

2. But also in *power* and the *Holy Spirit* and much assurance—this is what happened on the day of Pentecost and

what happens to every believer's life when they are filled with the Holy Spirit with the evidence of speaking in tongues, according to the scriptures.

(This is where the living *Church* needs to be *today*!)

As members of the body of Christ, *we all* need to be filled with the *word* and *power*, via *the Holy Spirit*! If you have only the word, you will dry up. Word and Spirit, you grow up!

We then will see the same results as the early Church did, by having three thousand souls believing in Jesus Christ as the only begotten Son of God, as on the day of Pentecost, then daily as the Lord adds to the Church.

The devout men where Jews, but once the word went out to them with the power of the Holy Spirit, it changed their lives forever! In another time five thousand souls were added to the Church. As for those who thirst and hunger for an early Church movement, get yourself baptized or filled with the Holy Spirit and His power, and see what happens. My wife and I have been in revival now for the past thirty-seven years. While revival may include a series of meetings, a series of meetings do not make a revival. Unless there is a true coming alive unto the things of God, with a continual thirst and hunger for the things of God, there is no true revival.

Was this Pentecost experience a onetime event to jump-start the Church, allowing her to grow as fast or as slow as she wishes? Or is it what the Lord expects to happen as the *norm* in the Church *today*? I gravitate toward the latter in my belief, and let me explain to you why I do.

The first time this Pentecost experience happened was in the upper room, where the one hundred and twenty were, basically, hiding from the Jews in fear of being killed themselves. Peter, who, just fifty-three days earlier, denied that he even knew Jesus, stood boldly in front of the very same people that crucified Christ earlier and preached the gospel according to the truths given to him by Jesus and the Holy Spirit.

Perhaps, Peter spoke of the things that impressed him the most, like the things found in First and Second Peter, the same way the things that impressed James and John and, eventually, Paul, by revelation from the Holy Spirit, showing up in the writings of the Epistles.

My point is, we now see a picture of a man who was scared to death to acknowledge Jesus, but stood boldly preaching to all who was seeing and understanding the marvelous works of God. And because of the gifts of the Holy Spirit that were in operation on that day, which were tongues and the interpretation of tongues, understanding of the *truth* was given to them who heard what was being spoken directly to God!

Then as if a switch had been turned on inside him, Peter cried, *"This is that which was spoken through the prophet Joel."* Denying Christ three times earlier, he now courageously stood to proclaim the gospel or good news of Jesus, with the boldness and anointing of the Holy Spirit. He was able to convince them of the truth, as Peter explained that which they were experiencing and where it came from. They too understood and acted upon the truth they received by calling upon the name of the Lord to be saved, and Jesus was faithful and more than happy to accommodate them with salvation.

What was the difference? Peter was now baptized or filled with the Holy Spirit and His power and was one of those one hundred and twenty in the upper room who was speaking in tongues!

(Power—*dunamis*—Greek word where we get our word *dynamite* from.)

As Peter tarried as Jesus commanded, he and the others trusted in Him to send the promise of the Holy Spirit. They did not know when or how, but they <u>believed</u> Him and were each <u>filled</u> by Jesus, who baptized those who believed and asked for the promise of the Father, with the Holy Spirit and fire.

So again, is this filling a onetime thing that a Christian can experience then be done with, to wear like a badge of honor? Absolutely not! We can be filled over and over with the Holy Spirit! Why? Because, we give to others of His power that we receive; His power flows through us and is not stored in us. Therefore, we are in need of being filled again and again. This is His design, and we build up ourselves on our most holy faith each time we pray in the Holy Spirit.

THE OPERATIVE

Nine (9) times, in the book of Acts, the same people, Jews and Gentiles, were either originally baptized with the Holy Spirit, with the evidence of speaking in tongues for the first time, or the same people being filled over and over, with others being baptized for the first time.

The Holy Spirit inspired men to write the Bible, which sets His precedence about being baptized with the Holy Spirit. Take special notice of the similarities that affected each of them all before, during, and after being baptized for the first time. As we search the scriptures, also pay attention to the number of times they each were filled (that is, *"as we were in the beginning"*), meaning *Acts 2:1–4*. There is only one baptism in the Holy Spirit, but there are many fillings after the initial baptism.

In chapter 6, I'll begin to expound on each of the nine separate occasions the believers were baptized with the Holy Spirit. In these, the Holy Spirit is revealed to the world and to the Church. The results that followed each time believers were either baptized initially or filled again with the Holy Spirit were simply amazing and surely believable, because it is God's holy word.

New believers are baptized with the Holy Spirit's precedence of speaking in tongues, along with the presence of joy and boldness, which are equated with the evidence of speaking in tongues by those who are baptized with the Holy Spirit and filled over and over again and again.

It's very important to see that not only are tongues spoken but also the results of tongues in a believer's life that are normally accompanied by joy and boldness, as they are baptized with the Holy Spirit.

Are you feeling the excitement concerning what happens each time the Holy Spirit is poured into a man or woman that receives power to be a witness in Jerusalem (hometown), Judaea (surrounding county), Samaria (state), and the uttermost parts of the earth (the world)?

The excitement still thrills me even after thirty-seven years of being baptized with the Holy Spirit, with the evidence of speaking in tongues and being filled again and again with the Holy Spirit of Jesus

Christ my Savior. I never grow tired of the wonderful works of God, for they are part of my abundant life.

Faith found in me becomes stronger each time I pray in tongues. I do not always receive interpretations, as they are not necessary for the building up of myself on my holy faith. I do, however, ask, and I am sure that answers will come later when I need to know them the most.

The wonderful works and mysteries of God—there is nothing like them. My prayer for you is that you too would partake of the fullness of His gift. If you have not yet been baptized with the Holy Spirit with tongues as the evidence, stay with me and find out more about the Holy Spirit of Jesus Christ. He is not to be avoided, but embraced with your spirit, soul, and body. You will never regret yielding yourself to Him in this capacity. He will literally take you around the world as He has with us.

For His plan and purpose for you is to obtain your expected end, and to do this, you must embrace Jesus's Holy Spirit with your whole being and enjoy the journey along the way.

"For I know the thoughts that I think toward you, saith the LORD, thoughts of peace, and not of evil, to give you an expected end." (Jer. 29:11, KJV)

The Holy Spirit has gifts for you! The Holy Spirit has fruit for you as well!

If you are already baptized with the Holy Spirit and speak in tongues, good for you! Pray without ceasing and keep reading, for perhaps, you will learn something not previously revealed to you or something that you can help somebody else with along both of your journeys through life with the Holy Spirit of Jesus Christ as your guide.

CHAPTER 6

There are nine (9) gifts of the Holy Spirit, and there are nine (9) fruit of the Holy Spirit. Each is found in the Bible, and I will be addressing each of these individually in later chapters. I do not think it coincidence that there were also nine (9) different times that people were said to be baptized and/or filled with the Holy Spirit with the evidence of speaking in tongues in the early Church and recorded in the book of Acts.

I also believe that numbers in the Bible are very significant and not coincidental. The following information by Matt Slick illustrates this thought in further detail:

> *"Whether or not numbers really have a significance is still debated in many circles. Nevertheless, I present the information for your examination."*[1]

The # 3—THE NUMBER OF DIVINE PERFECTION. The Trinity consists of Father, Son, and Holy Spirit. There are three qualities of the universe: Time, Space, and Matter. To exist (except for God) all three are required. Each quality consists of three elements. Therefore, we live in a trinity of trinities.

---

1. Article by Matt Slick—CARM

The three qualities of universe are each three:

TIME Is One	SPACE Is One	MATTER Is One
Yet Three	Yet Three	Yet Three
Past	Height	Solid
Present	Width	Liquid
Future	Depth	Gas

We live in a Trinity of Trinities: [Romans 1:20] says, "For since the creation of the world His invisible attributes, His eternal power and divine nature have been clearly seen, being understood through what has been made…"

If you are a trichotomist then man is made of three parts:

Body   Soul   Spirit

(The Bible, however, teaches the order as spirit, soul, and body.[2] I believe that there are no mistakes found within the Holy Spirit's order of revealing information to us throughout God's word—my words and not Matt Slick's.)

Human abilities are three parts:

Thought   Word   Deed

The divine attributes are three-fold:

God is:	God is:	God is:
Omniscient	Love	Holy
Omnipresent	Light	Righteous
Omnipotent	Spirit	Just

Three bear witness [1 John 5:8]:

Spirit   Water   Blood

---

2.   Thessalonians 5:23

THE OPERATIVE

Christ is Three Shepherds

*The Good Shepherd [John 10:14–15]—
speaking of His death
The Great Shepherd [Heb. 13:20]—speaking of His resurrection
The Chief Shepherd [1 Pet. 5:4]—speaking of His glory*

The Three appearances of Christ:

Past: *Has appeared [Heb. 9:26] to put away sin*
Present: *Is appearing [Heb. 9:24] in the presence of God*
Future: *Will appear [Heb. 9:28] to those who await Him*

The Father spoke from Heaven three times:

*—[Matt. 3:17], "This is My beloved Son, in whom I am well pleased."
—[Matt. 17:5], "This is My beloved Son, with whom I am well-pleased; listen to Him."
—[John 12:28],"I have both glorified it [the Father's name], and will glorify it again."*

Both the Tabernacle and the Temple consisted of three parts:

The Court   The Holy place The Sanctuary

Regarding the Tabernacle:

*The Holy of Holies was a cube
(10 cubits × 10 cubits × 10 cubits)*

Regarding the Temple:

*The Holy of Holies was a cube
(20 cubits × 20 cubits × 20 cubits)*

(End of Matt Slick Information)

Then there's also The Meaning of the Number 9. according to biblestudy.org [3]

The number 9 is used 49 times in Scripture and symbolizes divine completeness or conveys the meaning of finality. Christ died at the 9th hour of the day, or 3 p.m., to make the way of salvation open to everyone. The Day of Atonement (Yom Kippur) is the only one of God's annual Feast days of worship that requires believers to fast for one day. This special day, considered by many Jews to be the holiest of the year, begins at sunset on the 9th day of the seventh Hebrew month [Leviticus 23:32].

Nine also represents the fruits of God's Holy Spirit, which are Faithfulness, Gentleness, Goodness, Joy, Kindness, Long suffering, Love, Peace and Self-control [Galatians 5:22–23].

(End of biblestudy.org)

The number nine, as with many other numbers in the Bible, does seem to have significance. Whether or not we will ever be able to understand all their meanings in this life, I am not sure. Since numbers play a big part in the Bible, giving us insights into the divine design of God, we can realize that they show the validity of a divine design. In simplicity, we know that $3 \times 3 = 9$, and $9 \div 3 = 3$. But in the cosmos, as seen above, this simple formula seems to have its place in the order of many things.

Numbers are so important to God that He included an entire book in the Bible entitled *Numbers*. It's wrong to think that our God created the heavens and the earth and all that we see in the cosmos without using mathematics, calculus, physics, or trigonometry. I am further convinced that there must be an "ometry" or two that exist that we do not know about yet.

God created and set all things into motion and in correct order by using complex equations and formulas. This is not humanly possible, even if we gather all the geniuses on earth together and set them about the business of replicating the cosmos. It cannot be accomplished; they can never figure out where to begin, let alone where to end.

---

3. biblestudy.org

God's ability to create life that is reproducible after its own kind is a power only reserved for His Son, Jesus, and His Holy Spirit. I think you would agree that God is so amazing, isn't He?

So amazing that His Holy Spirit, who inspired the Bible, including the book of Acts, set a very important precedence concerning this powerful beginning of the early Church. This precedence continues to this day and will continue until Jesus returns for His bride, the Church, which each believer is a member of—the body of Jesus Christ our Savior.

As promised, it's time to take a look at the <u>first filling</u> found in the book of Acts and the details of His precedence. If you have not already figured it out, the words *baptism* and *filling* mean the very same thing.

"And they were all filled with the Holy Spirit, and began to speak with other tongues, as the Spirit gave them utterance." (Acts 2:4)

This is the event, action, or happening—call it what you will—that all the eight other times that believers were either filled for the first time or again and again was based on. This is the precedence of the baptism of the Holy Spirit. <u>They all spoke in tongues</u>. There is no scripture that eliminates this precedence, and this has not changed throughout the course of time. As a matter of fact, the apostle Paul confirms and solidifies tongues in First Corinthians 12:14.

"Jesus Christ is the same yesterday, today, and forever." (Heb. 13:8)

As we will also find out, this is not a onetime event for a believer, like water baptism. A believer can be baptized initially with the Holy Spirit and filled over and over and over again, with as much of the Holy Spirit that they wish to have flowing in and through them.

This is what Paul was talking about in *Ephesians 5:18–21 (KJV)*: *"And do not be drunk with wine, [as some falsely accused the disciples in the upper room of being drunk with wine] in which is excess; but be filled with the Spirit, speaking to one another in psalms and hymns and spiritual songs, singing and making melody in your heart to the Lord, giving thanks always for all things to God the Father in the name of our Lord Jesus Christ, submitting to one another in the fear of God."*

There will be more about all this later.

- The first detail we must realize is this: the daily routine of the disciples, since Jesus was taken up into heaven to the day of Pentecost, was filled with believing, talking about, or witnessing and praying about the same things that Jesus taught them, things concerning kingdom principles while walking with them before and <u>after His resurrection</u>.
- Secondly, their obedience to tarry until the promise from the Father would come upon them being fulfilled when the day of Pentecost had fully come. These fishermen and others, like Levi the tax collector, never went back to fishing or tax collecting again after Pentecost. As far as I could see in the scriptures, Paul only used his tent-making abilities not to be a burden to the local churches, concerning finances. This was <u>his</u> personal choice and not a commandment of the Lord.
- Thirdly, as the Holy Spirit of promise came into the room, each felt and saw the effects of the wind and the fire. (Both wind and fire are symbols of the Holy Spirit.) It's important to realize that the wind, symbolizing the Holy Spirit, is the result of His presence, the same way the wind is a part of our natural life. We see the trees moving in the presence of the wind and feel its force on our body, but we never actually see the wind, do we? Enough said.

Then, there is fire. As mentioned previously, the Holy Spirit's fire burns up that which is no longer needed or wanted in our lives. Fear on that day of Pentecost was burned out by the fire of the Holy Spirit's presence, while the wind of the Holy Spirit began to lead them to places they normally would not go. (His wind keeps us on the right course.)

Boldness replaced fear, allowing them to speak that which, just a few days before, were terrifying to utter. Anointed words flowed out of Peter's mouth as easily as water flows through a clean pipe, for this was now what was in his heart in abundance.

- The fourth thing we need to see is that <u>every believer</u>—and I do mean <u>every believer</u>—who was in that upper room was <u>baptized and filled</u> with the Holy Spirit. Each of them <u>spoke in tongues,</u> as the Holy Spirit gave them utterance or the words to speak, as promised by the Father as far back as the eighth or ninth century BC when Joel first told of this glorious day.

Notice here that Jesus *did not* choose this one over that one to baptize with the Holy Spirit, giving them utterance too. <u>Each</u> was baptized with the Holy Spirit, and <u>each</u> spoke the heavenly language of the Holy Spirit to God, speaking with boldness about the wonderful works of God and fearing nothing that man could do to them or say about them.

The Holy Spirit, being a perfect gentleman, will never override a believer's will. Acts 2 is an excellent example of believers yielding themselves to Him, as Jesus baptized each of them with His Holy Spirit and fire, giving them power and authority.

I previously told you that I believe that the devout men heard (understood) them in their own languages and were given the interpretation (understanding the message of tongues) by the Holy Spirit. This day of Pentecost started the early Church with a very powerful event. Jesus not only introduced His Holy Spirit to everyone, but He also introduced two of His nine gifts, and the results were that three thousand souls were born again and baptized with the Holy Spirit as well. This was the norm of the day and should be the norm of the day with today's Church.

We found out, and it bears repeating, that in *First Corinthians 14:4, 5 (KJV), "he that speaketh in an unknown tongue edifieth himself; but he that prophesieth edifieth the church. I would that ye all spake with tongues, but rather that ye prophesied: for greater is he that prophesieth than he that speaketh with tongues, except he interpret, that the church may receive edifying."*

According to these scriptures, tongues, once interpreted, <u>is equal to prophecy</u> and is spoken in a language known to all that are in a certain place or meeting. This is done for exhortation, edification, and comfort—the three indicators that the message is from God and not man.

Now let's put this thought into context.

"Follow after charity [love], and desire spiritual gifts, but rather that ye may prophesy. For he that speaketh in an unknown tongue speaketh not unto men, but unto God: for no man understandeth him; howbeit in the spirit he speaketh mysteries [wonderful works of God]. But he that prophesieth speaketh unto men to edification, and exhortation, and comfort." (1 Cor. 14:1–5, KJV)

So this promised gift from the Father, given by Jesus as the baptizer of the Holy Spirit, gives us believers weapons that are, literally, out of this world.

1. Those speaking in tongues are speaking directly to God Himself.
2. Those speaking in tongues are doing so by the Holy Spirit, as He gives them utterances or words to speak, and they are speaking the mysteries or the wonderful works of God.
3. Once interpreted by the same Holy Spirit that gives the words to speak the mysteries of God, the person giving the interpretation speaks in the language that is spoken and understood by all who stand by. The believer giving the message becomes an interpreter.
4. The devil and his demons <u>cannot</u> understand what we are saying directly to God unless an interpretation is given in a known language that they too understand.
5. The person speaking in tongues, while speaking to God and waiting for an interpretation, which may or may not be given (decided by the Holy Spirit), edifies or builds up himself spiritually on his most holy faith. (See also Jude 20–21.)

<u>There you have it</u>—five excellent reasons to believe that tongues and the interpretation of tongues are real and for today! Jesus is the one who baptizes in the Holy Spirit, and a believer must ask Him (Jesus) to fill them with His Holy Spirit and power. *Do not* ask God the Father or the Holy Spirit, as this responsibly belongs to neither

THE OPERATIVE

of them. The gift is from God, and Jesus only, is the baptizer of the Holy Spirit, while the giving of the tongues is the responsibility of the Holy Spirit.

Are you beginning to realize why the devil has worked so hard to discredit this gift freely given to *all* believers who believe that God exist and that He is a rewarder of those who diligently seek Him?

"But without faith it is impossible to please Him, for he who comes to God must believe that He is, and that He is a rewarder of those who diligently seek Him." (Heb. 11:6)

Wouldn't you try to discredit this gift freely given to all believers if you were the enemy of Christ and His believers? Wouldn't you do your best to convince them that this gift is not for today? Wouldn't you use any means necessary to discredit this gift, which contains God's power in His believers?

It's so sad that many believers of Christ—yes, even those who are supposed to know the word of God and are the shepherds of Jesus's flock—have fallen prey to these kinds of lies. If you have fallen prey to these lies, you may find yourself in a category of unbelief when it comes to the baptism of the Holy Spirit. You might as well turn to each of the scriptures concerning the baptism of the Holy Spirit and tear them out of your Bible. Not accepting them as truth and not acting upon them are the same as doing so.

While you're at it, tear out First Corinthians chapters 12–14 and parts of Ephesians too. Go back to the book of Joel, and find the promise, and tear it out, and place them in file 13. If you believe that the baptism in the Holy Spirit with the evidence of speaking in tongues is *not* for today or is of the devil or whatever reason that you have accepted these lies as truth, then why keep them in there? <u>That's right—tear them out of the Bible.</u>

Is speaking in tongues of the devil? Was he the one who inspired the writings of these scriptures? No! Can we find scriptures in the Bible to back up this theory that the baptism with the Holy Spirit with the evidence of speaking in tongues was inspired by the devil? No, of course not! Was Paul inspired by the devil to write First Corinthians 12–14? Of course, he was not! It was the Holy Spirit who inspired each writer of the Bible!

Maybe you believe that Paul was inspired by the devil when he wrote to the Ephesians not to be drunk with wine in excess but to be filled with the Holy Spirit? There is, of course, no scripture to back up any of that nonsense. Neither was Dr. Luke taking some strong potion he might have concocted for himself before writing the Gospel of Luke and the book of Acts! To think this way is to err from the scriptures the way that Jesus said that those *not* knowing the true revelation of them would do.

When we say we do not believe in the baptism of the Holy Spirit with the evidence of speaking in tongues according to the scriptures, we are saying the equivalent of these nonsensical, false statements.

Not believing this free gift given by our heavenly Father as being viable for today is the same as telling God that He is a liar. What person in their right mind would call God a liar?

"God is not a man, that He should lie, Nor a son of man, that He should repent. Has He said, and will He not do? Or has He spoken, and will He not make it good? Behold, I have received a command to bless; He has blessed, and I cannot reverse it." (Num. 23:19–20)

"If we are faithless, He remains faithful; He cannot deny Himself." (2 Tim. 2:13)

"In hope of eternal life which God, who cannot lie, promised before time began, but has in due time manifested His word through preaching, which was committed to me according to the commandment of God our Savior." (Titus 1:2,3)

Yet there are those who are brassy enough to call God a liar, every time they say that they do not believe what is in the Bible. <u>I am not one of them</u>. I believe Him and His Holy Spirit's inspired writings of His word, the Bible. Some things in it are not for us to practice in this dispensation, but being filled with the Holy Spirit and speaking in tongues as the Spirit gives the words to speak certainly <u>are!</u>

The Old Testament is given to Israel and to us as a tutor, to bring them and us to the knowledge and revelation of Jesus Christ. It still serves its purpose to give us teachings of wisdom and understanding of God and how He has planned and purposed everything to fulfill His plan and purpose for mankind.

THE OPERATIVE

The baptism in the Holy Spirit with the evidence of speaking in tongues is the most important part of the New Testament or the new covenant made between Jesus and the Father for the believer, second to salvation. Being filled with the Holy Spirit and speaking in tongues help us to realize the following reality in a believer's life:

"I am crucified with Christ: nevertheless I live; yet not I, but Christ liveth in me: and the life which I now live in the flesh I live by the faith of the Son of God, who loved me, and gave himself for me." (Gal. 2:20, KJV)

We will look further at a few other times that the Holy Spirit was given to them who believed and were willing to receive this free gift from God our Father in the chapters that follow. Instead of saying, "Thanks, but no thanks, Lord. I do not want to receive this free gift of your Holy Spirit from you," I would pray that you are saying, "*Yes*, Lord, *yes*, to your will and your way. I will trust and obey you, and I will answer you *yes*, Lord, *yes!*"

Continue your quest in searching for the *truth* that will set you free. Freedom comes as revelation continues regarding Jesus. Revelation continues with the close fellowship of the Holy Spirit flowing in us and through us. As you trust and obey Him, I am sure that you'll find the remainder of this book a blessing to you. You too can benefit from the presence of the Holy Spirit in your life, with a deeper fellowship than you have ever experienced before!

CHAPTER 7

May I start this chapter by saying, "I realize that none of you will literally take out your Bibles and begin tearing or cutting out scriptures. But isn't this what we are doing when we do not believe what the Holy Spirit inspired about Himself in the scriptures?"

All I am asking is that you do not throw out the baby with the bathwater just because somebody said this is not the way or that's not what the scriptures really meant. Do not try to explain Him away! Do not allow others to do this for you either. Do not fear Him, but embrace Him.

Allow yourself to be taught by the Holy Spirit of Jesus. Then let others confirm the truths that He has taught you. Study the Bible for yourself, and seek the Holy Spirit's interpretation of what He is saying.

Let's quickly recap what we know as facts so far:

a) We know that the event known as the day of Pentecost was foretold hundreds of years ago.
b) We know that John the Baptist informed us that Jesus was the one who baptized with the Holy Spirit and fire.
c) We know that Jesus walked with the disciples for forty days after His resurrection, teaching them about kingdom principles, including informing them of this promise of the Holy Spirit once He was gone.

d) We know that the disciples left their livelihoods behind them to focus on the kingdom principles of the gospel of Jesus Christ.
e) We know that the disciples were tarrying or waiting for the promise of the Holy Spirit, and on Pentecost we know that the gift promised was poured out.
f) We know, as they tarried, they were all in one accord—unity in what they believed, thought, and spoke regarding those kingdom principles taught to them by Jesus.
g) We know that the one hundred and twenty in the upper room felt and saw the results of the presence of the Holy Spirit by feeling the wind and seeing the results of His presence—the fire, burning out all the dross of the old man, during which the spirit of fear was the first to go.
h) We further know that each believer filled with the Holy Spirit had the evidence of speaking in tongues and received boldness to stand and speak before the very same people that crucified Christ Jesus just fifty-three days prior.
i) We know that once men hear the <u>wonderful works of God</u> by the power of the Holy Spirit, they are convinced, by the Holy Spirit Himself, of the goodness of God. Believing that Jesus is the only begotten Son of God activates the measure of faith given to us at conception to receive eternal life by becoming born again.
j) We know that Jesus Himself said, *"Nevertheless I tell you the truth. It is to your advantage that I go away; for if I do not go away, the Helper [Holy Spirit] will not come to you; but if I depart, I will send Him to you. And when He has come, He will convict the world of sin, and of righteousness, and of judgment: of sin, because they do not believe in Me; of righteousness, because I go to My Father and you see Me no more; of judgment, because the ruler of this world is judged"* (John 16:7–11).
k) We know that on the day of Pentecost, because of the boldness of the disciples speaking the wonderful works of God, three thousand souls were added unto them (Acts

2:41), and later five thousand souls were added (Acts 4:4). True Holy Ghost revival begins this way with the Holy Spirit in charge.

l) We also know that after this wonderful day, the disciples continued steadfastly in the apostles' doctrine and fellowship, in breaking of bread, and in prayers. And God gave them favor with all the people, and the Lord added to the church daily such as should be saved.

The disciples now had power or authority because of the Holy Spirit that now dwelled within them, as they prayed in the Spirit, building themselves up on their most holy faith, then reaching out to others, giving freely that which was given to them. One day while Peter and John were on their way to the temple to pray, they were met by a lame man, who asked them for alms.

Peter, being full of the Holy Spirit, asked the man to look upon him as he spoke, *"'Silver and gold have I none, but that which I have I give to thee in the name of Jesus of Nazareth, rise up and walk.' And the lame man rose up and walked and they all glorified God" (Acts 3:1–11).*

The lame man needed healing more than he needed silver and gold! The best gift that needed to be desired here was the gift of the working of miracles, which is what was given by the Holy Spirit through the apostles (details of this in "The Gifts of the Holy Spirit" following these nine events of being baptized or filled with the Holy Spirit).

Of course, we read that the Sanhedrin refuted this miracle and that Peter and John were brought before the rulers. Being afraid of the people for all men glorified God, they found nothing wrong with them but threatened them not to teach or speak in Jesus's name any further. Peter and John, being let go, went back to the other disciples.

Peter and John both were in the upper room on the day of Pentecost, and both were baptized or filled with the Holy Spirit and fire and spoke in tongues, as the Holy Spirit gave them utterance. The precedence of tongues as proof of being filled with the Holy Spirit and fire has now been established in Acts 2:4.

"And being let go, they went to their own companions and reported all that the chief priests and elders had said to them. So when they heard

that, they raised their voice to God with one accord and said: 'Lord, You are God, who made heaven and earth and the sea, and all that is in them, who by the mouth of Your servant David have said:

Why did the nations rage, And the people plot vain things? The kings of the earth took their stand, and the rulers were gathered together against the LORD and against His Christ. For truly against Your holy Servant Jesus, whom You anointed, both Herod and Pontius Pilate, with the Gentiles and the people of Israel, were gathered together to do whatever Your hand and Your purpose determined before to be done.

Now, Lord, look on their threats, and grant to Your servants that with all boldness they may speak Your word, by stretching out Your hand to heal, and that signs and wonders may be done through the name of Your holy Servant Jesus. And when they had prayed, the place where they were assembled together was shaken; and they were ALL filled with the Holy Spirit, and they spoke the word of God with boldness." (Acts 4:23–31) [Including Peter and John and others who were in the upper room].

Notice that when they gathered together, their prayer was a prayer of acknowledgment of who God is and what He has done (the wonderful works of God). They recognized that when they were initially baptized with the Holy Spirit and spoke in tongues, fear in their hearts left, and boldness to speak God's words replaced words of fear, doubt, and unbelief, <u>then</u> miracles began to happen.

As a result, not only were souls saved, but also the lame walked after Peter and John released the resurrection power of the Holy Ghost through their words. We, literally, become channels of the resurrection power of Jesus's Holy Spirit.

Notice that the Holy Spirit, through Dr. Luke, equates precedence of being filled with the Holy Spirit and fire and speaking in tongues. He repeats this in chapter 4 verse 31 in the words, *"And they were all filled with the Holy Spirit* [which means with fire as they spoke in tongues] *and they spoke the word of God with boldness."* As we will see, he uses this precedence several times throughout the book of Acts.

The Holy Spirit equates speaking the word of God with boldness, as the result of speaking in tongues as the Holy Spirit gives the utterance, the same as on the day of Pentecost. When it relates to being filled with the Holy Spirit, boldness comes as a direct result of being filled with the Holy Spirit while speaking in tongues. However, someone speaking boldly does not necessarily mean that they are filled with the Holy Spirit and speak in tongues.

Notice that *if* being filled with the Holy Spirit is a onetime event, why, then, were Peter and John and their companions filled again with the Holy Spirit, as they were asking to receive more boldness? They knew they had a continual need for boldness, and that boldness accompanied being filled with the Holy Spirit with the evidence of speaking in tongues. Boldness was needed to continually speak the wonderful works of God in the midst of all the unbelievers and the Jewish nation. Miracles began to manifest, and many people were being healed, with these supernatural signs and wonders that were being accomplished through this authority in Jesus Christ.

"And He said to them, 'Go into all the world and preach the gospel to every creature. He who believes and is baptized will be saved; but he who does not believe will be condemned. And these signs will follow those who believe: In My name they will cast out demons; they will speak with new tongues; they will take up serpents; and if they drink anything deadly, it will by no means hurt them; they will lay hands on the sick, and they will recover.'" (Mark 16:15–18)

Luke saw no need in repeating the same words, but in showing the same kinds of results. The key words are, *"And they were all filled with the Holy Spirit."* Later we will see words like, *"And they were filled with the Holy Spirit as we were in the beginning,"* meaning the same as on the day of Pentecost when they were each initially filled with the Holy Spirit and spoke in tongues, as the Holy Spirit gave them utterance.

This is evidence that once a man, woman, or child, for that matter, is filled with the Holy Spirit, it is not a onetime event. It is to be received and experienced over and over and over. As those that are filled with the Holy Spirit and speak in tongues will tell you, when God uses you to release His power, the power flows through you and is not retained or stored up within you. It is Jesus's resurrection power flowing through us to others and <u>cannot be stored or retained in any</u>

way. It is always fresh and always full of His resurrection—life of our risen Savior.

Just like batteries that need recharging once the energy is spent, the spirit of men and women are filled (recharged) with God's Holy Spirit again and again. By faith we release His power to do the wonderful works of God through us in Jesus's name (which is His *authority* given for us to use). Once this power is released, it leaves us and flows out of us to do that which needs to be accomplished for others, then we need to be filled again. Quoting Jude again, *"But ye, beloved, building up yourselves on your most holy faith, praying in the Holy Spirit."*

All the early disciples realized this truth and walked in its revelation by releasing God's resurrection power by faith in the authority given to them by the baptism of the Holy Spirit. The same Holy Spirit who raised Christ from the dead and convinced you and me of sin, righteousness, and judgment is the same Holy Spirit who drew you and me to Jesus, then worked on activating the measure of faith given to each of us at conception by hearing, and hearing by the word of God.

"For I say, through the grace given to me, to everyone who is among you, not to think of himself more highly than he ought to think, but to think soberly, as God has dealt to each one a measure of faith." (Rom. 12:3)

"So then faith comes by hearing, and hearing by the word of God." (Rom. 10:17)

He is also the very same Holy Spirit of God who hovered over the waters of the deep in Genesis. There is certainly nothing for you and me to be afraid of. I always like to say, "There is only one Ghost, and His name is holy." I write *Holy Spirit* for the sake of my readers, but I call Him Holy Ghost in our fellowshipping.

"The grace of the Lord Jesus Christ, and the love of God, and the communion of the Holy Spirit be with you all. Amen." (2 Cor 13:14)

He knows all. He takes all He knows about Jesus, which is everything since He is Jesus's Spirit, and teaches them to us. Are you afraid of Jesus? Why, then, be afraid of Jesus's Holy Spirit? He means no harm and only has our best interest in mind.

There is one last thing to notice. Fire and wind are now equated with "The place was shaken." When the wind and fire showed up, the upper room shook, perhaps, because the shaking and trembling they experienced were inside their spirits while they were being filled with the Holy Spirit of Christ. I know it was so for me. When I was filled with the Holy Spirit, I definitely trembled at the presence of the Most High God in my life.

"For the time is come that judgment must begin at the house of God: and if it first begin at us, what shall the end be of them that obey not the gospel of God?" (1 Peter 4:17, KJV)

Whether the wind and the fire felt and experienced on that day actually shook the building or just within their spirits or both, it does not really matter. Either way, it began working its way outwardly from within them through tongues, and now circumstances for them and others began to change, and none of them would ever remain the same. If this is not shaking things up, then I don't know what is.

I can only speak firsthand of my own experiences about the day that I was filled with the Holy Spirit and spoke in tongues. I felt the fire inside me beginning to burn out all that was not for Christ. I also felt the cool presence of the wind of the Holy Spirit moving through my spirit and soul like I never experienced before. I further felt the washing of the water, as He took the word of God and instructed me in righteousness. I even experienced boldness that accompanied this wonderful work of God. Prior to this experience, I could not speak in front of people at all!

Even my understanding each time I studied the Bible or heard a sermon was clearer after being filled with the Holy Spirit. The things of God seemed to draw me like a magnet draws metal. My thirst and hunger for them were, and still are, unquenchable. The more I partake, the more I want. I receive more of Jesus each time I pray in the Holy Spirit and studied the word of God.

Inward change took place quickly, and for the first time, it actually felt like I was working out my own salvation in fear and trembling. I was not trembling with the spirit of fear, but with a reverential acknowledgment of God for who He is. My heart (spirit) acquired a greater respect for the Creator of all things, including the cosmos and

His host. I had started a journey of the continual drawing from the Holy Spirit's substance as He revealed to me to "look here," "see this," "here is your answer," "do this and not that," and so forth.

I welcomed His presence in my life as my helper with open arms. The comfort I have because of His presence gives me peace that is unexplainable and certainly inexhaustible, especially during times when I should have no peace. His personal instructions and revelations given to me from His words could never be received as clearly by learning in a classroom unless, of course, if He were the instructor. Words, images, and clear visions flow sometimes like a cool brook flowing through the desert as my spirit and soul desire His endless times of refreshing.

It was and remains a life changer for me. After thirty-seven years of drinking in the Holy Spirit's presence in my spirit and soul, His gifts and fruit abiding and working through me, in Jesus's name, are felt stronger now than ever before imagined.

Each day I wake to yet another time of refreshing in the Holy Spirit, ready to share with others this great salvation included in the wonderful works of God. Oh, how wonderful, oh, how marvelous is my God, my Savior, to me!

In Acts 4:23–31 this was the second time that was recorded showing Peter and John being filled with the Holy Spirit again, along with other believers as well. There could have been many other times before and after this, as I am sure that Luke was not privy to every one of them, because he was not with them all 24-7.

I am further convinced that in each of their private times—while walking down a street, going to the market, or praying for others—they were in a continual need of more of Him and less of themselves. You know, just doing the day-to-day routines of life, they were praying in tongues, as the Holy Spirit gave them the words to speak directly to God, singing and making melody in their hearts in a heavenly language that only God understood all too well.

It's still the same today—as I drive down the road or while I am walking in the woods, operating equipment, or taking a shower, I pray in the Holy Spirit. I too have experienced the fire, wind, and water of the Holy Spirit, and I desire being filled more today than I previously was.

Armed with the knowledge that I am praying directly to God, the Holy Spirit makes further revelation of knowledge of the truths clearer, as they contain the words of God. His inspiration is just as real and alive in my life today as it was when He inspired each of the writers of the Bible. The word of God is full of life and can never be destroyed in any manner.

"For the word of God is living and powerful, and sharper than any two-edged sword, piercing even to the division of soul and spirit, and of joints and marrow, and is a discerner of the thoughts and intents of the heart. And there is no creature hidden from His sight, but all things are naked and open to the eyes of Him to whom we must give account." (Heb. 4:12–13)

This is how I wrote my first two books titled; "*Destiny in Time, Observations in the Light*" and "*The Original Thought.*" Now, I find myself writing about the baptism of the Holy Spirit, His gifts and fruit. Jesus continues to fill me over and over, and the fire of the Holy Spirit burns His way out of my upper room in my spirit and sends His message down into the streets to share with others who may or may not have received this knowledge. Whether it is through one-on-one witnessing, preaching, teaching, or life in general at my workplace, He always finds His way through me to others.

Presently, I find myself sharing His truths with as many people as I possibly can, words now filled with Spirit, life, meaning, and understanding. How wonderful it is to share these Spirit-filled words of life with others and watch the Holy Spirit take them and begin the life-changing process of taking them from where they are and begin transforming them into the likeness of Jesus Christ.

One of my goals in life is to be involved in making movies in whatever capacity that the Lord allows and opens a door for. There is nothing more powerful than streaming images with sound and music to move an audience. Why should the rest of the world be the only ones to use this effective media? We have the message that they need to see and hear. Great match, don't you think?

THE OPERATIVE

My heart's cry is to have God's presence in me bringing forth His substance that draws all men (inclusive) to Jesus. *This is true Holy Ghost revival*, folks! It takes the fire, wind, and water of the Holy Spirit of Jesus to ignite, blow, and flow inside each of us, which is the coming alive unto the things of God.

His fire burns out of us all that is not like Christ. The wind leads us to places in the world that we normally would not go to share the good news of Jesus Christ. Our desire should be to embrace the continual washing of the water by the word of God that gives us our compass in life, enabling us to stay on the course, as the Holy Spirit directs us as easily as we direct our automobiles. Let us learn to be that sensitive to His touch as our cars are to the movement of the steering wheel.

Sharing God's words comes easy when a believer is filled with the Holy Spirit, as this gift is designed by God to work its way from the inside out. Once His word is placed inside our spirit man that is being transformed into the likeness of His Son, I guarantee you the living word in you will find His way out to others. If this is not part of your daily life, then maybe it's time to pay more attention as to what you are allowing as the priorities of your life.

Containing God the Father, Jesus the Son, and the Holy Spirit inside our spirits and souls is an improbability. <u>It cannot be done</u>. We have been designed by God to be vessels, conduits, and channels of their presence to reach out to a lost and dying world, just like somebody reached out to us.

This is what being filled with the Holy Spirit with the evidence of speaking in tongues is all about. Speaking in <u>tongues</u> is just the evidence that a believer is filled with the presence of Jesus's Holy Spirit, and because of the tongues, we will speak about the wonderful work of God that is taking place within our own spirit. Would you be filled today with the Holy Spirit of Jesus? The Holy Spirit will come if you ask the one who sends Him, and that is none other than Jesus Christ, our Savior.

CHAPTER 8

By now it has been established that the baptism of the Holy Spirit, promised by our heavenly Father and given to us by Jesus, our Lord and Savior, is a very important gift given to each believer (Christians) who asks Jesus for it. The Holy Spirit's presence, operation of gifts, and His fruit are crucial for our spiritual well-being.

However, it is important to note here that the term *Christians* was not realized until as written in the following:

> "And the disciples were first called Christians in Antioch." (Acts 11:26) (This is the *only* time in the entire Bible that the term *Christians* is even mentioned.)
>
> "*Christianos* (khris-tee-an-os'); from NT:5547; a Christian, i.e. follower of Christ: KJV—Christian" (NT:5546).
>
> "*Christos* (khris-tos'); from NT:5548; anointed, i.e. the Messiah, an epithet of Jesus: KJV—Christ" (NT:5547).
>
> "*chrio* (khree'-o); through the idea of contact; to smear or rub with oil, i.e. (by implication) to consecrate to an office or religious service: KJV—anoint" (NT:5548).

If you call yourself a Christian, then you are saying, in essence, that you are a follower of Jesus Christ and His teachings and are anointed by God through His Holy Spirit through the idea of contact as smearing or rubbing with oil. (Oil is another symbol used for the Holy Spirit.)

THE OPERATIVE

This became the *gauge* or standard by which other people knew whether a person was a believer in Christ, not because somebody said that they believed in the way. Billy Sunday, an evangelist several decades ago, is famous for his quote, "Going to church no more makes a man a Christian, than walking into a garage makes him an automobile." I agree with Billy; however, going to church allows opportunity for you to become a Christian, the same as when a believer talks to you about Jesus in your house or on the street. God's word never returns to Him void.

But for the sake of this book, we take special note that all those being filled with the Holy Spirit were those who believed in Jesus and the works that God the Father had done through Him. Throughout the entirety of this book, the term *believer* is to be considered as Christian. But in reality, not all Christians are believers. They're believers in Jesus Christ as Savior, yes, but they are not believers of His total word. Otherwise, we all would be like the early Church—every believer filled with the Holy Spirit and speaking in tongues, with signs and wonders following—as we each release the resurrection power of the Holy Spirit, as He gives us directives to do so. Isn't this what the Lord began His Church with? Yes, of course! Isn't this what He wants to end His Church with? Yes, of course, He does!

Without a doubt, we know that Jesus was the baptizer with the Holy Spirit, as John instructed in his teachings that there was one coming whose shoe latches he was not worthy to unlatch; it was He that would baptize with the Holy Spirit and fire.

In Acts 2:4 we were shown that as the believers were filled with the Holy Spirit, <u>all began to speak in tongues</u>, as the Spirit gave them utterance. This was the <u>first filling</u> of the Holy Spirit.

Peter and John, after being told by the Sanhedrin never to teach or speak in the name of Jesus again, went back to their own company (many of which were some of the initial people filled with the Holy Spirit and who spoke the word of God with boldness from the upper room into the streets of Jerusalem).

"And when they had prayed, [read 4:23–30 to see what they prayed] *the place was shaken where they were assembled together; and they were ALL filled with the Holy Spirit [again] and they spoke the word*

of God with boldness." (Acts 4:31) This was the <u>second filling</u> of the Holy Spirit to many of the same people who were previously filled.

In the first filling, we saw each receiving boldness, taking the place of timidity and the spirit of fear. Now standing boldly, they spoke the wonderful works of God, and thousands of believers began to be added to them. Then after the second filling of the Holy Spirit, we read about miracle after miracle that were being done by the hands of the apostles and others.

Many things happened between then and Acts chapter 6, but for the sake of time and space, I will not go into detail concerning these miracles. I do, however, want to focus on two men who were <u>not</u> original apostles.

This gift from the Father, through Jesus our Savior, was not and is not only for a select few or those only in a position of authority—that is, apostles, prophets, evangelists, pastors, and teachers. These positions are the fivefold ministry gifts. Being filled with the Holy Spirit, according to the scriptures, makes those who are placed in these positions more effective spiritually.

(A quick note—these fivefold ministry positions are not titles for us to place beside our names lightly. These are positions of great responsibility and accountability, first to God through Jesus, then to those they serve.)

In Acts 6 we see a problem arising with the service to the Grecian widows. They were being neglected in the daily administration. Back then, these men fulfilled their duties with joy, but today, we find many thinking this office of waiting on tables below them. Notice what the apostles said were the qualifications that the seven candidates had to possess: (1) Choose seven men of honest report and (2) Choose men full of the Holy Spirit and wisdom. These were just the qualifications to wait on the tables of the Grecian widows. We find out that these two men actually did more in their lives than wait on tables.

While number 1 is just as important as number 2, we are introduced to another word being equal in status with being filled with the Holy Spirit—*wisdom*. Wisdom is now brought to the forefront as being another benefit or attribute of being filled with the Holy Spirit. It's a by-product, like boldness was as we saw earlier.

Of course, we know this wisdom is the wisdom that Jesus Himself has and continues to make available to us through His Holy Spirit. The disciples recognized it as one of the gifts of the Holy Spirit, which is the word of wisdom.

This truth was known by the disciples, as they were men filled with the Holy Spirit and operated in these gifts of the Holy Spirit, which included the word of wisdom.

The phrase *"full of the Holy Spirit"* can only be taken one way. And that way is determined by the precedence set by the Holy Spirit through Luke in Acts 2:4, which says, *"And they were all filled with the Holy Spirit, and began to speak in other tongues as the Holy Spirit gave utterance."* Anything short of this is not and should not be considered as being filled with the Holy Spirit. This precedence is the meaning and equivalency of all other mentions of being filled with the Holy Spirit in Acts, and other books of the Bible that speak to this topic, such as 1 Corinthians & Ephesians to name a couple.

Luke and Paul did not have to continually repeat themselves, as I am, by writing, *"And they were all filled with the Holy Spirit, and began to speak in other tongues as the Holy Spirit gave utterance."* The reason he did not have to repeat himself was because he and others knew that the early Church believers were *all* filled with the Holy Spirit, and they understood what he meant, just like we still set a precedence in writing today. Because of this fact, later on when Luke's words were read *("Wherefore, brethren, look among you for seven men of honest report, full of the Holy Spirit and wisdom, whom we may appoint over this business")*, they were each aware of the standard and considered it a prerequisite for this position.

I choose to repeat myself in this book several times because I want to place emphasis upon this most important topic and teach like the Bible says—line upon line, precept upon precept, here a little, there a little. Notice the repeat of *line* and *precept*? (See Isaiah 28:10-13 NKJV).

The seven men chosen were Stephen, Philip, Prochorus, Nicanor, Timon, Parmenas, and Nicolas, and each of them were filled with the Holy Spirit and all that implied. They each spoke in tongues and had boldness, faith, power, honest report, and wisdom, which are what this gift produces in our lives so men can prosper in the things of God.

This is the <u>third filling</u> of the Holy Spirit as in Acts 2:4; otherwise, they would not have been eligible to have been considered for this position at all. If they had to have such a high standard then for waiting on the tables, shouldn't our standard for those filling the pulpits in the church have, at least, the same qualifications?

Only two out of the seven mentioned were chosen for this task, and we know by the scriptures that it was Philip and Stephen. <u>The other five candidates were never mentioned again in the Bible.</u> Since they each were filled with the Holy Spirit, each had an honest report, was bold in their speaking, and was full of wisdom; I believe they still had a full life. Being worthy of a mention in God's word is an honor in itself as equals to those who were chosen.

I believe they symbolize the millions that do great things for Jesus through His Holy Spirit but never receive recognition in this life for all they have done by those who keep records of such things. Perhaps, Luke had not heard or seen what the other five men might have accomplished in their lives, but either way God took notice and recorded them all.

Philip conducted a revival meeting when he came to Samaria and preached about Christ. The Jews did not think well of the Samaritan people. The Bible is very clear about this fact. I am sure that for Philip to go there to preach, he received some evil looks and possible threats, and someone could have mentioned about ostracizing him from the Church. Of course, no true believers would ostracize another believer for preaching the gospel, right?

(But Jesus paved the way for this city when He ministered to the lady at the well, then spent two days in Samaria before going to Galilee. You can read this full account in John 4:1–45.)

I am sad to say that in our churches today, we still see the click mentality—"us four and no more" kind of thinking. According to the Bible, this kind of division and respect of person should not be going on. It is a product of men yielding to fleshly ways instead of listening to the Holy Spirit.

The Holy Spirit always had other plans as He does even today, as the people heard the message that Philip was preaching, which was about Christ crucified, raised from the dead, and His blood shed for the removal of sin, with the power of the Holy Spirit in Him producing miracles. Many believed, and unclean spirits, crying with loud voices, came out of many who were possessed. Others taken with palsies and the lame were healed. *"And there was great joy in that city." (Acts 8:8)*

You Think?

For those of you who desire to see revival in America and throughout the world, <u>this is how it is done</u>. It takes the Holy Spirit to stage a true revival—bringing life to the spoken word, calling men to Jesus, and operating His power and gifts to convince men that they need a Savior.

We dare not leave the Holy Spirit out of our meetings! He should be front and center in everything we do, as He is the one who teaches us the things of *Jesus* so we can apply them in our lives and share them with others.

While revival may contain a series of meetings, a series of meetings does not constitute a revival. True revival is men (inclusive) coming *alive* unto the things of God, which also includes changing their minds about Jesus, that He is truly the Son of God and that God sent Him to save all who call upon His name. (Take the time to read Psalms 119, which will clarify this for you. After reading it, find someone to share it with.)

Philip continued doing the work of an evangelist. In the middle of this successful revival in Samaria, the Holy Spirit instructed him to leave and go to Gaza. Upon his arrival in Gaza, he saw an Ethiopian reading Isaiah. He joined him and explained to him the meaning of the words that he was reading.

Philip instructed him that Isaiah was actually talking about Jesus and explained the way to him. The Ethiopian eunuch was enlightened and chose to be born again and asked what would hinder him from being water baptized. As Philip was bringing the Ethiopian out of the water, the Holy Spirit's power transported Philip to another location.

"Now when they came up out of the water, the Spirit of the Lord caught Philip away, so that the eunuch saw him no more; and he went on his way rejoicing. But Philip was found at Azotus. And passing through, he preached in all the cities till he came to Caesarea." (Acts 8:39–40)

Read the entire eighth chapter of the book of Acts for all the details. Philip was <u>transported approximately twenty-two miles away from where he was in Gaza</u>. Why does this not happen today? Or maybe it does happen! I believe it does, and we just don't hear about it. How many of you would tell if the Holy Spirit transported you to another location, like He did Philip? Jesus Christ is the same yesterday and forever, isn't He?

My point in sharing scriptures concerning Philip with you, as well as about Stephen, is to show you that both of them had the prerequisite of having an honest report and being filled with the Holy Spirit, just to wait on tables. How far from the truth of this prerequisite has the Church come?

Notice also that the Holy Spirit never left them waiting on tables but promoted them by using them as instruments of righteousness while operating in His gifts and power through them. As we are faithful over the little, He gives us more to be faithful over.

As for Stephen, once filled with the Holy Spirit with the evidence of speaking in tongues, he was a man full of *faith*. The Holy Spirit chose him for an assignment altogether different from that of Philip's. *(Remember Jude 20?)*

These seven men set before the apostles, and when they had prayed and laid their hands on them, what were the results? Acts 6:7 says, *"And the word of God increased, and the number of the disciples multiplied in Jerusalem greatly; and a great company of the priest were obedient to the faith."* Even those of the priesthood were getting born again and filled with the Holy Spirit.

There was no lack of candidates to replace Philip's and Stephen's positions. However, their replacements were not mentioned in the scriptures. I am sure the writers assumed the readers would realize that those chosen would eventually be sent out, and then replaced by other qualified believers filled with the Holy Spirit by those new converts who were convinced and brought fresh into the body of Christ and filled with the Holy Spirit with the evidence of tongues and all other qualifications that followed on a daily basis.

As Jesus directed the early Church by His Holy Spirit, I believe that He still desires to direct the modern Church in the same manner, calling in new converts, filling each of them with His Holy Spirit and fire, then maturing them for the work of ministry, with the help of His Holy Spirit teaching them, along with those who are already equipped by Him.

Once equipped, they too are sent out by the Holy Spirit to do their particular parts of the ministry. This process is to be repeated over and over until the last soul comes into the fold.

Notice the words "obedient to the faith." In context, these words are equivalent not only to believing in Jesus as the Savior but also to being filled with the Holy Spirit and speaking in tongues as the Spirit gives the utterance, which brings boldness, fullness of wisdom, fullness of faith and power, and honest report. The faith of Jesus includes the baptism of the Holy Spirit, according to the inspired scriptures of Jesus Christ.

Each time, the writer was saying the same thing, and for all those who heard or read these letters (scriptures), they understood what it meant to be filled with the Holy Spirit and the evidence of speaking in tongues, because every believer was filled with the Holy Spirit and spoke in tongues, along with all that this implied.

As time passed, knowledge of these things had been lost because of traditions of men, which, Jesus said, took the power out of God's word or made it noneffective.

"Making the word of God of none effect through your tradition, which ye have delivered: and many such like things do ye." (Mark 7:13, KJV)

It may be our own preferences (denominations) in worshipping God that are threats of removing the true context of what the Holy Spirit is saying. What is He saying to the Church today? He is revealing His truths when we spend time with Him as the author of the Bible. Asking

Him to reveal to us the meaning and understanding of what He actually wants and expects from us as the Church today is our duty as a believer.

Understanding what these statements and words mean and counting the cost of being equated with them were known by the believers in the early Church. They knew very well that their lives needed to be in total submission to Jesus and His Holy Spirit. It is still the same today. Believers who actually spend time reading the Bible know the cost.

In America today, we feel the sting of losing certain things like friendships, families, jobs, etc., because we are professing Christians. Take a good look around the world today in 2015. Many Christians are actually losing their lives because they have made Jesus Christ their Savior and are speaking boldly about it. God forbid that it ever starts happening here, but it very well could happen. I wonder, how many Christians would announce their Christianity, then?

In verse 8, it's recorded that "Stephen full of faith and power, did great wonders and miracles among the people." *Now wait just one minute!* Weren't Stephen and Philip both two of the seven men chosen to serve the tables of the Grecians widows? *Yes* is the answer you are looking for! He never left them there because of their willingness to be used in all the things of the Lord.

The Holy Spirit does not only use those in authority but also longs to use any member of the body of Christ who makes himself or herself available to Him. He has a plan and purpose for each of us, with nothing but good thoughts that accompany them.

"For I know the thoughts that I think toward you, saith the LORD, thoughts of peace, and not of evil, to give you an expected end." (Jer. 29:11, KJV)

Evidently, Stephen had prayed so much in the Holy Spirit, and the faith in him was strong enough that when he addressed the Sanhedrin, he spoke the truth to those that questioned him, and it did cost him his life. (Read Acts 6 and 7 for full details.)

This now leads us to the <u>fourth filling</u> of the Holy Spirit. As we continue to explore the details regarding the *Acts of the Holy Spirit*, keep in mind that Jesus longs to baptize you with His Holy Spirit today!

CHAPTER 9

It is true that there are nine different times in the book of Acts that the Holy Spirit reveals His baptism, promised by the Father and given to each believer who asks His Son, Jesus, the one who baptizes in the Holy Spirit.

If you are seriously pursuing this baptism, Jesus is the one to ask. He will fill you with His Holy Spirit with the evidence of speaking in tongues <u>as on the day of Pentecost</u>.

Let's now take a look at the <u>fourth filling.</u> The Holy Spirit recorded in the book of Acts that believers were all filled with the Holy Spirit. If you recall in the previous chapter of this book, Stephen, full of the Holy Spirit and faith, was speaking to the Sanhedrin, telling them the truth about the wonderful works of God, reminding them of what they did to Jesus. Obviously, this made them mad, to say the least. Usually the truth does this to a person who is not open to the things of God.

In Stephen's case, it worked against him. In Acts 7:54–60, his audience gnashed their teeth at him, and they actually ended up stoning him to death. Not everyone filled with the Holy Spirit is chosen for martyrdom, <u>thank God</u>. So do not get worked up, robbing yourself of the wonderful works of God.

Martyrs among believers have been chosen with and without being filled with the Holy Spirit through the centuries. If this is part of the plan and purpose for a believer's life, it will happen regardless of whether they are filled with the Holy Spirit or not. I would rather be filled with the Holy Spirit than not, especially if I were chosen to be a martyr for Christ.

Today, as in Stephen's day, there are believers who want more of God. They want to get closer to Jesus. Well, if you're filled with Jesus's Holy Spirit, you cannot get any closer than that, as He actually fills your spirit with His presence.

In Acts 8, we have a new character introduced, Saul of Tarsus. After Stephen's death, there was great persecution against the Church in Jerusalem, and Saul was right in the middle of it.

As they carried Stephen to his burial, it was Saul who kept stirring up havoc for the Church. He was actually the man standing and holding the garments of those who stoned Stephen to death. Simply holding their garments—the Lord considered this act of Saul as consent and approval to this stoning. We will learn more about him later.

I now want to draw your attention to this <u>fourth filling</u> of the Holy Spirit found in Acts 8:14–17: *"Now when the apostles who were at Jerusalem heard that Samaria had received the word of God, they sent Peter and John to them, who, when they had come down, prayed for them that they might receive the Holy Spirit. For as yet He had fallen upon none of them. They had only been baptized* [water baptism] *in the name of the Lord Jesus. Then they laid hands on them, and they received the Holy Spirit."*

Here we have yet another event directly associated with the baptism of the Holy Spirit. The Holy Spirit introduces another way that Jesus uses to fill believers with His Holy Spirit, and that is the laying on of hands. Simon, the sorcerer, wanted to buy this ability once he saw it work. Peter told him his money perished with him. <u>We never hear of Simon, the sorcerer, again in the Bible.</u>

These believers were the Samaritans that Philip was preaching to, and many souls were saved and delivered from the evil works of the devil, and these were the same Samaritans found here in Acts 8:14–17! The news traveled so fast to the apostles in Jerusalem, and they, being astonished by the news that Samaritans were born again, sent Peter and John to go verify its truth.

THE OPERATIVE

God had now made available to the Gentiles (Samaritans) His salvation, the very same salvation that the Jews were experiencing at that time. They were born again and added to the Church through Philip's Holy Spirit–planned services, and they were all baptized in *water*. Notice the distinction made by the Holy Spirit between being baptized in water and being baptized in the Holy Spirit.

Many in the Church today still believe that they are filled with the Holy Spirit when they are born again and water baptized. According to the scriptures, *this is not so*! They are two distinct *baptisms*.

Some still believe that the baptism of the Holy Spirit is of the devil, or it's passed away with the apostles. If this is the case, why are these Gentile believers in Samaria, being filled with the Holy Spirit <u>after</u> being born again and water baptized? The truth is right before our eyes, if we will only pay attention to it under the direction of the Holy Spirit who inspired it.

In Acts 11:15, 16, Peter was reviewing this very matter, which I will show as the sixth filling of the Holy Spirit. However, it is fitting to write what Peter says about <u>this</u> event upon the Gentiles: "And as I began to speak, the Holy Spirit fell upon them, <u>as upon us at the beginning</u>. Then I remembered the word of the Lord, how He said, John indeed baptized with water, but you shall be baptized with the Holy Spirit."

I do not think it can be any clearer than that! "The Holy Spirit fell upon them, as upon us at the beginning." What happened at the beginning?

"And they were all filled with the Holy Spirit and began to speak with other tongues, as the Spirit gave them utterance." (Acts 2:4)

Then Peter said, *"Then I remembered the word of the Lord, how He said, John indeed baptized with water, but you shall be baptized with the Holy Spirit."*

I feel such sorrow for you if you cannot see that these are two separate events that happen to believers. We recognize water baptism as symbolic of the old man becoming new after being washed in the blood of Jesus.

Why do we have so much trouble in recognizing the baptism of the Holy Spirit as a valid gift for each believer who asks Jesus for this promised gift from the Father? I believe it is because it is easier to believe a lie than the truth, and this is why the devil has had so much success in keeping the resurrection power out of most of the Church. But this is about to change.

The Holy Spirit never ceases to amaze me. I was reading a post online that read as follows:

> "Holy Spirit You Are Welcome Here,
> Come Flood This Place
> And Fill The Atmosphere."

I later discovered that these words are from the song titled "Holy Spirit", by Francesca Battistelli, which song I fell in love with the moment I heard it. However, we must always realize that each person can only work and present the truth from the revelations that they have at the moment of presentation. We must always allow room for growth in our knowledge and understanding of God's word in our lives, as we each are in a continual flux of spiritual growth.

At that time, something about these words did not set well in my spirit, and as I began to meditate upon and prayerfully consider them with the revelation that I had currently, I was given understanding, as the Holy spirit revealed to me that He did not come to change the atmosphere in our lives, but He came to change the *"inner-sphere"* of our lives.

That's it—the *"inner-sphere"* of our lives! It is the inner man made stronger by His power in us that changes us—first on the inside, then those changes are worked out of us to our soul and flesh, and the appropriate changes, then, can be realized within our lives.

On that day that the Holy Spirit was poured out on and into the believers in the upper room, His original "calling card" was the rushing mighty wind. The disciples had previously felt this wind when Jesus breathed on them, saying, *Receive ye the Holy Spirit.* Jesus knew this was how they would realize this event as the promised gift of the Holy Spirit, and they would not resist Him or run from Him in fear.

The result was that each believer was filled with the Holy Spirit and spoke in other tongues or what Paul later called tongues. Those who heard them speaking in tongues thought they were drunk with new wine, but eventually understood the wonderful works of God in their own language because of the two gifts of the Holy Spirit in operation, which were tongues and the interpretation of tongues. (See again First Corinthians 12, 13, and 14.)

It was not as some seemed to believe that they were actually speaking the languages of those devout men and women there in Jerusalem for the Passover Feast. As mentioned before, they heard them speaking in tongues—the devout men, by the Holy Spirit giving each of them the understanding, in their own language, of that which was being spoken.

This is what happens when the gift of interpretation of tongues is given. One understands in the language or languages that they speak and interprets accordingly so that the observers can also understand and profit from or be edified by the message interpreted.

Yes, the atmosphere changed on that glorious day but only to verify who it was entering the room. The Holy Spirit cannot be seen with our natural eyes, as Jesus's glorified body was when He entered the room after His resurrection. He revealed Himself in this capacity to confirm His resurrection. But when He sent the disciples His Holy Spirit on Pentecost, He had already prepared them to recognize His presence by the wind of His breath.

This wind was only mentioned in the book of Acts in the upper room, and Luke never mentioned this again, nor did any other writer in the New Testament. But tongues is mentioned more than once in the New Testament—thus, being the gauge of being filled with the Holy Spirit and fire as His new calling card.

<u>The Holy Spirit is the operative of the Church today and is given to us to change us from the inside out</u>, enabling each of us to become more like Jesus today than we were yesterday. As men (inclusive) are born again, they receive a new spirit, which enables the King of kings and the Lord of lords the ability to reside within them.

Jesus comes as a spiritual seed via His Holy Spirit and matures as the believer grows in the grace and knowledge of our Lord and Savior. This spiritual growth process of a born-again believer is strengthened and nourished by being filled with the Holy Spirit and fire. The same resurrection power used to raise Christ from the dead is <u>now</u> available to fill the born-again believer's new spirit, bringing Jesus Christ to life inside us.

Again, this baptism of the Holy Spirit is *not* a prerequisite for salvation. But it certainly is a growth enhancement, like plants receiving Miracle-Gro to keep them healthy, growing stronger while becoming more productive. Believers who are filled with the Holy Spirit thrive on the miraculous resurrection power of the Holy Spirit, filling them.

We have established that the calling card of the Holy Spirit is tongues, as of fire. He cools our spirits and souls from the consuming fire of God's presence with the refreshing water of His word—all this while the flaming fires keep burning inside us. The wind symbolizes His breeze that directs us to places that we should go, as He leads us in the paths according to God's plan and purpose for each of our lives.

The water of the Holy Spirit not only cools but also mixes with the word of God and cleanses us continually, changing our viewpoints, opinions, and who we are to line up with who we should be according to the scriptures.

The scriptures themselves are alive and sharper than any double-edged sword.

"For the word of God is living and powerful, and sharper than any two-edged sword, piercing even to the division of soul and spirit, and of joints and marrow, and is a discerner of the thoughts and intents of the heart." (Heb. 4:12)

They contain the brooks that our souls desire, the same as a deer pants for the water brooks.

"As the deer pants for the water brooks, So pants my soul for You, O God. My soul thirsts for God, for the living God." (Ps. 42:1–2)

They are the well of living water springing up from deep within our spirits and souls.

"On the last day, that great day of the feast, Jesus stood and cried out, saying, 'If anyone thirsts, let him come to Me and drink. He who believes in Me, as the Scripture has said, out of his heart will flow rivers of living water.'" (John 7:37–39)

THE OPERATIVE

The fire of the Holy Spirit transforms us from <u>our glory</u> to <u>His Glory</u> until we all come into the unity of faith and be not as children tossed here and there with every wind of doctrine.

The Holy Spirit is available to all who believes and asks Jesus to fill them. When this happens to a believer, the Holy Spirit pours the love of God into our hearts (spirit man) and begins the process of spiritual growth within us. We become more like Christ, which is our ultimate goal, is it not?

This *"inner-sphere transformation"* experience shows us what we will become once we receive our glorified body. This is what we experience today—not a changing of the atmosphere so much as the changing of our inner man being renewed daily! If we continue to look for the curtains to blow or houses and churches to shake, we might miss out on the best gift given to us since salvation.

Our natural eyes see the curtains and buildings. But it is our spiritual eye of faith that reveal to us that which cannot be seen in the natural. What works in the natural realm does not necessarily work in the spiritual realm! Stop looking at natural things to change to receive the spiritual things from God; it does not work that way.

What a closet to go into and pray and fellowship with the Lord. Could this be the closet that the Lord Jesus was talking about? When we pray, we have been instructed to go into our closet and pray to God in secret so that He can reward us openly. Your *"inner-sphere closet"* is the dwelling place of the Godhead bodily, and you cannot get any closer to God than this.

Have you experienced this inner-sphere event yet? If not, I highly recommend that you go to your Savior, Jesus, and ask Him to fill you with His Holy Spirit of promise, and let Him show you the evidence that is relevant for today.

Information revealed to us by the Holy Spirit is for our benefit to solidify our fellowship with the Father, Jesus, and the Holy Spirit. In order to know something from the Holy Spirit about a particular topic, He may have to give you pieces of knowledge before your understanding is complete in a matter. He uses revelation knowledge to accomplish this.

Revelation knowledge is what Jesus was talking about when He questioned His disciples, *"Who do you say that I am?"*

"He said to them, 'But who do you say that I am?' Simon Peter answered and said, 'You are the Christ, the Son of the living God.' Jesus answered and said to him, 'Blessed are you, Simon Bar-Jonah, for flesh and blood has not revealed this to you, but My Father who is in heaven. And I also say to you that you are Peter, and on this rock I will build My church, and the gates of Hades shall not prevail against it.'" (Matt. 16:15–19)

There are many believers who misunderstand these scriptures. Let's see what is being said. The topic is, *"Who is Jesus?"* He began by asking them a series of questions, first being *"Who do men say that I am?"* They answered, *"Some say Elias, and others said this or that."*

As Jesus turned the question back on them, He asked, *"Who do you say that I am?"* As they all stood by, trying to think of a satisfactory answer, Peter stood and said, *"You are the Christ, the Son of the living God."*

Bingo, the correct answer to the question was given. Now, here is where many lose out on the correct revelation. Jesus then used Peter's answer to change direction in the topic of their conversation. The topic now changed from *"Who do men and you say that I am?"* to *"How did you receive this knowledge?"* Jesus proclaimed, *"For flesh and blood has not revealed this to you, but My Father who is in heaven."* Can you see that the topic changed from who Jesus was to how Peter received this revelation?

Many believe that the Church is built upon Peter, but actually, it is built upon revelation knowledge from the Holy Spirit. Let me prove it to you.

First, we have Jesus saying that *"flesh and blood* [or men] h*as not revealed this to you, but my Father who is in heaven."* Secondly, the original words used for *Peter* are the following:

"*petra* (pet'-ra); feminine of the same as NT:4074; a (mass of) rock (literally or figuratively): KJV—rock" (NT:4073).

"*Petros* (pet'-ros); apparently a primary word; a (piece of) rock (larger than NT:3037); as a name, Petrus, an apostle. KJV—Peter, rock. Compare NT:2786" (NT:4074).

THE OPERATIVE

> "*lithos* (lee'-thos); apparently a primary word; a stone (literally or figuratively): KJV—(mill-, stumbling-) stone" (NT:3037).
> "*Kephas* (kay-fas'); of Aramaic origin [compare OT:3710]; the Rock; Cephas (i.e. Kepha), a surname of Peter: KJV—Cephas" (NT:2786).
> "*keph* (kafe); from OT:3721; a hollow rock: KJV—rock" (OT:3710).
> "*kaphaph* (kaw-faf'); a primitive root; to curve: KJV—bow down (self)" (OT:3721).

Each of the above words' definitions should be used in determining that Peter's name is a piece of larger rock and a derivative from the word used for small rock. Also, it is a derivative of words pointing to Cephas as the surname of Peter, as a hollow rock to curve or bow down. This is the meaning of *Peter* that Jesus used. Let's now take a look at what "upon this rock" means.

> "upon—*epi* (ep-ee'); a primary preposition; properly, meaning superimposition (of time, place, order, etc.), as a relation of distribution [with the genitive case], i.e. over, upon, etc.; of rest (with the det.) at, on, etc.; of direction (with the accusative case) towards, upon, etc." (NT:1909).
> "rock—*petra* (pet'-ra); feminine of the same as NT:4074; a (mass of) rock (literally or figuratively): KJV—rock" (NT:4073).

I believe Jesus's use of these words pointed to the rock as figuratively and not literally. To paraphrase what Jesus was saying based upon the meanings of the words used above, I have to come to this conclusion: Peter said; *"You are the Christ, the Son of the living God."* Then Jesus said, "No man has revealed this to you, Peter. This knowledge was revealed to you from my Father in heaven. I say to you, Peter (small portion of a larger rock), that you have received a portion (revelation knowledge) of the larger rock (foundation of the church), and upon this substance of revelation knowledge, I will build my Church, and the gates of hell will not prevail against it." Jesus, being the larger rock of our salvation and revelation knowledge, brings us pieces of these foundational truths for our beliefs to build upon.

Why are the gates of hell not able to prevail against the Church built upon this substance? Because the revelation knowledge that the Holy Spirit reveals to us brings convictions of the truth that does not change, unlike preferences, which do change. You will stand firm on the things that you have been convinced by the Holy Spirit as truth. Isn't this what we do with our salvation?

Preferences, however, do change. They are made from things preferred and accepted by men or women, either giving or receiving what others say is truth without finding out for himself or herself. Groups prefer to worship God as a Baptist, Methodist, Presbyterian, or perhaps, Catholic, etc., while other people worship God—or should I say *god*—through nature, intelligence, animals, etc., worshipping the creation more than the Creator.

I have seen firsthand, and you probably have too, the many ways that men think they can find God. Some even believe that *nothing* somehow accumulated from *nowhere* and that *nothingness* exploded by *nothing* that existed at that time with such force that *nothing* brought forth *everything* that exists today. As stupid as this may sound, it is just equally stupid to believe that the cosmos actually came into existence this way—from nothing. You who believe this have got to be kidding me, right?

We need to realize that revelation knowledge is the substance or the building material that the Holy Spirit uses during His preparation of the Church for Jesus's return to remove His bride from this world.

This you will see in more detail once we start exploring the gifts of the Holy Spirit, and one of them is actually the gift of word of knowledge, given to men supernaturally by the Holy Spirit for a specific reason and/or purpose.

I believe most of the revelations that I have been given are direct results of praying in the Holy Spirit or tongues. Then at the appointed time, the Holy Spirit gives me these words of knowledge to prosper me in my understanding of His spiritually discerned words found in the scriptures, equipping me for a fruitful work of the ministry and all that it implies.

By all means, *welcome* the Holy Spirit into your life, *not* just into a building! God; His Son, Jesus; and His Holy Spirit are mindful of each of us more than our buildings. He actually considers each believer as His temple, His abiding place.

"Jesus answered and said unto him, 'If a man love me, he will keep my words: and my Father will love him, and WE will come unto him, and make our abode with him.'" (John 14:23, KJV)

"Or do you not know that your body is the temple of the Holy Spirit who is in you, whom you have from God, and you are not your own? For you were bought at a price; therefore, glorify God in your body and in your spirit, which are God's." (1 Cor. 6:19–20)

"And I heard a loud voice from heaven saying, 'Behold, the tabernacle of God is with men, and He will dwell with them, and they shall be His people. God Himself will be with them and be their God. And God will wipe away every tear from their eyes; there shall be no more death, nor sorrow, nor crying. There shall be no more pain, for the former things have passed away.'" (Rev. 21:3–4)

He cares for our well-being more than that of our structures for us to gather together to worship Him. For we must worship Him in spirit and truth, as He has chosen for us not to worship Him while in buildings only when we come together. This is why we are not seeing the curtains move or the building shaking. He is more interested in moving you and me and shaking us, as His Holy Spirit transforms us into that which will be manifested for the whole world to see.

Welcome Him into the house made without hands of men (your spirit), a spiritual house, enabling the Almighty God, His Son, and His Spirit to abide there. Take some time to think about this. The Creator of the heavens and the earth and the possessor of the title and deeds thereof makes it possible to make His habitation in us through His Spirit, who is freely given to all believers requesting His presence in this capacity!

Oh, what a glorious day, in which to live, a time like never before in our history! I ask you, should we be spending it, building bigger buildings? Should we be spending it, fussing about our differences or the color of carpets, pews, chairs, etc? As for such a time as this, we were born! What are we actually doing with the time that the Lord has given us as the Church of the living God? Is the Church today turning the world upside down or turning the old carpets and pews into new ones? Invest in lives, please! Spend your time on things that matter the most, like souls!

Jewish believers were filled first with the Holy Spirit, with speaking in tongues. Then the Gentiles (common folk just like you and me) were filled and began to speak in tongues, as the Spirit gave them utterance. Yes, the twelve apostles were baptized in the Holy Spirit, with the same evidence of speaking in tongues, but so wasn't the other one hundred and eight Jewish believers in the upper room on Pentecost?

I cannot stress this enough; we have records of Gentile believers being born again, water baptized, and baptized with the Holy Spirit. And guess what? They all spoke in other tongues, as the Spirit gave them the utterance. This was not meant for the apostles alone, but for the whole Church of the living God.

All throughout the book of Acts, the early believers of the Church were filled with the Holy Spirit and spoke in tongues. This was the norm for them and should be the norm for today for every believer in Christ.

This is God's word, not mine. I believe it and experience it every day in my life. I am convinced and know, for a fact, that this is real! For me, this truth is equivalent to the truth that Jesus died for my sins. Nobody could talk me out of either of these!

What does the modern Church need today? <u>More conviction and less preference!</u> We need (His) boldness, (His) power, and (His) faith. Once a believer is filled with the Holy Spirit, evidenced by speaking in tongues, boldness, power (authority), faith, and much more come with Him. This life is available to every believer.

But what if we do not believe this?

Saul did not believe this because he preferred the Law of Moses. His beliefs brought anger and hatred toward believers, much like other religious leaders and atheists do today. This hatred motivated him to go to those in authority, making deals and drawing up agreement papers (approval to do what he wanted to do to the believers in Christ), permitting him legally to beat, imprison, and yes, even murdering many believers of Christ.

You may think it's not that simple. Our own lawmakers in America can change the way we live with a single stroke of a pen. Have you felt any of the results of their actions in your family's lives today? Take a closer look at what is going on today around the world toward Christians and what is trying to start happening here in America. God forbid that it gets worse.

<u>There is a good ending to Saul's sad beginning</u>. While on his way to Damascus to do his dirty deeds, he had an unexpected encounter with the very one he was persecuting—Jesus, the resurrected Christ.

(Another side note here—Those who mistreat, laugh at, mock, beat, and yes, even kill Christians are actually doing it to Jesus Himself. We are members of His body. Jesus lives within our spirits, and the Father lives within Jesus. Once a person becomes born again and is given eternal life, having Jesus living in their heart, whatever happens to them, Jesus considers it happening to Him as well.)

This leads us to the <u>fifth filling</u> of the Holy Spirit. A man's life was changed forever, and because of his changed life, much of the New Testament was made available for us to read. God, via His Holy Spirit, gave Saul revelation knowledge, changing his name to Paul. A man once known as Saul of Tarsus, angry and full of hatred toward all Christians, became Paul and joined the ranks of the believers to preach and teach the wonderful works of God to all he came in contact with.

Change in a person's life is not only the reward of being born again but also the proof that Jesus is alive within their heart. Becoming more like Jesus today than we were yesterday allows us to know that we are on the path of His righteousness and not our own.

Saul was on the path of his own righteousness, conformed to the law. Because of this conformation, he was filled with murderous deeds toward believers. However, there is *hope* for even the worst of the worst because of the *goodness* of God and His wonderful mercy and grace.

> Sometime in 2006, my wife wrote in her book of quotes the following: "A man or woman is worth more than the worst thing that he or she has ever done!"[4]

---

4. Rosalyn A. Hamrick

CHAPTER 10

Saul came to the forefront of the Church when he consented to the stoning of Stephen to death by holding the coats of the stone throwers who killed him. This made Saul just as guilty also.

It's important to say that our words can be just as devastating as the actual stones thrown at Stephen. Bullying and slandering are how many are being stoned today. Yes, this even takes place in modern churches. Of course, in other countries, Christians are literally still being stoned to death and much worse.

You may ask, "Why are you talking about stoning people?" Have you listened to the news lately or read a newspaper, a magazine, or an online post? I am sure that you have. I just want you to be aware of the devil' devices and not be ignorant of them.

Saul, who later was called Paul, is known by this new name even to this day. He obtained letters to do whatever he thought to be right in his own eyes, regarding the mistreatment of the early believers. He had already beaten some and placed some in shackles in the depth of the darkest prisons, and yes, he murdered in some cases.

While Saul and his fellow travelers were riding their horses along the road to Damascus, a very unique thing happened to him. The one he had been persecuting by beatings, imprisonments, and killings of the believers showed up in person. Whether in reality or in a vision, he later would say, that he could not tell. He just knew that he was in a situation he had never experienced before or even knew existed.

THE OPERATIVE

It was the glory of God that was revealed to Saul. His horse threw him off, and when he came to his faculties, he heard a voice saying, *"Saul, Saul, why persecutes thou me?"* Immediately Saul recognized authority in the voice, as he asked, *"Whom art thou, Lord?"* Jesus answered him by saying, *"I am Jesus, who thou persecutes, it is hard for thee to kick against the goads."* (Read chapter 9 of Acts for details.)

Knowing now He was the Lord Jesus who was raised from the dead, Saul immediately asked for instruction on what to do. Up to this point, Saul had done what he thought was right in his own eyes. The law that he was raised and trained under as a devout Jew had just failed him. His preference for the law was changing forever in his life, right before his very eyes and there was nothing he could do to stop it from happening. Jesus told him to "arise, and go into the city (Damascus), and it shall be told thee what thou must do."

Where once the law was his tutor giving him guidance and authority, from this point forward, it would be the Holy Spirit of Jesus, the resurrected Lord. His coveted law had finally brought him face-to-face with the Christ of the law, as the tutor was designed by God to do for all of Israel.

"Therefore the law was our tutor to bring us to Christ, that we might be justified by faith. But after faith has come, we are no longer under a tutor." (Gal. 3:24–25)

Imagine if you will—Saul's companions watching, speechless, hearing a noise but seeing no man. Saul rose from the ground, and upon opening his eyes, he realized that he could not see. The presence of the glory of Jesus was so bright that it had blinded him. This glory placed scales upon his eyes, hindering his vision, as he was led away by his companions.

After their arrival in Damascus, Saul remained for three days without sight, food, and drink. I am sure his mind raced with thoughts of what had just occurred: "Was this for real? Was this a vision, or did I actually just meet Jesus? I heard His voice, I saw His glory, and now I am blind. It must have been real? It's not a dream."

During those three days, I am sure that Saul reflected on the law that he was so familiar with. It probably seemed to him like time and space ceased to exist, as nothing else mattered in his life at this point. Once where there was light reflecting off his surroundings, giving him sight, the scales of darkness from the glory of the Lord now blocked his vision. Alone with his thoughts, all he had was the fact that Jesus met him on the road and the words He spoke to him. As he pondered upon these, they were changing his mind about all that he believed to date.

Perhaps, he began remembering what the prophet Joel said about the Lord's Spirit, along with countless other scriptures he knew, pertaining to the coming Messiah. Before this encounter, to him, Jesus was crucified as a false teacher at best. Now, he had just come face-to-face with the long-awaited Messiah. I am sure that his conclusion was that "the Lord Jesus had to be the Messiah, for there is no other possibility."

Jesus's words, few as they were, revealed to Saul that He knew everything that Saul had done to His believers whom he caught, imprisoned, beat, and murdered. Now Saul understood that by him doing those things, it was the same as if he had done them to Jesus Himself. Was this more than he could bear or comprehend? This fact alone remains the same unto this very day. All those who come against believers of Christ are actually coming against Jesus Himself, as if to poke God in the eye.

"He found him in a desert land and in the wasteland, a howling wilderness; He encircled him, He instructed him, He kept him as the apple of His eye." (Deut. 32:10)

"For thus says the LORD of hosts: 'He sent Me after glory, to the nations which plunder you; for he who touches you touches the apple of His eye.'" (Zech. 2:8)

"He permitted no man to do them wrong; Yes, He rebuked kings for their sakes, Saying, 'Do not touch My anointed ones, And do My prophets no harm.'" (1 Chron. 16:21–22)

"He permitted no one to do them wrong; Yes, He rebuked kings for their sakes, Saying, 'Do not touch My anointed ones, And do My prophets no harm.'" (Ps. 105:14–15)

Is it possible that our words can deeply touch other's lives in such a manner that harms the one speaking them? Sure, they can! We must remain aware of this fact when talking about others, whether in the Church or outside the Church. For how do we know who the anointed of God are, giving them the ability and commandment to do a particular thing?

"But you have an anointing [enabling] *from the Holy One, and you know all things. I have not written to you because you do not know the truth, but because you know it, and that no lie is of the truth." (1 John 2:20–21)*

Ananias, being one of the believers whom Saul was going to hunt down in Damascus, was also visited by Jesus. Jesus said to Ananias, *"arise and go into the street called Straight, and inquire in the house of Judas for one called Saul of Tarsus, for, behold, he prayeth. And hath seen in a vision a man, named Ananias, coming in and putting his hand on him, that he might receive his sight." (Acts 9:11,12 KJV).*

(Needless to say, I believe Ananias was a little apprehensive to go, as he pleaded his case to the Lord.) He knew of Saul and knew he had authority from the chief priest to bind all that called on the name of Jesus. The Lord's response to him was, *"Go thy way, for he is a chosen vessel unto me, to bear my name before the Gentiles, and kings, and the children of Israel, For I will show him how great things he must suffer for my name sake." (Acts 9:15,16 KJV).*

Be very careful of what you say and do to other believers. Your words and actions may come back to you in the same way you sent them out. Blessing or cursing, either way, the Lord hears and sees all. *"Death and life are in the power of the tongue, and those who love it will eat its fruit." (Proverbs 18:21).*

There are two things I want you to notice here: Number one, the previous introduction of the laying on of hands introduced by the Holy Spirit in the previous filling of the Holy Spirit is now used here again as "coming in and putting his hand on him that he might receive his sight."

We who are filled with the Holy Spirit are conduits of the power of God through the Holy Spirit of Jesus in us. Once filled with this power (Holy Spirit) and fire, and speaking in tongues, we must not think in terms of separating these actions, as they are connected together by His Holy Spirit in us. That which we touch, He touches.

When we speak, He is speaking through us (that is, as long as we stay on His word).

You may have asked before, "Why tongues?" "Why does this evidence have to be there to prove that I am filled with the Holy Spirit?" Well, I am glad you asked. Let's take a look at a couple of things about "the tongue" before moving on to the second thing that I want you to notice.

First, open your Bible, and read the entire sixteenth chapter of Proverbs, then turn to James 3, and read the entire chapter, then come back. I'll wait.

* * *

Now that you're back, here are three things that should stand out to each of us: (1) All of us are *not* perfect. Sorry, but this is true. (2) James talks about bits in horse's mouths and big ships with little helms, giving those controlling them the ability to turn the horse or ship wherever they desire. (3) The tongue is a fire and a world of iniquity. *Wow* to this one!

Notice any similarities with the topic of baptism of the Holy Spirit and fire that John said Jesus would baptize us with? How about this: "And there appeared unto them cloven tongues as of fire, and it sat upon each of them. And they were all filled with the Holy Spirit, and began to speak with other tongues as the Spirit gave them utterance"?

According to James 3:1–18, the tongue is already a fire and a world of iniquity. This is what everyone who is born into this world has—everyone! *"Behold, I was brought forth in iniquity, and in sin my mother conceived me." (Ps. 51:5)*

Nobody is immune to this. The fall of man in the Garden of Eden brought this to everyone born in the past, present, and future. Believing in Jesus as the only begotten Son of the Father is the only way that gives us the eternal life we need and the deliverance from iniquity we are brought forth in life and the sin that we all were conceived in. As we call upon His name to be saved, Jesus accepts us as we are, and once born again, with our sins forgiven and washed by His blood, we now become qualified to be filled with His Holy Spirit and fire.

It could not be clearer; every person who believes that Jesus is God's Son whom He sent to save us can be born again. Then, is every believer qualified to receive the baptism of the Holy Spirit and fire? <u>Yes, they are!</u> But the reality is that today, not every believer is filled with the Holy Spirit as the early Church was in the book of Acts. Why? Because every believer does not believe this is for today. Either they refuse to believe because they try to understand it with their natural minds (which cannot be done), or they just outright believe the lies fed to many by the devil. Either way, I pray this information will help change your mind, thus changing your preference in believing.

Notice "cloven tongues." <u>The word *cloven* simply means "to be divided."</u> When a believer is baptized with the Holy Spirit and begins speaking in tongues, present is the fire when the Holy Spirit comes, which John and Jesus talked about. His fire begins the annihilation of the iniquity of the tongue by consuming the fire of the world of iniquity we were born with and replacing it with the fire of the Holy Spirit of truth.

As we pray in tongues, speaking the wonderful works of God, the Spirit of truth separates the fiery darts that satan previously had us to use with our tongues, thereby helping us to speak truths and not lies. Our speech, in times past, was a vehicle of lies, rumors with fiery darts toward others, and cursing in more ways than one.

Being filled with the Holy Spirit and praying in tongues give us the fire of God to burn out that which we were born with, replaced by speaking the truths of God in new boldness. We, in essence, yield our tongues to be cleansed by His fire, as we speak the wonderful works of God via His Holy Spirit filling us.

This baptism of Holy Spirit and fire separates the good from the bad and the wheat from the chaff and begins a journey of speaking and acting more like Jesus every day. This is why "He gets sweeter and sweeter as the days go by, oh what of love between the Lord and I, I just keep falling in love with Him, over and over and over and over again!" (I Keep Falling In Love With Him, By Lanny Wolf)

Unlike water baptism, the baptism in the Holy Spirit contains His *resurrection power* that actually fills us each time we pray in the Holy Spirit. We can receive as much of Him as we want or as little of Him as we want. Praying in the Spirit is always accompanied by tongues, speaking directly to God about His wonderful works. Remember, this is God's design as to how this is to be done, not man's and surely not from the devil.

It is my hope that as you read this book, you will acquire enough knowledge to overcome any fear or wrong belief that would keep you from His resurrection power. Realizing who you are in Christ will bring an added stability in your fellowship with His Holy Spirit.

Experiencing a personal relationship not only with the Father and His Son, Jesus, but also with their Holy Spirit as well, is the true fellowship that we have, and John talks about this type of fellowship in his first Epistle.

"That which we have seen and heard we declare to you, that you also may have fellowship with us; and truly our fellowship is with the Father and with His Son Jesus Christ. And these things we write to you that your joy may be full." (1 John 1:3–4)

Our joy is made full when we realize that we join the apostles' fellowship when we truly fellowship with the Father and the Son through His Holy Spirit. This vertical fellowship must happen first and continue before any horizontal fellowship with other people can be productive and truly positive. If not, most horizontal fellowships with other members of the Church, and others, is superficial and lacking in depth of the love of God.

It is said, "There is power in numbers." What better team could a believer have than the Father, Son, and Holy Spirit living inside you, making the fourth person!

"Though one may be overpowered by another, two can withstand him. And a threefold cord is not quickly broken." (Ecc. 4:12) We actually have a fourfold cord scenario if we have this kind of fellowship present in our lives, and nothing can break it but us.

Being the perfect gentlemen that He is, the Holy Spirit never forces us to do anything against our will. He will continue to give us information and instructions for us to make our own decisions for ourselves, to partake of the full gifts of God or not.

Actually, this *power* is what threatens the very operation of all the demons and the devil. Once the Church (all believers in Christ) finally catches the vision of this, it's just a matter of time, as it was in Acts 2, that the Holy Ghost revival breaks forth, and it's all over but the shouting. The Church will leave in the same *power* that she arrived with.

The moment the Holy Spirit is expressed in us, many will reach out to Him as He draws them unto Jesus, convincing them of sin, righteousness, and judgment. They too will be saved and can be filled with the Holy Spirit and fire, only if they ask Jesus for it. This is the process of reproducing and making disciples as Jesus commands us to do until He returns for us all. Can you see now why the devil fights against this truth as hard as he does?

Finally, we come to the second thing I want you to notice about Saul's born-again experience. The acts that Saul was doing while persecuting the believers became many of the very things that happened to him during his ministry. He was beaten, imprisoned, and eventually killed for the faith of Jesus Christ. This is proof that we should be mindful of our treatment toward others, for God will not be mocked.

In studying the life of Paul, we also discover that he endured other things like hunger, lack, and even a shipwreck. I believe these to be direct results of what Jesus said of how Saul must suffer great things for the sake of His name. What he was sowing was what he reaped.

<u>Now I am not saying this is an absolute for everyone</u>; thank God for His grace. Those who persecute Christians—well, let's just say, if you live by the sword, you will die by the sword, and you will reap what you sow. How have you treated or how are you treating God's anointed? Are your words touching them in the right ways of blessing, or are your words touching them in a wrong manner of slander, gossip, and hatred (cursing)?

Ananias was obedient to that which the Lord asked him to do, and he entered into the house where Saul was praying and placed his hands on Saul and spoke these words:

"'Brother Saul, the Lord, even Jesus, that appeared unto thee in the way as thou camest, hath sent me, that thou mightest receive they sight, and be filled with the Holy Spirit.' and immediately there fell from his eyes as it had been scales, and he received sight, and arose, and was baptized." (Acts 9:17–18)

Some may say this is talking about water baptism. I beg to differ! If this was water baptism, why would Ananias say, "That thou mightest receive thy sight, and be *filled* with the Holy Spirit"? If this was talking about water baptism, why would he not say, "That thou mightest receive thy sight, and be baptized in the name of Jesus for the remission of your sins"?

I'll tell you why he did not. The dispensation changed, and Ananias understood that being baptized in water was only then as it is today, symbolic of not only the old man becoming new after having his sin washed away but also that it was symbolic of another baptism—that of the Holy Spirit, evidenced by speaking in tongues directly to God, submerged in the presence of the Almighty!

Being baptized or filled with the Holy Spirit holds the same weight as that of Act 2:4. It should be recognized as such when Ananias laid his hands on Saul to receive his sight and to be baptized with the Holy Spirit. I believe that Paul had already repented days before and asked Jesus to forgive him of his sin of not believing that Jesus was the promised Messiah, the Son of God, who sent Him to die for all mankind's sin. Jesus was faithful and did so.

As Saul regained his sight, he was ready to be filled with the power of the Holy Spirit, who would see him through his coming trials and tribulations. Paul endured such great trials and tests like none other since Job's experience.

Once he received the gift of working of miracles by the hands of Ananias through the Holy Spirit in him, Saul was filled with the Holy Spirit and spoke in tongues according to the scriptures. The scales that blinded him were removed by the resurrection power flowing through Ananias and transferring into Saul by the laying on of hands, the same way it was with Peter and John in Samaria in chapter 8 of the book of Acts.

There is no water baptism here. I am sure that Saul, who became the apostle Paul, was baptized in water, but it is not here. This is the baptism of the Holy Spirit filling him. Filled to the point of overflowing, he who once persecuted believers now became a true believer himself, preaching and teaching with boldness.

THE OPERATIVE

Continue reading Acts, and you will see this power of being filled with the Holy Spirit and fire, over and over again. This power kept Paul everywhere he went while doing everything he did for the rest of his life.

My suggestion in reading the book of Acts is reading it in its entirety, all at one sitting. This power will become more obvious, and all these truths will become more apparent than reading one or two scriptures here and there.

Read also First Corinthians chapters 12, 13, and 14 in one sitting after reading the book of Acts. In 14:18 Paul says, *"I thank my God, I speak with tongues more than ye all."* This was his sustaining power throughout his days. This is what kept Paul strong and built up spiritually, giving him strength for endurance, and longevity in his walk with Christ.

It is important for us to recognize that this supernatural transformation changed Saul of Tarsus into Paul. This event began to anoint him to become an apostle as a direct result of the baptism of the Holy Spirit with the evidence of speaking in other tongues, just like on the day of Pentecost. Also within his credentials was the coming face-to-face with Jesus.

(More details of the gifts of the Holy Spirit that accompany those filled with the Holy Spirit and fire will be in future chapters. Also, we'll be taking a closer look at the *fruit* of the Holy Spirit to see how all these connect with one another, giving us believers the advantage over our flesh and the devil.)

In chapter 11 we will be taking a look at the <u>sixth filling</u> of the baptism of the Holy Spirit that is revealed to us as found in Acts 10:44–48.

You'll see that by asking Jesus to baptize you in the Holy Spirit, with the evidence of speaking in tongues, you are yielding yourself to Him, including your tongue. I can tell you of my own personal experience with this when I was first filled with the Holy Spirit. Let's do this now before continuing on to Chapter 11.

I was at the altar, praying, a couple of weeks after being born again. Once I acquired the knowledge about this baptism in the Holy Spirit, it was all I could think and pray about. At the altar in our midweek service, I faintly heard in my spirit words that I did not understand. I recognized this as the tongues spoken of in Acts 2. I yielded my tongue to the Holy Spirit by repeating those words even though I did not understand their meaning; He began flowing into me.

As He gave me the words to speak, I realized they were His words coming through me, and as I repeated them, I felt His strength and boldness flowing in my spirit. I prayed for what seemed like an hour or more in tongues.

When I arose from the altar, there were others around me, doing the same. I had stepped into another realm with God and knew this was so from my studies. I had spoken His heavenly language, talking directly to God about His wonderful works.

I have been speaking in tongues for over thirty-seven years now, and as mentioned before, you're way too late to try to convince me that this is not real, let alone that it is not relevant for today! I have been blessed to give messages in tongues, and I have interpreted messages in tongues (details of both these and other gifts will also be covered in upcoming chapters).

Pray and ask Jesus to baptize you in the Holy Spirit, and you too can hear His words in your spirit man, words that you will not understand, sounds that you never heard before. Those are the words of the Holy Spirit speaking the wonderful works of God, echoing within your spirit, longing to flow through you like water down a stream.

Jesus is waiting for you to ask Him to baptize you with His Holy Spirit and fire. Say yes to Him today, just the way you did when you asked Him for the forgiveness of your sins and the assurance that you make heaven your eternal home. His Spirit is not to be feared, but embraced.

Be not filled with wine in excess, but be filled with the Holy Spirit and power in excess. The evidence is tongues, as you hear them ever so softly being spoken in your spirit. Yield your tongue to the Holy Spirit of Jesus today, and start speaking the wonderful works of God.

CHAPTER 11

We now come to the recording of the <u>sixth filling</u> of the Holy Spirit mentioned in Acts 10. Peter was on the housetop, praying around noon, when he saw a vision of a vessel descending in front of him as if it had been a great sheet knit at the four corners and let down to the earth. This great sheet knit is similar to our parachutes today.

Inside this vessel were all manner of four-footed and wild beasts and creeping things of the earth and fowls of the air. Peter heard a voice speaking to him, saying, *"Rise, Peter, kill and eat."* Peter, being the devout Jew that he was, answered, *"Not so, Lord, for I have never eaten anything that is common or unclean."*

Prior to Peter's vision, unknown to him, a certain man in Caesarea, called Cornelius, a centurion of the Italian band and a devout man who feared God, had seen an angel of God, appearing to him, saying, "Cornelius, thy prayers and thine alms are come up for a memorial before God. Send men to Joppa and call for one Simon, whose surname is Peter."

While Peter was receiving his vision, the men sent by Cornelius were knocking on the door of the tanner whose house Peter was staying. After Peter had received the same vision for the third time and being perplexed to what this vision meant, he was informed that there were men here from Cornelius's house, asking for him.

Prior to being informed of these men, the Holy Spirit said unto Peter, "Behold, three men seek thee, arise, therefore, and get thee down, and go with them, doubting nothing, for I have sent them."

We now see that not only is the Holy Spirit active in the believer's lives by filling them with faith, power, and other languages, but <u>He is also now speaking directives to them,</u> giving specific instructions. He spoke to Peter and Cornelius, and previously, we read where He spoke to Ananias and Saul of Tarsus.

(Details are in chapter 10 of the book of Acts.) We see that Peter goes to Cornelius's house and finds them gathered together to hear the words that he would speak to them. Peter begins with his time of prayer on the housetop and tells all that the Holy Spirit had said to him, and verse 34 says that Peter opened his mouth and said, *"Of a truth I perceive that God is no respecter of persons."*

Prior to this, Peter, evidently, was thinking that God was a respecter of persons.

Since salvation came to the Jews first, his thinking was that God had respect for a man's person, especially a Jewish man. <u>But God</u> was doing a new thing in the earth that Peter, at that time, had no understanding of. He continues:

"But in every nation whoever fears Him and works righteousness is accepted by Him. The word which God sent to the children of Israel, preaching peace through Jesus Christ—He is Lord of all—that word you know, which was proclaimed throughout all Judea, and began from Galilee after the baptism which John preached: how God anointed Jesus of Nazareth with the Holy Spirit and with power, who went about doing good and healing all who were oppressed by the devil, for God was with Him.

And we are witnesses of all things which He did both in the land of the Jews and in Jerusalem, whom they killed by hanging on a tree. Him God raised up on the third day, and showed Him openly, not to all the people, but to witnesses chosen before by God, even to us who ate and drank with Him after He arose from the dead. And He commanded us to preach to the people, and to testify that it is He who was ordained by God to be Judge of the living and the dead. To Him all the prophets witness that, through His name, whoever believes in Him will receive remission of sins." (Acts 10:35–43)

And here it is, the <u>sixth filling</u> or baptism of the Holy Spirit for others than just those in the upper room on the day of Pentecost, not a house full of Jews, but a house full of Gentiles, a Centurion soldier, along with his family and servants. Pay special attention to every word the Holy Spirit records here about this gift given *now* to this Gentile family (a gift given no longer only to the Jews).

"While Peter was still speaking these words, the Holy Spirit fell upon all those who heard the word. And those of the circumcision who believed were astonished, as many as came with Peter [Jewish believers filled with the Holy Spirit] because the gift of the Holy Spirit had been poured out on the Gentiles also. For they heard them speak with tongues and magnify God [speaking the wonderful works of God].

Then Peter answered, 'Can anyone forbid water, that these should not be baptized who have received the Holy Spirit just as we have?' And he commanded them to be baptized [baptized in water after they believed and was filled with the Holy Spirit] in the name of the Lord. Then they asked him to stay for a few days." (Acts 10:44-48) Peter and all his companions, were astonished as they heard them [speak in tongues and magnify God].

Now, I don't know about you, but I believe this blows the theory and all speculations completely out of the water that the baptism of the Holy Spirit with speaking in tongues went away with the apostles. These were not Jewish apostles or Jewish disciples. They did not see Jesus (except on the inside of their spirit man), but they embraced the truth of Peter's message. If the Acts 2:4 experience passed away with the apostles, this is the scripture that refutes its passing away as being a false teaching altogether.

<u>God is not a respecter of men!</u> With this fact, Peter and his companions had no other choice but accept this action of the Lord as truth, because they were witnessing it with their own eyes and ears. They, evidently, thought the Jewish believers were specifically chosen to be the only ones to receive the Holy Spirit in this manner, so God had to correct Peter's wrong thinking, thereby correcting all doubters of the reality of the baptism or filling of the Holy Spirit for all times.

In Peter's message to the people in the house of Cornelius, he said, *"Him God raised up on the third day, and showed Him openly, not to all the people, but to witnesses chosen before by God, even to us who ate and drank with Him after He arose from the dead."*

Peter, as well as other Jewish believers, was thinking that since God did not choose everyone to show Jesus openly to, he then assumed that God chose them only. Could they have been thinking that this gift was for the Jews only? I believe so.

Peter and the others with him from Jerusalem had to have their thinking and perspective changed according to the will of God, concerning this matter of Jesus's Holy Spirit. Only the Holy Spirit is able to accomplish a change of this magnitude! Cornelius asked them to stay for a few days, and they did. I would love to have heard some of the conversations during those few days, wouldn't you?

It is easy for the devil to keep these truths from believers today, because he has been successful in selling his lies against the Holy Spirit to the world and even within the Church. Practically, every mainstream denominational church today does not teach or preach about this power, because they do not believe God's word when it comes to the baptism of the Holy Spirit. They choose, rather, to explain it away, and they are able to get by with it because most people will not search out the truth on their own.

What is it that the devil does not want believers to realize? It is that there are actually two baptisms that the Bible teaches us about. Water baptism, which contains *none* of God's power accompanying it, and does not saves us, nor does it wash our sins away, because it is a symbolic act of what actually does, which is the blood of Jesus. It is the water of the word of God and the blood of Jesus that saves us and washes our sins away, respectively. However, the baptism in the Holy Spirit, with the evidence of speaking in tongues, contains the resurrection power that accompanies it.

In warfare (natural or spiritual), if you had the wisdom to do so, wouldn't you remove your enemy's power to destroy you as quickly as you could? Can you see the devil's device in removing the power from the Church through lies? He shivers every time a believer is filled with the Holy Spirit and fire (power, authority, boldness, faith, good report, joy, or strong fruit of the Holy Spirit, etc.).

How is it, then, that many church leaders have failed to see this truth for so many years? How is it that they can persecute those who are filled with the Holy Spirit and fire and teach others to do the same?

Explaining it away while teaching others that this baptism is not for today or that it has passed away with the apostles is simply foolishness. As mentioned previously, some go as far as saying it is of the devil! How they do err from the truth! How is it that many believers, who are responsible for their own walk with the Lord, have not taken the time to search out this truth? Do they err from the truth as well?

Comparatively speaking, those who proclaim to be filled with the Holy Spirit, with the evidence of speaking in tongues, according to the scriptures, are few compared to the total number of believers of Christ in the world today.

For me, this is *the revival* that needs to take place within the *church* first, before there is an influx of multiple numbers of souls that are yet to be born again. This is the revival that the devil fears most, because when it happens, there will be no stopping the number of new converts in the last days of harvesting souls. The devil knows his time is short.

"Therefore rejoice, O heavens, and you who dwell in them! Woe to the inhabitants of the earth and the sea! For the devil has come down to you, having great wrath, because he knows that he has a short time." (Rev. 12:12)

I have to admit he has used his time wisely so far. But you know what? The Holy Spirit is wiser and more powerful than the devil ever was, can be, or ever will be. The jig is up! The truth is coming out! And many believers will recognize the truth for who the devil really is, and that Jesus Christ is the way, the truth, and the life!

According to the scriptures, we <u>now</u> have Gentile believers born again and being filled with the Holy Spirit and speaking in tongues. For these Gentiles, water baptism in Jesus's name came after they were filled with the Holy Spirit and spoke in tongues. Again, notice in verse 47: *"For they* [Peter and those who came with him to

Cornelius's house] *heard them speak with tongues and magnify God." Then Peter answered, "Can any man forbid water that these should not be baptized, who have received the Holy Spirit, as well as we?"*

Are you convinced yet that this <u>baptism</u> is a reality for today? Are you convinced that this baptism is a valuable gift given to us by our Lord and Savior, Jesus Christ? The same Holy Spirit that convinced you that you needed a Savior is revealing to you right now the truth about being baptized in the Holy Spirit and speaking in tongues and the fact that it is real and is for today and is yours for the asking. This realization is my prayer for everyone who is reading this book who has not yet been baptized or filled with the Holy Spirit of promise and all that it implies.

These descriptions of the baptism of the Holy Spirit in detail are not by happenstance or placed in the Bible to take up space. They are not there just to move the story forward. Each is specific and a directive from Jesus Himself, as He introduces the third person of the Trinity—the helper, comforter, counselor, and teacher, the Holy Spirit as His operative of the Church as well as the world today!

After reading First Corinthians 12, 13, and 14, verses 37–40 of chapter 14 states, and I quote, *"If anyone thinks himself to be a prophet or spiritual, let him acknowledge that the things which I write to you are the commandments of the Lord. But if anyone is ignorant, let him be ignorant". Therefore, brethren, desire earnestly to prophesy, and do not forbid to speak with tongues. Let all things be done decently and in order."*

The whole purpose of these three chapters is to bring the Church at Corinth and today's Church, the body of Christ, out of being ignorant concerning the spiritual gifts of the Holy Spirit. Paul begins chapter 12 of First Corinthians verse 1 by stating the same thing that I just quoted: *"Now concerning spiritual gifts, brethren, I do not want you to be ignorant."*

If the Corinthian believers weren't being ignorant about the spiritual gifts of the Holy Spirit, no instructions would have been needed. But because there was instruction to them, the believers there were ignorant of the correct operation of them when they came together. Sadly, many remain ignorant (or unlearned) of the very same spiritual gifts of the Holy Spirit today.

The greatest fuel that feeds fear is the lack of knowledge. People are afraid of that which they know little or nothing of. Remove this fuel from a fire of ignorance concerning *the* Holy Spirit of *truth* and all He has to offer, then the fire of ignorance will go out!

Paul ends chapter 14, starting at verse 38 through 40, with, *"But if anyone is ignorant, let him be ignorant. Therefore, brethren, desire earnestly to prophesy, and do not forbid to speak with tongues. Let all things be done decently and in order."*

If I were to visit your church as the guest speaker, and the Holy Spirit gave me a message for *your* church with the interpretation, would your pastor, elders, board members, deacons, or other parishioners forbid me to speak in tongues? Would the Holy Spirit be welcome to operate His gifts there?

Again, keeping church members ignorant or unlearned concerning the baptism of the Holy Spirit with the evidence of speaking in tongues is one of the devil's goals and deceptive plans to keep <u>the power of God short-circuited within the Church</u>. *No*, the devil does not care if we go to church! He just does not want us to come with <u>the resurrection power of the Holy Spirit.</u> Please answer this question honestly: has your church fallen prey to his devices?

"Now whom you forgive anything, I also forgive. For if indeed I have forgiven anything, I have forgiven that one for your sakes in the presence of Christ, lest satan should take advantage of us; for we are not ignorant of his devices." (2 Cor. 2:10-11)

I can only answer for myself, as the Holy Spirit has taught me His truths. I take His knowledge and understanding and apply them to my personal life first. Then, I become confident in presenting them to others, allowing them to decide for themselves to do the same thing.

All of Cornelius's prayers to God and alms (giving to the poor) were brought before the Lord as a memorial. God wanted him to be a part of this gift given to all who believed in Him, as He rewarded those who diligently sought Him.

"But without faith it is impossible to please Him, for he who comes to God must believe that He is, and that He is a rewarder of those who diligently seek Him." (Heb. 11:6)

Yes, there is much controversy over this topic of being baptized or filled with the Holy Spirit with the evidence of speaking in tongues. But the Bible is crystal clear on the subject, if you have the Holy Spirit giving you the clarity. Many, for years now, have been robbed of this special gift simply because of past traditional thinking or not knowing the truth concerning the Lord's miraculous gift.

"Yeah hath God Said?"—these four simple words, which are as old as the Garden of Eden, have brought more doubt and unbelief not only into the world but also within the Church, concerning the things of Jesus. This reality is because an individual believer's mind and heart do not have the truth, but a lack of knowledge on the subject.

Questioning every truth is a device the devil uses even unto this day. It is when those truths are questioned that if the believer does not know the truth according to God's word already to respond with, they lose their argument and begin down the path of doubt and unbelief even in their own lives. There are those who even challenge believers, questioning as to whether the God of the Bible is alive or dead. How do you respond when you are questioned about that?

Be it known today unto all that read these words: the God of the Bible is *alive* and *well*, and this gift from His Son, Jesus Himself, is as real as it gets! Doubt and unbelief in no way diminish the truth of this second baptism. The only thing that doubt and unbelief do is cause those who listen to them to lose out on the many things pertaining to an abundant life through Christ and His Holy Spirit.

You and you alone will have to decide whether or not you will be a partaker of this blessing and begin to reap the benefits, whether it is building up yourself on your most holy faith (Jesus) by praying in the Spirit, thereby praying directly to God (the wonderful works of God) or receiving a specific message or information from God to share with others. It's for all to benefit, thereby!

The Holy Spirit with all His benefits are never forced upon any believer by God the Father or Jesus, His Son. Whatever your viewpoint has been regarding this subject, you are *now* being given a boatload of information from the Holy Spirit and His word, and from this point on, *you* are accountable to God, concerning its contents and what you should do with them. He loves you so much! He wants you to have this information to apply to your personal life, and this is the motive of His direction for me to write this book.

There remain three more events of the baptism or filling of the Holy Spirit left to research plus the information on the nine (9) gifts of the Holy Spirit. Then there is the fruit of the Holy Spirit. We dare not forget the gifts given unto men by Jesus, which are apostles, prophets, evangelists, pastors, and teachers. All these are direct results of Jesus giving us His Holy Spirit beginning on the day of Pentecost. Isn't this exciting?

The Holy Spirit, by no means, takes away anything from God the Father or Jesus the Son. On the contrary, He enhances their works and characteristics by taking the things of Jesus, who took the things of the Father to show us the Father, and revealing them to us as reality for us to apply in our hearts and daily living.

The Holy Spirit of Jesus is the operative of the Church today! He started the early Church on its powerful path full of miracles by giving instructions and directions to those who would hear and obey. Once these were followed, lasting fruit were the results.

In Jesus's day, the Sadducees and the Pharisees missed Jesus as being sent from God as the Messiah. Again I ask, "Are our Church leaders doing the same thing today with the Holy Spirit whom Jesus sent to us as the other helper, comforter, counselor, and teacher as well as being the operative of the Church? Are they missing the one who has the resurrection power the Church so desperately needs today?

During a discussion with a well-versed teacher of Israel, concerning the topic of being born again, he questioned Jesus: *"Nicodemus answered and said to Him, 'How can these things be?' Jesus answered and said to him, 'Are you the teacher of Israel, and do not know these things?'"* (John 3:9–11).

Look closely at Jesus's answer to Nicodemus: *"Are you the teacher of Israel, and do not know these things?"* Jesus reveals to us that the teacher of Israel should have known the things concerning these spiritual matters, and if this is the case then, it is still the case today. Are you the teacher of the Church, and do not know these things?

You may ask, what things? The things of Jesus, concerning His promised gift of His Holy Spirit once He went away to fulfill His position on the throne at the right hand of the Father. This action did not limit Him, as He was well able to send us His Holy Spirit, which He did on the day of Pentecost in Acts 2 and continues to do so even today.

Fear Him? No, run to Him and embrace Him. Seek His presence in your heart and life. Ask for His wisdom, knowledge, and understanding that He has for us from Jesus. Allow Him to comfort you in troubled times, as He gives you God's peace that surpasses all understanding that is able to keep our hearts and minds through Jesus Christ.

Are you in need of comfort, guidance, or help? This is what the Holy Spirit brings with Him, as we are baptized or filled with His presence and power. If you haven't already asked Jesus to baptize you with the Holy Spirit and fire, please do so now. Giving you this gift is His good pleasure, as you yield your life wholly and totally to Him.

Jesus is patiently waiting to give more of Himself to you through His Holy Spirit, which is given to all who believes, and asks Him for His powerful gift, promised and poured out on the day of Pentecost, over two thousand years ago.

Next we will be researching the <u>seventh filling</u> of the baptism in the Holy Spirit, evidence of the Holy Spirit as proof of being filled with His presence and power. The book of Acts is so rich with the Holy Spirit's actions on every page, miracle after miracle recorded for us to read and experience so that Jesus's faith can come to us, giving each of us the opportunity to act upon it or just let His words drop by the wayside.

Which one do you choose?

CHAPTER 12

The <u>seventh filling</u> of the Holy Spirit is written by Luke once again, under the inspiration of the Holy Spirit. With all the precedence about being filled with the Holy Spirit with the evidence of speaking in tongues, they reveal to us the truths that Jesus and His Father want us to know and understand.

He understood that the readers of that day would understand what the meaning of the words "were filled with the Holy Spirit" meant. Every believer knew perfectly well what this entailed, because they too were speaking in tongues to God about His wonderful works.

On one of my online accounts, I posted a video about a doctor's MRIs of a preacher while speaking in tongues. Here is the page site if you would like to take a look at it. I do hope it is still available: *https://www.youtube.com/watch?v=NZbQBajYnEc.*

I love it when science proves the Bible to be correct and when the Bible proves science to be correct as well, which both happen more often than we realize. God created science, and it is one of the many hosts that Jesus is Lord over. He keeps total control over all things by the word of His power.

"God, who at various times and in various ways spoke in time past to the fathers by the prophets, has in these last days spoken to us by His Son, whom He has appointed heir of all things, through whom also He made the worlds; who being the brightness of His glory and the express image of His person, and upholding all things by the word of His power,

when He had by Himself purged our sins, sat down at the right hand of the Majesty on high." (Heb. 1:1–3)

Scientific minds have been trying, for centuries, to understand what holds all things together in the cosmos. Simply put, it is Jesus! He upholds <u>all things</u> by the word of His power. If this is all the information given to me about this topic, it is all that I need to understand how <u>He</u> holds all matter together and makes every equation work as they do. In other words, it's because He gave His word when He created all things, and all things must obey Him until He is finished with each of them.

In Acts chapter 13, we find that the Holy Spirit separated Paul and Barnabas for the work unto which He had called them to (verse 2). He sent them to Cyprus to preach the word of God in the synagogues of the Jews, along with John, who was their helper.

They were obedient to the Holy Spirit. But when the Jews heard these words, they left the synagogue angry. The Gentiles were glad and sought them to share these words with them on the following Sabbath. We begin at verse 43.

"Now when the congregation had broken up, many of the Jews and devout proselytes followed Paul and Barnabas, who, speaking to them persuaded them to continue in the grace of God.

On the next Sabbath [almost the whole city came together to hear the word of God]. But when the Jews saw the multitudes, they were filled with envy; and contradicting and blaspheming, they opposed the things spoken by Paul. Then Paul and Barnabas grew bold and said, 'It was necessary that the word of God should be spoken to you first; but since you reject it, and judge yourselves unworthy of everlasting life, behold, we turn to the Gentiles.' For so the Lord has commanded us: 'I have set you as a light to the Gentiles, That, you should be for salvation to the ends of the earth." (Acts 13:43-47)

[This message, I am sure, could have come through the gift of tongues and interpretation of tongues. Possibly, there are a couple of others found in First Corinthians 12, but I do not want to get ahead of myself.]

THE OPERATIVE

"Now when the Gentiles heard this, they were glad and glorified the word of the Lord. And as many as had been appointed to eternal life believed." (Acts 13:48).

[It is God's will that none should perish, but all should come to repentance. The reality or truth of this is, not all will believe. He knows who will and will not believe in Him and His Son. This "appointed to eternal life" statement were the Gentiles who heard the word preached who received it with gladness and believed it and acted upon its truth, so they were saved.]

"The Lord is not slack concerning His promise, as some count slackness, but is longsuffering toward us, not willing that any should perish but that all should come to repentance." (2 Peter 3:9)

"And the word of the Lord was being spread throughout all the region. But the Jews stirred up the devout and prominent women and the chief men of the city, raised up persecution against Paul and Barnabas, and expelled them from their region.

But they shook off the dust from their feet against them, and came to Iconium. And the disciples were filled with joy and with the Holy Spirit." (Acts 13:49-52)

The disciples were filled <u>again</u> with the Holy Spirit because they were giving out the word of God with resurrection power. People believed because of the words they were speaking. People were getting healed because of them. Even a whole Gentile town was glad when they heard that God included them in salvation and in this wonderful gift of the Holy Spirit.

The scriptures don't say here that the Gentiles of Antioch heard and were glad and were filled with the Holy Spirit. Brought to our attention here by the Holy Spirit is the *joy* of being filled with the Holy Spirit. Why would it not be the same here also as on the day of Pentecost? Think in terms of the Holy Spirit's precedence established in previous scriptures of this event. I see this as the <u>seventh filling</u> of the Holy Spirit.

Notice that Paul and Barnabas were once again speaking by the inspiration of the Holy Spirit, and they too were filled with joy and the Holy Spirit.

In a previous chapter of this book and in the book of Acts, we saw that Saul, who later became Paul, was filled with the Holy Spirit (Acts 9:17–20, which we have already covered). For any doubt that Barnabas was baptized or filled with the Holy Spirit with tongues as evidence, here is the proof that he was:

"Then news of these things came to the ears of the church in Jerusalem, and they sent out Barnabas to go as far as Antioch. When he came and had seen the grace of God, he was glad, and encouraged them all that with purpose of heart they should continue with the Lord. For he was a good man, full of the Holy Spirit and of faith. And a great many people were added to the Lord." (Acts 11:22–24)

Both Paul and Barnabas were filled again with joy and the Holy Spirit—further proof that being filled with the Holy Spirit is more than just a onetime event in a believer's life, which brings many attributes like faith, good report, joy, etc., with this gift. Thus, this is our <u>seventh filling</u> of the Holy Spirit.

In this meeting, salvation came, joy came, gladness came, and the Holy Spirit came as well. However, in the midst of all this, persecution also came. There is a message many of us preachers give about Paul being shipwrecked and swimming to the island after. Once there, they built a fire with the sticks they had gathered. From within the sticks that the fire was burning, a snake came out and bit Paul on the arm. He just shook it off back into the fire.

Assuming that he would die, the island people thought that he must have been a murderer. Fact being, before he was born again and baptized with the Holy Spirit, he was a murderer, but he was still able to be used mightily by God because of the wonderful works of Jesus that he accepted in his life by grace, through faith. Often, God has to put distance between the past and the present to bring balance into someone's life, and Paul's time for judgment had not come, as the islander's reasoned. However, Paul did not <u>die,</u> and because of this miraculous incident, it presented a powerful, open door for them to minister to the village chief the gospel of Jesus Christ.

The sermon is entitled, *"When the Fires of the Holy Spirit Are Built, the Snakes Will Come Out."* I have seen this firsthand. When true Holy Spirit fires are manifested in believer's lives, the snakes (doubters, unbelievers, and liars) always come out.

The snakes (demons) of the world cannot abide in the fire of God. Opposition will come—expect it. But opposition will never put out the fire of the Holy Spirit, which leads us to the <u>eighth filling</u> of the Holy Spirit.

The account of the <u>eighth filling</u> of the Holy Spirit is found in Acts 15:1–12. While this is a recount of a previous filling, I count it as one because of the words that are used, which are, "Giving them the Holy Spirit, even as he did unto us." Peter was referring to the day of Pentecost, when this gift of the baptism of the Holy Spirit was given to the Jews first. The Gentiles later became recipients of this gift, which God had planned to do all along. Speaking in tongues was and always is the evidence that a believer of Jesus has been filled with His Holy Spirit.

This <u>eighth filling</u> of the Holy Spirit is proof that each time "They were filled with the Holy Spirit" is mentioned, we should always reference back to Acts 2:4 with the understanding that speaking in tongues is always present when this statement is made. They all understood this back then; why shouldn't we understand it today?

"And it shall come to pass afterward that I will pour out My Spirit on all flesh; your sons and your daughters shall prophesy, your old men shall dream dreams, your young men shall see visions. And also on My menservants and on My maidservants I will pour out My Spirit in those days." (Joel 2:28–29)

<u>"Those days,"</u> my friends, have been happening now for over a couple of millennium and will continue to happen to all who believe in Jesus Christ as their Savor and ask Him for this marvelous and miraculous gift from the Father.

What is the undeniable evidence of this free gift in your life, according to the Bible? It's speaking in tongues. This is the evidence of the baptism of the Holy Spirit that we look for. If it was good enough for the early Church, then it should be good enough for today's Church, <u>which we are!</u> Wouldn't you agree?

It's the Holy Spirit who brings Jesus to us and convinces us that we need Him as our Savior and makes Him a reality in our hearts.

But being filled with the Holy Spirit and fire does not automatically come to a believer at the time they are born again or baptized in water. Jesus baptizes the believer with the Holy Spirit and fire if we *believe* and *ask* Him for this baptism.

"*God's word be true, and every man, a liar.*" As you can see, this is not my opinion or preference. It is God's own words that I have given you. It will take His Holy Spirit to help you understand it. The New Testament of the Bible was written by many who actually were there on the day of Pentecost and lived through all the events written in the book of Acts. Surely, we can take their words as truth. Can't we? After all, they were eyewitnesses to everything written in Acts!

Besides all this, Peter, who prayed in tongues in the upper room and several other times afterward, is clearly found in the book of Acts, written by Luke, who, in turn, was inspired (directed) by the Holy Spirit to pen each of these accounts that he was personally aware of as examples so that there would be no misunderstandings. Each of these accounts should be considered as enough proof for sure, but I have one other example to share with you.

There is one other group of scriptures that I want to bring to your attention, concerning this most important topic of being baptized in the Holy Spirit with the evidence of speaking in tongues, which deserves to have full disclosure.

I did not count it as one of the baptisms in the Holy Spirit for this simple reason. The precedence of the baptism in the Holy Spirit was clearly understood by those of that time. They had clarity concerning the evidence of tongues, which proved that a believer was actually filled with the Holy Spirit.

However, there are some Christians today who think that there is too much read into these scriptures to assume that the original precedence of tongues should be applied here. I submit to you that it fits perfectly, and not to consider this as one more time that a believer was baptized in the Holy Spirit, with the evidence of speaking in tongues, would be a big mistake.

"*And a certain Jew named Apollos, born at Alexandria, an eloquent man, and mighty in the scriptures, came to Ephesus. This man was instructed in the way of the Lord; and being fervent in the spirit, he spake and taught diligently the things of the Lord, knowing only the baptism of John. And he began to speak boldly in the synagogue: whom when Aquila and Priscilla had heard, they took him unto them, and expounded unto him the way of God more perfectly. And when he was disposed to pass into Achaia, the brethren wrote, exhorting the disciples to receive him: who, when he was come, helped them much which had believed through grace: For he mightily convinced the Jews, and that publickly, shewing by the scriptures that Jesus was Christ."* (Acts 18:24–28, KJV)

The apostle Paul, who, we know, was filled with the Holy Spirit and spoke in tongues, wrote to the Corinthians, *"I thank my God, I speak with tongues more than ye all,"* along with, *"Wherefore, brethren, covet to prophesy, and forbid not to speak with tongues."* Paul had previously stayed at Aquila and Priscilla's house for a year and a half, working with them, making tents. (Read Acts 18:1–28.) They would go with Paul to the synagogue every Sabbath, hearing him persuade both the Jews and the Greeks.

Because of this, we must conclude that they too were baptized with the Holy Spirit with the evidence of speaking in tongues, first because every early believer was baptized in like manner as before, meaning on the day of Pentecost, and, secondly, because Paul would have made sure of it, as he did with all the other believers.

So when the Holy Spirit reveals to us that Aquila and Priscilla took Apollos aside to "expound unto him the way of God more perfectly," there could be only one reason. They taught him about being baptized in the Holy Spirit with the evidence of speaking in tongues. Why else would water baptism be mentioned?

For until they clarified this to him, Apollos only knew about the baptism of John, which, we know, is about being submerged in water and is symbolic in nature as to the old man dying and the new man coming alive. We also realize that it is symbolic of this greater baptism where the Holy Spirit fills our spirits with His power to release to others.

In the fourth account of being baptized in the Holy Spirit (Acts 8:14–17), we saw that the believers at Samaria had only been baptized with John's water baptism as well. When Paul laid hands on them, they received the Holy Spirit, which, by all the other scriptures, confirmed to us that this meant they each spoke in tongues, as the Holy Spirit gave them the utterance.

Are you familiar with the scientific principle of Occam's razor? The principle states that among competing hypotheses, the one with the fewest assumptions should be selected. Other more complicated solutions may ultimately prove correct, but—<u>in the absence of certainty</u>—the fewer assumptions that are made, the better.

We can apply this scientific principle to prove that this assumption in the Bible is correct. Based upon the precedence set by the Holy Spirit, it absolutely would <u>not</u> be wrong to assume that Aquila and Priscilla acquired this information from Paul during the time that he spent working and living with them for a year and a half. They experienced this gift in their own lives, thereby being able to reveal this truth to Apollos as well.

Furthermore, it would also be <u>correct</u> to assume that the laying on of hands was the method that Paul used. This practice was previously revealed to us as a valid method, whereby believers who had not been baptized in the Holy Spirit would receive the baptism of the Holy Spirit, along with the evidence of speaking in tongues. Besides, Ananias laid his hands on Saul, who became Paul, and he too was baptized in the Holy Spirit in like manner.

This gives us a better understanding that the Holy Spirit longs to fill each believer, as we ask Jesus to baptize us or fill us with His Holy Spirit. It truly is an amazing gift from an amazing Savior, Jesus Christ, our Lord.

This now leads us to our <u>ninth filling</u> of the Holy Spirit and our <u>final example</u> of being filled (baptized) with the Holy Spirit with the evidence of speaking in tongues. This account is also found in the book of Acts.

I can hear the critics now saying, "See, if the scriptures do not mention speaking in tongues when a person is filled with the Holy Spirit, then it must mean that it (tongues and this baptism) has been done away with." The last account will settle this speculation and false teaching once and for all.

The Holy Spirit knew there would be this kind of opposition against His power. He saved the best for last, proving that He set the precedence of speaking in tongues and not having to continually write it again each time the baptism of the Holy Spirit is mentioned or occurs.

Let's read it together, shall we?

"And it happened, while Apollos was at Corinth, that Paul, having passed through the upper regions, came to Ephesus. And finding some disciples he said to them, 'Did you receive the Holy Spirit when you believed?'

So they said to him, 'We have not so much as heard whether there is a Holy Spirit.' And he said to them, 'Into what then were you baptized?' So they said, 'Into John's baptism.' [John's baptism was in water—*no power*, just symbolic even today.]

Then Paul said, 'John indeed baptized with a baptism of repentance, saying to the people that they should believe on Him who would come after him, that is, on Christ Jesus.'

When they heard this, they were baptized (filled with the Holy Spirit) *in the name of the Lord Jesus. And when Paul had laid hands on them, the Holy Spirit came upon them, and they spoke with tongues and prophesied. Now the men were about twelve in all." (Acts 19:1–7)*

Now, I don't know how to make this any clearer or plainer for you. This last and final account of being filled or baptized with the Holy Spirit has the evidence of speaking in tongues and prophecy and should be the proof—that is, the nail that keeps the lid of the coffin of doubt and unbelief nailed shut for the rest of time. It's been in the Bible since it was written.

Many Church leaders are overlooking this information today. How is this even possible? I will tell you. It's because many are studying the Bible intellectually instead of studying the Bible with the Holy Spirit of truth teaching them and giving them the understanding that is so desperately needed to correctly understand the spiritual content of God's word.

I am not naive, I know that there will still be many who will not believe in the baptism of the Holy Spirit with this evidence of other tongues even after all this evidence is given. Poor judgment in choosing to miss out on the power of God's third person, the Holy Spirit, is a sad reality within the Church today. I can only say the same thing as Paul did: *"But if a man be ignorant, let him be ignorant."*

These twelve men that the apostles came across in Ephesus were already believers in Christ. They appeared to have been baptized according to John's baptism. Paul asked them plainly, "Have you received the Holy Spirit since you believed?" Believed in what or who? They were baptized with the water baptism unto John's baptism, but their answer was, *"We have not so much as heard whether there is any Holy Spirit."*

Wow, folks, I am going to repeat myself, how much plainer and clearer can the Holy Spirit, Dr. Luke, and I make it?

When they heard this *good news*, they were baptized in the Holy Spirit in the name of the Lord Jesus, and when Paul laid his hands on them and prayed, the Holy Spirit came on them, and they spoke with tongues and prophesied. They did it God's way and missed out on *nothing*!

I have to wonder, how many believers in Christ who are not filled with the Holy Spirit, with the evidence of speaking in tongues according to the scriptures, would be offended or maybe even quit and get mad if a man of God would ask them today, "Have you received the Holy Spirit (implying as having the evidence of speaking in tongues) since you believed?"

Now, not only do we have an account of them receiving the Holy Spirit after believing in the one who would come after John (Jesus), but we also have all twelve of them speaking in other tongues as on the day of Pentecost and prophesying as well.

I am convinced that the Holy Spirit inspired me to write this book just for you and that many Christians will become enlightened because of the truth of its contents. Perhaps, for some, it will be the first time they will have seen or heard of these scriptures and the Holy Spirit in this manner at all.

Many of you will be born again and baptized in the Holy Spirit and fire, speaking in tongues and prophesying just as these twelve believers did in Ephesus. How the Holy Spirit chooses to use this book is totally up to His plan and purpose for it!

THE OPERATIVE

Dear reader, all that is expected of you is to be obedient to Him by doing your part, and He will do the rest!

During the accounts of the baptism in the Holy Spirit, we were introduced to <u>three</u> of the <u>nine gifts</u> of His Holy Spirit. This sets the stage for later chapters concerning the gifts of the Holy Spirit. So far we have seen these three gifts in operation:

1. Tongues.
2. Interpretation of tongues.
3. Prophecy.

As you read the book of Acts during your private time, you will see it could have easily been entitled, "The Acts of the Holy Spirit." The Holy Spirit's dispensation or season is now! As mentioned before, He is the operative in the Church and world today. When Jesus walked on the earth during His life and ministry, He was full of His Holy Spirit without measure. Jesus, then, was the operative.

For us now, Jesus sent us His Holy Spirit, and the Holy Spirit is the operative of the Church and the world today. He will remain the operative of the Church and the world until He is taken or removed out of the way.

"For the mystery of lawlessness is already at work; only He who now restrains will do so until He is taken out of the way. And then the lawless one will be revealed, whom the Lord will consume with the breath of His mouth and destroy with the brightness of His coming." (2 Thess. 2:7–8)

The antichrist cannot be revealed to the world until the Holy Spirit is removed, along with the bride or the Church of Christ. He continues to keep the plan of God on schedule, on time, and in order so that all will come to pass as prophesied.

This verse pertains to worldly events and operations. In the book of Revelation, the first three chapters talk about the Church. Beginning at chapter four, the Church is not mentioned again till the end when the Church becomes the bride of Jesus.

Do you desire true Holy Ghost *revival* in America and in the entire world? The Holy Spirit is the one to ask and follow. Church, look to Jesus, the author and the finisher of our faith, and ask Him for the gift of the Holy Spirit with the evidence of speaking in tongues, and begin your Holy Spirit–filled journey today! Let's make a difference in the lives of others together, shall we?

This ends the accounts of the baptism of the Holy Spirit recorded in Acts. However, the entire book is filled with His actions, as He lived through the believer's lives, just like you and me. Do we dare to be the ones whom the Holy Spirit helps to turn the world upside down?

I conclude this chapter with a testimony of a person, who gave me permission to share it with you—her personal experience concerning being filled with the Holy Spirit with the evidence of speaking in tongues as the Spirit gives utterance.

Following this testimony, in chapters 13 and 14, we research the gifts Jesus gives to men. In these two chapters, we will study to gain understanding about what we call the fivefold ministry gifts for today. Enjoy her testimony, and I will join you again in chapter 13.

PERSONAL TESTIMONY

I was 12 years old when I was born again. I was a church bus kid. We all know them, don't we? They are the little ones who go to church because of an outreach from a local church. Kids whose families do not attend church for one reason or another.

My story begins in a small Baptist church in rural West Virginia. During Vacation Bible School, I was made aware that many of the youth would be leaving soon for church camp. I wanted to go and someone sponsored me, so off I went.

At camp, I was born again. I was so happy that I would one day go to heaven. I knew very little about the Holy Spirit. It was not until I was married with 2 children that I was introduced to the Holy Spirit. My husband faithfully attended a spirit filled church that I visited now and then because I still considered myself a Baptist.

He spoke a lot about this Holy Spirit, of being filled with Him, along with the fruit of the Holy

Spirit and even the gifts of the Holy Spirit. I listened to him but I was not convinced. My heart was tender towards God so I was open but with much reserve. The one thing I knew was that the man I first met and the man that I was married to and living with were quite different. I knew it had to be God and His influences in his life.

One Sunday he asked me to go with him to a revival meeting, (which lasted by the way for thirteen weeks). Instead of going to my church, I went with him to his church. The Evangelist talked a lot about the Holy Spirit as well. This made me feel a little uncomfortable.

Fear left as I saw no signs of demonic activity like it was rumored to be. No fire was shooting out of their eyes, no shaking, or rolling down the isles. There were no snakes, and no swinging from the chandeliers. Those were all lies that I believed might be true.

By the 3rd evening I recognized some familiar faces in the congregation and was less uncomfortable. Everything was still in order. I still made my husband and kids sit in the back of the church where I felt safer being next to the exit sign.

We attended every night and the list of scriptures on my notepad grew larger and larger. I needed some time to investigate this Holy Spirit especially if I was going to prove this young Evangelist wrong. For I was told that I already had the Holy Spirit when I was born again. I believed the baptism in the Holy Spirit was not true and definitely not necessary. I was told that they only believed like that because their denomination did.

There were only a few more nights of Revival and I needed to get started on my quest. My husband worked 11–7 at a local coal mine and after tucking the boys into bed and saying our prayers and goodnights, he left for work. I would then get out his Strong's Concordance, Vines Commentary and my Bible to do my research to prove my point of view as fact. I would study the scriptures extensively from the previous meetings.

However, by the end of the Revival, I got to know a part of God I thought I already knew. The 3rd person of the Trinity or what became known to me as the third character of God that longed for my close fellowship with Him.

It was one service of the revival and yes, we still sat in the back by the exit, that the Evangelist did something different. He got up to the podium and said, "I am going to do something a little different tonight. The Holy Spirit is saying that there is someone here that understands the Holy Spirit like never before and would like to be filled with the Holy Spirit with the evidence of speaking in tongues."

As he said this, my heart leaped but my flesh hesitated. He prayed and some went forward, but I did not. After a few moments, which seemed like an eternity, I yielded. I did not go up front but stayed right in my pew. I said "Lord Jesus, if this is of you, fill me here where I am and baptize me with Your Holy Spirit." I no sooner got those words out of my mouth, when I started speaking in tongues and this evidence solidified to me that I was being filled with the Holy Spirit. Even as I do to this very day.

I can only describe to you what I felt. I was 2/3 full, lacking the other 1/3 that made me completely full. As I continued speaking in tongues, an overflow happened. Glorious times between my God and I during my times of praying in the Spirit. Communicating like never before, and when and where I wanted to pray in the Spirit, I could. For the first time I felt full, lacking nothing, without breakdown in communications. I felt whole, new and I was being equipped. I was speaking the language of God!

All of the sayings that it is of the devil and all his deception WERE NOT TRUE. First, if tongues were of the devil, then wouldn't we be hearing it in all the local bars and on the streets? The ungodly would be speaking it. But no, the tongues found in the Bible, happens when a believer is filled with the Holy Spirit and Fire.

Secondly, it is not possession! The Holy Spirit is God's Spirit, and He is Holy. I invited Him after He revealed His truth in the matter through His Word. It was not what other people thought about Him, or even what I thought about Him. The omission of biblical truth kept this from me for a long time and it did not prosper me in my Christian life the way the truth of it did.

After the baptism of the Holy Spirit, the truths about His gifts and fruit, became so clear and more relevant to me in my day to day Christian walk.

One encouragement, "love someone towards the truth about the Holy Spirit, like my husband Jim did. The Holy Spirit is not to be argued about." "Just be yourself!"

END OF TESTIMONIAL

You may have guessed that it was my wife, Rosalyn, who shared her testimony and experience about being filled with the Holy Spirit with the evidence of speaking in tongues. Rosalyn and I encourage you to share your testimony with others about Jesus's baptism in the Holy Spirit with the evidence of speaking in tongues.

You may contact us at catchthevm@gmail.com, and share your experience concerning the baptism of the Holy Spirit. We would love to hear from you today!

Write your experience down, and refer back to it from time to time for encouragement. This is an excellent tool for stirring up the gift that is within you, which Paul encouraged Timothy to do, which is this baptism of the Holy Spirit.

"Therefore I remind you to stir up the gift of God which is in you through the laying on of my hands. For God has not given us a spirit of fear, but of power and of love and of a sound mind." (2 Tim. 1:6–7)

Here is yet more proof that another believer, Timothy, received the baptism of the Holy Spirit with the evidence of speaking in tongues by the laying on of hands. He was originally filled, but Paul knew that Timothy needed to encourage himself by praying again and again in the Holy Spirit. This is what Paul was telling Timothy—to stir up or encourage yourself by praying in the Spirit.

(In every example given where the apostles laid hands on believers who were not filled with the Holy Spirit and fire with the evidence of tongues, each were filled with the Holy Spirit and spoke in tongues or prophesied.)

Paul, in essence, was telling Timothy, "Remember when we first met, and I laid hands on you, and you were filled with the Holy Spirit and spoke in tongues? Boldness, faith, joy, along with power and authority, were transferred to you, as you were filled. Stir that gift up, Timothy, when you are feeling low or weak. Pray in the Holy Spirit, and build up yourself with your most holy faith by praying in the Spirit."

Now I paraphrased a little here, but that is what precedence does. Once set, you don't have to assume—*you know*! Praise the Lord Jesus forevermore!

Are you filled with the Holy Spirit of Jesus?

So there you have it—nine different times that believers were either baptized or filled with the Holy Spirit for the first time and filled again many times after that, as they built up their most holy faith praying in the Holy Spirit.

What are your thoughts now toward the baptism of the Holy Spirit? Have you read with an open mind and heart? Have you

THE OPERATIVE

changed your mind yet, or perhaps, has your mind been changed for you? Knowledge about a subject will do this. The more knowledge you acquire, the more fear of something will take wings and fly away.

It's up to you what you will do with this knowledge given to you about Jesus's gift of *His* Holy Spirit.

There is much more to share with you about the Holy Spirit that is directly connected to this baptism. In the remaining chapters, I will be sharing with you about Jesus's gifts to men—the gifts of the Holy Spirit and the fruit of the Holy Spirit.

A common mistake that's made is to think that any of these are separated in any way. You cannot have one without having the others unless you are not whole—spirit, soul, and body.

Each of these gifts that pertain to the Holy Spirit of Jesus is for our prosperity in the matters of the things of God. Of course, if these things do not matter to you, then they will have no further meaning to you than that which you allow.

But if they do matter to you, then you will find that they will take you to higher heights and deeper depths than you have ever gone before with the Lord. As the Holy Spirit fellowships with you with His Word, give them permission to come alive to you in ways that you have not yet experienced.

Continue your journey by continuing your knowledge of Jesus's Holy Spirit and the many responsibilities that He has as the operative <u>of the Church and world today!</u>

CHAPTER 13

Gifts Jesus Gives to Men
Part 1

As I have mentioned before, and it bears repeating, being filled with the Holy Spirit and fire is not a prerequisite to making it into heaven. The only prerequisite to obtain access into heaven is believing that Jesus Christ is God's only Son, sent to die for all mankind's sins. Believing also that God sent Him to die for our sins and to be raised from the dead, with the resurrection power of the Holy Spirit, is part of that truth. Taking action by recognizing that you have need of a Savior by calling upon Jesus's name to be saved is the deciding part of being born again.

"For with the heart one believes unto righteousness, and with the mouth confession is made unto salvation. For the Scripture says, 'Whoever believes on Him will not be put to shame.' For there is no distinction between Jew and Greek, for the same Lord over all is rich to all who call upon Him. For 'whoever calls on the name of the LORD shall be saved.'" (Rom. 10:10–13)

When a person does this, their sins are forgiven, and their name is written in the Lamb's book of life, and they are now born again with a new spirit to house Jesus. Without your name in this book, you cannot enter heaven and partake of His glory! Your <u>heavenly eternal life</u> begins the moment you believe and act upon that belief.

Nothing else—no other name, no other way, no other person, no other thing, no other god or religion—will get you there. That is what the Bible says, and it's a matter of fact that is undeniable, as you read it with the one who inspired it, the Holy Spirit of truth.

Once you become a child of God, Jesus begins to equip you as one of His children growing in the grace and knowledge of Him.

"And He Himself gave some to be Apostles, some Prophets, some Evangelists, and some Pastors and Teachers." (Eph. 4:11)

These offices of responsibility held by men (inclusive) are not titles that we, ourselves, can add to our names, but they are positions of responsibility and accountability unto God. What responsibility and accountability, you ask? The answer is found right here in the Bible:

"For the equipping of the saints for the work of ministry, for the edifying of the body of Christ." (Eph. 4:12)

Beloved, once a person is born again, we <u>all</u> are supposed to be equipped for <u>the work of ministry</u>. The responsibility of this equipping lie with the ones who hold the offices of apostles, prophets, evangelists, pastors, and teachers, who have previously been equipped themselves. We are to see to it that each believer is equipped for the ministry to fulfill the plan and purpose of God for each member of the body of Christ to accomplish as their part, whatever that may be.

This ministry then extends to <u>the edifying of the body of Christ.</u> For how long is this to be done? Did this commandment cease sometime during the last few centuries? Verses 13–16 reveal the answer:

"Till we all come to the unity of the faith and of the knowledge of the Son of God, to a perfect man, to the measure of the stature of the fullness of Christ; that we should no longer be children, tossed to and fro and carried about with every wind of doctrine, by the trickery of men, in the cunning craftiness of deceitful plotting, but, speaking the truth in love, may grow up in all things into Him who is the head—Christ—from whom the whole body, joined and knit together by what every joint supplies, according to the effective working by which every part does its share, causes growth of the body for the edifying of itself in love."

Has this happened yet to the Church today? Have we arrived at each of those destination points and goals found in verses 13–16 above? I submit to you that many ministries are too busy building bigger buildings and adding more programs and ministries instead of building up the Church that is already in their care.

The Church needs more qualified members who are sent out to replicate this process again and again. This is the plan of God, not the same members remaining in the same Church building, their entire life and, in some cases, generation after generation.

It seems to me that the Church has settled for far less than what Jesus intended her to be and to do. These position should be filled with believers who are anointed to operate in them as called by God and are gifts given unto men by Jesus. They should be teaching and training every new convert how to correctly understand the word of truth, as the Holy Spirit did, to teach and train them.

"To rightly dividing the word of truth, so that they need not be ashamed while becoming a workman unto God." (2 Tim. 2: 15—paraphrased)

How about it, folks, are we seeing this being done in *all* our churches and ministries today? Our born-again existence was never intended to be a spectator sport, but rather with every team member skillfully trained in doing his or her part in the body of Christ and in the big picture of things.

It must be possible to reach this point of maturity, or the Holy Spirit would not have given us this directive, would He? Are we anywhere close to being in "unity of faith and the knowledge of the Son of God"? You judge this by trying on the spirits of those who are influencing your life.

As revealed in previous chapters, Jesus fills His believers with the Holy Spirit, and we know this by the evidence of speaking in tongues, according to the scriptures, helping each of us in our endeavors to become the men and women whom the Lord intends us to be. It is the Holy Spirit's power in the believers of the early Church that turned the world upside down, <u>making the things of God more precious and predominate than the things of the world.</u>

THE OPERATIVE

The apostle Paul was saved by Jesus and also baptized by Him with His Holy Spirit and all that implied. Writing to the Church in Corinth in AD 56, Paul gave instructions about Christian conduct, grace, and fellowship.

At the time of his writing this, half a century had passed since that powerful day of Pentecost and his new birth in Christ. Since then the operation and power of the Holy Spirit had been manifested many times always changing people's lives in the process.

Expounding on the details about being filled with the Holy Spirit and the order in which these gifts are to operate in a Christian's life and in the Church structure, Paul gives us all the information we need to know to realize they are real and still relevant for today.

It is clear that those who are filled with the Holy Spirit, at a given time, are chosen by the one who they are filled with (the Holy Spirit) to operate within certain anointed offices—not only to fill that office(s) of responsibility and accountability to Jesus, but also to operate in a way and manner that is *not* conducive to traditional thinking in the modern-day Church. <u>These gifts are His and His alone.</u> The Holy Spirit chooses when and how they are to be used.

Be prepared for the arguments that are most commonly used to deny the validity, the existence, and the operation of these gifts and this baptism. For this reason, I am sharing a few of them with you as preparation for any opposition you may face, including your own belief system.

Let's look at the scriptures most commonly used by those who oppose the baptism of the Holy Spirit with the evidence of speaking in tongues, as they try to explain it away because of their lack of knowledge and personal experience in the matter:

"But earnestly desire the best gifts. And yet I show you a more excellent way. Though I speak with the tongues of men and of angels, but have not love, I have become sounding brass or a clanging cymbal. And though I have the gift of prophecy, and understand all mysteries and all knowledge, and though I have all faith, so that I could remove mountains, but have not love, I am nothing. And though I bestow all my goods to feed the poor, and though I give my body to be burned, but have not love, it profits me nothing." (1 Cor. 12:31–13:3)

The following is another verse used by many to deny the resurrection power of the Holy Spirit's filling and operations in believers today:

"When I was a child, I spoke as a child, I understood as a child, I thought as a child; but when I became a man, I put away childish things. For now we see in a mirror, dimly, but then face to face. Now I know in part, but then I shall know just as I also am known. And now abide faith, hope, love, these three; but the greatest of these is love." (1 Cor. 13:11–13)

Their argument against the validity of these gifts today is that as we mature in Christ, we are to put away childish things. Are you kidding me? After studying the many believers who were filled with the Holy Spirit and were speaking in tongues, are we now to accept this as a valid argument? What about the notable and supernatural miracles that took place—were they childish?

If you could ask any of the recipients of them if they thought they were childish, they would tell you different. Better yet, ask somebody like me who has received healing after healing of my body for the past thirty-seven years. No, these gifts are not childish at all. I too have seen many miracles that others have received from these gifts operating in anointed men chosen for these offices.

Was the boldness that came with being filled with the Holy Spirit childish? Was the resurrection power that raised Christ from the dead childish? Do you think all those people who were healed and delivered from demons by the hands of not only Jesus but also of those filled with the Holy Spirit and fire thought them childish?

At best their argument is very weak and falls flat on its face in the light of all the scriptures pertaining to this. Even God's *love*—which, they say, is greater than these gifts—is what we should be desiring rather than a healing or deliverance from demon control. They go as far as to say that God's *love* is a more excellent way than that of the gifts of tongues or discerning of spirits or working of miracles, etc. Can they not see that it is because of God's *love* that these gifts have been given, and they are totally motivated to operate because of His *love*?

In no way are these scriptures saying that God's love takes away the validity of His gifts. Their claim concerning these gifts being childish and that they should be put away or that we should not desire after these gifts is just plain foolishness.

Let me show you what these critics do not say and do not want you to know. First, let's take God's *love* for example. As a Holy Spirit–filled man of God, I will be the first to tell you that nothing—including being filled with the Holy Spirit, operating in any previous offices mentioned, or operating in one or more of His nine gifts—can function without His *love*.

It is God's *love* that is the motivating force that enables a man to turn his heart toward Jesus for salvation, because He first loved us. His love is the reason a man will bestow his goods upon the poor. His love is the reason a man will lay down his life for another, for there is no greater action of love than this.

I could go on, but my point is that Paul is telling us that *love* is the reason the gifts are given and why they operate in those who have this love of God, which, by the way, is poured into their hearts.

"The love of God is poured out IN our hearts by the Holy Spirit who was given unto us." (Rom. 5:5)

We cannot love others like the Lord does, except we love them through His supernatural *love* being poured into us each time we pray in the Spirit. I am convinced that the lack of this love being poured into the hearts of believer's that are not baptized or filled with the Holy Spirit, is why there is so much contention between Christians, and non-believers. Those unsaved in the world, see this, and want no part of it, because, they already have enough contention, and a lack of God's love, in their own lives.

But this love is poured into each believer, as they pray in the Holy Spirit as often and as much as they can receive, to share with others. If you're not being filled with the Holy Spirit according to the scriptures thus far, then how is the love of God being poured into you?

Secondly, verse 31 of chapter 12 says, "But covet earnestly the best gifts [plural]; and yet show I unto you a more excellent way."

Here is a truth that many believers fail to recognize. There are nine gifts of the Holy Spirit that Paul talks about in First Corinthians 12:8–11. They are the word of knowledge, word of wisdom, faith, gifts of healing, working of miracles, prophecy, discerning of spirits, various kinds of tongues, and interpretation of tongues. *"ALL these works that one and the very same Spirit, dividing to every man SEVERALLY as HE* [the Holy Spirit] *wills."*

Each of these nine gifts performs a specific task directed by the Holy Spirit, which is the *will* of the Trinity, consisting of the Godhead body, which is God the Father, Jesus the Son, and the Holy Spirit. Remember the fire triangle? In order to have a fire, you must have three things: (1) source of fuel, (2) source of Ignition, and (3) oxygen. If any one of these is removed, the fire goes out.

(See page 147 to view the spiritual fire triangle.)

It's the same thing with the gifts of the Holy Spirit. Remove any one of the Trinity from the gifts, and they do not operate, because they each have their part in the gifts of the Holy Spirit.

"There are diversities of gifts, but the same Spirit [Holy Spirit]. *There are differences of ministries, but the same Lord* [Jesus]. *And there are diversities of activities, but it is the same God* [God the Father] *who works all in all. But the manifestation of the Spirit is given to each one for the profit of all." (1 Cor. 12:4–7)*

THE OPERATIVE

FIRE TRIANGLE

FATHER — **SON** — **HOLY GHOST**

Remove Any Of The Above And The FIRE Goes Out!

[I Corinthians 12:4-6]

"There are diversities of gifts, but the same Spirit. There are differences of ministries, but the same Lord. And there are diversities of activities, but it is the same God who works all in all."

© 2015 - Revised - James J. Hamrick - Printed by Permission

I will be expounding on each of these individually and show you that Jesus Himself operated in them, as He has the Spirit without measure. We, on the other hand, have the Holy Spirit with measure while living here on earth.

This measure is determined by how much we pray in the Spirit. How full of the Holy Spirit we are, at any given moment, will determine the amount of His power available to flow through us.

<u>Critics of God's power do not want you to know that</u> these gifts are given out of love. They operate because of love, and we are to desire or covet earnestly the *best gifts*, not God's love, as this is what is poured into us, as we are filled with His Holy Spirit.

If I ministered in a meeting at your church and you needed, let's say, a miracle, which of the gifts listed above would meet your need? Would it be love? Of course not! It would be the working of miracles! Why, then, as a visiting evangelist, would I covet love for you or, say, desire the gift of discerning of spirits or various tongues if you needed a miracle?

The design of the operation of the gifts of the Holy Spirit is to get your need met, and it's that plain and simple. And the knowledge of the operations of each gift will guide us into which gift is best to be desired. Without the correct knowledge, you will not know which gift is best to meet the need.

Furthermore, why would I want to limit the Holy Spirit by just allowing Him to use me in just one or two of His gifts? If I did limit Him, wouldn't you miss out on your miracle?

You see what I am talking about? Desiring the best gifts is not talking about desiring *love* over these gifts. It's talking about the best gifts that will meet the need of the person, people, or circumstances at hand. Besides, the Holy Spirit had Paul write *best gifts* plural, not singular, which is what love is, right? Sometimes more than one gift will be needed to operate to meet the need(s) at hand.

I believe these gifts are given from and by the Holy Spirit, showing us that we, as individuals, <u>do not</u> have ownership of them. Some believers call them their own gifts. I have heard many Christians say, "I have the gift of healing" or "I have the gift of whatever"—<u>no, a million times no!</u>

Men or women can't rightly claim one of these gifts as being their gift and never should. They are the gifts of the Holy Spirit. He decides to whom He will share them with. Private ownership is so out of order. According to the scriptures, we are commanded to do everything decently and in order.

I believe they do this because of a lack of knowledge or revelation, possibly because of those who have trained them improperly. They need to know the truth about these gifts that are part of the wonderful works of God, especially those we call the fivefold ministry gifts—the apostles, prophets, evangelists, pastors, and teachers—who, certainly, should know these truths. What if they do not?

Apart from these ministry gifts, each believer is held responsible individually, as they are being trained for the ministry, to rightly divide the word of truth with the *help* of the Holy Spirit.

"Beloved, do not believe every spirit, but test the spirits, whether they are of God; because many false prophets have gone out into the world." (1 John 4:1, read also verses 2-6)

Each believer is responsible for knowing what is from God and what is not. Are you able to tell false teachings? Would you know if false teachers were interpreting the Bible incorrectly? Would you know if they were forming their own private interpretation?

It is the Holy Spirit alone, according to the Bible, who divides to every man severally as He wills. We do not pick and choose what gifts we like at our leisure. We are only to covet or desire earnestly the best gifts that will meet the need.

Our part is to make ourselves available to be used in a variety of ways as conduits of His supernatural power. This allows His power to flow through us to others, as we continue to build up ourselves on our most holy faith, praying in the Holy Spirit.

Got it? Good, let's move on.

Four years later, in AD 60, Paul revealed more to us in his writings to the Church of the Ephesians:

"And be not drunk with wine, in which is excess, but be filled with the Spirit, Speaking to yourselves in psalms and hymns and spiritual

songs, singing and making melody in your heart to the Lord, Giving thanks always for all things unto God and the Father in the name of our Lord Jesus Christ, submitting yourselves one to another in the fear of God." (Eph. 5:18)

Some have wrongly used this scripture to instruct *not* to drink alcohol. Before I was born again, I drank some. When I was drunk, I liked to sing. Many people who get drunk sing, even if they can't sing at all, like me. Paul's comparison of being drunk with wine in excess with being filled with the Holy Spirit in excess shows us that the more we pray in the Spirit, the greater the possibility one could actually be mistaken as being drunk. This, simply, is because you would be operating in ways that are not natural, but supernatural, in joy and not in unhappiness, and in faith and not doubt.

Hmm, where have we heard this before? Remember Acts 2:13? *"Others, mocking said, these men are full of new wine."* They were so full of the Holy Spirit that their words and actions were mistaken to be of somebody who was drinking all night long. But Peter, of course, having the boldness he never had a few days prior, stood up and said… (You remember the words, right? If not, go back and read it again.)

Lack of knowledge is a very dangerous tool that is cunningly used by those who want to keep others in the dark. A lack of knowledge allows one to be swayed easily and controlled to some extent. This is what the devil does, and this is what some politicians, family members, friends, and even people in powerful positions count on. Manipulative people count on others having a lack of knowledge. This gives them a false sense of power that they will continue to use against you, if you let them.

Receiving revelation from the Holy Spirit about the actual meaning of the scriptures He inspired is truly enlightening. Words of knowledge and words of wisdom fall under this category of receiving revelations from the Holy Spirit.

You too can operate in the gifts of the Holy Spirit if you ask Him and desire them as the best gift needed while meeting the need that presents itself.

For example, when I read the Bible, I ask for His revelations and understanding of what I read. They sometimes come in the form of words of knowledge or words of wisdom, and sometimes understanding comes because of His ability to teach me in the way that He knows I will understand. It is the Holy Spirit giving me the interpretation of the Bible, not me having my own interpretation of what I think the Bible is saying and should be able to teach each of us, as the divine teacher that He is.

<u>Do not limit the Holy Spirit in your life.</u> He is our comforter and should be, to each of us, our divine teacher. He (the Holy Spirit) takes the things of Jesus and shows them to us, and we become more familiar and more like Jesus with each teaching accepted and applied in our lives.

Jesus also informed us that the Holy Spirit would show us things to come. Did He not do this with John when he inspired the book of Revelation? John was caught up in the Spirit, but I think it's safe to say that the Spirit of Jesus was giving him words of knowledge and words of wisdom. Even the gift of prophecy was in operation in the writing of the book of Revelation.

When I am giving a message, or writing a letter or book, the Holy Spirit is the one who gives me the words to say and write, because I call upon Him to do so.

"But whatever is given you in that hour, speak that; for it is not you who speak, but the Holy Spirit." (Mark 13:11)

Now, I am a human being and realize that the purity of any message may change a bit when it comes through a believer. He takes this into account and still works with all our characteristics and oversees the results, because God's word never returns void back to Him.

"It is the Spirit who gives life; the flesh profits nothing. The words that I speak to you are spirit, and they are life." (John 6:63)

"Then Jesus said to them, 'When you lift up the Son of Man, then you will know that I am He, and that I do nothing of Myself; but as My Father taught Me, I speak these things.'" (John 8:28)

"I speak what I have seen with My Father, and you do what you have seen with your father." (John 8:38)

You <u>cannot</u> harm a man who knows the truth. Sure, you can do physical abuse to him, even unto his death, but he always triumphs and comes out smelling like a rose on the other side because he knows the truth and applies it in his life.

And no, I am not only talking about heaven. Circumstance can hurt men greatly, yet it is up to each believer how we choose to either <u>respond</u> or <u>react</u> to them. A man who knows the truth <u>responds,</u> and a man who does not know the truth <u>reacts</u> more often than not!

Jesus said in *John 8:32, "And you shall know the truth, and the truth shall make you free."* (That is the truth you know and apply that will set you free.) Are you a free man or woman today? If not, you surely can be.

It is commanded of us to try on or test the spirit of what we read, see, and hear as to whether or not it is of God. How do we do that, especially if we, ourselves, do not know what the word of God says and means? This is how we try on or test the spirit of a matter, by seeing if it lines up with <u>two or more witnesses</u> in God's word.

I'll give you an example. Once I receive a new revelation from the Lord, I do not teach, preach, or write about it until I have found those two or three witnesses of someone else saying and/or revealing the same principle in the Bible. This is how you stay true to the word of God and stay out of trouble with God. However, this check and balance system that God has given us does not ensure that we will stay out of trouble with men as we proclaim His truths.

Generally, most people do not like change. This, however, is what revelation-knowledge speaking does. It's the spiritual fabric that transforms us by using the scriptures. I have found that when a revelation diverts from traditional teachings, men, especially leaders in the Church, do not care very much for it. But it's the very substance that Jesus builds His Church with, by challenging believers to go deeper into the things of God.

This practice of finding the two or more witnesses has served me well over the years. Read the verses again for yourself in Matthew 16:15–19.

Revelation knowledge comes one way, and it is from God the Father because of Jesus, His Son, via the Holy Spirit. He chooses where and when to use a *word of knowledge.* Here I go, jumping ahead of myself again.

THE OPERATIVE

I pray that while you are reading this book, the gifts of the Holy Spirit become operational through you, as you are filled with the Holy Spirit with the evidence of speaking in tongues.

Operating in the gifts of the Holy Spirit is not only available to the fivefold ministry gifts, but is also available to <u>every man</u> (inclusive) to prosper, as the Holy Spirit chooses who operates and with which gift to operate.

"Beloved, I pray that you may prosper in 'all things' and be in health, just as your soul prospers." (3 John 2)

Your soul must prosper first! How? It is with the knowledge and application of Jesus's word. Then prosperity, on every level, follows. Let your soul prosper, by believing in God's whole word, which contains each of these gifts mentioned within this book and confirmed by the Bible.

To recap, the fivefold ministry gifts of apostles, prophets, evangelists, pastors, and teachers are *offices* of responsibility to mature the Church with accountability directly to Jesus. These are *not* just titles we place on our business cards, letterheads, and Web sites. Nothing is wrong with this, but having knowledge of the truth helps you to never lose sight of it.

This will also keep humility in your life. Pride often follows advancements in life, like more power or authority at your position in life. One may lose sight of the fact that it is God's blessing and not your own self that has gotten you this authority.

I believe those holding positions of authority need to realize the truth of their stations. When the world sees more of Jesus and less of each of us, including the ministry gifts, the Holy Spirit will have an easier task of drawing men unto Jesus without men being in the way. Pride is a horrible downfall in one's life, don't you agree?

I appreciate those in these offices today. I am, however, opposed to impostors who are placed in these positions in the Church by the vote of men instead of the appointment of God. Personalities and being a yes-man will only carry one so far.

I have recently been made aware of well-known music directors in churches today who do not stay for the message once their part (performance) is completed. They leave once they have sung in the worship service. Call me old-fashioned, but I thought we praised Him with singing and worshipped Him in spirit and truth.

This is one reason the Church is not shining as brightly to the world—because there are many in the modern Church who are hirelings (tares among the wheat) instead of appointees by the Holy Spirit.

How would you know if you, yourself, don't have the right knowledge to ascertain this? Each of us will give account of these works, and you want to be found on the side of the wheat who knows and not on the side of the tares who are in hiding.

The fivefold ministry gifts given to men by Jesus, according to the scriptures, I believe, are clear; that they should be filled with the Holy Spirit with the evidence of speaking in tongues. If those who waited on tables had to be filled with the Holy Spirit and have a good report, then anything short of this does not bring the power into God's word, except for times of a sovereign move of God in certain services. Only God can choose this grace and not man. He gives grace unto whom He will give grace.

Is this what today's Church should be waiting for—that is, a sovereign move of God now and then (like the man waiting at the side of the pool for somebody to come and carry him to the water once the angel came and stirred the waters for a miracle)? Or should the Church be experiencing special moves of God continually by the power and anointing of the Holy Spirit? *(Jesus gave us the example when he told the man to "rise, take up your bed, and walk.")* I believe the latter; how about you? *(See John 5:1–9.)*

In chapter 15, we will begin looking into each of the nine gifts of the Holy Spirit. Taken individually, we will find out what they are, how they operate, and for what purpose they serve in our lives.

We will learn more about how others operated in them in the past, giving us the ability to know how to yield ourselves in the present to be willing vessels or conduits of the flow of the supernatural resurrection power of the Holy Ghost.

But first let's finish with "Gifts Jesus Gives to Men—Part 2," concerning the fivefold ministry gifts, which continues in chapter 14.

CHAPTER 14

Gifts Jesus Gives to Men Part 2

"Then Peter said to them, 'Repent, and let every one of you be baptized in the name of Jesus Christ for the remission of sins; and you shall receive the gift of the Holy Spirit. For the promise is to you and to your children, and to all who are afar off, as many as the Lord our God will call.'" (Acts 2:38, 39)

Now, if we were to take these two verses by themselves, I would have to come to the conclusion that everyone who is born again automatically receives the baptism of the Holy Spirit. I am concerned that this is what happens to many who have been trained by denominational thinking only. They simply are not taking into account all the other verses in the Bible that the Holy Spirit has used to set His precedence about this most important event, second to salvation, in a believer's life. *Scripture interprets scripture!*

If believers are trained wrong and placed into positions of leadership—such as being an apostle, prophet, evangelist, pastor, and teacher—they are more likely to reproduce false teachings that simply are not truth according to the other scriptures. The danger is that if another gospel is being preached other than that what we read about, according to the scriptures, this happens:

"But even if we, or an angel from heaven, preach any other gospel to you than what we have preached to you [including all the scriptures of the New Testament covenant between God the Father and Jesus, His only Son], let him be accursed. As we have said before, so now I say again, if anyone preaches any other gospel to you than what you have received, let him be accursed." (Gal. 1:8–9)

I am not advocating throwing the Old Testament out the window. On the contrary, as we have seen through Paul's teachings, it was the tutor who brought the Jewish believers to Christ. There is a tremendous amount of wisdom and knowledge that we can glean from the Old Testament, which helps us not only to know God better, but also to see how He accomplished things in times past, and what future events that are still to come.

But, it is very important for every believer to realize that we are no longer under the curse of the law. Jesus has delivered us from it, because in the Old Testament Law of Moses, no man could keep them all, so if one law was broken, then that person was guilty of all of them as being broken in God's eyes. Thank you, Father, that you made a new covenant with Jesus, whereby believers are set free from the curse of the law, because He is responsible for us as our Lord and Savior. That is true *hope* and *peace of mind*!

Anytime scriptures are repeated, this should get our attention as being important. For this very reason, I have been repetitious with certain scriptures, reminding you of their importance, as did the writers of the Bible, as in Galatians 1:8, 9.

As we continue with this second part of "Gifts Jesus Gives to Men," my intention is to help you see the importance of knowing the person(s) you are submitting yourselves unto and what their responsibilities are according to the word of God.

"But this spoke He of the Spirit, whom they that believe on Him should receive; for the Holy Spirit was not yet given, because Jesus was not yet glorified." (John 7:39)

Jesus had to be crucified and raised from the dead in order to receive His eternal, glorified body that had no restrictions whatsoever, in any realm that He enters. Not only did this enable Him to give us salvation and eternal life, but also when that day comes, we Christians will receive our glorified body, just like Jesus did.

He could not have given us His Spirit while He was still in the flesh, because the Holy Spirit was inside Jesus, just like your spirit is inside you. It was His Holy Spirit that kept His flesh alive until all sin was placed upon it, to destroy the power of sin in our lives. However, after He was glorified, all limitations were removed, and *now* Jesus came to His body of believers as the operative of the Church in the person of His Holy Spirit.

"Beloved, now we are children of God; and it has not yet been revealed what we shall be, but we know that when He is revealed, we shall be like Him, for we shall see Him as He is." (1 John 3:2)

"Love has been perfected among us in this: that we may have boldness in the day of judgment; because as He is, so are we in this world." (1 John 4:17)

This act of love, the giving of His life for us, enabled Him to give unto His body of believers Himself, through His Holy Spirit, without lack of enough power to continue God's will. He now gives the members of His body in a measure that we each believe concerning this baptism, allowing Him to live His life in each believer in the capacity that each believer permits Him to.

"For as he thinks in his heart, so is he." (Prov. 23:7)

Just like a person cannot operate in life past what they know unless they are smart enough to listen to the advice of others who have already been through what they are struggling with, believing is the same way. We cannot and will not operate in <u>faith</u> past that which we know and believe. That which we believe, we speak, and that which we speak, we become.

I learned a very important lesson when I was first born again, and I am mindful of it almost daily. I heard this from one of the guest speakers at Fishnet back in 1978: *"Sow a thought, reap an action; sow an action, reap a habit; sow a habit, reap a lifestyle."* I pray you can see the truth in this and now have a greater understanding why certain things in your life are the way that they are.

As believers, we can make our decisions based upon God's word as to whether or not we will move past that which we knew and believed yesterday. No one person makes another person believe anything, and certainly, the Holy Spirit will never make you, because He reveals it to you, and you decide what to do with it.

One of the many things that I appreciate greatly about the Trinity is that neither God the Father, Jesus the Son, nor His Holy Spirit makes or pushes us to do anything. They never override our will. There is no dictator mentality within the Trinity of God!

Unlike the devil, who is a taskmaster, pushing sinful opportunities in our faces and without Christ, man is powerless to say no. Even then, sometimes our will has the final say-so as to whether we will partake or not. The flesh has been weakened by sin that entered through Adam. During life, some people have learned to hold at bay some thoughts and feelings they have been tempted with. This is mainly because of a morality choice as they mature, but it is impossible for mankind not to yield to temptations without help.

This is why the devil loves abortions. If he can snuff out a life before it hears God's word and has the opportunity to become born again, he can stop many great men and women from coming into the world, killing them off before they become his enemy.

The last statistic I read was that there were over four thousand recorded abortions every single day. And now, there are proofs and videos of those who, after aborting the child, are dissecting the bodies and selling the body parts.

Father God in heaven, please put a halt to these murders and demonic activities that are killing Your children all over this world, in Jesus's name. This begs the question to be asked: who and what could have each of these children become?

Maybe one would have been the scientist who would find a cure for cancer or one who would find the breakthrough in self-sufficient energy. Perhaps, some would have become doctors, lawyers, or contractors, and the list goes on.

What the devil fears most is that some could have become anointed men and women of God for this last-day Holy Ghost revival and harvest of souls that are upon us. We may never know in

THE OPERATIVE

this life. But our hearts cry should be, "Holy Spirit of the Most High God, convince these *women* to stop killing their children, we ask this in Jesus's name, amen."

There are even some in the modern Church who believe that the ones holding the offices of the fivefold ministry gifts are the only ones whom the Lord can use in the operation of the supernatural gifts of the Holy Spirit. We must be careful not to seek out these men and women. By doing so, many have placed them on a pedestal, making them think that they are somebody when they are not. Instead, we need to keep Jesus on the pedestal, His throne in our hearts and lives, and be sure to keep each man and woman in their respective place.

Jesus definitely is somebody! It is Jesus who gives these gifted men and women to the Church and to the world. Some He anoints to operate as apostles; some, prophets; some, evangelists; some, pastors; and some, teachers. Those anointed for these tasks have a responsibility not to man, but directly to Jesus for rightly dividing the word of truth, then to teach others to do the same.

Their reason for being is for the perfecting (maturing) of the saints (believers) so the mature believers (you and me) can do the work of the ministry. Through this work the body of Christ is edified (built up). Throughout this process of spiritual growth, we must make sure that it's the Holy Spirit teaching us, even if it is through a man. They should teach us the ways of Jesus, correctly, above men's opinions of what they think the word of God is saying.

Each believer has a large degree of personal responsibility to grow in the grace and knowledge of Jesus. The ministry gifts are there as examples and guides to ways that the Holy Spirit has already matured them in their own experiences, being guided by Him throughout their lives.

Each of these offices should have men and women trained correctly, equipped by the Holy Spirit with His anointing, power, and gifts operational, as He appoints them to the various offices, instead of them merely being trained and appointed by men. The latter happens when you have a group of people choosing not to be trained by the Holy Spirit. They make their selections of those holding these positions from their own intellect and not from the direction of the Holy Spirit. This is why there are so many hirelings within the Church today.

Hopefully, each would be yielded to the Holy Spirit, allowing Him to use them in one or two or all the nine gifts outlined in First Corinthians 12. Sadly, there is a large percentage of those holding these positions in the modern Church who are <u>not</u> filled with the Holy Spirit with the evidence of speaking in tongues, let alone, not operating in the gifts of the Holy Spirit.

Even for them there is still *hope*. They only have to be enlightened to the truth about the Holy Spirit and all that He is and has for the Church today. As with the early Church, the modern Church should be full of His power, with supernatural miracles happening daily so others can see the goodness of God. Believers would no longer have to go from meeting to meeting, searching for the power of the Holy Spirit to find a miracle.

Many in the pulpits in the modern Church do not believe in the operation of the gifts of the Holy Spirit. Maybe their denomination does not believe this way, or personal beliefs get in the way. Therefore, those who are trained and are behind the pulpits will train and teach the congregation the same. Like produces like. We multiply after our own kind. There is a danger of circumventing the benefits of the Holy Spirit's operations.

If we recognize that it is Jesus who gives the anointing (ability) through His Holy Spirit, then we can seek His anointing for ourselves. Each member of His body has this right and ability to do so if they choose to exercise it.

"For the gifts and the calling of God are irrevocable." (Rom. 11:29)

"So the last will be first, and the first last. For many are called, but few chosen." (Matt. 20:16)

I believe, the reason that <u>few are chosen</u> is *not* because they are found unworthy, but because many do not hear the calling from Jesus and His Holy Spirit in the first place. Then, there are also those who do not know they are capable of hearing the voice of God and are not being trained to know how to hear Him.

THE OPERATIVE

Being filled with the Holy Spirit with the evidence of speaking in tongues helps tremendously with hearing His voice and hearing directions from the Lord, as He uses His Holy Spirit to do these.

It is true that once the Lord calls a person for His plan and purpose, He never changes His mind and never removes the call, no matter what we choose to do or not do. That is why the gifts and callings of God are irrevocable. Being called to these offices is the highest calling in one's life. Each believer is called once they recognize their need of a Savior. As we have seen in Ephesians, we are all called to the work of the ministry, are we not? Whether we heed the call is another matter. This is between us and the Lord.

In my lifetime and ministry, I have had the privilege of being chosen by the Holy Spirit to hold and operate in each of these five listed positions. For each position, His anointing, or the enabling to function in the capacity needed, was given to me by His Holy Spirit. As with the nine gifts of the Holy Spirit, He picks and chooses everything. Let me share with you some of my fivefold ministry gift experiences.

There was a season when I traveled to other countries, taking food, financial, and medical aid to churches in need. I have even worked with new, start-up churches, which are some things the apostle did by taking relief to the churches and establishing new works throughout the land. (While I never have seen Jesus face-to-face in the natural, like Saul who became Paul, I have certainly seen Him in my spirit and each time I read His word. He is ever before me, and there is no way to move away from this truth, even if I wanted to, and I never want to leave His presence.)

As it pleased Him, the anointing would change, and the prophetic office was needed. Modern-day prophets do not, so much, foretell the future, but tell forth the word of God with His anointing and through His gifts, bringing forth miracles, healing, knowledge, wisdom, etc. There have been worldly events revealed to me by the Holy Spirit that came to past as well, as Jesus has promised me that He (the Holy Spirit) would also show me things to come. These revelations are shared only with my inner circle.

During revival meetings or just out on the street in my daily life, the anointing comes for evangelism. Reaching out to the lost and believers alike are key parts of my life. The anointing is different for an evangelist than that of a pastor, but similar in the fact that the work of an evangelist is really for those who do not know Jesus as their Savior, while a pastor's anointing is to watch over those entrusted in his/her care as they mature.

"For since, in the wisdom of God, the world through wisdom did not know God, it pleased God through the foolishness of the message preached to save those who believe." (1 Cor. 1:21) There will be more on this in later chapters.

Then, there was a season that I was asked to spend some time, teaching and ministering to a group of men in a local prison. The anointing of a pastor/teacher, was operating through me for three-and-a-half years. There were times when I proclaimed the word of God, which was preaching, and there were times that I explained the word of God.

To meet the need of the office that I was operating in, to either preach or teach the word of God, the Holy Spirit adjusted His anointing accordingly. The anointing for a pastorate is for longevity and maintenance of the congregation being trained for the work of the ministry. There are times of evangelism also when the Holy Spirit requires it.

I determined years ago that I would *not* limit God, Jesus, or His Holy Spirit in any way in my life to the best of my ability. This is why I can say with all conviction that these ministry gifts given to men are not permanent positions, but temporary and can be changed at any given moment, just as the anointing needed to operate in them changes by the Holy Spirit.

I believe the Church would be healthier if its leaders would allow the Holy Spirit the same freedom to do His work through them the way He sees fit. We need the anointing of each of these gifts, saturating our lives, flowing to and through us to others, and producing a fervent living body of Christ. It takes all five of these anointing's, to make the Church whole, according to the Bible!

THE OPERATIVE

By now, I believe that you know more about the fivefold ministry gifts. They should be under the directive of the Holy Spirit and not man or their board of directors or governments. Each of these has their place but should not be relied upon to be the final directive for the <u>operation of spiritual matters</u>. Jesus has placed this responsibility in the sole hands of the extremely qualified Holy Spirit Himself.

A man or women chosen by God should have the freedom and liberty to give themselves wholly to the Holy Spirit, allowing Him to pick and choose the anointing for which office He needs them to operate in. Gifts flow through them, along with the number of fruit others can partake of, because of the Holy Spirit's operations. Jesus's abundant lifestyle depends totally upon a believer's willingness to be used in this capacity.

The Holy Spirit will also work with the check and balance of the governing boards held by men and women, who should also be filled with the Holy Spirit to keep any one individual from going away from the word of God and His principles. <u>This is why it is extremely important to have those filled with the Holy Spirit and full of faith, with a good report, holding these positions as well.</u> (The two enemies to watch out for, concerning these offices, are pride and power.)

Continue to look to Jesus, the author and finisher of our faith, who writes the pages of our lives, as we yield ourselves wholly unto Him to fulfill that good, perfect, and acceptable will of God.

Fact being, it is God, through Jesus, who sets each of us in positions of the Church.

First Corinthians 12:28 says, *"And God has appointed these in the church: first apostles, second prophets, third teachers, after that miracles, then gifts of healings, helps, administrations, varieties of tongues."* Notice—*varieties of tongues*, or various tongues. According to some, this practice has been done away with, but <u>not</u> according to the word of God! He is still appointing believers to these positions, as He needs them, and as they yield to His Holy Spirit's directions.

<u>What if</u> the Holy Spirit wants to use you in His gift of tongues, would you say yes or no? Worse yet, what if you do not believe in

the gift of tongues or any other of His gifts? Many people depend on what we do; give us the strength, dear Lord, to go on with You!

Paul asked a series of questions, <u>which he did not answer</u>. Why? Because he knew the Corinthian readers, along with all other readers of this letter, would know the answer to the questions.

"How is it then, brethren? Whenever you come together, each of you has a psalm, has a teaching, has a tongue, has a revelation, has an interpretation. Let all things be done for edification." (1 Cor. 14:26)

When we get to the gifts of various kinds of tongues and the interpretation of tongues, there will be more details on both of them. However, in First Corinthians 14, Paul was giving instructions about keeping things in order within Church meetings. I am not talking about the buildings or denominations, but the spiritual gifts and the operations of the Holy Spirit in the body of Christ, fellowshipping with Him in our collective services.

Paul knew the believers were all filled with the Holy Spirit in the early Church and were yielding themselves to be used by the Holy Spirit in these capacities. They allowed the Holy Spirit to flow through them when they came together continually.

Paul continued with these questions, and based on his teachings in First Corinthians 12, 13, and 14, along with Ephesians 4:11-16, I am able to give you the answers that everyone knew <u>at that time</u> and should realize today.

Here are the questions that Paul asked in First Corinthians 12:29,30 and what, I believe, are the answers:

Are all apostles?	Answer—No, but they could be.
Are all prophets?	Answer—No, but they could be.
Are all teachers?	Answer—No, but they could be.
Are all workers of miracles?	Answer—No, but they could be.
Do all have gifts of healing?	Answer—No, but they could have.
Do all speak with tongues?	Answer—No, but they could.
Do all interpret?	Answer—No, but they could.

Paul gives us instructions to earnestly desire the best gifts, and he will show us a more excellent way to do this.

THE OPERATIVE

We dare not mix up the gifts of the Holy Spirit with the members of the body of Christ. God places each member of the body of Christ within His body. Each of those members can and are chosen by Jesus and His Holy Spirit to fill positions of authority, and each member can be chosen by the Holy Spirit to operate in His gifts severally as the Holy Spirit wills.

Many are called, but few are chosen. Again, I believe it's because many have not been told that they are being called, resulting in no time being spent in preparation and not giving his or her lives wholly to God—spirit, soul, and body. The body of Christ is designed to replicate itself in love by the power of the Holy Spirit. This reproduction, I believe, has been stunted by a lack of knowledge and the unwillingness of Church leadership to teach this truth. They have the love partially right, but many seem to be denying the power.

<u>Paul knew this important fact about the Church members.</u> He knew that everyone was not on the same level of spiritual growth in grace and knowledge of Jesus. Many were added to the Church daily, some having already matured into teaching and instructing others, concerning the operations of the Holy Spirit, while others where learning.

His questions imply, are all apostles? <u>Not yet, but they could be once they mature in the things of Jesus and His Holy Spirit.</u> He understood that the Church was in a constant flux of growth. This knowledge allowed him to lead them properly to earnestly desire the best gifts. The more excellent way of obtaining them was to allow the Holy Spirit to pour God's love into them each time they built themselves up on their most holy faith, praying in the Holy Spirit, as Jude revealed.

These gifts given to men by Jesus (and His Holy Spirit) are gifts of mature Christian men and women, who, according to the scriptures, should be filled with the Holy Spirit and fire and all that implies. They are to be positioned by the Holy Spirit because they were trained by Him to further the kingdom of heaven here on earth while maturing other believers to do the <u>same work of the ministry</u>.

Apostles, prophets, evangelists, pastors, and teachers are called by the Holy Spirit and have accepted the call on their lives for His purpose of maturing other believers, as they have been matured. The yielded believers are not only called but also chosen to these ministry offices by the Holy Spirit, as they mature. It is His anointing that enables those placed into these offices by Him to train other men and women to do the same, thus allowing the body of Christ, the Church, to continue to grow up in Jesus. This is God's perfect process of maturing His bride spiritually for his Son, Jesus.

In <u>First Corinthians 12</u>, Paul tells what the gifts are. <u>In chapter 13</u>, he tells why they are given and the motivation that makes them work, which is *love*. <u>Then in chapter 14</u>, he gives detailed instructions on the *how* and *why* they operate.

I believe it is clear that all those currently operating in one or more of these fivefold anointed ministry positions should be filled with the Holy Spirit, according to the information revealed to us in the scriptures that we have covered thus far.

If the ministry gifts are not believers filled with the Holy Spirit, I do believe it takes away from the congregation's spiritual health, by not receiving the power of the Spirit and life of the word of God that He intended for them to receive. They are simply relying upon their own abilities, or abilities of others, instead of relying upon the Holy Spirit.

An unhealthy Church gives way to reasoning things out according to intellect and traditions of men, bringing into the Church things that need not be there. The Church must be more than a social gathering place and a blending pot.

"But know this, that in the last days perilous times will come: For men will be lovers of themselves, lovers of money, boasters, proud, blasphemers, disobedient to parents, unthankful, unholy, unloving, unforgiving, slanderers, without self-control, brutal, despisers of good, traitors, headstrong, haughty, lovers of pleasure rather than lovers of God, having a form of godliness but denying its power. And from such people turn away! For of this sort are those who creep into households and make captives of gullible women loaded down with sins, led away by various lusts, always learning and never able to come to the knowledge of the truth. Now as Jannes and Jambres resisted Moses, so do these also resist the truth: men of corrupt minds, disapproved concerning the faith; but they

will progress no further, for their folly will be manifest to all, as theirs also was." (2 Tim. 3:1–9)

"Beloved, do not believe every spirit, but test the spirits, whether they are of God; because many false prophets have gone out into the world. By this you know the Spirit of God: Every spirit that confesses that Jesus Christ has come in the flesh is of God, and every spirit that does not confess that Jesus Christ has come in the flesh is not of God. And this is the spirit of the antichrist, which you have heard was coming, and is now already in the world." (1 John 4:1–3)

In chapter 15 we begin the exploration into these miraculous gifts of the Holy Spirit, showing forth the wonderful works of God. I wonder, will you be a part of this last day's miraculous move of the Holy Spirit, or will you still believe that all this has passed away with the apostles? Perhaps, you are not even acknowledging that there are still anointed apostles, prophets, evangelists, pastors, and teachers today.

My prayer is that the Holy Spirit is able to reveal to you these things of Jesus to be true and worthy of acceptance in all faith and hope of Christ within you. After all, He is the one who gave them all to us, is He not?

CHAPTER 15

Gifts of the Holy Spirit Part 1

I begin this teaching by placing these <u>nine gifts</u> into <u>three categories</u>. This categorization I first heard in a message over twenty-five years ago by an evangelist friend of ours from West Virginia. This teaching gave us such clarity and made such an impact in our lives that I've had the privilege of literally teaching it around the world over the years of our ministry, concerning this topic of the gifts of the Holy Spirit.

We will take each individual gift and show how they operate, for what purpose do they operate, and some examples of them being used in the scriptures. These are found in First Corinthians 12:1–11. (Please read them now then return to this teaching.)

In the first category we have the following:

1. word of wisdom
2. word of knowledge
3. discerning of spirits

These three gifts help us to <u>think</u> like God.

In the second category we have the following:

4. faith
5. gifts of healing
6. working of miracles

These three gifts help us to <u>act</u> like God.
And in the third category we have the following:

7. prophecy
8. various kinds of tongues
9. interpretation of tongues

These three gifts help us to <u>talk</u> like God.

As we look at each of the gifts individually, keep in mind that it is the Holy Spirit who chooses who and which gift is used, not the person operating in the gift. We are to only desire the best gift, and He chooses to allow either us to operate within it or somebody else, depending upon His knowledge of the things to meet the need(s).

First is the gift of the word of wisdom. It's not the wisdom we learn over the years from trial and error, then correcting our mistakes. On the contrary, it is the wisdom of God, made available to each believer in Christ and through His Holy Spirit.

Let's first take a look into *word* and see what the original Greek word means for this teaching.

> "*logos* (log'-os); from (NT:3004) *lego* (leg'-o) a primary verb, properly, to "lay" forth, i.e. (figuratively) relate (in words [usually of systematic or set discourse]); something said (including the thought); by implication a topic (subject of discourse), also reasoning (the mental faculty) or motive; by extension, a computation; specifically (with the article in John) the Divine Expression (i.e. Christ): KJV—account, cause, communication, concerning, doctrine, fame, have to do, intent, matter, mouth, preaching, question, reason, reckon, remove, say (-ing), shew, speaker, speech, talk, thing, none of these things move me, tidings, treatise, utterance, word, work" (NT:3056).

Next let's look at "of wisdom."

"*sophia* (sof-ee'-ah); from (NT:4680); wisdom (higher or lower, worldly or spiritual): KJV—wisdom" (NT:4678).
"*sophos* (sof-os'); akin to *saphes* (clear); wise (in a most general application): KJV—wise (NT:4680).

Each of us, drawing from the depths of Jesus's wisdom, depends upon what we believe and what limitations we place upon the Holy Spirit's gifts in our lives. For instance, what if we were taught something contrary to the word of God, and we accept it as truth? God forbid, but this has and does continue to happen today. Knowing the fact that He <u>never</u> overrides our will, we can truthfully say that the limitations to how God is able to use each of us in the work of the ministry are according to that which we believe.

"If we are faithless, He remains faithful; He cannot deny Himself." *(2 Tim. 2:13)*

<u>God's faithfulness</u> to His words and promises does not depend upon whether or not we believe them. He remains faithful because He swore by Himself, as there is no other greater than Himself to swear His oath too. So for Him to deny His own words would be the same as denying His own existence, which He cannot do. If He did, the result would be that we would immediately cease to exist. Are you still here? I am!

"For when God made a promise to Abraham, because He could swear by no one greater, He swore by Himself, saying, 'Surely blessing I will bless you, and multiplying I will multiply you.'" (Heb. 6:13–14)

Jesus operated in the word of wisdom each time he spoke. As He pointed out, He *only* spoke what words He heard the Father say. So then, we can safely say that all the red-letter words in the Bible that signify Jesus speaking are words of wisdom.

"Then Jesus said to them, 'When you lift up the Son of Man, then you will know that I am He, and that I do nothing of Myself; but as My Father taught Me, I speak these things.'" (John 8:28–29)

"I can of Myself do nothing. As I hear, I judge; and My judgment is righteous, because I do not seek My own will but the will of the Father who sent Me." (John 5:30)

In fact, we can go one step further and say that the Bible is written of continual words of wisdom. Since all the words written in the Bible are inspired by the Holy Spirit, they too must be considered words of wisdom, words of knowledge, and prophecies as well.

"And so we have the prophetic word confirmed, which you do well to heed as a light that shines in a dark place, until the day dawns and the morning star rises in your hearts; knowing this first, that no prophecy of Scripture is of any private interpretation, for prophecy never came by the will of man, but holy men of God spoke as they were moved by the Holy Spirit." (2 Peter 1:19–21)

No matter what book you read, whether it is Proverbs, Psalms, Kings, Matthew, Mark, Luke, or John, they are <u>all</u> inspired by the Holy Spirit, who is full of the wisdom and knowledge of Jesus Christ, because He is the Holy Spirit of Jesus.

We need to be aware of the fact that false teachers in the Church use this next scripture (1 Cor. 2:9–16) below to discredit the validity of the Holy Spirit's operation within the body of Christ today. (I believe, false teachers are called by men and placed into offices by men for their own selfish purposes, stacking the odds in their favor with "yes" personnel, if you would.)

I have sat under a pastor that had a "you scratch my back, and I will scratch yours" mentality. His statement to me was, "Jim, I can either open doors for you, or I can close them." Since I believed, and still do, that Jesus only held this responsibility in my life, the Holy Spirit did not leave me there.

Some do this because they lack the confidence in their calling. And if questions are raised, challenging the status quo, they often explain away why they do not know the answers to those weightier questions that are asked. <u>The Bible was not written for people to use as an excuse not to believe in God and His ways, but rather to believe in God and His ways!</u>

"But as it is written: 'Eye has not seen, nor ear heard, Nor have entered into the heart of man The things which God has prepared for those who love Him.'" (1 Cor. 2:9)

This verse is being used by so many to explain to multitudes of congregations that we are *not* supposed to know these things. Why, because they are not understanding the spiritual content of the spiritual word of God.

They only have to read a little further and not stop at this verse in their sermons. If verses 10–16 are read within their message, they seem to have a perfect explanation as to why these are not valid for today, or they do not address them at all in their preaching or teaching.

<u>But God</u> are my two favorite words in the Bible. The word *but*, as you know, is a conjunction that connects two thoughts together, and the word *God*—well, that covers everything, doesn't it?

In First Corinthians 2, there are four thoughts connected by this conjunction *but*, concerning the wisdom of God and how He has changed the process whereby we can receive His wisdom. Each thought is important and adds another level of understanding to the next thought.

In First Corinthians 2:1–8 Paul explained that he did not come to the Corinthian church, using excellence of speech to declare the testimony of God. Neither did he use enticing words of man's wisdom. He came in the demonstration of the Spirit and of power so that their faith would not stand in the wisdom of men, but in the power of God. Verses 7 and 8 ended the thought with, "Had the princes of this age known the wisdom of God in Jesus and His crucifixion, they would not have crucified Christ."

In verses 1–8 we find the comparison of the wisdom of God versus the wisdom of men. Please take the time and read Verses 1-8 on your own, then come back. Paul quotes Isaiah in verse 9, concerning the wisdom of God. Notice, the first word in verse 9 is *but*, connecting the first thought about God's wisdom to what was mentioned by Isaiah in the Old Testament.

The <u>two thoughts</u> I want you to pay particular attention to begin at verse 9 and continue through 16.

"But as it is written: Eye has not seen, nor ear heard, Nor have entered into the heart of man The things which God has prepared for those who love Him."

The thought here is that nothing, which man has seen or heard or has entered into his heart up to that point of the original writing found in Isaiah years ago before Christ, compares with the things that God has prepared for those who love Him (God).

"For since the beginning of the world men have not heard nor perceived by the ear, nor has the eye seen any God besides You, Who acts for the one who waits for Him." (Isa. 64:4)

This first thought of Isaiah was connected to the next by <u>"but God,"</u> meaning that God did something that changed the original thought that was previously not understood, one way, but now could be understood another way.

It tells us that since we have Jesus as our Savior, and He gives us His Holy Spirit, <u>we now can know</u> "the things that God has prepared for those who love Him."

Here are the remaining verses 10–16:

"But God has revealed them to us through His Spirit. For the Spirit searches all things, yes, the deep things of God. For what man knows the things of a man except the spirit of the man which is in him? Even so no one knows the things of God except the Spirit of God. Now we have received, not the spirit of the world, but the Spirit who is from God, that we might know the things that have been freely given to us by God.

These things we also speak, not in words which man's wisdom teaches but which the Holy Spirit teaches, comparing spiritual things with spiritual. BUT the natural man does not receive the things of the Spirit of God, for they are foolishness to him; nor can he know them, because they are spiritually discerned. BUT he who is spiritual judges all things, yet he himself is rightly judged by no one. For "who has known the mind of the LORD that he may instruct Him? "But we have the mind of Christ."

Let's break all this down so that we can see what God has done.

1. That which was previously hidden from man, God has revealed to us now.
2. He accomplishes this through His (Holy) Spirit giving revelation knowledge.
3. The Holy Spirit searches all things, even the deep things of God.

("Deep calls unto deep at the noise of Your waterfalls" [Ps. 42:7])
4. It's the spirit of man that knows the truth but can be deceived by lies.
5. No one knows the things of God except the Holy Spirit, who teaches us.
6. We have received the Holy Spirit of God, not the spirit of the world.
7. Since we received the Spirit of God, we might *know* things freely given unto us by God.
8. We speak these things of God given to us by the wisdom of what the Holy Spirit teaches and not what man's wisdom teaches us.
9. This wisdom compares spiritual things with other spiritual things.
10. A natural man (fleshly or not born again) cannot receive spiritual things, for they are foolishness to him.
11. A natural man cannot know this wisdom, as this wisdom is spiritually discerned.
12. A spiritual man knows them and judges all things with and by God's wisdom.
13. A spiritual man is judged by no one except the wisdom of God.
14. A spiritual man has the mind of Christ (available to him in his new spirit).

These are fourteen different insights received by men and women, as the Holy Spirit gives them to us. If we stop reading and/or believing, after First Corinthians 2:9, we miss out on the power of God once again and miss out on what is available to us. Quoting verse 9 only, we see what we don't have. Remember, he is quoting the Old Testament scripture in Isaiah, of what we now have because of Christ and His Holy Spirit. Are you seeing the importance of embracing our new covenant that is full of better things, including His wisdom and power?

"And we have such trust through Christ toward God. Not that we are sufficient of ourselves to think of anything as being from ourselves,

THE OPERATIVE

but our sufficiency is from God, who also made us sufficient as ministers of the new covenant, not of the letter but of the Spirit; for the letter kills, but the Spirit gives life." (2 Cor. 3:4–6)

During Isaiah's time men did not have these things available to them for ministry; they only had the letter of the law. Paul quoted this scripture to educate his readers that we <u>now</u> had them and could know what things God had in store for us and that they were revealed to us by the Holy Spirit. This could not be clearer, could it?

After reading verses 9–16 this way, I challenge you to think of them as you did before! Breaking them down like this gives the *wow* factor, doesn't it? Seeing them in the correct light of their intended meaning is most informative. <u>Does this ever reveal the spiritual strength and validity of the Holy Spirit's revelation knowledge at its best?</u>

Can you see that God <u>does</u> want us to know the truth about Him? We are living in the day and age where His Holy Spirit's revelation knowledge about things is given to those who love Him. If we love Him, we will believe His word the way that His Holy Spirit gives us His revelation knowledge.

His Holy Spirit's use of the scriptures, which include His nine gifts, allows us to see that which in times past was hidden from man, but now they are revealed unto the children of Jesus Christ, whom we are.

Is there any further question or doubt that God actually wants us to know the things about Him that He has in store for us? Is there any doubt that they are given to us by His Holy Spirit? His knowledge and understanding on matters come to us so that we might be changed from who we were to who He wants us to be.

Let's now take a look at a believer operating in the word of wisdom and word of knowledge. These two are so closely related that a word of wisdom may include a word of knowledge as well and vice versa. To do so, there is no better place to look than in the book of Acts, chapter 6. This chapter is full of the wisdom of the Holy Spirit.

Stephen, full of faith and power, did great wonders and miracles among the people. As mentioned before, Stephen was one who waited on the tables of the Grecian widows, yet the Holy Spirit used him mightily.

The Libertines, Cyrenians, Alexandrians, and others were disputing with Stephen. In verse 10 it says, "And they were not able to resist the wisdom and the Spirit by which he [Stephen] spoke." Here is an excellent example of a person operating in the gift of word of wisdom.

They realized that Stephen had received knowledge of the truth, and they could not resist or dispute the wisdom of the Holy Spirit presented through him. This was so foreign to their beliefs that in order to stop this message, they found false witnesses who would speak against him, and the end result was that Stephen was stoned to death.

This next statement bears repeating: not everyone full of the Holy Spirit and who operates in the word of wisdom is stoned to death. You have heard it said—one word from God can change your life forever. This is true! Whether you are persecuted for it or not is ultimately up to the Lord.

But by all means, please do not shy away from being used by the Holy Spirit in the gift of word of wisdom, or any of the gifts for that matter, because of the spirit of fear.

"For God has not given us a spirit of fear, but of power and of love and of a sound mind." (2 Tim. 1:7)

A word of wisdom is the word or words given by the Holy Spirit to someone, assisting them in applying *His* wisdom to their decision making. The difference between word of wisdom and word of knowledge is that wisdom is always the application of knowledge given. For this reason, the gift of word of knowledge is, many times, accompanied by a word of wisdom for application purposes. Look for it; you may very well miss it!

Some believers have a tendency of saying, "I got this gift, but not the others." Let me be clear here; we do not have any of these gifts as our own. The Holy Spirit, according to the scriptures, gives the nine gifts.

THE OPERATIVE

Being sent to Rome, Paul was under arrest for preaching the gospel and was given a word of knowledge by the Holy Spirit during the course of his journey there.

"Now when much time had been spent, and sailing was now dangerous because the Fast was already over, Paul advised them, saying, 'Men, I "perceive" that this voyage will end with disaster and much loss, not only of the cargo and ship, but also our lives.'" (Acts 27:9, 10) How we see things (our perception) can be changed or altered by these gifts.

This word of knowledge that Paul acquired was the knowledge from the Holy Spirit of a disastrous storm causing the shipwreck with loss of life. It was given for Paul and the others to prosper by its revelation. This situation of the loss of life changed when he was praying and was given a word of wisdom as instructions on what to do, which was <u>for everyone to remain on the ship.</u> In verse 31 Paul says, "Except these abide in the ship, ye cannot be saved." (KJV) This application to the knowledge of the shipwreck saved all their lives.

Can you see the advantage of having these gifts operating in our lives as parents, business owners, employees, or ministers, and the list goes on and on. All the times, when we as parent's, just knew that our children should not partake of this, or that, or that they should not go here, or there. Time always reveals how many of their lives are spared by these gifts in operation for our children and in our own lives as well as in other people's lives.

Here is a modern-day example of a word of wisdom given to a son from his mother. A pastor's wife shared this with us one Sunday afternoon. God had given to her what she thought to be a word of wisdom from the Holy Spirit.

After Sunday services, as with many of us, she would take a nap. On this particular Sunday, her son approached her, asking to go outside and ride his bicycle. She told him not to while she was napping, but to stay inside till she was able to be outside with him. He disobeyed and went outside, while his mother was napping, and rode his bike without his protective gear. This action cost him his young life. She believes he would be alive today if he had listened to her, simply by obeying his mother's wisdom given to her from God.

Our hearts were saddened, as she told us of her experience, but it was one that we will <u>never forget</u>. After that testimony, we *did not* allow our boys to wear us down by changing our minds. When we felt the Holy Spirit was directing us, we stood firm!

Paul's life lesson had a different outcome. The application of knowledge given to him with the wisdom on how to survive the shipwreck was applied, and when you read the rest of the story, you'll find that even though the ship was broken into pieces, because they remained in it till it was, they all were saved. I like to describe it like this: *application of the revelation changes the situation.*

This shipwreck scenario is an excellent example of the first two gifts of the Holy Spirit in operation, a word of knowledge and a word of wisdom. The word of knowledge, given to Paul by the Holy Spirit before sailing, concerning the disaster, was not heeded to by those in charge. He tried his best to advise against the trip, but since he was in bonds, he couldn't do anything about stopping them. If he was not in bonds, I am sure he would have made other arrangements for both him and his companions, especially after being warned by the Holy Spirit about the shipwreck.

This miraculous event would not have taken place if Paul was not, first, born again and, second, filled with the Holy Spirit and, third, learning about Jesus's gifts given to men to prosper them. Luke wrote them down for us to read, giving us excellent insights to these two miraculous gifts in operation.

We have these same benefits as children of God. What disasters in our lives or, better yet, what blessings in our lives are we missing out on because we are not filled with the Holy Spirit and are not operating in His gifts? If we're not making ourselves available to be used in these gifts, we have to ask ourselves, "What are we truly missing out on?" and "What is my reason for not believing in them?"

Learning to be sensitive to the Holy Spirit by yielding our lives to Him in this way, I believe, could spare ourselves and others a lot of heartaches and bring more joy that is unspeakable and full of glory into our lives, don't you think?

You may have begun to recognize other examples of the supernatural gifts of the Holy Spirit that are available to each believer now that you know what to look for. Pay close attention to the Holy Spirit in your own life, pertaining to a word of wisdom and a word of knowledge, so that you too can be saved from the shipwrecks of life.

Keep this in mind: knowledge = knowing information. Wisdom is the application of the knowledge received. Knowing how to apply knowledge that one has acquired in their life is not always easy. For this reason, when one is given a word of knowledge, it is wise to listen for or also ask for a word of wisdom so that you will also know the application of the revelation to change that situation.

If it were easy, Einstein would not have come up with the definition of insanity, which he defined as "doing the same things over and over while expecting different results." This is a perfect example of those wishing and hoping for their lives to change for the better, but they continue doing the same thing over and over, trying to get a different result, which, obviously, will not happen.

As we learn more about these gifts, I believe you will see that each of them can help us prosper in our personal lives and the lives of others. That prosperity brings much more fullness than just money.

The third gift in this first category is discerning of spirits. You might ask yourself, why is this gift so important, and how can we benefit from it?

"But a certain man named Ananias, with Sapphira his wife, sold a possession. And he kept back part of the proceeds, his wife also being aware of it, and brought a certain part and laid it at the apostles' feet.

But Peter said, "Ananias, why has satan filled your heart to lie to the Holy Spirit and keep back part of the price of the land for yourself? While it remained, was it not your own? And after it was sold, was it not in your own control? Why have you conceived this thing in your heart? You have not lied to men but to God.

Then Ananias, hearing these words, fell down and breathed his last. So great fear came upon all those who heard these things. And the young men arose and wrapped him up, carried him out, and buried him.

Now it was about three hours later when his wife came in, not knowing what had happened. And Peter answered her, 'Tell me whether you sold the land for so much?' She said, 'Yes, for so much.' Then Peter said to her, 'How is it that you have agreed together to test the Spirit of the Lord? Look, the feet of those who have buried your husband are at the door, and they will carry you out.' Then immediately she fell down at his feet and breathed her last. And the young men came in and found her dead, and carrying her out, buried her by her husband. So great fear came upon all the church and upon all who heard these things." (Acts 5:1–11)

This is an example of Peter operating in discerning of spirits, concerning two believers pretending to be like the other disciples by saying they gave *all* to the apostles when they sold some land they owned. At that time, many of the disciples that had land were selling them and turning the total amount over to the apostles. Peter was shown that they were lying because of the operation of the gift of discerning of spirits. The Holy Spirit revealed to him the lying spirit talking from out of their hearts.

One could argue the point that he was given a word of knowledge here, and you would be right. In addition, Peter was seeing or understanding the type of spirit or discerning of spirits that were lying to him about this matter. This gift enabled him to know that they did not give 100 percent of the proceeds from the selling of the land, like the others did, and he was also able to perceive the spirit in which they acted upon.

Ananias and Sapphira were trying to elevate their status as being in the same category of giving as the other disciples. The honor that was given to those who gave 100 percent of the proceeds from the sale of their property was quite high, I am sure. They desired to receive equal honor while giving less than the 100 percent of the proceeds. Had they said, "We have need of some of this money to pay a debt,"—or something like that—"but we are willing to give this much," I am sure that they would not have died. Peter even gave Ananias's wife the opportunity to say this, but she chose to tell the same lie as her husband did, and it cost her life also.

They chose to tell a lie, thinking the apostles would not find out, not considering that the Holy Spirit, who knew *all things*, would expose them. Because of their choice, they both were carried out by the disciples and were buried.

THE OPERATIVE

This gift gives the ability to recognize the person(s) spirit(s) once you come in contact with them. While the Holy Spirit may not reveal every detail, He can and will give you enough information concerning the kind of spirit influencing a person, such as boastful, prideful, lying, unclean, murderous, sabotaging, etc.

In Acts 16:16-18 (KJV), we find yet another example when a certain maid possessed with a spirit of divination met Paul and his group. For many days she followed them, crying out loud, *"These men are the servants of the Most High God, who show unto us the way of salvation."* Now many might say, "What, in the world, is wrong with that? What she is saying is true. I am getting free publicity from others, which in worldly marketing applications, word of mouth is the best advertisement, right?"

Watch what happens. After many days of this free advertisement, Paul, being grieved, turned and said to the spirit in the woman, *"I command thee, in the name of Jesus Christ, to come out of her,"* and *he came out the same hour."* Of course, Paul and his companions got in trouble with her masters by cutting off their livelihood because she could no longer divine for them.

The act of divining or divination is forbidden with the Lord. Divination uses things like familiar spirits and witchcraft, which are the devices of the devil. In this case, the woman was using <u>familiar spirits</u>, which were very <u>familiar</u> with Paul and his actions. (She was full of the spirit of divination.)

> *{Question: "What does the Bible say about divination?"*[5]
>
> *Answer: The word divination comes from the Latin divinare, meaning "to foresee" or "to be inspired by a god." To practice divination is to uncover hidden knowledge by supernatural means. It is associated with the occult and involves fortune-telling or soothsaying, as it used to be called.*

---

5. From gotQuestion.org online questions about the Bible.

From ancient times, people have used divination to gain knowledge of the future or as a way to make money. The practice continues as those who claim supernatural insight read palms, tea leaves, tarot cards, star charts, and more.

God tells us His view of divination in Deuteronomy 18:10: "There shall not be found among you…anyone who practices divination or tells fortunes or interprets omens." First Samuel 15:10 compares rebellion to the "sin of divination."

Practicing divination is listed as one of the reasons for Israel's exile (2 Kings 17:17). Jeremiah 14:14 spoke of the false prophets of the time, saying, "They are prophesying to you a lying vision, worthless divination, and the deceit of their own minds." So, compared to God's truth, divination is false, deceitful, and worthless.

As Luke traveled with Paul and Silas in the city of Philippi, he recorded an encounter with a diviner: "We were met by a slave girl who had a spirit of divination and brought her owners much gain by fortune-telling" (Acts 16:16). The girl's ability to penetrate mysteries was due to a demon that controlled her. Her masters received "much gain" from their slave. Paul eventually exorcised the demon (verse 18), freeing the girl from her spiritual bondage and angering the slave owners (verse 19).

Divination in any form is sin. It is not harmless entertainment or an alternate source of wisdom. Christians should avoid any practice related to divination, including fortune-telling, astrology, witchcraft, tarot cards, necromancy, and spell-casting. The spirit world is real, but it is not innocent. According to Scripture, those spirits that are not the Holy Spirit or angels are evil spirits.

THE OPERATIVE

Christians need not fear the spirits involved in divination; neither are Christians to seek wisdom from them. The Christian's wisdom comes from God (James 1:5).}

(End of gotQuestion.org.)

Paul, being troubled in his spirit about her comments, was given by the Holy Spirit the gift of discerning of spirits and, seeing this was not from God, he commanded the familiar spirit to leave in Jesus's name. The spirit had to obey, <u>as they always do, even though they might tell you different</u>.

Nowhere in the Bible is there mention of a gift of discernment or one that has keenly selective judgment, good taste, or judgment like some believers claim to have. There are some believers that go as far as to say, "I have the gift of discernment" or "I have the gift of healing," etc.

Let me speak frankly once more: no, you do not have any such thing. Let's rightly divide or interpret the Bible scriptures with their meaning and understanding that the Holy Spirit inspired so that the true knowledge can be heard, believed, and acted upon in our lives and others.

<u>No one gift or any of the nine gifts of the Holy Spirit belongs to any believer!</u>

I cannot stress this enough! They belong to the Holy Spirit, and He alone decides who gets what, when, where, and how many. We cannot pick and choose the gift(s). We can only covet or desire the best gift we believe to be needed, then He takes it from there, as we make ourselves available to be used in them. His will, not ours, is what matters in the operation of His gifts.

In this first category we learned about the following:

1. word of wisdom
2. word of knowledge
3. discerning of spirits

These three gifts help us to <u>think</u> like God. This wisdom, knowledge, and discerning of spirits come from the Holy Spirit to us and are not the natural wisdom, knowledge, or discernment one acquires in life experiences. No, these gifts are supernaturally given to us, as the Holy Spirit of Jesus sees the need for them.

Before going onto the next category of the "Gifts of the Holy Spirit—Part 2" in chapter 18, I would like to take the time and share with you an example of an experience that I had while ministering in a revival meeting in chapter 16. It aligns perfectly with the information pertaining to the use of the word of wisdom, word of knowledge, and discerning of spirits. After reading it, I believe that you will agree.

Then in chapter 17 the answer to the long-asked question "Where do demons come from?" is revealed from the scriptures of the holy Bible of our Lord and Savior, Jesus, with His Holy Spirit teaching us once again from His inspired word.

CHAPTER 16

My Personal Experience

I was preaching a weeklong revival, from Sunday to the following Sunday. It was in the Wednesday service that a particular woman who had been coming to each of the previous services was there once again. I never noticed her before, for whatever reason, but was told after this particular service that she had attended each service since Sunday morning. What I am about to tell you really happened, for it was a true event.

After about forty-five minutes into the meeting, the Holy Spirit said to me, "You're done, you can sit down now." So I turned the service back over to the pastor and sat down beside my wife, who was sitting on the front pew. The pastor seemed a little taken back by this, as he knew that I usually ministered longer than I did that night.

He stood in front and said, "If anyone would like to come around the altar and pray, feel free to do so now." Many came up, including this lady, who is the subject of this experience. She was praying directly in front of me and to my right. I started to go up and join in prayer when the Holy Spirit stopped me, as I heard Him say in my spirit, "Stand here and pray in front of the pew because I want to show you something."

It's important that you understand that I did not hear an audible voice. It was the knowing that one received like when words of knowledge and words of wisdom came. As a matter of fact, it's pretty much the same as a couple other gifts. When you receive the information from the Holy Spirit that comes from His still, small voice within your spirit and, occasionally, in word pictures or in dreams and visions, you always know that it is from Him and not yourself.

Almost everyone was praying out loud in a low tone of voice; however, with many people praying like this, it was a little noisy at times. Some were praying in English, and some, in tongues. But in this particular lady's case, she was praying fairly loud and using words that <u>sounded like</u> someone praying in tongues or the Holy Spirit.

As I stood, softly praying in tongues, inside my spirit, I knew that something was not quite right, like Paul with the lady of divination each time she spoke. I had my eyes closed while praying, and the Holy Spirit's instruction was to open my eyes. When I did, what I saw happen next was like watching something out of *The Exorcist*.

As I scanned the sanctuary to find out what the Holy Spirit wanted me to see, I saw almost everyone else's eyes were closed while praying. I wondered what it was that He wanted to show me. Then it was revealed <u>right before my eyes</u>. This lady I am talking about, while standing straight up, in what seemed like slow motion to me, sat down on her rear without even bending her knees. Now, you know as well as I do that this was not natural at all.

I looked around the room to see if anybody else saw what I just did; however, nobody else seemed to have noticed. Suddenly, as she sat on the floor, facing the front of the church, she began to turn her head. She turned it from looking forward to looking straight back, one hundred and eighty degrees, with her eyes closed. I immediately thought, *That is not you, God,* and the Holy Spirit said, "No, it is not."

I immediately asked Him what He wanted me to do. Within my spirit a word picture of myself walking up slowly, not drawing any attention, and laying my hands on her came to me. I tried to do this as discreetly as I could. So quietly I left my place in front of the pew and went and stood beside her.

THE OPERATIVE

At that time, she turned her head back around toward me, with her eyes closed, and looked up at me as if to say, "What do you think are you doing?" I leaned slowly over and laid my right hand on her shoulder, and immediately, I was shown by the Holy Spirit, using His gift of discerning of spirits, that there were two spirits that had control of her. I perceived the first one was an unclean spirit. The second spirit I could not identify at this point, but I asked the Holy Spirit what He wanted done.

The reason I asked the Holy Spirit what to do was because one other time, in a McDonald's, the Holy Spirit instructed me to cast out a demon from a homeless man I was ministering to, as I bought him lunch. He screamed out very loud, "You do not know who I am, I need these demons." In that case my instructions from the Holy Spirit at that point was, "Get up and leave him alone, this was his last chance." He did not want to be set free from them, and every time I cast them out in Jesus's name, they left, but he would ask them to immediately come back in. The last I had seen of him, the police was taking him to jail.

So as I asked the Holy Spirit what He would have me do with this lady, He instructed me to cast them out. As quietly as I could (screaming loudly at demons does not make them hear you any better), I leaned over and said to her discreetly in a whisper, "Come out of this woman, you unclean spirit, in the name of Jesus." At this point, you could have heard a pin drop, as everybody heard it. Then the other spirit began to speak. With a loud voice, we all heard, "I am not going to do it," blurted out of the woman's mouth.

Now, all attention was on what I was ministering to this lady. The people began to slowly return to their seats, and the pastor walked over to where we were. She remained sitting on her rear, with her feet and legs straight out toward the altar, and her eyes remained closed.

I was so excited because *I knew* that no lying demon could ever tell the truth. I also knew the name of the second demon that I had seen in her spirit, and I said once more, "I command you in Jesus's name, you unclean and lying demons, to come out of the woman and set her free."

I was so happy for this lady that I started dancing in the Spirit, and the more I danced and praised God, the more they cried out, "We are not coming out." The more they cried out that they were not coming out, the more I praised Jesus's name for setting this woman free!

While I continued dancing, praising, and thanking Him for His wonderful power in His name, she cried out with a loud shriek and fell backward onto the floor of the church. By now the only people who were at the altar were the pastor, this lady now lying still on the floor, and me. Of course, the Holy Spirit of Jesus was there also.

As the congregation began to praise the Lord and thank Him for His goodness toward this lady (about five minutes or so), she began to slowly move, and the pastor and I helped her to stand. The Holy Spirit prompted me to allow her to give a testimony about what just happened to her and what the Lord did for her, which I did.

She began crying so much that she had a very hard time talking at first. After gaining her composure, I was led by the Holy Spirit to ask a series of questions, which, once answered, explained everything.

Two years previously, she said she was going through a tough time in her life, and it seemed like she was not getting any help from God. So she took it upon herself to go to a local palm reader. The reader began telling her things about herself, using familiar spirits (which they listen to, telling them things about a person to draw them in). This is why the Lord forbids Christians to go to palm readers and such, because Christians would be giving permission to these demons to enter their life and, sometimes, to possess them, as was in this case. (She gave place to the devil.)

She said, for the past two years, she let herself go, not bathing or taking care of herself physically. Her body had a very strong, distasteful odor. Her hair was tangled in small knots. Her clothes were dirty as well. I never noticed this before, because, I do not categorize people by their appearances in my mind or heart. The Holy Spirit since has shown me to pay close attention to some of these details. What is going on inside men and women sometimes reveals itself by outward characteristics. These experiences, however, are not absolutes in people's lives. But they are guideposts along the way.

THE OPERATIVE

She said, for the past two years, she was also having stomach problems. There were only a few foods that she was able to eat. *Remember First Timothy 4:1–5?*

"Now the Spirit expressly says that in latter times some will depart from the faith, giving heed to deceiving spirits and doctrines of demons, speaking lies in hypocrisy, having their own conscience seared with a hot iron, forbidding to marry, and commanding to abstain from foods which God created to be received with thanksgiving by those who believe and know the truth. For every creature of God is good, and nothing is to be refused if it is received with thanksgiving; for it is sanctified by the word of God and prayer." (1 Tim. 4:1–5)

This had been the work of the deceiving spirits and doctrines of demons in this lady's life. Long story short, the following service, she returned, and I literally did not recognize her. Others made the same comments, as her hair was untangled, and she bathed and used perfume, with makeup on her face. She also testified that when she went home after her freedom meeting, she had her husband make a pizza, and she ate it with no problem.

She was set free from that which brought her into this bondage because of the fact that she lost faith in God's timing and took it upon herself to try and seek answers where she should *not* have been looking. She now had a beautiful, humble spirit, and the Lord continued to minister to her.

"Therefore, putting away lying, 'Let each one of you speak truth with his neighbor,' for we are members of one another. 'Be angry, and do not sin': do not let the sun go down on your wrath, nor give place to the devil." (Eph. 4:25–27)

What if I was not filled with the Holy Spirit, and He was not able to use me in His gifts? How many church meetings within this two-year period do you think she had attended? Only the Lord knows where she would be today. Oh, how marvelous is the resurrection power of the Holy Spirit, giving us authority over the devil and his devices in Jesus's name.

WARNING—Do not try to do this if you do not have a close relationship with Jesus through His Holy Spirit filling you and doing His work through you. Four words of advice to you—"seven son of

Sceva." Read Acts 19:11–20 and learn, because the natural man cannot partake of the spiritual things of God.

I would have never realized any of this if the Holy Spirit had not trained me prior to this event, to hear His voice and His prompting. It was not until the Holy Spirit opened my spiritual eye that I was able to recognize this lady was bound by these demons. Praises unto God for His grace and mercy toward each of us.

The same applies for today. There are many spirits that would overtake unbeliever's lives whether by influence or possession. These gifts allow a man or a woman of God to operate with such precision that people's lives can be changed forever. He desires to set the captives *free*.

The original Greek meaning of discerning of spirits is the following:

"discerning *diakrisis* (dee-ak'-ree-sis); judicial estimation: KJV—discern (-ing), disputation" (NT:1253).

"spirits *pneuma* (pnyoo'-mah); a current of air, i.e. breath (blast) or a breeze; by analogy or figuratively, a spirit, i.e. (human) the rational soul, (by implication) vital principle, mental disposition, etc., or (superhuman) an angel, demon, or (divine) God, Christ's spirit, the Holy Spirit: KJV—ghost, life, spirit (-ual, -ually), mind" (NT:4151).

So you see, the spirits are subject to us in His name, as Jesus said.

"Nevertheless do not rejoice in this, that the spirits are subject to you, but rather rejoice because your names are written in heaven." (Luke 10:20)

Rejoice in the fact that our names are written in heaven's book of life, but know that the spirits are subject to us because of His name and authority (power) given to us by His Holy Spirit.

They must obey us in His name, for the power of the Holy Spirit contains Jesus's authority. Being led by the Holy Spirit is hard to do if you are not filled with the Holy Spirit with the evidence of speaking in tongues, simply because of disbelief in His ways and operations. With doubt and unbelief flooding your thoughts, you may listen to their lies instead of listening to Him.

THE OPERATIVE

The Holy Spirit's way of operation will be foreign to you as well. And when you hear of others yielding to Him, you can become judgmental and critical, thus building a wall of unbelief and doubt within your heart, concerning these gifts.

The Holy Spirit is whom Jesus left in charge when He left for heaven and sat down at the right hand of the Father. His faithfulness to send the promised gift of His Holy Spirit should increase our trust in Him and His word.

Don't you think it wise to get to know Him better? The way you do this is to be filled with the Holy Spirit, qualifying yourself to be used in these kinds of ways that help men, women, and children. Then they too can be born again and receive the baptism of the Holy Spirit with speaking in tongues as the evidence. This should be the first priority for all new converts unto Christ. But what if they are taught something else?

The early Church disciples knew that these miraculous events *could not* be accomplished without being filled with the Holy Spirit. The believers who will, once again, turn the world upside down are the ones who are truly filled with the Holy Spirit and are led by Him in the operation of His gifts and the maturity of His fruit in their lives.

Currently, the number of those who are filled with the Holy Spirit may seem small compared to the many believers in Christ who are not filled with the Holy Spirit today. But this will change, as this last-day Holy Ghost revival floods the Church, bringing the Holy Spirit to the forefront, where Jesus planned for Him to be all along.

Will you join the rank and file of other spirit-filled believers who will, *once again*, turn the world upside down? Do good everywhere you go, just like Jesus did while here on earth! Then rejoice in hearing, "Well done, thou good and faithful servant, enter now into the presence of my joy."

CHAPTER 17

Origins of Demons

I believe that the Bible contains all the information we need to know; however, we will have to take the time to find it. Information about evil spirits or demons was given to us, and we can further our knowledge concerning the operations of the Holy Spirit's power over them through us, because of the authority of Jesus Christ.

By no means am I claiming to be an authority on demons. Furthermore, all spirit-filled believers should never be thought of as an exorcist when casting out demons. We are men and women of like passions who believe in the Bible as *truth*, along with its principles, while acting upon the instructions given by the Holy Spirit. We apply them, and the results of our applications are totally up to God the Father, His Son, Jesus, and His Holy Spirit, giving amazing and incredible results.

My goal in this chapter is to enlighten you with the truths about demons that are contained in the Bible. Once known, these truths will set you free from the spirit of fear as well. Understanding what the Bible says arms us with the truth about any subject. As we apply this knowledge and understanding of the Holy Spirit's revelations, we can live a life of freedom.

THE OPERATIVE

I have been asked over the years, and you may have been asked as well, "Where do demons come from?" For the longest time I too needed the answer to that question. When I first asked the Lord this question, I did not receive an immediate revelation on the matter. There are several standard scriptures that are used when teaching about demons. After several years of study and fellowship with Jesus and His Holy Spirit, one by one, revelations came that gave answers to questions that I, and others had, concerning the origins of demons. I can now reveal them to you by sharing what the Bible says about where the demons come from, in a biblical context.

I have found that the Bible does not always need to be read chronologically. Clues are hidden in verses throughout the Bible that tell us things about a variety of topics that need to be searched through with the Holy Spirit. He will give revelation to say, "This is the answer." Together with Him, we connect the dots, so to speak.

First, we must realize that no creation, which is everything contained in the cosmos, was made without Jesus and that all things were made by and for Him. Scriptures teach this clearly.

"He was in the beginning with God. All things were made through Him, and without Him nothing was made that was made." (John 1:2) (Read verses 1-4 for complete thought.)

"For by Him all things were created that are in heaven and that are on earth, visible and invisible, whether thrones or dominions or principalities or powers. All things were created through Him and for Him." (Col. 1:16)

The next thing to be realized about demons is that they are spirits—evil in nature because the one that governs them is the epitome of evil, the devil himself. In order to present a solid case, I must also exclude the possibility of where many believe demons come from—that is, the fallen angels. This could not be farther from the truth, and here is why:

"For if God did not spare the angels who sinned, but cast them down to hell and delivered them into chains of darkness, to be reserved for judgment." (2 Peter 2:4)

"And the angels who did not keep their proper domain, but left their own abode, He has reserved in everlasting chains under darkness for the judgment of the great day." (Jude 6)

You see, they cannot possibly be the demons, because the fallen angels are held captive in chains under the darkness for the judgment of the great day. Do we actually think that God would allow his created angels who fell with Lucifer, now known as the devil, to roam the earth, seeking whom they may devour as does the devil?

Absolutely *not*! Armed with the knowledge that one angel of the Lord killed one hundred and eighty-five thousand Assyrians in one night, how quick do you think the devil would wipe us all off the face of the earth if he had access to the fallen angels? No, the fallen angels are not the demons.

"And it came to pass on a certain night that the angel of the LORD went out, and killed in the camp of the Assyrians one hundred and eighty-five thousand; and when people arose early in the morning, there were the corpses—all dead." (2 Kings 19:35)

Again, mankind would not have a chance if the demons were the fallen angels! The fact is, these created angels are very powerful. With the devil and one-third of fallen angels under his control in the spirit realm, well, trust me, the earth would be a very different place today.

Besides, God be true and every man a liar. The Bible says in 2 Peter and Jude that they are being held "in chains of darkness under the darkness till the judgment day." They too have already been judged at Calvary and will take their place alongside of the devil in the lake of fire, to be tormented forever.

So with this information, we can safely rule out the delusion that the demons are fallen angels. I can only say that those who believe this simply have not done their research with the Holy Spirit as their helper.

During the original creation of everything, the how and when are not relevant to this topic;[6] a place called Hades (also known as

---

6. Explanation in *Destiny in Time, Observations in the Light* and *The Original Thought* by James J. Hamrick.

Sheol) was created. It later became known as what we call hell today. There was a specific reason hell was created. The Lord had to have a place to hold the spirits of all the dead animals. They did not live forever, you know!

Even when the larger animals roamed the earth, all kinds of creatures were alive and would eventually, one way or another, die. Many were killed because of the food chain, and many died after living their life expectancy. It is my understanding that archeologists have found remains of a T-rex, with another animal's remains, still within its stomach, confirming them as meat eaters and that there was a food chain in operation at the very beginning of life on earth.

After the earth was struck by an unidentified object wiping out all living things upon the earth and flooding it totally, many other dead animals fossils, confirms this event. This was the first flood. All previous life was destroyed, and every living thing became extinct. Read the following scriptures that will guide us in this proof from the Bible:

"So they and all those with them went down alive into the pit; the earth closed over them, and they perished from among the assembly." (Num. 16:33)

"In which are innumerable teeming things, Living things both small and great. There the ships sail about; There is that Leviathan which You have made to play there. These all wait for You, That You may give them their food in due season. What You give them they gather in; You open Your hand, they are filled with good. You hide Your face, they are troubled; You take away their breath, they die and return to their dust." (Ps. 104:25–29)

"Who knows the spirit of the sons of men, which goes upward, and the spirit of the animal, which goes down to the earth?" (Ecc. 3:21)

"And the LORD God formed man of the dust of the ground, and breathed into his nostrils the breath of life; and man became a living soul." (Gen 2:7, KJV)

"And so it is written, The first man Adam was made a living soul; the last Adam was made a quickening spirit." (1 Cor. 15:45)

"Now may the God of peace Himself sanctify you completely; and may your whole spirit, soul, and body be preserved blameless at the coming of our Lord Jesus Christ." (1 Thess. 6:23)

"But if he will not hear, take with you one or two more, that 'by the mouth of two or three witnesses every word may be established.'" (Matt. 18:16)

"This will be the third time I am coming to you. 'By the mouth of two or three witnesses every word shall be established.'" (2 Cor 13:1)

"How you are fallen from heaven, O Lucifer, son of the morning! How you are cut down to the ground, You who weakened the nations! For you have said in your heart: 'I will ascend into heaven, I will exalt my throne above the stars of God; I will also sit on the mount of the congregation On the farthest sides of the north; I will ascend above the heights of the clouds, I will be like the Most High.' Yet you shall be brought down to Sheol, To the lowest depths of the Pit." (Isa. 14:12–15)

"You were the seal of perfection, Full of wisdom and perfect in beauty. You were in Eden, the garden of God; Every precious stone was your covering: The sardius, topaz, and diamond, Beryl, onyx, and jasper, Sapphire, turquoise, and emerald with gold. The workmanship of your timbrels and pipes was prepared for you on the day you were created." (Ezek. 28:12–13)

"You were the anointed cherub who covers; I established you; You were on the holy mountain of God; You walked back and forth in the midst of fiery stones. You were perfect in your ways from the day you were created, Till iniquity was found in you." (Ezek. 28:14–15)

"And He said to them, 'I saw satan fall like lightning from heaven.'" (Luke 10:18–19)

"Be sober, be vigilant; because your adversary the devil walks about like a roaring lion, seeking whom he may devour." (1 Peter 5:8)

"I know a man in Christ who fourteen years ago—whether in the body I do not know, or whether out of the body I do not know, God knows—such a one was caught up to the third heaven." (2 Cor. 12:2)

"All Scripture is given by inspiration of God, and is profitable for doctrine, for reproof, for correction, for instruction in righteousness, that the man of God may be complete, thoroughly equipped for every good work." (2 Tim. 3:16–17)

THE OPERATIVE

"Knowing this first, that no prophecy of Scripture is of any private interpretation, for prophecy never came by the will of man, but holy men of God spoke as they were moved by the Holy Spirit." (2 Peter 1:20–21)

Based on what you just read in these scriptures, and there are others in Job and Ecclesiastes as well, man was made a living soul, according to Genesis. Since man was a living soul in Genesis, what were the remains of the Neanderthals that have been uncovered by the archeologists? They did live, and there is proof of their existence.

I submit to you that while they had an appearance like man, they definitely had no living soul. So I believe we can safely say that their souls were not only dead, but it is also quite possible that they had no soul at all, just like the animals that, according to the Bible, have a body and spirit. I have yet to find a scripture that speaks about animals having a soul.

I believe that before the Genesis account of the creation of man, anything that resembled man did not have a soul, just a spirit and a body. In these same scriptures you just read, we find that when a man dies, his body returns to the ground, which eventually turns back to dust, because this is the substance God used to originally form or create man with.

Once the body dies, the spirit and (living) soul (in the Old Testament dispensations) go to either paradise or hell. Paradise was also referred to as Abraham's bosom by Jesus, which was a place created by God to hold the souls of righteous men who believed God, even while following the law. Those who did not believe in God or follow the law, when they died, their spirits and souls did not go into paradise; rather, they were placed into hell by the angels that did not fall with Lucifer. Both the righteous and unrighteous men's bodies remain in the grave until the last trump of the Lord, or the white throne judgment of the Lord, respectively.

Today as believers, when we die, our spirit and soul go directly to be with the Lord, not to paradise. Jesus emptied paradise on His way from collecting the keys of death and the grave from the devil in hell. Whether or not Paradise remains across the gulf that Jesus spoke of in Luke 16:26, I do not know. However, I do know, that Jesus eluded to this same spiritual area in *Revelation 2:7* when He said: *"He that hath an ear, let him hear what the Spirit saith unto the churches. To him that overcometh will I give to eat of the tree of life, which is in the midst of the paradise of God." KJV (Read also Rev. 22)*

Our bodies are still buried. Unbelieving spirits and souls still go to hell, waiting for the judgment day, along with all others found there. To confirm this, we only have to read the following scriptures:

"There was a certain rich man who was clothed in purple and fine linen and fared sumptuously every day. But there was a certain beggar named Lazarus, full of sores, who was laid at his gate, desiring to be fed with the crumbs which fell from the rich man's table. Moreover the dogs came and licked his sores. So it was that the beggar died, and was carried by the angels to Abraham's bosom. The rich man also died and was buried. And being in torments in Hades, he lifted up his eyes and saw Abraham afar off, and Lazarus in his bosom.

Then he cried and said, 'Father Abraham, have mercy on me, and send Lazarus that he may dip the tip of his finger in water and cool my tongue; for I am tormented in this flame.' But Abraham said, 'Son, remember that in your lifetime you received your good things, and likewise Lazarus evil things; but now he is comforted and you are tormented. And besides all this, between us and you there is a great gulf fixed, so that those who want to pass from here to you cannot, nor can those from there pass to us.'

Then he said, 'I beg you therefore, father, that you would send him to my father's house, for I have five brothers, that he may testify to them, lest they also come to this place of torment.' Abraham said to him, 'They have Moses and the prophets; let them hear them.' And he said, 'No, father Abraham; but if one goes to them from the dead, they will repent.' But he said to him, 'If they do not hear Moses and the prophets, neither will they be persuaded though one rise from the dead.'" (Luke 16:19–31)

"Though one rise from the dead"? Jesus did just that and walked for forty days among the people with His disciples, and many still did not believe though He came back to them from the dead. This is a true story because Jesus used the beggar's name, <u>Lazarus.</u> This fact alone tells us that it is not a parable, but a real story concerning a rich man and Lazarus, in their eternal state of being.

THE OPERATIVE

The time from Jesus's death to His resurrection was three days. During these three days Jesus went into hell and took the keys of death and the grave away from the devil. He then crossed over the great gulf between hell and paradise, preaching to those held in captivity there since the death of Abel. His message was that He was the one they were looking for.

He then took their spirits and souls to heaven with Him, waiting to meet with their glorified bodies when the last trumpet sounds. Jesus emptied paradise, and today it remains empty of any spirits and souls of men (inclusive).

Imagine, for a moment if you can, those in hell being in torment, seeing and conversing with those in paradise, from hell, like the rich man did with Abraham, screaming for help but receiving none. One moment, they saw them all in paradise, desiring to be there with them, only realizing that it was too late.

The next moment they saw Jesus walking across the gulf fixed, which separated the two places (which they never had seen anyone do, including the devil, as I am sure he tried more than once), with keys in His hand, proclaiming His good news to them, as He emptied Paradise, and they all left with Him to go to heaven.

As if their torment weren't enough, they now saw them leave for a better place than paradise was for them, just like all those drowning unbelievers did when they saw the door close on the ark.

(The same thing will happen again, as this precedence of delivering His children has already been established. When the last trump of God will sound, we shall be changed, and those who died before will receive their glorified bodies. And we believers, who remain and are still alive, will be changed and meet Him in the sky, so shall we forever be with Him.)

What additional torment this must have been for all those lost souls seeing a pleasant place just across the way yet never able to escape their place of torment. The same feeling will come over everyone who is left behind after they see us in the sky with Jesus and our glorified spirits, souls, and bodies.

"Indeed, because he transgresses by wine, He is a proud man, And he does not stay at home. Because he enlarges his desire as hell." (Hab. 2:5)

The phrase <u>"enlarges his desire as hell"</u> informs us that hell's spiritual structure and perimeters are expandable because of man's sins that multiply over time. The many spirits there, along with the spirits and souls of men, remain tormented there until judgment day. Soon, the day will come when hell and the grave will have to give up their dead and be judged and found unworthy to enter into heaven.

"The sea gave up the dead who were in it, and Death and Hades delivered up the dead who were in them. And they were judged, each one according to his works [not believing in Jesus as the Son of God and the Savior of mankind]. Then Death and Hades were cast into the lake of fire. This is the second death. And anyone not found written in the Book of Life was cast into the lake of fire." (Rev. 20:13–15)

The lake of fire is the eternal existing place of torment, not hell as some suppose. There are those who have said, "I will rule with devil in hell." Good luck with that one, as Revelation is clear that both Death and Hades (Hell) are to be cast into the lake of fire, becoming the second death. There will be no rulers there!

If you are reading this book and have not given your heart to Jesus Christ, I pray that you realize that it is not too late. Do not play Russian roulette one moment longer with the eternal state of your spirit, soul, and body. You may turn to the back of this book and read the plan of salvation and find out what you must do to be saved. You will never regret it, my friend. Do it now! Do not hesitate. Now is the acceptable time; today is the day of salvation. I will wait for you to return from "What Must I Do to Be Saved?"

* * *

Excellent, I take it that you have returned a new creature. Praise God forevermore! So that we can come to a solid and believable answer to the question "Where do the demons come from?" let's use a scientific formula or principle to gain further confirmation of this truth before giving the answer.

Normally, I do not use this kind of method, as I rely upon the Holy Spirit to reveal the truths contained within His written word, but for the sake of those who may need a more scientific method of reaching a conclusion, I offer the following:

THE OPERATIVE

Remember the principle used earlier in this book, concerning Occam's razor? Let me briefly explain it again, as we will be using this method to apply all the scriptures we have previously read in this chapter to find out the answer to "Where do the demons come from?"

> *Occam's razor (also written as Ockham's razor and in Latin lex parsimoniae) is a problem-solving principle devised by William of Ockham (c. 1287– 1347), who was an English Franciscan friar and scholastic philosopher and theologian. The principle states that among competing hypotheses, the one with the fewest assumptions should be selected. Other, more complicated solutions may ultimately prove correct, but—in the absence of certainty—the fewer assumptions that are made, the better.*[7]

By applying Occam's razor's problem-solving principle to our question, we can find the path of the fewest assumptions by basing the facts of the Bible from the scriptures above containing what we know as truth from God.

Let's begin, shall we?

1. We know that Adam became the first living soul, and the last Adam (Jesus) became a quickening spirit, or one that makes alive.
2. We know that man is spirit with a soul and has a body housing them both.
3. We know that when a man dies, his body goes to the ground, and his spirit and soul go either to be with the Lord as a believer or to hell as an unbeliever.
4. We also know according to the scriptures that animals do not have a soul, just a spirit and body.
5. We also know that we are shown that when animals die, their body goes in the ground as does man's, but their spirit stays confined somewhere.

---

7. Wikipedia

6. We also know that since paradise is empty, there is only one other place that is mentioned in the Bible that would be compatible to hold the spirits of men (inclusive) and the spirits of animals, and that is the realm of hell.
7. We also know that the fallen angels <u>cannot</u> be the demons because God has them held in chains of darkness till judgment day.
8. We also know that based on the entire Bible, <u>nowhere</u> does the Bible teach us that the devil has any creative powers. So he cannot create demons. They have to come from somewhere, because they are real, and I have seen their activities firsthand many times in others.
9. We also know that Jesus gave us a very powerful guide of establishing a truth—that by the mouth (testimony) of two or more witnesses, a truth shall be established. With all the scriptures used to establish this truth, I think we all can agree there are more than two or three.
10. We also know that Lucifer was cast out of heaven's realm and incarcerated in the realm of Sheol or today's hell for his rebellion against God, along with one-third of the angels that decided to follow him. He was the anointed cherub that lost his covering when he hit the earth at the speed of lightning (possibly in unison with a meteor, or it was the action of his impact, instead of a meteor stopping abruptly at the speed of light, causing the destruction that many think was because of a meteor). Jesus saw him fall as lightning.
11. We also know that Lucifer, who became known as the devil, was fourth in the chain of command, because of his anointing, and all the music sung by the other creatures went through his timbrels and pipes or his vocal cords till iniquity was found in him.
12. We also know that Lucifer was cast down into the pit and incarcerated where the spirits of all the animals were being held, where they remain unto this day, and it would stand to reason that with his knowledge (limited and less than

God, I might add), he would be smarter and have more knowledge than all the other spirits, except the spirits of men and women who are confined to the perimeters of hell and cannot get out, because they did not believe in Jesus Christ as the Son of God or was not keeping the law in Old Testament times. These all are held captive within the confines of hell's perimeters, being tormented until judgment day.
13. We know that the word of God was given by His Holy Spirit inspiring anointed men to write kingdom truths, which are intertwined so that no one scripture can be taken on its own and receive a meaning without the others interpreting the truth contained therein.
14. Furthermore, we know that <u>nobody,</u> to date or ever will be, can prove the Bible not to be true. To the contrary, there are hundreds of millions of people who will testify of the truths contained in the Bible, that it has given them not only hope, but also a personal relationship with the one who created the cosmos and all its host, in which Jesus Christ is the Lord of them all.

This is where I hope I do not make some people mad at me, but I must tell the truth, as I see it according to the scriptures. I base my answer upon these fourteen (14) facts that I have found in the Bible, which is the word and will of God Almighty, the Creator of the heavens and the earth.

There may be more, but to date, these are the ones that I have found. Taking these fourteen (14) facts into consideration and using the problem-solving principle of Occam's razor, at this point, I believe the following to be the true answer to the question asked, "Where do demons come from?"

<u>The answer is, simply, with all conviction and revelation by the Holy Spirit, that they are the spirits of the animals, including the Neanderthals, that have died over the years since creation.</u>

It stands to reason, taking all known facts and truths of the Bible and using Occam's razor's problem-solving principle, which states <u>that "among competing hypotheses, the one with the fewest</u>

<u>assumptions should be selected.</u> Other, more complicated solutions may ultimately prove correct, but—in the absence of certainty—the fewer assumptions that are made, the better."

I know that many of you, including me, have had or do have pets. This should not make your love or care for them, in any way, be diminished. God created them for our pleasure in the proper biblical context. They are to be treated with love and respect as one of the hosts that Jesus is Lord over.

I believe that once Lucifer was cast down, he began to organize the only kingdom he had access to at the time. His evilness against God forcibly took charge of all the spirits that were being held in Sheol (Hades) or hell, whichever name you like to call it.

This is what seemingly makes him as though he is omnipotent even though we know that he is not. He is no match for God the Father, Jesus the Son, and their Holy Spirit, or any of the other heavenly beings like angels. Remember, he has already been defeated at Calvary's cross. His only weapon is deception to get you to believe his lies.

Having yielded to the Holy Spirit to be used in casting demons out of several possessed people, for whatever reasons the possession took place, I can say they do exist. Some people, even some believers, do not believe that they are real.

This should not take us by surprise because there are many people who still say that they do not believe that the devil is real. I guess this eases their conscience concerning the fact that they do not believe in God either. The word of God has much to say about both of their existence and their actions, and <u>for this reason,</u> we should not be ignorant about either of them.

This also explains the reason the demons in Legion wanted to be cast out of the man into the swine. The compatibility of their spirits made it possible for them to continue their evil presence within the realm of man. In this event, the swine were smarter than the man called Legion, who yielded himself to evil possessions! The swine ran themselves off the cliff and drowned.

It's important to remember, we are dealing with spiritual matters here that manifest in people's lives and that we cannot see with our natural eyes. We can, however, see their side effects. Now concerning the particular lady whom I gave testimony of and casting out those two demons, the unclean and lying spirits, I preached five meetings that she attended and did not see them. However, it was only when the Holy Spirit opened my spiritual eye that I even realized their presence. They were brought to the surface by the anointing and had to act and speak in a manner that gave up their disguise.

You decide. Do you take your scissors and cut out these scriptures, making an attempt to void their existence? Or do you choose to embrace the truth of God's words and deal with them when you come in contact with them, according to the directions of the Holy Spirit?

Even though He has only given us half of that which is to be told, the fact is, the half of the information given is enough for the Holy Spirit to guide us through this life and for us to run the race set before us, still reaching the mark toward our goal!

The Bible gives us all we need to know about how to conduct ourselves in this world. We do not have to study other people's bibles or beliefs to know what we need to do to reach our mark, in getting us to our expected end.

My prayer is that you learn to embrace God's word regarding all subjects. Then take that knowledge with His understanding, and apply it to your everyday life circumstances. You may never come across people who are possessed with demons, but you will never know for sure until the Holy Spirit reveals them to you anyway.

What happens to the animal spirits after judgment day? This is not totally clear to me yet, but my hope rests in the fact that they are included in the earnest expectation of the creation eagerly waiting for the revealing of the sons of God. As to whether they make it into heaven or not, at this point in time, I must trust the Lord that it is so. For if they were subjected to futility unwillingly, they were given no choice, then God's grace is sufficient to sustain them—that I am sure of.

As for the fallen angels, evidently, they made a choice, as did Lucifer, and because of their choice, they too were cast out, waiting to be judged with the devil, the antichrist, and the beast and then cast into the lake of fire for eternity.

"For I consider that the sufferings of this present time are not worthy to be compared with the glory which shall be revealed in us. For the earnest expectation of the creation eagerly waits for the revealing of the sons of God. For the creation was subjected to futility, not willingly, but because of Him who subjected it in hope; because the creation itself also will be delivered from the bondage of corruption into the glorious liberty of the children of God. For we know that the whole creation groans and labors with birth pangs together until now. Not only that, but we also who have the firstfruits of the Spirit, even we ourselves groan within ourselves, eagerly waiting for the adoption, the redemption of our body. For we were saved in this hope, but hope that is seen is not hope; for why does one still hope for what he sees? But if we hope for what we do not see, we eagerly wait for it with perseverance.

Likewise the Spirit also helps in our weaknesses. For we do not know what we should pray for as we ought, but the Spirit Himself makes intercession for us with groanings which cannot be uttered. Now He who searches the hearts knows what the mind of the Spirit is, because He makes intercession for the saints according to the will of God.

And we know that all things work together for good to those who love God, to those who are the called according to His purpose." (Rom. 8:18–28)

Oh, praise the Lord for His infinite knowledge and wisdom! *"Trust in the Lord with all your heart, do not lean on your own understanding, acknowledge Him in all your ways, and He will direct your paths." (Proverbs 3:5,6 paraphrased)*

In chapter 18, we will be taking a closer look at the second category of the "Gifts of the Holy Spirit—Part 2." His gift of faith, gifts of healing, and working of miracles are exciting, to say the least. Will you continue with me on this journey, finding out about more power than we had ever dreamed about?

CHAPTER 18

Gifts of the Holy Spirit Part 2

In chapter 15 we were introduced to the first of three categories of the gifts of the Holy Spirit found in First Corinthians 12:1–11. They are the following:

1. word of wisdom
2. word of knowledge
3. discerning of spirits

These three gifts help us to <u>think</u> like God.

Now let's take a look at the second category, which contains the following:

4. faith
5. gifts of healing
6. working of miracles

These three gifts help us to <u>act</u> like God.

Faith is the <u>fourth gift</u> of the Holy Spirit. This gift of faith is imparted in a moment, by the Holy Spirit, for the specific purpose of obtaining results that will be supernatural as well. This gift of faith should not be confused with the measure of faith that is given to every man.

According to the Bible, we are told that every man is given a measure of faith, and I believe this measure was given to each man (inclusive) at conception and is activated by hearing God's word. This faith is given to us in measure, where the gift of faith is not.

"For I say, through the grace given unto me, to every man that is among you, not to think of himself more highly than he ought to think; but to think soberly, according as God hath dealt to every man the measure of faith." (Rom. 12:3, KJV)

This small seed of faith was designed within each of our spirits by God and is what gets activated, as we hear the word of God spoken, through preaching, teaching, TV ministry, CD ministry, videos, reading, or even as we look upon God's creation. The measure of faith given to each of us at conception contains a portion of the substance of the gift of faith but is not given to us in full measure.

This faith is the faith that the Holy Spirit is able to lead us to Christ, with gentle line upon line. I like to label this faith as our faith, as it was given to us during our conception by God. This is the place in our spirits that men and women try to fill with things, only to find out that only Jesus can ever occupy its volume.

"Whom shall he teach knowledge? and whom shall he make to understand doctrine? them that are weaned from the milk, and drawn from the breasts. For precept must be upon precept, precept upon precept; line upon line, line upon line; here a little, and there a little: For with stammering lips and another tongue will he speak to this people. To whom he said, This is the rest wherewith ye may cause the weary to rest; and this is the refreshing: yet they would not hear. But the word of the LORD was unto them precept upon precept, precept upon precept; line upon line, line upon line; here a little, and there a little; that they might go, and fall backward, and be broken, and snared, and taken." (Isa. 28:9–13, KJV)

"The heavens declare His righteousness, and all the peoples see His glory."(Ps. 97:6)

THE OPERATIVE

"For since the creation of the world His invisible attributes are clearly seen, being understood by the things that are made, even His eternal power and Godhead, so that they are without excuse." (Rom. 1:20)

Faith comes so that our faith can grow, and it contains the substance that we build ourselves upon as our most holy faith, according to the scriptures in Jude. Jesus likened this kind of faith to a small grain of mustard seed that, when it's planted (by God in our spirits at our conception), would grow so large that birds would be able to land on its limbs. Of course, He was speaking metaphorically. This kind of faith, He said, is all we need to move mountains from where they are to yonder sea—meaning, getting them out of our way.

"So then faith comes by hearing, and hearing by the word of God." (Rom. 10:17)

"Another parable He put forth to them, saying: The kingdom of heaven is like a mustard seed, which a man took and sowed in his field, which indeed is the least of all the seeds; but when it is grown it is greater than the herbs and becomes a tree, so that the birds of the air come and nest in its branches." (Matt. 13:31,32)

"So Jesus said to them, 'Because of your unbelief; for assuredly, I say to you, if you have faith as a mustard seed, you will say to this mountain, "Move from here to there," and it will move; and nothing will be impossible for you.'" (Matt. 17:20)

"It is like a mustard seed which, when it is sown in the ground, is smaller than all the seeds on earth; but when it is sown, it grows up and becomes greater than all herbs, and shoots out large branches, so that the birds of the air may nest under its shade." (Mark 4:31, 32)

"It is like a mustard seed, which a man took and put in his garden; and it grew and became a large tree, and the birds of the air nested in its branches." (Luke 13:19)

"So the Lord said, 'If you have faith as a mustard seed, you can say to this mulberry tree, "Be pulled up by the roots and be planted in the sea," and it would obey you.'" (Luke 17:6)

"But you, beloved, building yourselves up on your most holy faith, praying in the Holy Spirit." (Jude 20)

This type of faith comes to us, as we hear the word of the Lord. Once activated, faith grows inside us each time we hear the word of the Lord until we are born again. Then once we are baptized or filled with the Holy Spirit, we build up our most holy faith, which is the strong foundation that we build ourselves upon, as we continue to pray in the Spirit or in tongues.

This faith is also directly related to the faith that is found in the fruit of the Spirit.

"But the fruit of the Spirit is love, joy, peace, longsuffering, gentleness, goodness, faith, Meekness, temperance: against such there is no law." (Gal. 5:22–23, KJV) (There will be more detailed information given on each of the nine fruit after the nine gifts of the Holy Spirit.)

This faith became the anchor to our soul during both good and troubled times. It is the type of faith that takes us from our beginning as a new believer, sustaining us throughout our lives. It's the kind of faith that assists us in reaching our expected end.

"For I know the thoughts that I think toward you, saith the LORD, thoughts of peace, and not of evil, to give you an expected end." (Jer. 29:11, KJV)

It is <u>not</u> the type of *faith* that the gift of the Holy Spirit gives to men, according to First Corinthians 12:9. This *faith* is a gift, and it is supernatural faith. It's the kind of faith that is already matured and is straight from the Holy Spirit and Jesus Himself. It is the exact same faith that Jesus operated with when He walked on the earth during His life and ministry. This kind of faith is void of doubt and unbelief. This faith is given to us to use personally or to share with others, thus making a difference in the many lives and circumstances that we experience.

Peter briefly tapped into it while walking on water, going toward Jesus, who was already walking on the water. This supernatural faith is given to believers, as the Holy Spirit chooses, just like Jesus answered Peter's request to come to Him.

"Now in the fourth watch of the night Jesus went to them, walking on the sea. And when the disciples saw Him walking on the sea, they were troubled, saying, 'It is a ghost!' And they cried out for fear. But immediately Jesus spoke to them, saying, 'Be of good cheer! It is I; do not be afraid.'

THE OPERATIVE

And Peter answered Him and said, 'Lord, if it is You, command me to come to You on the water.' So He said, 'Come.' And when Peter had come down out of the boat, he walked on the water to go to Jesus. But when he saw that the wind was boisterous, he was afraid; and beginning to sink he cried out, saying, 'Lord, save me!'

And immediately Jesus stretched out His hand and caught him, and said to him, 'O you of little faith, why did you doubt?' And when they got into the boat, the wind ceased. Then those who were in the boat came and worshiped Him, saying, 'Truly You are the Son of God.'" (Matt. 14:25–33)

As a young minister, I preached a message of the faith that Peter was the only man in that boat, other than Jesus, to have enough faith to walk on water. I was wrong! It was not Peter's faith growing inside him that he was using to walk on water. It was the *faith* of Jesus, as He commanded Peter's spirit, soul, and body to "Come."

Fear came upon Peter when he looked at the winds and the waves, and his doubt broke the connection that Jesus made with Peter through His *faith* when He had commanded Peter to walk on water and come to Him. Are you seeing the difference in whose faith is being drawn upon here?

This truth makes all the difference in the world and is a game changer once you see its revelation in your spirit. Peter's faith growing within his spirit sank him, while Jesus's *faith* controlled the winds, waves, and Peter's ability to walk on water.

When Jesus gave the command for Peter to come, Peter had no choice but to step out of the boat and start walking toward Jesus. Jesus is the Lord of hosts, and every host obeys His commands, including Peter and each of us.

"Now in the morning, as He returned to the city, He was hungry. And seeing a fig tree by the road, He came to it and found nothing on it but leaves, and said to it, 'Let no fruit grow on you ever again.' Immediately the fig tree withered away.

And when the disciples saw it, they marveled, saying, 'How did the fig tree wither away so soon?'

So Jesus answered and said to them. 'Assuredly, I say to you, if you have faith and do not doubt, you will not only do what was done to the fig tree, but also if you say to this mountain, 'Be removed and be cast into the sea,' it will be done. And whatever things you ask in prayer, believing, you will receive.'" (Matt. 21:18–22)

There is no doubt or unbelief in the <u>faith of Jesus</u>. The only way that doubt and unbelief are removed from us completely is through the supernatural gift of *faith* from the Holy Spirit, which is the same as Jesus saying, "Come."

The faith that we were saved by operates daily in our lives and continually comes to us, thereby growing in our lives based upon what we hear and believe concerning Jesus's accomplishments through Calvary. This faith contains doubt and unbelief because of our belief system (the way we believe the Bible—is it absolute truth, or is it not for today? etc., etc. Not everyone believes the Bible in the same way). This is where trust comes in.

<u>Let's review</u>. Based on the scriptures researched thus far, there are two types of faith: There is the faith that comes when the word of God is heard (this is the faith that activated our measure of faith to believe for salvation. It grows within us each time we hear the word of God and pray in tongues). Then there is the faith of Jesus, which is *His faith* that is without measure and is one of the gifts of the Holy Spirit. His faith contains no doubt or unbelief, thus having no limitations. His faith is the source of all faith given to men and women. It is the faith that actually moves mountains and performs the doing of His word. We will learn later about the fruit of faith, which is also a derivative of Jesus's supernatural faith.

Now, it is our faith that, Jesus said, could grow to the point that we too can move mountains, but it must mature to the point of no doubt and unbelief operating within it. I do not know if this is ever possible in this life for most, because of the doubt and unbelief many place upon themselves. But this one thing I do know—that with Jesus's faith, when given to a believer by the Holy Spirit to meet the need of moving a mountain in a believer's life, nothing is impossible.

Our faith is the faith that is directly connected to the fruit of the Holy Spirit and matures. The goal of this faith is to <u>trust in God's words</u> contained within the Bible, as we mature, becoming more like Jesus with each and every day. We use and acquire more of it by

THE OPERATIVE

hearing the word of God, receiving revelations from the Holy Spirit, and acquiring His understanding, thereby learning and growing in the grace and knowledge of Jesus. There are times before we reach this goal, if we do at all in this life, <u>that we will need His supernatural faith to help us.</u>

This is where the gift of faith comes into play, and the Holy Spirit operates within those who make themselves available to Him for this operation. Read this verse, and see what you can glean from it, pertaining to which faith we are actually supposed to be using in our daily lives:

"I am crucified with Christ: nevertheless I live; yet not I, but Christ liveth in me: and the life which I now live in the flesh I live by the faith of the Son of God, who loved me, and gave himself for me." (Gal. 2:20, KJV)

Our mark, which is our goal, should be to mature our faith to be like His! Until this is accomplished, we must learn that it is Jesus's faith we have available for us to live by.

"Here is the patience of the saints; here are those who keep the commandments of God and the faith of Jesus." (Rev. 14:12)

When this gift of faith is imparted to men and women, as mentioned before but it bears repeating, all doubt and unbelief are completely void, and the resurrection power or the anointing flows through them, and the gift of faith changes the circumstances.

"And believers were increasingly added to the Lord, multitudes of both men and women, so that they brought the sick out into the streets and laid them on beds and couches, that at least the shadow of Peter passing by might fall on some of them." (Acts 5:14–15)

"This man heard Paul speaking. Paul, observing him intently and seeing that he had faith to be healed, said with a loud voice, 'Stand up straight on your feet!' And he leaped and walked." (Acts 14:9,10)

This gift of faith, once imparted by the Holy Spirit, makes a connection from the resurrection power to Jesus's supernatural faith, and miracles take place. Not the faith of the man or of Peter, but Peter, now filled with the Holy Spirit, <u>made himself available</u> to be chosen for these gifts operation, and once the Holy Spirit made the connection, everything changed.

Why? Because they tapped into the Holy Spirit's gift of faith, which is Jesus's supernatural faith given for all to prosper. How far in our believing have we come from His power? Are we craving and desiring for these types of events? Are we looking for opportunities for *the supernatural power of His faith* to be released through us?

Wouldn't it be awesome, God forbid, if a loved one finds out that they have cancer or any other sickness or disease, that just the power alone, in our shadow, because of His faith, would heal them? Even our handshake or just a simple touch can be the channel or conduit to release the cure to them. Wouldn't it be wonderful for a body of believers to start emptying hospitals full of the sick and infirmed?

I know He was talking about the topic of money when Jesus said, "With men it is impossible, but with God ALL THINGS ARE POSSIBLE!"

Oh, that we, the believers, would catch the vision of this and begin to allow the Holy Spirit of Jesus Christ to work and operate through each of us! There are several other examples of Jesus releasing His faith, healing the multitudes. I believe that you too can think of a few other examples in the Bible since now you know what to look for.

What a challenge to step away from ministering from our level of faith and begin ministering from His level of faith, containing *no* limitation, *no* doubt, or *no* unbelief. Oh, what a day and age to be living for Christ!

So we now know that our faith that is activated for our salvation is in measure and growing, and Jesus's faith is without measure and mature, having no doubt or unbelief of any kind. Call upon Jesus to bid you to come, and see what His response will be.

The next gift of the Holy Spirit contained in the second category for us to research is the gifts of healing. Notice the word *gifts* is plural. The reason for this is because there are no limits to how the gifts of healing can operate.

(Jesus heals a man in this manner.) *"And he took the blind man by the hand, and led him out of the town; and when he had spit on his eyes, and put his hands upon him, he asked him if he saw ought. And*

THE OPERATIVE

he looked up, and said, I see men as trees, walking. After that he put his hands again upon his eyes, and made him look up: and he was restored, and saw every man clearly." (Mark 8:23–25, KJV)

Two operations were used by Jesus to get this man whole or completely healed. First, Jesus spit on the man's eyes then put His hands upon him. When the man regained his vision partially, Jesus, I am sure, thought, *This will not do,* so He placed His hands upon the man's eyes, and his eyesight was restored and he saw clearly.

This first result of the blind man, seeing men as trees, meant that his vision was stretched out of proportion, and for most of us, we would probably give up right then and there, thinking, *Why did I even think I could get this man healed?* Perhaps, we might think, *Well, they are better than they were before I prayed for them.* But Jesus knows that all things must obey His words spoken by *faith,* which, for Jesus to speak, there is no other way but <u>faith-filled words.</u> I personally believe that He did this healing in two parts to be an example to us. If it takes a second prayer of faith, so be it!

Then in another time He spoke by faith!

"And she said, 'Yes, Lord, yet even the little dogs eat the crumbs which fall from their masters' table.' Then Jesus answered and said to her, 'O woman, great is your faith! Let it be to you as you desire.' And her daughter was healed from that very hour." (Matt. 15:27–28)

Even though He said, "Great is your faith," it was <u>His faith</u> she was tapping into that made it so great. So <u>His faith</u> was released to her, and her daughter was healed from that very hour.

Just as Peter asked Jesus to command him to come, this lady was doing the very same thing by her statement about the crumbs. A person would not allow the dogs to come over and eat the crumbs if they did not want it to be so. Jesus recognized that the lady knew that if He commanded it to be so, <u>it would be so.</u>

<u>Nothing</u> can disobey Jesus once He speaks, and He can speak through His believers, especially through the gifts of His Holy Spirit!

Were these two people tapping into the faith of Jesus? You bet they were, making their act of faith in believing to be healed a conduit to the reception <u>of Jesus's supernatural faith.</u>

Remember, the Holy Spirit was not yet given when these two examples were accomplished, so in times like these, Jesus revealed to us what would be available to each of us once He left. How could this be? <u>Because He sent back His Holy Spirit with all His gifts and fruit.</u>

This lady's daughter was actually healed from the very hour Jesus gave His command for her to be healed. The man's eyes were healed after His second touch. So we find that the gifts of healing are progressive in nature, and a period of time may elapse from the initial release of the gift till the healing is actually manifested. Once the healing is manifested, it may be considered a miracle, especially if the doctors say there was nothing else that could be done.

Peter walked on water because Jesus commanded him to, revealing the gift of faith from Jesus, that points us to the next gift that we will be looking at, which is called the working of miracles. Are you observing how all these are connected together?

During His earthly ministry, Jesus revealed to us examples of the gift of faith, along with gifts of healing, and now the working of miracles that would be coming with His Holy Spirit. He would send His Holy Spirit as our personal helper, comforter, and teacher, concerning not only these matters but also all matters of life and godliness.

He informed us, concerning Him, whom He was sending back to us, the same way the prophets revealed through the scriptures pertaining to His coming to the world as the Messiah, our Savior.

We now know that being healed is progressive, and the difference between a <u>healing</u> and a <u>miracle</u> is, the gifts of healing can and will happen over time. Some gifts of healing may happen faster than others, but the healing always comes when the believer stays on the word of God and stays connected to the faith of Jesus.

On the other hand, the gift of working of miracles is instantaneous. *Immediate* or *sudden* are the words that are associated with miracles. No waiting is to be endured, just the sudden change of the circumstances.

I have been healed many times over the years, but I have only had what I consider the working of miracles to happen to me once. However, I have seen this gift in operation for others, both in Cuba and Mexico. During an outdoor meeting in Cuba, a woman's deaf ear popped open so she could hear as I was preaching. Praise God forevermore. In Mexico as a photographer for my evangelist friend, I saw cataracts fall off a man's eyes and a bulging tumor fall from another man's stomach. Praise the Lord Jesus forever. All these were instantaneous, thus being a miracle.

As for my miracle, last year my wife and I were watching a minister on TV, as he conducted a revival meeting. During the meeting the evangelist looked into the camera and said, "The Holy Spirit wants to give you a miracle, and if you will do what He says, you will receive it." When the broadcast was over, we turned off the TV. My wife went upstairs, and I sat thinking about his words. These are the scriptures that the Holy Spirit brought to my attention:

"So they rose early in the morning and went out into the Wilderness of Tekoa; and as they went out, Jehoshaphat stood and said, 'Hear me, O Judah and you inhabitants of Jerusalem: Believe in the LORD your God, and you shall be established; believe His prophets, and you shall prosper.'" (2 Chron. 20:20)

As I believed God's anointed prophet, the Holy Spirit gave me instructions to lie on my stomach on the floor in a word image—meaning, I saw myself getting up and lying on the floor on my stomach. When I did this, my lower back popped, on which I had a ruptured disk from an auto accident about ten years ago, and I had been in one level of pain or another since.

Those who know me can give account to the validity of this pain I was in. After my back popped, the pain left immediately, and now I could do things that for several years I was unable to do because of this ruptured disk. Today, I am pain free, and I thank the Holy Spirit for the gift of working of a miracle in my life.

Over the years, I have had the privilege of seeing many miracles done through other ministers, whom I am associated with as well. I know these gifts are very prosperous to the recipients. I challenge you to talk with someone who has received a miracle, and you will find that you cannot tell them that these gifts are not for today.

"And a certain man was there, which had an infirmity thirty and eight years. When Jesus saw him lie, and knew that he had been now

a long time in that case, he saith unto him, Wilt thou be made whole? The impotent man answered him, Sir, I have no man, when the water is troubled, to put me into the pool: but while I am coming, another steppeth down before me. Jesus saith unto him, Rise, take up thy bed, and walk. And immediately the man was made whole, and took up his bed, and walked: and on the same day was the Sabbath." (John 5:5–9, KJV)

The words *"covet earnestly the best gift"* take on a whole new meaning when you begin to see and operate in these gifts. If you need a miracle, why would you or I covet the discerning of spirits or speaking in tongues? Your immediate change needed would take place with the working of miracles. So the best gift to covet to operate for you to receive the change in your life that is needed would be the gift of working of miracles.

To covet the best gift is to desire to have the gift that will meet the need of the moment in your life or in the lives of others. Of course, if you do not believe in these gifts and that they are relevant for today, then the Holy Spirit will not be able to use you in them, right?

These gifts are real and have not passed away. It stands to reason that if we say that speaking in tongues along with interpretation of tongues have passed away, that would mean that the other seven gifts have passed away also. The good news for us is that they all are still available and operational through us, as the Holy Spirit wills.

Why not take the sum of the Bible and believe that God is true and every man a liar? If it is not represented within the Bible as the inspired word of God, then we should not be filling our minds and spirits with it when it comes to spiritual matters.

There is nothing wrong with having other information in your mind and spirit or even having feelings from your body and soul. Just be sure that it is information that will not cast doubt and unbelief upon that which you know as truth from God's word.

We have now covered two out of the three categories concerning the gifts of the Holy Spirit, and we have discovered that the first category contains the following:

1. word of wisdom
2. word of knowledge

3. discerning of spirits

These help us to think like God.
In the second category, we learned about the following:

4. faith
5. gifts of healing
6. working of miracles

And they help us to act like God.
In chapter 19 we will study the last three of the nine gifts given by the Holy Spirit, found in the third category, and those are the following:

7. prophecy
8. various kinds of tongues
9. interpretation of tongues

These three gifts help us to talk like God.

Here is another important question that I would like to ask you now: have you ever heard the Holy Spirit gently speaking to you, giving you word pictures as instructions, such as, "Pick up that book" or "Take your briefcase with you" or, to save yourself a trip back to your garage, you see yourself picking up that extra hammer? Many times I missed the little things only to realize later it was the Holy Spirit speaking to me, trying to help me out. Yet other times I listened and was blessed because I did.

He does this as part of training us to hear and to know His voice. He trains us to hear His voice so that in times of necessity, like life-and-death decisions and situations, we will know His voice and do the right thing. Remember Paul and the shipwreck? The Bible could have possibly read a little differently today if he had not learned to follow the leading of the Holy Spirit.

"Then He said, 'Go out, and stand on the mountain before the LORD.' And behold, the LORD passed by, and a great and strong wind tore into the mountains and broke the rocks in pieces before the LORD, but the LORD was not in the wind; and after the wind an earthquake, but the LORD was not in the earthquake; and after the earthquake a

fire, but the LORD was not in the fire; and after the fire a still small voice. So it was, when Elijah heard it, that he wrapped his face in his mantle and went out and stood in the entrance of the cave. Suddenly a voice came to him, and said, 'What are you doing here, Elijah?'" (1 Kings 19:11–13)

"*But your eyes shall see your teachers. Your ears shall hear a word behind you, saying, 'This is the way, walk in it,' 'Whenever you turn to the right hand Or whenever you turn to the left.'" (Isa. 30:20–21)*

The still, small voice of God is found today and contained within Jesus's Holy Spirit's communications with us. His voice and word pictures play a big part of His communication with each of us if we will just take the time to hear Him. You must find what works for you, as you pay attention to the little things. Hear His voice, and compare it to the word of God to see if it is from Him or not.

For you, skeptics, I am not talking about schizophrenics hearing voices. In <u>some</u> of these cases, I believe this is demonic activity, and only the power of Jesus and His Holy Spirit can deliver them.

No, I am talking about recognizing and knowing the voice of God through His Son's Holy Spirit. He can speak to us in so many ways and languages, for He is the creator of all communication. He has spoken to me, using various avenues like a cartoon or a portion of a movie or directing me by something that somebody else says. He often does this to confirm a word I've been thinking about, given to me from Him. The key to them all is that they each line up with what His word already speaks about in thought or principle.

If we will not limit Him, He is limitless to work in our lives. This brings us to a whole new dimension of living with Him, not just going through the traditional motions of having a form of godliness, but also denying the power of it or attending another meeting or program, but being used to change the lives of others as well as our own life!

"*But know this, that in the last days perilous times will come: For men will be lovers of themselves, lovers of money, boasters, proud, blasphemers, disobedient to parents, unthankful, unholy, unloving, unforgiving, slanderers, without self-control, brutal, despisers of good, traitors, headstrong, haughty, lovers of pleasure rather than lovers of God, having a form of godliness but denying its power. And from such people turn away!" (2 Tim. 3:1–5)*

Do you know anyone who fits into any of these categories listed in Second Timothy? I am not only talking about those outside the Church. I am also talking about those that are in the Church. Sure, they are there! They are called "tares." I mentioned them before, and it bears repeating.

"'Explain to us the parable of the tares of the field.' He answered and said to them: 'He who sows the good seed is the Son of Man. The field is the world, the good seeds are the sons of the kingdom, but the tares are the sons of the wicked one. The enemy who sowed them is the devil, the harvest is the end of the age, and the reapers are the angels. Therefore as the tares are gathered and burned in the fire, so it will be at the end of this age. The Son of Man will send out His angels, and they will gather out of His kingdom all things that offend, and those who practice lawlessness, and will cast them into the furnace of fire. There will be wailing and gnashing of teeth. Then the righteous will shine forth as the sun in the kingdom of their Father. He who has ears to hear, let him hear!'" (Matt. 13:36–43)

While some may consider this to be only a parable, I believe the answer Jesus gave to their question gave insight into the true events that took place in the spirit realm and takes place during these end times that we find ourselves in now. But like Jesus said, *"He who has ears to hear, let him hear!"*

Are you exercising your spiritual ear and spiritual eye?

"The hearing ear and the seeing eye, The LORD has made them both." (Prov. 20:12)

Both of these are singular for a specific reason. They prove that this scripture is not talking about our natural ears and eyes. Rather, the Lord created within each of us <u>a</u> spiritual ear to hear His Spirit and <u>a</u> spiritual eye to see the revelations and directives from His Spirit.

They are singular in origin, as they are tuned in to His voice only and only see His visions through them. Nothing else can operate them except His communications with us via His gifts. They each are closely connected to the gift of faith because faith is a prerequisite in believing that you have them available to you before they can effectively operate properly in the first place.

Once a believer realizes the gifts of the Holy Spirit are available to them, exercising them comes more easily, as you will increase in desiring to be used by the Holy Spirit in their operations. Sadly, these created spiritual communication tools sit dormant in many believers today mainly because they have never been taught that they have them, let alone how to use them.

From this time forward, you, the reader, will have no excuse because the Holy Spirit is training you, concerning the use of your spiritual ear and eye. I pray that you are yielding and open to what the Lord reveals to you through His Holy Spirit.

Communication with the Father, His Son, and His Holy Spirit is a vital part of our Father–child of God relationship. Giving honor and praise to Him in the form of trusting Him while spending time with Him by praying in the Holy Spirit. My time with Him has become so precious and joyful that I have to sing in the Spirit and dance with Him, as David danced with Him.

What an exciting time to be alive. Don't you agree?

CHAPTER 19

Gifts of the Holy Spirit Part 3

We have now arrived at the third and final category of the gifts of the Holy Spirit that is found in First Corinthians chapter 12, which are the following:

7. prophecy
8. various kinds of tongues
9. interpretation of tongues

These three gifts help us to <u>talk</u> like God.

I do not think it is by accident or chance that these three were written last and together. It is evident here that these three are in harmony, <u>as tongues being interpreted is equivalent to prophecy!</u> This book, from chapter 1 to the end, focuses on one thing—the operations of the Holy Spirit. His operations are sure and steadfast throughout eternity.

With so much written about the Holy Spirit in the New Covenant (New Testament)—a covenant made by and between God the Father and Jesus, His Son, not to mention what is found in the Old Testament (Old Covenant)—it can be a little overwhelming.

I am amazed how little His name is mentioned even among many believers. When His name is mentioned, the context alludes to the third party of the Trinity without any qualifiers of His person or operations.

Jesus said, He *had to* leave to make room for His Holy Spirit. He also said, it would be His Holy Spirit who would take His (Jesus's) things and teach them to the believers in Christ. My concern is that we have replaced the Holy Spirit with men and women teaching us only their points of view about the Bible, instead of the one who inspired it, each trying to be each other's Holy Spirit, instead of allowing Him to do His job.

Each Gospel gives us insight into His operations throughout Jesus's life and ministry. Jesus also gave instructions about His Holy Spirit's coming presence. The book of Acts is filled with His actions, as we have found out, along with His presence, instructions, and operations. While loving the Lord, the modern Church needs to be more mindful and yielding to Jesus's Holy Spirit.

Scriptures tell us to honor and love the Lord with all our soul, and with all our mind. Are we honoring His Holy Spirit in our lives as well? I am unaware of any scripture that reveals to us that Jesus and His Holy Spirit have been separated. Since they are not, can we safely say that we are honoring and loving the Lord with all our strength, with all our soul, and with all our mind?

As we each desire more of Jesus's presence in our lives, it will involve being directed by the one whom He knows will bring help to each of us—His Holy Spirit. Jesus further knows what it will take for us to change inside personally and what it will take for us to change our worship services from just formalities and programs to the spontaneity of joy and the excitement of His Holy Spirit's presence.

While we have our Father God in His place in our minds and hearts, and we have Jesus in His place as our Savior with all that implies, we cannot hold back the honor that is due Him. I believe that many within the Church have fallen short by not allowing the Holy Spirit His honorable place in the day-to-day operations of not only our individual lives, but also when we assemble together for praise and worship as well.

THE OPERATIVE

In many places of worship, they strictly follow a preplanned agenda on a printed program. This, I am sure, is done to honor everything being done decently and in order, but this is nothing more than formality. There is nothing wrong with this in and of itself <u>unless</u> there is no room for the Holy Spirit to change the order in the services. This takes leadership under the direction of the Holy Spirit. As the Holy Spirit orchestrates His Spirit-filled believers who have knowledge of His operations, anointing, and gifts, His presence can be seen, felt, and heard, as we conduct the service decently and in order, according to His ways of operation and not ours.

How often do changes in the preplanned program happen in your church? The perfect gentleman that He is, the Holy Spirit will never override our wills. So if this kind of structure is what is desired, then this kind of structure is what you will get, <u>until</u> the Holy Spirit is allowed to minister as He wills.

Instead of worshipping Him in spirit and truth as instructed, many choose to worship in formality. Somehow I do not believe that formalities are worshipping God in spirit and truth. According to His word, God must be worshipped in spirit and truth. This is true worship as described in the Bible. We are worshipping God by receiving a promised gift from Him, as we are filled with His Son's Holy Spirit.

Now God will work in a limited environment, as He always works with what He is given. However, freedom comes when He is allowed unlimited access to operate His will within His own house of worship!

What would you think of somebody, if you purchased him or her a valuable gift that cost you everything you valued, only to find out that when you gave them the gift, they picked and chose portions of that gift into pieces by saying, "I'll take this, but this and this I do not want!" Isn't this what many in the Church <u>are doing,</u> concerning the promised gift of the Holy Spirit from God the Father and Jesus, His Son?

Diligently seeking the Lord over the years, we have seen His presence in our own lives and in the lives of many others, as well as in our meetings. Both individually and collectively, He makes Himself known <u>when He is welcomed</u>.

His presence always meets the needs, gets to the root of the problems, and changes our hearts and minds. He knows <u>best</u>. The fact being, His way is far superior to our ways.

"Without counsel, plans go awry, But in the multitude of counselors they are established." (Prov. 15:22)

"There are many plans in a man's heart, Nevertheless the LORD's counsel—that will stand." (Prov. 19:21)

> The multitude of counselors that we should have
> first and foremost, is the Father, Son, and Holy Spirit!

One word of wisdom given by the Holy Spirit can give direction to our decision-making, guaranteeing the best-case scenario outcome to all situations. That word of wisdom keeps us in line with that good, perfect, and acceptable will of God, and our transformed mind is proof of this fact. As we yield to His directions, His word of wisdom will remind us of Jesus's words in the garden: "Not my will, but your will be done." He always knows what is best for us.

The next supernatural gift of the Holy Spirit is gift number 7, prophecy. Prophecy is a prediction or a foretelling of something that has not yet happened but will come to pass at a given point in time in the future. This is God's will coming to pass.

For example, every scripture in the Bible, foretelling Jesus's coming and all that He would accomplish, was told thousands of years ago and by several people. They each came to pass, meaning they actually happened the way they were foretold.

We know that the Holy Spirit is the one who came upon these men of old, and since Jesus is the same yesterday, today, and forever, His Holy Spirit has not changed either. God did, however, change the way He interacted with men. Instead of coming upon them, because of Jesus's accomplishments at Calvary's cross and His resurrection, He (the Holy Spirit of Jesus) dwells within men and women alike as was foretold by Joel and others, concerning the last days that we are living in. Jesus's obedience gives us *His* Holy Spirit, as He baptizes every believer who asks Him for *His* Spirit in this capacity, according to the scriptures.

THE OPERATIVE

<u>Here are a few examples for you to look up:</u>

Prophecy		Fulfillment
Genesis 3:15	*"would be the seed of a woman"*	*Galatians 4:4*
Micah 5:2	*"place of birth"*	*Matthew 2:1*
Deuteronomy 18:15	*"as a prophet"*	*John 6:14*
Isaiah 50:6	*"beaten and spit upon"*	*Mark 14:65*
Isaiah 53:12	*"crucified with sinners"*	*Matthew 27:38*

<u>These are just a few that came to pass,
but there are many more!</u>

In First Corinthians 14, Paul tells us in verse 1, *"Follow after love, and desire spiritual gifts* [Are you desiring these spiritual gifts yet?], *but rather that you may prophesy."*

Verses 2–5 give us the clues or the directives answering why we should desire spiritual gifts in the first place:

"For he who speaks in a tongue does not speak to men but to God, for no one understands him; however, in the spirit he speaks mysteries. But he who prophesies speaks edification and exhortation and comfort to men. He who speaks in a tongue edifies himself, but he who prophesies edifies the church. I wish you all spoke with tongues, but even more that you prophesied; for he who prophesies is greater than he who speaks with tongues, 'unless' indeed he interprets, that the church may receive edification."

"Therefore, brethren, desire earnestly to prophesy, and do not forbid to speak with tongues. Let all things be done decently and in order." (1 Cor. 14:39–40)

I realize that these scriptures are repetitious, but they all are connected to many topics and cannot be separated. Since scriptures interpret other scriptures, they must each remain in context of the topic. They each must be interpreted by the Holy Spirit and understood so that other scriptures that are given can be understood more clearly.

These are the things that need to be done decently and in order—the spiritual things of the Holy Spirit that He wants to bless us with as Jesus's believers individually and each time we come together. These gifts have a certain and precise way of operation by the Holy Spirit. He should be the one in control of their distribution, not men or women.

Let's notice some details here in these scriptures, shall we?

1. Paul points out that there are going to be those who speak in tongues.
2. Those who speak in tongues speak directly to God the Father and not to men.
3. Those who speak in tongues are speaking about the mysteries of God—that is, the wonderful works of God and all that they imply (Acts 2).
4. Those who speak prophecies edify, exhort, and comfort men.
5. Prophecy is spoken in a known language of the locality. (I do not speak Spanish, and if I heard a prophecy given in Spanish, I will not be edified, exhorted, and comforted because I do not know the Spanish language, unless it is interpreted in English, I would have no understanding, and therefore, I cannot be edified, exhorted, or comforted. The same principle applies to those who speak in tongues.)
6. He that speaks in tongues edifies himself, building himself up on his most holy faith (according to Jude 20).
7. Prophecy in a known language (locality pending) is to be desired so that all can be edified, exhorted and comforted by the language that they understand.
8. Paul wished that *you all* spoke in tongues (which edifies and builds up one's self). Do you speak in tongues? Paul wrote he wished we all did, even as he did.
9. Paul wished even more that *all* prophesied, "for he who prophesies is greater than he who speaks with tongues unless (please take notice of this *unless*) indeed he interprets, that the church may receive edification."

10. Paul also wrote, "And do not forbid to speak with tongues." Then why do we forbid this in our lives and gatherings?

The above ten details may be easily overlooked today, concerning these gifts, especially if you do not believe that they are actually for today's Church. Isn't it amazing how each stands out when we break them down like this? Within the first five verses of First Corinthians 14, all three of these gifts in this last category—prophecy, tongues, and interpretation of tongues—are mentioned and are explained in detail, both the differences and how each gift is to be used.

The gift of prophecy edifies, exhorts (builds up all the hearers with the prophetic words spoken), and comforts them with *His* message. There is a difference, however, between Old Testament prophecies and New Testament prophecies.

New Testament prophecy has a tell as to whether or not it is real. If prophecy is spoken over your life and if what is being said does not <u>edify, exhort, or comfort</u> you, <u>it is not a true</u> New Testament prophecy. That's the tell. The message given as prophecy today *must* <u>edify, exhort, or comfort</u>.

Old Testament prophecy was foretelling, or <u>looking ahead</u>. The tell of the Old Testament prophecy was whether or not what was spoken came true. Most times it took longer than a lifetime to be realized as true prophecy. We, however, have the privilege today of knowing that every prophecy in the Bible is true, because most of the events foretold have come to pass.

New Testament prophecy is forthtelling, which is more along the lines of speaking forth the existing word of God over the people and circumstances. See the difference?

For example, previously, we read Isaiah 53:12 foretelling that *"Jesus would be crucified for sinners."* It came to pass in Matthew 27:38. This is the Old Testament prophecy of foretelling. *Today*, the gift of prophecy forthtells that which has already been spoken of by God.

For another example, if a person has cancer. Today, New Testament prophecy proclaims to that person, *"By the stripes of Jesus, you are healed."* As the cancer leaves their body, the forthtelling of God's word comes to pass, and they are healed. (There are reasons some do not receive a healing that I will not take the time to teach here, but suffice to say that doubt and unbelief can play a major part in not receiving their healing. This is why it is instrumental we learn to stay in the faith of Jesus, which always agrees with the word of God in the Bible.)

<u>New Testament prophecy</u> is speaking forth that which God has already said about the situations or circumstances in our lives. Whether you do it for yourself, your family, or others, we must recognize that it is the Holy Spirit who brings to our attentions what God's word already has said about it. For this is His will in the matter. It is He who takes the things of Jesus and teaches them to us, and we benefit by their revelation in our lives.

Also, <u>New Testament prophecy</u> is full of grace and mercy. This is the dispensation that the Lord is operating in now. This will soon change when the last trump of God is heard, and the Church no longer finds herself here on earth.

Grace and mercy are indicators of New Testament prophecy, along with the edification, comfort, and exhortation of the recipient. That is never to say that there may not be warnings, but those warnings should always be accompanied with the hope of being able to come out of or away from the negative result of not following the Lord's instructions given.

We now look at the gift of various kinds of tongues, which is also for edification, exhortation, and comfort. The individual speaking in tongues (because they are speaking the mysteries or the wonder works of God) is speaking *His* words directly back to God the Father. As this is done, the power of His (Jesus's) word builds those speaking in tongues up on their most Holy faith, which is <u>Jesus's faith</u> contained within Him, and He is living in us. He ever lives to make intercession for us. This is one way He accomplishes this intercession, through *His* Holy Spirit speaking the will of the Father in our lives.

When someone is chosen by the Holy Spirit to operate in the gift of interpretation of the tongues, it is so that the explanation of what is being said directly to God the Father is understood by those listening to the interpretation. This too has a tell as to its validity.

THE OPERATIVE

Actually, there are two tells listed below as to whether or not it is a true gift of interpretation of tongues:

1. The interpretation will be in a known language and *must* edify, exhort, and comfort each hearing the interpretation. Remember, the interpretation of a message in tongues is *equal* to prophecy, according to scripture, once it is interpreted into a known language. When this happens, it is as <u>great or equal</u> to any prophecy spoken in a language that is understood by all.
2. The message given will line up with what scripture already says about the wonderful works of God and the topic of the interpretation. If not, it should not be considered a valid interpretation of the message. This holds true for prophecy as well. If it does not line up with God's word, be careful of what is being said and being heard.

Are you seeing the importance of knowing the word of God for yourselves? It is instrumental to your spiritual health and well-being. Do not listen to just anything (every wind of doctrine) that comes along. Make your calling and election sure.

Knowing the truth for yourself and applying it to your life sets you free, which is your obligation.

Take the time now to read again *First Corinthians chapters 12, 13, and 14*. As you do, you will find all the <u>instructions</u> that you need for the operation of all these gifts, especially in chapter 14 as Paul goes into great detail about their operations.

For example, *14:22–25* says, *"Wherefore, tongues are for a sign, not to them that believe, but to them that believe not; but prophesying serveth not for them that believe not, but for them who believe. Therefore, if the whole church comes together in one place, and all speak with tongues, and there come in those who are uninformed or unbelievers, will they not say that you are out of your mind? But if all prophesy, and an unbeliever or an uninformed person comes in, he is convinced by all, he is convicted by all. And thus the secrets of his heart are revealed; and so, falling down on his face, he will worship God and report that God is truly among you."*

Paul is not saying here not to speak in tongues. On the contrary, he is giving instructions that <u>when tongues are spoken out loud</u> in a meeting, there must be an interpretation of the message in tongues, not that everyone in the meeting should begin to speak in tongues.

Speaking in tongues becomes a sign to the unbeliever(s) in our meetings when the contents spoken directly to God are interpreted in a message in a known language for all that hear to understand, just like prophecies spoken in a language that is understood by all reveal the secrets of their hearts. Remember, tongues interpreted is equal to prophecy, and the unbelievers or unlearned will fall down on their faces and worship God and report to others that God is truly among you.

Is this happening within your Church services? Are the wonderful works of God supernaturally, through Him, revealing the secrets of the hearts of those hearing the interpretation of what is being spoken to God?

Paul instructs that all should not speak with tongues in our services, because there would not be understanding for edification, exhortation, and comfort to all at the meeting. He does instruct us to interpret tongues, which should be by two or three people <u>at the most,</u> using the gift of interpretation of tongues by yielding ourselves to the Holy Spirit to do so. If more than one interprets, the message will have the same instructions of edification, comfort, and exhortation.

It has been my experience that when more than one person are used in interpreting a message in tongues, the interpretation may or may not be a continuous interpretation, in which the interpretation will make up one combined thought. They will, at least, be saying something close to the same thing and should line up with God's word.

<u>When everything is done decently and in order,</u> according to the biblical principles outlined, others will not be able to legitimately call us fanatic or demonic. If they do, the truth is not in them, and it will take the Holy Spirit of truth to convince them of sin, righteousness, and judgment, not us. Many Churches today are governed by what they believe others will think.

THE OPERATIVE

This should not be! The things of the Spirit are spiritually discerned and should be understood by those mature believers who know how to operate in them and instruct other believers in the correct way. This is how more souls will be added to the Church daily.

We know of churches filled with believers who say they believe and practice speaking in tongues and interpretations but forbid it when strangers come into their meetings, in fear of offending them. In no way is Paul teaching this in these passages of scriptures.

Then there are those who forbid speaking in tongues altogether, because they believe it is of the devil or no longer needed for today. Some others believe that these gifts have passed away with the apostles. They each err from the scriptures (truth).

Beloved, this is not what the Holy Spirit wants and certainly is not what the word of God teaches us in the Bible. As a result of these kinds of thinking, there are closeted spirit-filled believers who are unable to experience their true freedom of worshipping in spirit and truth in many congregations today. One day they will have to come out of the upper room and speak the heavenly language to the public, regardless of the consequences.

This is why it is imperative that we learn to lean upon the Holy Spirit for correct revelation, interpretation, and understanding of His word. The use of sound references—like *Strong's Concordance* and Vine's *New Testament Word Studies*, just to name a couple—assists us as believers to clarify a lot of misconceived ideas, <u>if we would just take the time to study.</u>

I highly recommend *PC Study Bible* that includes concordances and many commentaries, enabling us the study of the original Hebrew and Greek words quickly and easily without having to spend decades of our lives, learning the original languages. <u>Invest in yourself</u> by ensuring that you are rightly dividing the word of truth, instead of just taking other people's word for it.

By all means, listen to your pastors, your teachers, and your friends at your church, especially if you know they are rightly dividing the word of truth. Try on the spirits, and see if they are of God by first knowing the scriptures yourself and comparing new revelations given to you by the Holy Spirit. This way, you will know the truths that are confirmed by one or more witnesses. <u>Always research for yourself as to whether or not something is truth and a sound doctrine of the Holy Spirit–inspired word of God.</u>

Jesus gives apostles, prophets, evangelists, pastors, and teachers to man. Do you remember why He did? Let me refresh your memory.

"And He gave some to be apostles, some prophets, some evangelists, and some pastors and teachers, for the equipping of the saints for the work of ministry, for the edifying of the body of Christ, till we all come to the unity of the faith and of the knowledge of the Son of God, to a perfect man, to the measure of the stature of the fullness of Christ; that we should no longer be children, tossed to and fro and carried about with every wind of doctrine, by the trickery of men, in the cunning craftiness of deceitful plotting, but, speaking the truth in love, may grow up in all things into Him who is the head—Christ—from whom the whole body, joined and knit together by what every joint supplies, according to the effective working by which every part does its share, causes growth of the body for the edifying of itself in love." (Eph. 4:11–16)

Do any of those words sound familiar to you—work of the ministry, edifying, faith, knowledge, etc? None of these offices have passed away, and certainly, their anointing that comes from the Holy Spirit, enabling men and women to fill them, has not! These offices are available to be filled with qualified believers till we all come in the unity of faith and of the knowledge of the Son of God, to a perfect man, etc., etc.

Based upon what we know so far, none of the nine gifts of the Holy Spirit or the fivefold ministry gifts have passed away. So why are many believers living their lives as though they were? The Bible is very clear about what their purpose is, who is supposed to operate in them, and how men are supposed to <u>correctly</u> operate within these gifts given to us by Jesus. Our thinking and believing concerning them have to change <u>now!</u> Prosperity for *all* in *all* areas of our lives that pertain to life and godliness is the motto of the Holy Spirit and not just for a few.

The fivefold ministry gifts and those holding these positions are given by God alone, I might add, and are *not* the only ones who can operate within the nine gifts of the Holy Spirit that are given to every man severally, as He wills. Shouldn't our Church leaders be teaching the members of the body of Christ these truths?

The actions of those operating within these ministry offices as <u>gifts to men</u> must reproduce the likeness and truth of Jesus Christ within the hearts of every member of His body. If each member isn't being prepared for the work of the ministry by receiving from their leaders the correct instructions and examples of operations of these gifts of the Holy Spirit, then the leadership is not correctly fulfilling *Ephesians 4:11–16.*

I have always said that if a church is full of the same people decade after decade, we are looking at an unhealthy church stunted in the grace and knowledge of our Lord and Savior, Jesus Christ.

<u>Unless</u> believers are being trained for the work of the ministry and sent out to do the same, that church is not patterning after the example that was given to us by the early Church. Modern churches that are filled with followers of personalities, instead of followers of Jesus and His Holy Spirit, are falling way short of God's best for them and certainly *not* the will of God.

(As I am writing, my wife just brought to my attention yet another church closing their doors and the building sold for a business to operate in it. Their membership, like so many churches today, were full of the elderly, with no children or new converts coming in to continue the vision of Ephesians 4:11–16. It was doomed for this reason, because the leadership was not being directed by the Holy Spirit and not following God's vision and plan for the body of Christ.)

God's instructional manual for us is the Bible. It teaches us that once a person is born again, we are to make them a disciple by training them in the word of God <u>properly</u> and according to all the scriptures, especially those in the New Testament. The New Testament is our pattern for today. The Old Testament contains examples of the earthly Church, which is considered Israel. We can learn a tremendous amount of wisdom from Israel's examples and the law that brought many of them and the early believers to Christ. But now we are to follow after Him (Jesus) and fashion His body as He instructs us in the New Testament, <u>by His Holy Spirit.</u>

Once trained to rightly divide the word of God for ourselves, we will learn how to hear the voice of God via His Holy Spirit. Once this witness of solid discipleship is confirmed, the Holy Spirit, at the appointed time, will choose and anoint those to be sent out for ministry. Where? He will give guidance for that. Why? So that they can replicate that which was invested in them according to the plan and purpose of that individual from God. *This is the blueprint of the book of Acts and Ephesians 4:11–16.*

There are further scriptures that give us more details concerning the structure of elders who reveal that they should not remain the same throughout the years. With enough said on this topic, let's move on.

I have done my best in following the leading of the Holy Spirit in providing this information and have written what I believe as to be as accurately conveyed from Him as I possibly could.

<u>The Holy Spirit is the operative of the Church today, concerning both individually or collectively,</u> not men and women learning a form of godliness, only to deny the power of the Holy Spirit and His presence, and placed within an office of authority within the Church by men.

It is the Holy Spirit who brings conviction to men and women's hearts and changes their minds. He builds them up by being the very substance of God and all that He is, and Jesus uses this same substance to fill His believers, giving them power and every advantage over their enemy, the devil, thus spoiling all his plans to steal, kill, and destroy us.

The Holy Spirit makes real to us the redemption we have been given. He applies the blood of Jesus continually, cleansing us from all unrighteousness. He takes the knowledge of Jesus and teaches us the ways of God Himself as revealed to us through Jesus, His Son. He gives us Jesus's wisdom to know how to apply *His* knowledge in our lives. He gives us the peace of God that surpasses all understanding that is able to keep our hearts and minds through Christ Jesus.

He is the Holy Spirit who makes real to us all things that pertain to life and godliness provided to us through Jesus. He pours into our hearts the *love* of God so that we can love others the way that He loves them—<u>unconditionally.</u> He is the part of the Godhead body who gives us directions and instructions in life because of His foreknowledge pertaining to all things.

I can go on and on about all the caring for us that the Holy Spirit does, but I believe that you're getting the message of how important He is, not only in each of our daily lives, but in our assemblies as well. He is the one who should be orchestrating our personal lives and conducting our services when we come together.

Are we allowing Him this honor? Are we withholding the power of God from our lives and in our meetings by not allowing Him His due place? Are we grieving Him by doing so?

"And do not grieve the Holy Spirit of God, by whom you were sealed for the day of redemption." (Eph. 4:30: read also verse 29)

As we look to Jesus, the author and finisher of our faith, we see the Holy Spirit in the midst of everything that pertains to Him in our lives. He is making sure that every word, every good thought of God, and every plan and purpose are fulfilled in each of us in reaching our expected end! His word remains true, whether we believe it or not or have understanding of it or not.

<u>It is the Holy Spirit who is responsible to see to it that we each reach our expected end.</u> He empowers those <u>who allow Him</u> in their circumstances. He brings Jesus unto them through His word, which is alive and sharper than any sword, piercing and dividing unto the soul and the spirit and the joints and the marrow and discerns the thoughts and intents of our hearts.

It is the Holy Spirit who knows everything about each of us and knows what's next in our lives, while moving us forward at the same time. He talks to us in that still, small voice of God, confirming all God has planned for us, <u>His children.</u>

If you desire Him to be active in your life and in your Church, then you will have to yield your life to Him and start doing things His way, which always lines up with His word. He wants for us what God the Father wants for us—<u>nothing but goodness.</u>

With the Holy Spirit's help, we can think, act, and speak like God. *His* gifts of a word of wisdom, word of knowledge, and faith will help you and me to <u>think like God.</u> The gifts of healing, working of miracles, and discerning of spirits help us to <u>act like God</u>, and operating in the gift of prophecy, various kinds of tongues, and the interpretation of tongues help us to <u>speak like God</u>.

My prayer for you is that you now understand more about His gifts, our great need for them, and their use in our lives and in our churches. Hopefully, you will choose to be available to operate in one of these gifts or in all of them, to be a blessing to you and others.

I remember when I was first asked by the Holy Spirit to give a message in tongues. The congregation was singing praises and worshipping the Lord. There was a pause in worship, as the voices softened, and my pastor began to yield the service to the Holy Spirit by recognizing that He wanted to speak to us. As I stood there listening, I felt an overwhelming desire to speak in tongues. I knew the order of things, and at that time, nobody else was speaking out loud in tongues.

As nervous as I was, I yielded myself to Him to operate in this church service, giving a message in tongues. I was filled with the Holy Spirit and was praying in tongues in my own devotions but never in a public service. However, I felt relaxed enough to begin, and so I did.

Yielding to the Holy Spirit, I began speaking out loud in tongues for what seemed to be a minute or two. I remember thinking as I did, *Please give me the interpretation if nobody else will yield* <u>to keep things decently and in order</u>. I did not want to be out of line, especially on my very first time that I spoke in tongues out loud in church.

(I am sure that He was chuckling when I asked Him to be sure to have an interpretation, as if He said, "Jim, I've got this!") When I stopped praying in tongues, He did give me the interpretation. Before I could speak it though, He had already instructed another person in the congregation to give the interpretation. It was almost verbatim to what I was given as the interpretation by the Holy Spirit. Confirmation had come to me for my training, and this brought forth a confidence within me to trust Him more, removing any doubt that I might have had previously.

<u>Faith soared</u> as my newfound confidence was applied like never before in my life. The message edified, comforted, and exhorted all

who was in that meeting. Since that time, I have been used in all nine of these gifts in one way or another, to the glory of God, my eternal Father, Jesus Christ.

Will you too make yourself available for these gifts, knowing that the Holy Spirit knows when you are ready to be chosen? You can covet the gifts that are best for the circumstances. He will build your confidence, just as He did mine.

After a while, as you or others, desire the best gift(s) to meet the need, you will know that tongues may not get the miracle you or another may need, so you will desire the gift of working a miracle instead.

<u>Remember, you cannot make these gifts operate through you.</u> You cannot pick and choose which gift you like best. Your part is to be filled with the Holy Spirit, with the evidence of speaking in tongues, and desire the best gift that will meet the need(s).

Be willing for the Holy Spirit to operate them through you when and wherever He calls upon you to do so. It will be Him who will release His power through you to operate the working of miracles or any other gift that He chooses. Then there is no pressure in the applications of these gifts. For it is <u>His</u> workmanship; we are just the yielded vessels of honor unto Him. With anxiety gone, just raise your hands and say, "Holy Spirit, use me!"

It is also my prayer and desire that this basic information given so far will instruct you with a better understanding of the baptism of the Holy Spirit with the evidence of speaking in tongues and that you receive His authority and power through this filling to express the supernatural wonderful works of God through the gifts of the Holy Spirit.

In Acts 1:8, the Greek word for power is "*dunamis* (doo'-nam-is)—force (literally or figuratively); specially, miraculous power (usually by implication, a miracle itself): KJV—ability, abundance, meaning, might (-ily, -y, -y deed), (worker of) miracle (-s), power, strength, violence, mighty (wonderful) work."

The <u>power of God</u> to show forth His wonderful works, *dunamis* is the Greek word that we fashioned the word *dynamite* from. <u>The Holy Spirit is someone you run to, not stay away from.</u> I further desire that since you are armed with this knowledge, you are no longer fearful of the things of the Holy Spirit and are now equipped and seeking to be used in whatever way He deems fit and necessary for <u>any</u> task at hand.

Become comfortable in His presence. Enjoy each other's company, as He makes real to you the true fellowship that is between God the Father, Jesus, His Son, and Jesus's Holy Spirit. Receiving this vertical fellowship will enhance your horizontal fellowship with others.

Saying all this, I conclude this portion on the nine gifts of the Holy Spirit, <u>which help us to think, act, and speak like God.</u> I certainly hope that you have enjoyed learning about the Holy Spirit of Jesus as much as I have enjoyed presenting it.

In the remaining chapters of this book, we will study the <u>fruit of the Spirit</u> that help us to <u>live like God</u>. Stay with me to the end, as we find out what happens when we allow the Holy Spirit to take control of our growth in the grace and knowledge of Jesus, our Savior, through His everlasting fruit, planted and growing inside each of us.

Working together is how the Holy Spirit and us can make a difference in other people's lives. And isn't this what the world needs a whole lot more of?

"Beloved, now we are children of God; and it has not yet been revealed what we shall be, but we know that when He is revealed, we shall be like Him, for we shall see Him as He is." (1 John 3:2)

"Love has been perfected [matured] among us in this: that we may have boldness in the day of judgment; because as He is, so are we in this world." (1 John 4:17)

CHAPTER 20

Fruit of the Holy Spirit
LOVE

"But the fruit of the Spirit is LOVE, joy, peace, longsuffering, kindness, goodness, faithfulness, gentleness, self-control. Against such there is no law." (Gal. 5:22–23)

We have learned that according to biblical scriptures, after being born again and water baptized, there is still another baptism available to all believers. It is the baptism of the Holy Spirit with the evidence of speaking in tongues.

We also found out that certain things change inside a person filled with the Holy Spirit. Where fear once resided, it is replaced with boldness. Doubt and unbelief are replaced with faith. We also found out that the fire of the Holy Spirit burns out the dross or anything that is not Christlike in our life.

Miracles begin to happen through those filled with the Holy Spirit, as they release His *dunamis*, or dynamic resurrection power. This power is received, as Jesus fills those believers who ask Him to, with the Holy Spirit and His presence, found in Acts 1:8 and 2:1–4.

As a direct result of this baptism of the Holy Spirit, we found out that a believer is more apt to operate in one, many, or all the nine gifts of the Holy Spirit, found in First Corinthians 12, with detailed instruction concerning their operation in chapters 13 and 14. These gifts operate and are administered by the Holy Spirit and are outside the realm of natural thinking, speaking, and man's abilities.

In addition, we now understand that believers are called by the Lord to fill positions of authority with accountability to the Lord Himself as mature believers are called to work the works of the ministry, either as one of the fivefold ministry gifts or all of them, as the Holy Spirit sees the need. Those holding these offices have a great responsibility to Jesus in fulfilling Ephesians 4:11–16. They operate in these positions as apostles, prophets, evangelists, pastors, and teachers because of the anointing that comes with His authority from God through Jesus and His Holy Spirit.

These ministry gifts have an anointing from the Holy Spirit to train others, helping them to mature for the work of the ministry so that the body of believers will be edified or built up by their ministering efforts. Once matured, they are to be sent out, as the Holy Spirit directs to replicate that which was deposited in them as a disciple. Then the Church grows and multiplies under the direct supervision of the Holy Spirit, as He chooses those to operate in His gifts.

Those releasing the miraculous, wonderful works of God will be both seen and heard. This is the deep that calls to the depths of a man's spirit and soul. This calling is what the Holy Spirit uses to convince all of sin, righteousness, and judgment. This conviction brings godly sorrow that needs not be repented of, thus calling men, women, and children to their destiny as children of the Most High God, our eternal heavenly Father.

We also learned to <u>think like God</u>, <u>act like God</u>, and even <u>talk like God</u> through the gifts of the Holy Spirit. Now we look for understanding that there is yet another directive from the Holy Spirit to <u>live like God!</u>

Growing inside each of us believers is the good fruit of the Holy Spirit. Our goal is to have nothing but good fruit growing inside us. However, since we are still in this earthly tabernacle, the reality is that both good and bad have a tendency to be present. The kind of fruit we display in our lives reveals to others what kind of person we are.

THE OPERATIVE

Sometimes both are seen, as we work out our own salvation in fear and trembling. Desiring to have only good fruit growing within us in the process of discarding the bad is the act of dying daily to self, as we live less like our old self and more like Jesus, pleasing Him as a new man or, we could say, the new and improved version.

The <u>fire of the Holy Spirit</u> works toward eliminating the bad fruit that had been growing in our lives since conception. He waters and increases the good fruit planted by Him, for spiritual maturity purposes within each believer. This was what Jesus was talking about when He said that "we shall know them by their fruit."

The fact is that fruit trees bear fruit! When I look at an apple tree, I don't call it a pear tree, because I know it by the fruit it bears. The fruit of that tree is an apple; therefore, I know what kind of tree it is. Even if I do not partake of the fruit, I know what to expect.

I know what it looks like, tastes like, smells like, and feels like. I know all the attributes of the fruit because I know what the tree produces. This fact applies to every fruit tree, and Jesus likens us to them in His analogy.

As a matter of fact, this is the <u>only judgment</u> that Jesus has placed into our hands. This judgment <u>does not</u> determine whether a person enters heaven or if they should be thrown into hell.

This judgment is <u>only</u> for us to judge someone's character as to whether a person should be considered a good person or an evil person and anything in between. Our character reveals more about us than we realize. For example, whether or not we are reliable, trustworthy, patient, kind, wicked, mean, etc.

According to Jesus, <u>we are</u> in control of what type of fruit (or character) we produce. I believe that this is mainly done by the choices we make in life. Also by our repetitious lifestyles, we reinforce those characteristics to grow larger and stronger, whether good or bad. This enables others to know exactly the type of person we are, especially as we spend time with each other.

"Beware of false prophets, who come to you in sheep's clothing, but inwardly they are ravenous wolves. You will know them by their fruits. Do men gather grapes from thorn bushes or figs from thistles? Even so, every good tree bears good fruit, but a bad tree bears bad fruit. A good

tree cannot bear bad fruit, nor can a bad tree bear good fruit. Every tree that does not bear good fruit is cut down and thrown into the fire. Therefore, by their fruits you will know them." (Matt. 7:15–20)

This brings us to the <u>fruit of the Spirit.</u> We will discover many things about this fruit that is inside us and all that that implies. Let's look once again to the Bible, for it is our guidebook of the truth.

"For you were once darkness, but now you are light in the Lord. Walk as children of light (for the fruit of the Spirit is in all goodness, righteousness, and truth), finding out what is acceptable to the Lord." (Eph. 5:8–10)

As with the gifts of the Holy Spirit, there are also nine (9) <u>fruit of the Holy Spirit.</u> Looking at each fruit character individually, let us pay close attention to how they each are connected to being filled with the Holy Spirit and the gifts of the Holy Spirit.

"But the fruit of the Spirit is love, joy, peace, longsuffering, kindness, goodness, faithfulness, gentleness, self-control." (Gal. 5:22–23)

Notice the scripture does not say *fruits* (plural), but *fruit* (singular). It's because the fruit of the Holy Spirit is the outgrowing of Jesus's Holy Spirit's character. This is accomplished, as He takes the things of Jesus's character and teaches them to us. Our minds are changed, and now the way we determine right and wrong is according to the word of God, no longer emphasizing the ways of the world, but cherishing the ways of the Spirit, according to His scriptures.

In essence, He transforms us to look just like Jesus, who looks just like the Father. In the new heaven and the new earth <u>after</u> we receive our glorified bodies, each of us will look exactly like the Holy Spirit, who looks exactly like Jesus, who looks exactly like the Father in character and action. We will all have a family resemblance!

<u>There will be one massive family of God,</u> with each believer looking exactly as our heavenly Father. On earth in our own reproduction, our DNA enables our children to take on certain characteristics and even looks from their parents. Spiritual DNA enables us to be exactly like our heavenly Father, through Jesus, His Son, because of His Holy Spirit.

When we are born again, our new spirit contains this spiritual DNA of Christ, and He begins this wonderful transformation of us becoming like our heavenly Father. This process continues, as we grow in the grace and knowledge of our Lord and Savior, Jesus Christ, and continues throughout the remainder of our lives till each believer receives their glorified bodies, <u>just as</u> Jesus did when He was raised from the dead.

The Holy Spirit gave me this chorus to sing, and as my wife can tell you, I sing it often! It was influenced by and based upon First John 4:17.

It goes like this:

> I'm just like my Heavenly Father,
> I'm so like my Heavenly Father,
> For as you are, Jesus, so I am,
> As you are, Jesus, so I am,
> As you are, Jesus, so I am, in this world!
> (Repeat chorus as often as you like.)
> (Copyright 2014 James J. Hamrick)

Jesus is the expressed image or exact copy of the Father, and the Holy Spirit is the expressed image or exact copy of Jesus! <u>After all, the Holy Spirit is Jesus's Spirit.</u> How can He be anything else but like Jesus? This is why no Christian should be afraid of the ministry of the Holy Spirit. He is the Spirit of Jesus! If you love Jesus, you should love His Holy Spirit too!

Part of our working out our own salvation in fear and trembling is the growing process of the Holy Spirit in our new spirit that changes us into the likeness of Jesus Himself. If you're not filled with the Holy Spirit, I believe this growth process will be much slower and can be a more difficult journey than if you are filled with the Holy Spirit, which could be the answer to the question "Why do some Christians remain the same for twenty, thirty, or forty years or more without changing after being born again?"

"Therefore, my beloved, as you have always obeyed, not as in my presence only, but now much more in my absence, work out your own salvation with fear and trembling; for it is God who works in you both to will and to do for His good pleasure." (Phil. 2:12–13)

I have found that in my own life, as I stay in communion with the Holy Spirit, He never allows me to remain the same. I have said it before, and it bears repeating, "The me that I used to be before I was born again is nothing like the me today." Believers in Christ remain in a state of flux, which many may find very uncomfortable to be in from time to time, but the end results will be out of this world!

Jesus Christ is full of love, joy, peace, long-suffering, kindness, goodness, faithfulness, gentleness, and self-control. These fruit characteristics describe Him accurately. The attributes of His character growing inside our spirits have been designed to be exposed to the outside so that others can see them and identify us as children of God.

<u>Remember,</u> the whole body of Christ is not at the <u>exact same spiritual growth level with God</u> at the same time. There will be some who seem to be very similar, as God always has "at least seven thousand who has not bowed the knee to Baal." This saying means that no matter where you are in your spiritual growth of the grace and knowledge of Christ, there are at least seven thousand others who are in the same place spiritually that you are, for you are not there alone.

No one person should ever feel elite in his or her current position of spiritual growth. God always will have many others right where you are with the knowledge, understanding, spiritual growth, and anointing as well.

This, I believe, is another reason there are so many denominations. Believers who believe the same way are called like faith. They will gravitate together. The danger here is to make sure you are gravitating to the word of God and not the philosophies of men.

Several years ago I heard a minister—I believe it was Kenneth Copeland—use this example while describing the different churches. I would like to share his example with you.

"Some churches are plumbing churches, and some, electrical churches, while others may be painting churches." He went on to say, "It may not be a bad idea to have the plumbers that may find themselves in an electrical church and direct them to the plumber's church and so on."

This is a great analogy, but I do see one little notion to add. <u>Does the Holy Spirit want us to remain a plumber, electrician, or</u>

painter for the rest of our lives? I am not talking about occupations in the natural realm, and neither was he. I am talking about this spiritual analogy of churches.

I am sure that there are times when the Holy Spirit sends plumbers into electrical churches for the purpose of challenging others in their spiritual growth. There may even be times that He wants a believer to be a plumber and an electrician at the same time.

See what I mean? Dividing the body of Christ in any manner is never OK! We are all members of the same body. We should never be separated in any way, including through denominational thinking or preferences!

The problem is that churches that are electrical churches do not want to associate with those attending a plumber's church and vice versa. This is because the body of Christ is not in unity of faith yet, as Ephesians says, and this unity of faith should be our goal and reason for being. But it soon will be in the unity of faith, as the Holy Spirit is currently training those who will not be afraid to teach others all they know so they too can reproduce in like fashion.

How sad these separations are, as we are *all* members of the same body of Christ if, indeed, we believe in Jesus's saving grace according to the scriptures and that He is our Savior.

There is nothing wrong remaining where you are as long as you are growing in the grace and knowledge of our Lord and Savior, while you are doing the work of the ministry so that the body of Christ can be edified, exhorted, and comforted. But the most important reason of all is that it's the Holy Spirit's will for you to remain there instead of being sent out. This choice should always be up to Him and not us; as we are bought with a price (life of Jesus), we are not our own.

"For ye are bought with a price: therefore glorify God in your body, and in your spirit, which are God's." (1 Cor. 6:20, KJV)

"Ye are bought with a price; be not ye the servants of men." (1 Cor. 7:23, KJV)

As long as that work of the ministry is training other new converts in some way to do the work of the ministry, it remains in line with Ephesians. Remember the scriptures in Ephesians? "For the perfecting of the saints, to work the work of the ministry till we all come in the unity of faith, for the edification of the church that we be no more children tossed here and there by every wind of doctrine."

One of the problems is that many believers remain the same spiritually as they were when they were first born again years ago. There are many members of the body of Christ who are not being trained properly according to the will of God, and they, definitely, should never be the ones who are training others, until they are trained properly themselves.

Each believer has the right to be stubborn and choose to remain the same. But if this is their choice, then they should never speak evil of those whom have been filled with the Holy Spirit with the evidence of speaking in tongues, operating in the gifts, and sharing His fruit with others. In reality, their choice to remain the same is resisting the Holy Spirit and His truths.

This scenario is what happened to those listening to Stephen. If you recall, the Jewish leaders resisted the wisdom by which he spoke and stoned him to death. He was telling those leaders the truth, and they could not bear it.

"And they were not able to resist the wisdom and the Spirit by which he spoke. Then they secretly induced men to say, 'We have heard him speak blasphemous words against Moses and God.'" (Acts 6:10–11)

Have you—or, perhaps, I should say—are you speaking blasphemous words against your brothers and sisters who are filled with the Holy Spirit and who operate in the gifts of the Holy Spirit? Or, for that matter, are you filled with the Holy Spirit and speaking blasphemous words against those who are not? Words can be just as damaging as actual stones. How can this, in any way, be any part of God's love?

A quick warning here: *"When they went from one nation to another, And from one kingdom to another people, He permitted no man to do them wrong; Yes, He rebuked kings for their sakes, Saying, 'Do not touch My anointed ones, And do My prophets no harm.'" (1 Chron. 16:20–22) This principle is repeated in Psalms 105:13–15.*

Love, joy, peace, long-suffering, kindness, goodness, faithfulness, gentleness, self-control—against such, there is no law. The letter (*law*) kills, but these fruit give *life*!

THE OPERATIVE

Isn't this just like Jesus?

Now, having said all this, let's take a closer look at *love*. This love found in the fruit of the Spirit is not your everyday type of love. No, this <u>love</u> is the <u>agape love</u> or the God-like love that chooses to love even when others are not lovable.

"But God demonstrates His own love toward us, in that while we were still sinners, Christ died for us." (Rom 5:8) There was a time when each of us was not that lovable. Maybe some still are not. But we must thank Him for His inexhaustible love always!

The distinctions of the different types of love are best read and studied in the Gospel of John 21:15–19, where Jesus was asking Peter if he loved Him. Jesus used the word *agapao*, which means "to love in a deeper sense morally." Peter replied with, *"You know I phileo you,"* which means "as a friend" and "being fond of another." Jesus uses the word *agapao* two times, and both times Peter replied with the *phileo* type of love. The third time Jesus uses *phileo*, Peter replied, *"You know I phileo you, Lord.*

Jesus was trying to get Peter to understand that there was another type of *love* needed when it came to tending His flock (which Peter and the other disciples were lacking at this time). It is the God kind of *love*, which is poured into our hearts (spirits) by the Holy Spirit, as Jesus fills His believers with His Spirit.

"Now hope does not disappoint, because the love of God has been poured out in our hearts by the Holy Spirit who was given to us." (Rom. 5:5) He brings God's *love* with Him, as Jesus fills us with His very own Spirit.

The original Greek word for love in Romans 5:5 is "*agape* (ag-ah'-pay)—love, i.e. affection or benevolence; specially (plural) a love-feast: KJV—(feast of) charity ([-ably]), dear, love."

There are three types of love governing or motivating men and women:

1. Agape—Godlike love.
2. Phileos—Friendship fondness.
3. Eros—Fleshly or sexual.

I believe each of these to be self-explanatory.

The agape type of *love* found in the fruit of the Spirit of Jesus is the same *love* that was God's motivation for His Logos, beginning with the creation of the angels, seraphim, and cherubim. During the creation of the foundations of the earth and all that it implies, to date and throughout the future of man, God's *love* remains the motivating factor that guides and moves His being.

We are keenly aware of how to love others with the *phileo* and *eros* types of love. But agape love can only be manifested from God through His Son's Holy Spirit and through us to others. As believers are filled with His Holy Spirit, He brings this agape love that the Father, the Son, and the Holy Spirit are full of and pours it into our hearts (spirits), as Jesus fills us with His Holy Spirit.

The fruit we are discussing is the character of Jesus's Holy Spirit, which is exactly the same as the Father's. Why do some think that they are three separate God's? The Trinity is very easy to understand and accept through the eyes of the Holy Spirit. Love comes with the Holy Spirit because He is full of the Father's love, because God is love, and Jesus is that expressed image of God's love.

We cannot love (agape) others like God, except we love (agape) others through His agape *love* that is poured into us! Without this *love* to share with others, we simply will be angry toward them, disappoint and be disappointed by them, and in some cases, even hate others because we will not be able to look past their offenses. We must learn to receive His *love* and release it toward others.

Some believers still have the "you scratch my back, and I will scratch your back" or "I'll love you if you do this or that" mentality. It is the most dangerous kind of love (*phileos*) there is because it allows those using it to have control over others who allow this type of love to dominate their lives.

Have you ever had somebody say, "If you love me, you will _____ (you fill in the blank)." Be very careful; run from this kind of love because God considers this as manipulation and is a form of witchcraft.

Eros, or sexual love, has its dangers as well. This is why we should be teaching our sons and daughters these three different types of love that exist. Teach them that just because somebody says that they love you does not mean it's OK to have sex with them. Let's see what God's word says about this topic.

The term *fornication*, which is having sex before marriage, means very little today. If this practice is in your life, you will have to deal with it as sin. Communing with the Holy Spirit is a great way to sustain from practicing acts of a sinful nature.

"Now the works of the flesh are evident, which are: adultery, fornication, uncleanness, lewdness, idolatry, sorcery, hatred, contentions, jealousies, outbursts of wrath, selfish ambitions, dissensions, heresies, envy, murders, drunkenness, revelries, and the like; of which I tell you beforehand, just as I also told you in time past, that those who practice such things will not inherit the kingdom of God." (Gal. 5:19–21)

> "fornication—*porneia* (por-ni'-ah); from NT:4203; harlotry (including adultery and incest); figuratively, idolatry: KJV—fornication" (NT:4202).
>
> "*porneuo* (porn-yoo'-o); to act the harlot, i.e. (literally) indulge unlawful lust (of either sex), or (figuratively) practise idolatry: KJV—commit (fornication)" (NT:4203).

The Holy Spirit's *love* never—I repeat, *never*—does for us if we do for Him. He loved (agape) us first, even while we were yet sinners, and never stops loving us. Nothing can remove us from His agape love—nothing!

We need to be courageous enough to see things and call them as though they were already accomplished. Forgiving ourselves as well as others will help us and them to find hope during the difficult conditions we both may find ourselves living in. God's love always produces positive change.

"For I am persuaded that neither death nor life, nor angels nor principalities nor powers, nor things present nor things to come, nor height nor depth, nor any other created thing, shall be able to separate us from the love of God which is in Christ Jesus our Lord." (Rom. 8:38–39)

> "love—agape (ag-ah'-pay); from NT:25; love, i.e. affection or benevolence; specially (plural) a love-feast: KJV—(feast of) charity ([-ably]), dear, love" (NT:26).
>
> "*agapao* (ag-ap-ah'-o); perhaps from *agan* (much) to love (in a social or moral sense): KJV—(be-) love (-ed)" (NT:25).

Imagine how heart-wrenching it must be on the Spirit of Jesus and the Father when a soul is thrown into hell to be held till the judgment day, soon to be cast into the lake of fire to be tormented forevermore.

This is why the Holy Spirit strives with us, speaks to us, convicts us, teaches us, and above all, *loves* us! He is not willing that none should perish, but all come to repentance.

What type of *love* is growing inside you and motivating you? Is it the *phileo* love, the friendship kind that Peter had before he was baptized in the Holy Spirit? Perhaps, it may be eros love, the sensual or sexual love of self-gratification (they are always thinking, *Me, me, me!*) or a combination of both of these?

Our goal is to have the <u>agape love of God</u> that shines through for others to see and partake of. This *love* is the love that you want growing and operating in you for the work of the ministry. Yes, there is room for all three to be active in a believer's life, but they always need to be in the correct setting and context based upon scriptural knowledge found in the Bible.

I would now like to share with you an example of this kind of love in operation. Before moving to Virginia twenty-seven years ago, our youngest son did something that just blew both my wife and me away. On our last Christmas there, he received a new bike, on which he would go outside and ride every day, weather permitting. He was eight, and he sure loved this bike. We taught our boys everything we knew at that time, concerning God's *love*, which is only what one can do. Little did we know how receptive our little man was.

One day the neighbor's boy came over to play with our son. He was a year or two older than our son, but they played well together. Excited to go out to play, our son hurriedly put on his boots and coat. After being outside for a short while, he came back in with a huge smile on his face. We noticed the neighbor's boy crossing the street with our son's new bike.

We questioned him as to why our neighbor was taking his new bike to his house. He simply replied, "God loved us so much that <u>He gave that which He loved so</u> much, and I just wanted to do the same thing." That was that! He went upstairs to his room, and not another word was ever said about it. Out of the mouth of babes, right? God's love is not from this world!

His agape love can only be received one way, and that is to have it poured into us by His Holy Spirit each time we pray in the Spirit. This is according to His word and not my opinion. You can read it again for yourself in Romans 5:5 if you like. This is God's chosen method of giving unto us His love that cannot be counterfeited by either *phileos* or *eros* love that each of us were born with in the flesh.

God's agape love can only be learned about through intellect to a certain degree, but while knowledge may be there in our minds, it does not guarantee that we are capable of operating within its perimeters. The limitations of the *phileos* and eros love that are in our flesh will keep us from giving our last one hundred dollars to the evangelist.

Perhaps, that automobile or that house and land that the Holy Spirit is speaking to us about to give to a man or woman of God will never be realized as seed sown into the anointing, because of these fleshly limitations we will reason away the thoughts with our minds. (Remember Ananias and Sapphira who sold their land and lied to Paul and the Holy Ghost? Perhaps, they were not filled with the Holy Spirit; therefore, they had not had the same agape love poured into them, like Barnabas and others did.)

For this very reason is why the Lord designed His agape love to only come from His Holy Spirit, as He pours it into our hearts, because it is attached to His being that is being poured into us. Its design is that as He fills us with His love, His love has to work its way out of us and to others.

Which gift are you being motivated by?

This now takes us to chapter 21, as we advance to the next fruit. What could we possibly learn about the Holy Spirit's fruit of *joy*? Join me and let's find out!

CHAPTER 21

Fruit of the Holy Spirit
JOY

"*But the fruit of the Spirit is love, JOY, peace, longsuffering, kindness, goodness, faithfulness, gentleness, self-control. Against such there is no law.*" (Gal. 5:22–23)

What *joy* we felt in our spirits, as we watched our eight-year-old son give his new bike to his friend who did not have one. The *joy* that was seen in his friend's face with his new bike each time he would ride it over was priceless. Our son never wavered, and I am sure the *joy* he felt enabled him to rejoice with his friend, who now could say that he had a bike of his very own!

Chapter 20 introduced us to the fruit of the Holy Spirit and gave us a closer look at the first fruit, which was *love*. In this chapter we are taking a closer look at *joy*, finding out what the Holy Spirit has to say, as we peel back each layer of His wonderful fruit.

As mentioned before, Jesus said that we "*shall know them by their fruit.*" This fruit or character of a person can easily be recognized by one's actions or reactions to things that occur to us as well as to the people around us, like our family and friends. I believe that <u>men of faith</u> should respond to things good and bad, instead of reacting.

Responding implies that some time has already been taken concerning preparation as what to do when life's challenges confront our hearts and minds. Reacting implies more along the line of impulses such as anger, bitterness, etc. and is predominately negative, where responses are more positive in nature.

As the fruit of the Holy Spirit, growing within our spirit, prepares us for responses, it also exposes our Christian character in spite of the circumstances. By not partaking of the fruit of the Holy Spirit growing inside us, we are vulnerable to lean more toward that of reacting to situations, instead of responding. So sweet is the investment of the Holy Spirit in our lives, amen!

Responding to situations actually takes a conscious effort on our part, where reacting does not. In a believer's case, our thoughts and words should line up with what God's word has to say concerning the matter at hand.

For example, I have been healed many times by the Lord. As a Christian, there is an overwhelming *joy* that accompanies being healed. Previously, I was going through one of those times of physical battles.

I had a choice to make. I could either react with negative thoughts and words, even agreeing with the injury as having the final word. Or I could continue to respond to this attack on my health with positive thoughts and speak words that God has already spoken over me, words such as, "By His stripes I am healed" and "Beloved, I wish above all things that you prosper and be in health, even as your soul prospers" and many others.

What did I do here? I chose to think like God, speak like God, and act like God, calling those things that weren't mine as though they were already mine, because they actually are mine, according to God's word. Now I am living like God when I respond in this like manner. This is the life He wants each of us to live like, one that honors His word and releases the healing virtue or whatever is needed to be released to meet the need. This is always done according to His riches in glory by His Son, Christ Jesus, and not according to our abilities whatsoever!

THE OPERATIVE

In the midst of the lack, debt, pain, sickness, or disease, we *must* realize that we are the blessed and the well, and our enemy, the devil, that comes to steal, kill, and destroy, is <u>trying</u> to rob us of our resources and our health.

"The thief does not come except to steal, and to kill, and to destroy. I have come that they may have life, and that they may have it more abundantly." (John 10:10)

In the same scripture, Jesus said that He came to give us life and life more abundant. That, which Jesus gave to us, is what the devil tries to take from us in any way that he can.

You may ask, "How long do you quote scriptures?" Well, I (you) do it as long as it takes for my (your) healing or miracle to be manifested. It's all in His hands, and the timing is always perfect in His will. This principle is the same for every need we have.

I would like to say here that if you are under a doctor's care and taking medications or treatments, <u>by all means, continue them until your healing arrives.</u> Once your healing arrives, it becomes equivalent to a miracle in your life. After your miracle manifests, then witness this to your doctor, and let him remove you from any medications or treatments. He placed you on them, and he is the one who should take you off them.

<u>God does not want us to be stupid about things, but wise as serpents and harmless as doves.</u>

"Behold, I send you out as sheep in the midst of wolves. Therefore, be wise as serpents and harmless as doves." (Matt. 10:16)

The fruit of *joy* helps us to choose to respond with God's words in our thinking and speaking and is revealed by our actions. It gives us the strength that we need to push through.

"Do not sorrow, for the JOY of the LORD is your strength." (Neh. 8:10)

The fruit of the Spirit of *joy* is planted and cultivated within each believer by the Holy Spirit of promise. *Joy* grows, as we receive more and more of Jesus's Holy Spirit, as we pray in tongues or in the Spirit, as Jude revealed. The *joy* of the Lord gives us the strength to draw from. Having this fruit inside us gives us an inexhaustible supply, and when we need the character of Jesus that the Holy Spirit produces within each believer, it is always available.

He chooses to watch over His word to perform the doing of it. His ministering spirits (angels) also have His power to minister unto each believer who becomes the heirs of salvation. There may be tears through the night, but *joy* comes in the morning. We are strengthened and encouraged by the fruit of His *joy*.

"Bless the LORD, you His angels, Who excel in strength, who do His word, Heeding the voice of His word." (Ps. 103:20) (What we believe we say, and they agree with God's word and obey them, so stay on what God's word says.)

"But to which of the angels has He ever said: 'Sit at My right hand, Till I make Your enemies Your footstool'? Are they not all ministering spirits sent forth to minister for those who will inherit salvation?" (Heb. 1:13–14)

"For His anger is but for a moment, His favor is for life; Weeping may endure for a night, But JOY comes in the morning." (Ps. 30:5)

The fruit of Jesus's Holy Spirit helps us to respond with steadfastness and with the strength of the Lord, which is a substance within our spirit, called *joy*. The strength of *joy* enables us to respond as a child of God instead of reacting with worldly weaknesses of the flesh. The fruit of *joy* is there long before the circumstances that try His faith within us. Learn to draw from this supernatural substance of the fruit of *joy*.

Have you ever gone through something that you asked God, "Are you sure there is no other way?" Jesus did in the garden, but He knew He had to walk His via dolorosa all the same.

"For the JOY of the LORD is your strength." (Neh. 8:10)

"JOY—*chedvah* (khed-vaw'); from OT:2302; rejoicing: KJV—gladness, joy" (OT:2304).

"*chadah* (khaw-daw'); a primitive root; to rejoice: KJV—make glad, be joined, rejoice" (OT:2302).

The *joy* that is mentioned in the book of Galatians as the fruit of the Spirit is the following New Testament Greek word:

THE OPERATIVE

"JOY—*chara* (khar-ah'); cheerfulness, i.e. calm delight: KJV—gladness, greatly, (X be exceeding) joy (-ful, -fully, -fulness, -ous)" (NT:5479).

Notice the similarities in these words above: gladness, joy, make glad, be joined to, rejoice, cheerfulness, calm delight. When times are good and easy, these words and actions flow from us like streams of water. These are all normal reactions, as you experience a respite from warfare. Please keep in mind, though, that the Lord is just as concerned about watching what we do when the trials of life come.

Our actions and words should match the character or fruit of the Holy Spirit, flowing just as easy as in the good times. If not, perhaps, they are dammed up by our fear, pain, doubt, or just lack of knowledge? Being filled with the Holy Spirit and speaking in tongues are great remedies to remove these dams from our lives.

As we realize that the fruit of the Holy Spirit of love, *joy*, peace, long-suffering, kindness, goodness, faithfulness, gentleness, and self-control is actually the character of the Holy Spirit of Jesus, I believe we will look at them in a different light.

The Holy Spirit longs to bring to the forefront the character of Jesus in the midst of our trials of life here on earth. Knowing this, I believe we can be more mindful of the power of *joy* being released upon our situations and circumstances.

Like desiring the best gift for the need, we should look for the best fruit to release its power in every circumstance. Sometimes it may be more than one fruit or character of the Holy Spirit released, like love, coupled with joy and peace. If the trial lingers, then we will need to release long-suffering with some self-control and so on.

You have heard it said that "knowledge is power." This is true. Let me prove it by the word of God.

You now have the knowledge of the baptism of the Holy Spirit, along with the gifts of the Holy Spirit. Couple them both with the fruit of the Holy Spirit, and watch the miraculous results.

All this knowledge has one common thread. It is the resurrection power of the Holy Spirit! It's the very same power that raised Christ from the dead. Without this power operating in our lives, it's like trying to start a car without a battery. It will never start, let alone turn the engine over. If we remove the key elements of something, it becomes nonusable and, therefore, useless to us. (Removing one of the three key elements of a spiritual fire, the fire goes out and is no longer usable by us.)

Many believers have removed one of the three key elements in the Godhead body. Therefore, there will be no *power* flowing. It's just not activated! Like with an electrical light circuit, as long as the power company has no breaks in the lines, the voltage remains constant in the electrical wires. It sits and waits for a demand to be placed upon it, before it can move through the wires. Amperage is what pushes the voltage through the wires but is not allowed to do so until someone or something throws the switch to the ON position. Once this happens, a demand for electricity is made, and the amps push the voltage through to the light that is consuming the wattage found within the electricity, and presto, you have light in a dark room.

Likewise, the Holy Spirit remains available to believers until a demand is placed upon His resurrection power. Each believer is in control of the switch of faith within them. What we believe we speak, and what we speak we do. Being filled with Jesus's Holy Spirit allows this switch of faith to operate more smoothly and more frequently. As we allow this flow of His resurrection power to meet the needs of others and even ourselves, the demand or need draws on the power of the Holy Spirit and results in miracles taking place.

Like the lightbulb consumes the energy of wattage contained within the voltage, the demand of change or miracles is produced by the resurrection power of Jesus's Holy Spirit flowing through us to others. As this power is dispelled in various ways, we believers need to continually pray in the Spirit as did the early Church believers, to build ourselves up again on our most holy faith, remaining ready for when the Holy Spirit needs to touch again through us, as we are His hands extended to others.

Many believers, sadly, have removed the Holy Spirit, who is the *power*, from the equation, because of either poor training or lies from others they believe to be true or acceptance of these false teachings without finding out for themselves. By not believing that Jesus actually promised the gift of His Holy Spirit, they are short-circuiting their results.

This is how God designed His Son's Holy Spirit's power to operate, and according to His scriptures, His power does not operate in any other way except in times of providence, when He throws the switch of faith Himself. I do not believe the Church should be waiting for the providence of God when He has already provided for us all that we need through His Son, Jesus, and His Holy Spirit.

"But if the Spirit of Him who raised Jesus from the dead dwells in you, He who raised Christ from the dead will also give life to your mortal bodies through His Spirit who dwells in you." (Rom. 8:11)

Wow, do you have the same Spirit, who raised Christ from the dead, dwelling in you? Of course, each believer has the Holy Spirit who brought the seed of Jesus Christ into our spirits, but He cannot dwell or abide as a living entity with a believer's spirit until Jesus is able to baptize or fill a believer with His Holy Spirit and power. But you, the believer, must seek the Lord by asking Him to baptize you, because He will not make you speak in tongues until you, as a believer, give Him permission to allow this to happen.

Remember, He is a perfect gentleman and will never override a believer's will! He is waiting for you to believe in His promise and ask Him personally for it, the same as you asked Him for forgiveness of your sin, especially for not believing in Him as the Son of God. His Spirit continued to strive with you and me until He was able to activate the measure of faith we received at conception, and then, He still could not do anything with it till we gave permission. Receiving the baptism of the Holy Spirit with the evidence of tongues is the exact same scenario.

Couple all this *knowledge* together by believing God's word as the final authority on the matter and by acting upon it, along with the following:

"And we know that ALL THINGS work together for good to those who love God, to those who are the called according to His purpose." (Rom. 8:28) And you will be one strong, unwavering believer.

This is why knowledge is power, and there is an enemy who does not want you to know any of this. He also does not want you to know that this power becomes available to flow through you once you have been filled with the Holy Spirit, according to the scriptures. He does not want you to realize the investment of God's power that is available to you as a believer in Christ.

Knowledge brings joy! Doesn't this bring *joy* to know that all things are temporary and that they too will come to pass in our lives (including our times of trials and tests)? And pass they will, and nothing but good things will come from them. Don't wait till the other side of your trial to rejoice. Rejoice in the midst of the circumstances, and release the power of *joy* that brings forth the changes needed in your life.

Now that is power, folks! Praising and thanking Him in the midst of our trials and tests release His power to bring to pass that which we need.

"Be anxious for nothing, but in everything by prayer and supplication, with thanksgiving, let your requests be made known to God; and the peace of God, which surpasses all understanding, will guard your hearts and minds through Christ Jesus." (Phil. 4:6–7)

The knowledge of this scripture comforts us that no matter what we go through in life, all things become our employees, working for us to bring us *good* and not bad. It is through this knowledge found in Jesus's words and His works that we can draw from the resurrection power through His Holy Spirit. If the same Spirit who raised Christ from the dead is alive and well within each believer, He will bring Jesus to the forefront, showing the world <u>who He is in us</u> through <u>His joy, which is our strength</u>.

From the very beginning, when God created the angels, cherubim, and seraphim, His goal was to reveal Himself through His *word*—His <u>Logos</u>. His word later became flesh, and we know Him as Jesus. Presently, He is still revealing Jesus through each of His children, as we each allow His Holy Spirit to do so within our lives.

In the natural we say, "That boy has his father's looks" or "She acts just like her mother." This is what the Holy Spirit longs to say: "Don't they look just like their heavenly Father, Jesus?"

By resembling our heavenly Father, we have the confidence in knowing that all things will work for our good because we love Him and are called according to His purpose. What purpose might that be? Why, for us to allow Jesus to be revealed in our lives to the world, of course! He is the hope of glory to the world. Are you allowing Jesus to be revealed in you by His Holy Spirit?

The sooner we realize that the fruit of the Holy Spirit is the actual character of Jesus growing within us, we will be more at peace and full of *joy* while we grow in the grace and knowledge of our Lord and Savior, Jesus Christ.

Again, it is His fruit/character that enables us to respond to situations instead of reacting. This is called maturity in a Christian's life. Have you ever heard, "Therefore you be perfect, just as your Father in heaven is perfect"? This word *perfect* is not a sinless state of being, but rather a place of spiritual maturity.

"Therefore you shall be perfect, just as your Father in heaven is perfect." (Matt. 5:48)

> "perfect—*teleios* (tel'-i-os); complete (in various applications of labor, growth, mental and moral character, etc.); neuter, completeness: KJV—of full age, man, perfect" (NT:5046).

Do you need the sincere milk of the word? If so, be encouraged and recognize that you will eventually become a mature Christian. Just continue to study the word of God, and apply to your life what you learn, and you'll become more like your heavenly Father, as you grow in His grace and knowledge of His Son, Jesus, who is living His life now through you and each believer, just as countless others have before us.

If you are partaking of the meat of the word, then you have matured past needing the milk and are partaking of the deeper things of God's word and are closer to <u>thinking, acting, and speaking like Jesus than you were before.</u> We are all at one level of maturity or another. Whether on milk or meat or somewhere in between, we each are being encouraged by the same power of the Holy Spirit who continues to mature His fruit within each of us.

If you have not seen it yet, let me tell you that this is what the baptism of the Holy Spirit, His gifts operating in our life, and His fruit maturing <u>do for us</u>. It bears repeating: if this power is removed from our lives, the fire of God goes out! Do not let the fire of God go out of your life! Ask Jesus today to baptize you in His Holy Spirit.

A believer errs by considering the baptism of the Holy Spirit, the gifts of the Holy Spirit, and the fruit of the Holy Spirit as being three separate things or events happening in their lives.

In fact they are one continuous relationship with the Most High God through His Son, Jesus, revealed by His Holy Spirit. He is the same Spirit who is mentioned in First Corinthians chapter 12. If separated, the Godhead body becomes fragmented in our thinking. In essence, you are living a life of faith with no power. Remember the scripture "Having a form of godliness, but denying the power thereof"?

By separating them, the mainstream way of thinking makes them issues of arguments as if this *power* is not relevant for today or whether it too has passed away or is no longer needed. This should not be the case within His church, because we believers have a very privileged life! Many have not realized this yet.

Separation or even a hint of any part of the Holy Spirit's character as being passed away makes Him weak at best within a believer's walk of faith that does not agree with the fullness of the Holy Spirit's operations in their life. Since Jesus Christ is the same yesterday, today, and forever, then it only stands to reason that His Holy Spirit is too.

Let me show you something about being whole:

"Though one may be overpowered by another, two can withstand him. And a threefold cord is not quickly broken." (Eccl. 4:12)

I believe, with everything that is within me, that God actually gave Adam and Eve the opportunity never to taste sin by reason of reproduction. If they had been obedient and reproduced before the fall, Cain would have been born with a glorified body housing his spirit and soul, like his mother and father, Adam and Eve. And he most likely would have never murdered his brother, Abel.

If this reproducing had been accomplished while Adam and Eve still remained in the glory of God, the spiritual principle of *"a threefold cord is not quickly broken"* would have been implemented, and life, as we know it, would not have happened. This plan was God's

THE OPERATIVE

best for His man, but He is God, and in the end, He receives His family anyway.

Giving choice through man's freewill was the only way to prove true love toward God, the Creator. The power to choose to love another, even when they are not lovable, was what *God* chose to do by loving us first. Adam and Eve's choice sent us all down the path of sin, and the rest is history. Thank you, Father God, that you did not change your mind about loving us even when we were not too lovable.

<u>Good news,</u> though, this fall became man's employee and has been working for all mankind since. In the end, it will be as if every believer came out of Eve's womb with glorified bodies, and it will be as if none of this even happened.

You may ask, how is this possible? Because of the wonderful works of God through His Son, Jesus. We believers ultimately receive our intended glorified body, and it will be as if none of this ever happened. How is this so? Thank you for asking; now if you will allow me to show you:

"There is no remembrance of former things, Nor will there be any remembrance of things that are to come By those who will come after." (Eccl. 1:11)

When the preacher pinned these words long ago, little did he know that he was prophesying about all of us believers in Christ, receiving glorified bodies! "I need more proof!" you say. I am glad you do. Let me show you some more:

"For behold, I create new heavens and a new earth; And the former shall not be remembered or come to mind. But be glad and rejoice forever in what I create; For behold, I create Jerusalem as a rejoicing, And her people a joy. I will rejoice in Jerusalem, And, joy in My people; The voice of weeping shall no longer be heard in her, Nor the voice of crying." (Isa. 65:17–19)

When the Lord is finished with the heavens and the earth as we know it, judgment will come, and all the cosmos will be destroyed with the consuming fire of God's presence. As the new heavens and the new earth are given for our occupation, it will be as if none of our lives even happened: *"And the former shall not be remembered or come to mind."* Do you need more proof? Here is a third witness to help establish this truth:

"And God will wipe away every tear from their eyes; there shall be no more death, nor sorrow, nor crying. There shall be no more pain, for the former things have passed away." (Rev. 21:4)

The writers of Ecclesiastes and Isaiah both informed us that the "former things will not be remembered anymore." If we will have no memory of any of our lives (former things), then will it not be as if it never happened? Absolutely! This too should bring us great *joy* by knowing this wonderful truth in God's plans for us.

These writers looked across time with the help of the Holy Spirit and had seen this outcome. If Adam and Eve had been obedient to multiply and subdue the earth as commanded, God would have had His glorified family already here on earth. Knowing God, this fall did not take Him by surprise, because He too had seen all events of His Logos, from the creation of the angels and everything that would occur after that.

I shared earlier in the book what Logos meant. Basically, it was God having one complete thought of every detail in every person's life, including knowing every decision that we each would make. Looking down through the time line, He already knew Jesus, His Logos, and that this would be the image that He made His first man from, including the glorified body that was representative on the mount when Jesus was transfigured. Man started in glory, and man will finish this life in glory and step into eternity as the tabernacle of his God!

Not only will the former things of this life pass away, according to scriptures, but all memory of it as well passes away. All things become new! Glory to the highest God!

Because God is a responsible Creator, He knows the results of Jesus holding all things together by the word of His power, with the help of His Holy Spirit, and that all things turn out good for us who love Him and are called according to His purpose. This ought to tell us about the intelligence of God. He always wins—always!

What does this have to do with the fruit of *joy*? Well, I don't know about you, but having this revelation knowledge gives me great comfort and *joy*, unspeakable and full of glory. The half that has been told to us is enough for the Holy Spirit to reveal to us all that we need to know until we receive the other half of God's Logos, half of which contains our eternity without limitations in Him, as God dwells once again within each of His children. *Wow!* If this is not *joy*, unspeakable and full of glory, I do not know what is.

Now, I believe some of you might be saying, "But, James, how then will we know each other if we do not remember this life?" You asked another great question, and again I am more than happy to answer.

Remember the scripture about what Jesus said on <u>how</u> we would know each other? Why, of course, the answer is by their *fruit*. Then take a look at this:

"But if any man love God, the same is known of him". (1 Cor. 8:3, KJV)

"For now we see in a mirror, dimly, but then face to face. Now I know in part but then I shall know just as I also am known." (1 Cor. 13:11)

"For no other foundation can anyone lay than that which is laid, which is Jesus Christ. Now if anyone builds on this foundation with gold, silver, precious stones, wood, hay, straw, each one's work will become clear; for the Day will declare it, because it will be revealed by fire; and the fire will test each one's work, of what sort it is. If anyone's work which he has built on it endures, he will receive a reward. If anyone's work is burned, he will suffer loss; but he himself will be saved, yet so as through fire." (1 Cor. 3:11–15)

After reading this, what is the answer to the question? We will know each other by our <u>fruit and our works,</u> which are what defines how we are known for all eternity. When the glory comes, it will burn up all the wood, hay, and stubble within our lives, and only the precious things done by His Holy Spirit's power will remain. You see, <u>it's in there;</u> if we will just take the time with the author, He will reveal a great deal to us. His name is the Holy Spirit or, as I still like to call Him, the Holy Ghost!

Some of you may remember this, and some may not. Several years ago there was a TV commercial for Prego spaghetti sauce. The theme was, "It's in there!" I preach a revival message entitled, "It's Prego," because no matter what you are looking for pertaining to mankind, it's in the Bible—"It's in there!"

What fruit and works are you going to be known for?

Our responsibility is to rightly divide the word of truth. It is one of the Holy Spirit's responsibilities to see to it that we do this, if we allow Him to. If we allow Him to be active in our hearts and lives, His fullness will bring the revelations necessary for us to become members of the body of Christ whom He wants us to be. The body of Christ suffers today because of the lack of unity of faith and wholeness of the Spirit of Jesus.

The helper and comforter sent to us by Jesus (as He sat down at the right hand of the Father) is the operative today. He is the operative both in the Church and in the world! We only need to allow Him His rightful position, and He will get the job done better and quicker than we could ever think of doing in our own abilities.

The fruit of joy in our lives brings the assurance and joyfulness in the midst of troubled times because we know every end result will be for our good. As we draw from Jesus's strength through the fruit of *joy*, we may not know when or how or understand why, but we know that at the end of each trial, only good will come out of it. Then it is God's *good pleasure* in us that will be seen by all.

"Do not fear, little flock, for it is your Father's GOOD PLEASURE to give you the kingdom." (Luke 12:32)

"Blessed be the God and Father of our Lord Jesus Christ, who has blessed us with every spiritual blessing in the heavenly places in Christ, just as He chose us in Him before the foundation of the world, that we should be holy and without blame before Him in love, having predestined us to adoption as sons by Jesus Christ to Himself, according to the GOOD PLEASURE of His will, to the praise of the glory of His grace, by which He made us accepted in the Beloved [Jesus]." (Eph. 1:3–6)

"In Him we have redemption through His blood, the forgiveness of sins, according to the riches of His grace which He made to abound toward us in all wisdom and prudence, having made known to us the mystery of His will, according to His GOOD PLEASURE which He purposed in Himself, that in the dispensation of the fullness of the times

He might gather together in one all things in Christ, both which are in heaven and which are on earth—in Him." (Eph. 1:7–10)

"For it is God who works in you both to will and to do for His GOOD PLEASURE." (Phil. 2:13)

"Therefore we also pray always for you that our God would count you worthy of this calling, and fulfill all the GOOD PLEASURE of His goodness and the work of faith with power, that the name of our Lord Jesus Christ may be glorified in you, and you in Him, according to the grace of our God and the Lord Jesus Christ." (2 Thess. 1:11–12)

Joy remains growing stronger in our hearts, evidenced by the smiles on our faces and the strength to share the gospel of Jesus Christ with others in bringing them hope. This process is the Holy Spirit pouring God's love in us, watering and giving "Son-light" to our spirit, allowing the power of the fruit of joy to be drawn from Jesus's character, as our strength, for we can do all things through Christ, who continues to strengthen us.

"I can do all things through Christ who strengthens me." (Phil. 4:13)

Embrace His eternal *love* and *joy* in your life, as they grow, and do not think it bad when He wants to show you off to the world when trials come your way, as well as in the absence of them.

"Now the God of hope fill you with all joy and peace in believing, that ye may abound in hope, through the power of the Holy Ghost." (Rom. 15:13, KJV)

In chapter 22 we will take a closer look at the next characteristic of the Holy Spirit through *peace*, gaining more knowledge and understanding about this resurrection-power fruit in our lives and how we each benefit from His presence of *peace* within us.

CHAPTER 22

Fruit of the Holy Spirit
PEACE

"But the fruit of the Spirit is love, joy, PEACE, longsuffering, kindness, goodness, faithfulness, gentleness, self-control. Against such there is no law." (Gal. 5:22–23)

In this teaching on the Holy Spirit's presence, power, character, and operations, we look at the fruit called *peace*. This third characteristic of the fruit of the Holy Spirit is another example of the characteristics of Jesus Christ.

Like *joy*, in times of turmoil in our lives, we can find the *peace* of God that surpasses all our understanding that sustains us through them.

"Be anxious for nothing, but in everything by prayer and supplication, with thanksgiving, let your requests be made known to God; and the PEACE of God, which surpasses all understanding, will guard your hearts and minds through Christ Jesus." (Phil. 4:6–7)

Take special care to notice what the peace of God guards. It guards our *hearts* (spirit men, whom we really are) and our *minds* (the battleground arena).

THE OPERATIVE

"But I fear, lest by any means, as the serpent beguiled Eve through his subtilty, so your minds should be corrupted from the simplicity that is in Christ." (2 Cor. 11:3, KJV)

There you have it—the battlefield where all battles are either won or lost. Thus far, we found out that in *Proverbs 23:7 (KJV)*, *"As a man thinks, in his heart [spirit] so is he. eat and drink, saith he to thee; but his heart is not with thee."*

If we allow the wrong stuff into our spirit's belief system, it could be affecting the way that we view the things of God. Junk in! Junk out! This is why "out of the abundance of the heart [spirit] the mouth speaks." Our mouths reveal that which is in our hearts in abundance, thus telling others who we really are.

Remember, it is our mind that is the battleground and the filter of that which we accept as truth or lies. It is our mind that feeds our spirit and soul, and for this reason, our minds must be renewed after we become born again, renewed by the truth contained within the scriptures of God's holy Bible. As we study them and practice their application in our lives, they enable us to be transformed into the persons we are supposed to be, instead of remaining who we were.

I placed a comma after *thinks* to prove a point. As mentioned before, as we are born again, our heart (spirit man) was fed and formed by what we allowed our brains to processes as being the truth or a lie. The brain is where all prejudices are birthed. We intellectually determine what is truth and what is a lie based upon our own prejudices concerning that which we want to be our truth, even if it is a lie.

In other words, "As a man thinks in his mind [brain], his heart [spirit man] follows suit along that line of thinking and so he becomes that which he believes or does not believe and lives his or her life accordingly."

The scripture reads in *Proverbs 23:7*, *"For as he thinks in his heart, so is he."* This is correct because before we are born again, this is how it operates. The sin that we are conceived in reversed the order in which God intended us to determine what is truth or a lie, as we are born into this world. But God has *the way* to bring us back.

Once we are born again, this process reverts back to the original intent that God wanted for man in determining what is truth or lie. Our spirits actually know the truth when we hear and see it. This is where we get our conscience from, as well as our gut feeling. A lifestyle of tolerance and compromise numbs both of these, and we live according to what we believe is right in our own eyes.

Prior to our new birth, this process remains short-circuited by the brain and the prejudices acquired along the way, as we mature. Many of these prejudices are passed along to us from family members and friends, as we accept them as being right and the truth even though they may be wrong or a lie.

However, a man or woman that is born again, after receiving his or her new spirit, becomes compatible to have Jesus abiding in him or her. A believer is now ready to grow to maturity. Acquiring the truths of God's words contained in the Bible feeds our heart (spirit man), and as our heart grows with increased knowledge of the truths of God's words, Jesus in us continues His renewing of our minds by changing them. Isn't this what repentance actually is—the changing of our minds?

Maturity happens as our new spirit thirsts and hungers for the things of God that are found within His word, which contains spirit and life. The need for the substance within God's word, which is Spirit and life, becomes stronger than the desires of our fleshly mind. The more we read, study, and hear the words of God, the more our brains become renewed by all the truth that flows through it from God's word.

No matter how many times a lie sticks its ugly head up, we have the fruit of *peace* in knowing the truth we learned from God's word that sets us free and keeps our minds and hearts through Christ Jesus.

No longer are we to have a life of being tossed here and there with every wind of doctrine.

For example, reincarnation is one of those lies that many want to be true, so they think by believing it to be so, it will become reality for them once they die. In my youth and before I was born again, I too used to believe this way. So I know this statement is fact. But I realized from God's word that "it is appointed unto men to die once, after this the judgment."

"And as it is appointed for men to die once, but after this the judgment, so Christ was offered once to bear the sins of many. To those who eagerly wait for Him He will appear a second time, apart from sin, for salvation." (Heb. 9:27–28)

My heart (spirit man) recognized truth when he heard it even though my mind had convinced me of this lie of reincarnation. But because faith was coming to me by hearing the word of God, His word started the transformation process, and once I accepted Jesus as my Savior, the *truth* was confirmed. It is Jesus that finishes the work in every believer by His Holy Spirit.

After becoming born again, if we are not trained correctly, our minds can't be properly renewed. This becomes a very important issue because many battles are lost more than won because of inadequate training by leadership within many churches. As a result, we see many new converts falling away. Many believers who remain in fellowship are lacking spiritual maturity, so they remain on the milk of the word, instead of progressing to the meat of the word. They remain untrained to do the work of the ministry for years after being born again. In some cases, it may be decades, and in other cases, they remain immature in Christ for the rest of their lives.

Once born again, the devil's task is to get the new convert to throw away all benefits of our salvation as soon as he possibly can. New believers that struggle, wondering why they cannot have victory over certain things pertaining to their lives, do so because of a lack of knowledge.

However, once knowledge of these benefits is acquired and applied in a believer's life, they begin to walk away successfully from living in the conflict of the flesh and into the newness of the spirit (inner man). Jesus then can fill them with His Holy Spirit if they ask Him to. This begins the revelation of His character and making His gifts available for operation through the believer as more than a conqueror.

As the fruit of the Spirit matures within the believer and the force of this fruit is applied to the believer's life, they acquire more and more knowledge of truth to apply. More battles are won, and we are made more than conquerors through Christ.

"Yet in all these things we are more than conquerors through Him who loved us. For I am persuaded that neither death nor life, nor angels nor principalities nor powers, nor things present nor things to come, nor height nor depth, nor any other created thing, shall be able to separate us from the love of God which is in Christ Jesus our Lord." (Rom. 8:37–39)

"I can do all things through Christ who strengthens me." (Phil. 4:13)

"The sting of death is sin, and the strength of sin is the law. But thanks be to God, who gives us the victory through our Lord Jesus Christ." (1 Cor. 15:56–57)

Believers must be instructed and made aware of our adversary, the devil, that always comes to us in the first person. He teaches his lying spirits to do the same. They never whisper to us, "You're not feeling good" or "What do you think that pain is?" No, they whisper, "I am not feeling good" or "This pain feels like I might have…," and the next thing you know, your mind entertains it as your own thoughts. If you do not cancel it out with the word of God, you may sign for the package that is a special delivery to your body or circumstances.

In doing so, our spirit man follows suit, and our bodies have no choice but to listen and agree with these lies coming to pass, simply because we <u>have not</u> been trained to reverse the process. Here is some insight on how this operates:

"But the unbelieving Jews stirred up the Gentiles and poisoned their MINDS against the brethren." (Acts 14:2)

"But their MINDS were blinded. For until this day the same veil remains unlifted in the reading of the Old Testament, because the veil is taken away in Christ." (2 Cor. 3:14)

"But even if our gospel is veiled [hidden], it is veiled to those who are perishing, whose MINDS the god [satan] of this age has blinded, who do not believe, lest the light of the gospel of the glory of Christ, who is the image of God, should shine on them." (2 Cor. 4:3,4)

Do you see it? We were conceived in sin and shaped in iniquity. Because of sin, we grow up in the natural world with a blind-

THE OPERATIVE

fold over our <u>spiritual mind's eye</u> so that we cannot see the truth, mainly because we do not know that it exists. Man's intellect has no choice but to take over and try and figure out what is right and wrong for themselves.

This spiritual mind's eye (the seeing eye that God created in each of us) is connected to our brains via our soul (the seat of all our emotions and feelings). Our soul is connected to our spirit (that which knows).

It takes the <u>Holy Spirit</u> to remove this blindfold, so the light of the glorious gospel of Christ is shown to us, because no man comes to Jesus except when they are called or drawn by <u>Him.</u>

"No one can come to Me unless the Father who sent Me draws him; and I will raise him up at the last day." (John 6:44)

It's the <u>Holy Spirit</u> who does the convincing men (inclusive) of sin, righteousness, and judgment. *He* alone is given the power to remove that blindfold, <u>as they give Him permission to do so!</u>

It is the <u>Holy Spirit</u> who also gives the godly sorrow needed for one to see who they are, in the light of who Jesus is, with the end result being for you to call upon Jesus's name to be saved.

"For godly sorrow produces repentance leading to salvation, not to be regretted; but the sorrow of the world produces death." (2 Cor. 7:10)

"But without faith it is impossible to please Him, for he who comes to God must believe that He is, and that He is a rewarder of those who diligently seek Him." (Heb. 11:6)

What do all these scriptures about the *mind* have to do with the fruit of the Spirit of Jesus called *peace*? Excellent question—let's find out, shall we?

As seen from the scriptures above, we find that our *mind* is the battleground of our faith in God. We either win or lose battles right there.

"Likewise the Spirit also helps in our weaknesses. For we do not know what we should pray for as we ought, but the Spirit Himself makes intercession for us with groanings which cannot be uttered. Now He who searches the hearts knows what the mind of the Spirit is, because He makes intercession for the saints according to the will of God." (Rom. 8:26–27)

As we pray in the Holy Spirit or in tongues, this allows the one praying to pray the will of God in all matters concerning them, because the Holy Spirit knows the will of the Father. Believers praying in tongues are building up themselves on their most holy faith.

You are not only having the love of God poured into you when you pray in the spirit, but also the faith of Jesus is growing stronger inside you each time you do.

This faith is the faith of Jesus that brings the *peace* of God to us, which keeps both our hearts and minds through the presence of Jesus's Holy Spirit's fruit of *peace*.

The Greek word here for *peace* is "*eirene* (i-ray'-nay); probably from a primary verb *eiro* (to join); peace (literally or figuratively); by implication, prosperity: KJV—one, peace, quietness, rest, set at one again."

Webster's Dictionary defines *peace* as the following:

1. n. A state of quiet; freedom from disturbance; calm.
2. Public quiet, order, and security.
3. Harmony between peaceful persons or nations.

This is the same peace of God that comes to Jerusalem and that we are commanded to pray for. Have you ever wondered who is driving all the hatred against the Jews? It is the devil himself, because he knows that those who pray for and love Jerusalem will prosper. This infuriates him!

When God answers these prayers, Jerusalem finally receives the *peace* of God during the one thousand years of *peace* spoken of in the book of Revelation. This *peace* begins after the tribulation period and ends prior to the battle of Armageddon. Those who love and pray for Jerusalem will be reigning in *peace* with Jesus as well for those one thousand years.

"*Pray for the peace of Jerusalem: May they prosper who love you. Peace be within your walls, Prosperity within your palaces. For the sake of my brethren and companions, I will now say, 'Peace be within you.' Because of the house of the LORD our God I will seek your good.'" (Ps. 122:6–9)*

THE OPERATIVE

For this very reason, I know the world cannot be destroyed until after the battle of Armageddon. Ask yourself, if the last trumpet of God would sound today, activating the rapture of the Church, would you be in the number of believers who would receive their glorified bodies and meet with the Lord in the air? I sure hope so, for your eternal well-being! After the rapture of the body of Christ, it still will take an additional one thousand and seven years before this world is destroyed by fire and never seen again. This truth is contained in the Bible and is how I know of this as reality.

Peace—is it any wonder, then, that when a trial or test comes to us, this is the first fruit to be attacked? The devil knows that if he can steal (John 10:10) the *peace* in our *minds*, then in our *hearts* (spirit men), who we really are, along with our bodies, we will most likely fall prey to the lies and deceptions he offers, and he is more likely to have a victory over the believer. Once our *peace* is gone, all other fruit struggle to get back into the fight.

But God has His Holy Spirit teaching us how to reverse this process by being transformed by the renewing of our minds. Instead of our minds telling us what to feel and believe, we acquire the knowledge of God's word while feeding on it as truth or knowing the correct way of living within our new inner man.

The new man (you and me), who is being renewed daily, accepts the word of God as truth telling his brain, "GOD SAID IT, THAT SETTLES IT, AND OH, BY THE WAY, I CHOOSE TO BELIEVE IT!" Now, this new man will gauge all matters by comparing them to what the Bible has to say about the topic concerning day-to-day living.

"And do not be conformed to this world, but be transformed by the renewing of your mind, that you may prove what is that good and acceptable and perfect will of God." (Rom. 12:2)

The carnal or fleshly mind's way is for us to gather information through our five senses. We are even taught this early in school (seeing, hearing, smelling, tasting, and touching). Then we process this information in our brains, and the things that we like best we accept as truth to build our own belief systems or a code to live by. This is great for learning how to operate in the world that we live. However, this method falls way short of God's best for us. It actually short-circuits faith in our lives by the countless religious beliefs steeped in man's own theories of what's right and what's wrong. They each have their way and always speak to the outward man and his fleshly desires.

But God's way for us is to see and hear with our spiritual eye (seeing) and our spiritual ear (hearing), concerning the processing of the knowledge of His word. Faith to believe and accept His word as truth, allows us to receive His promises as yes and amen. Faith, once activated by hearing the word of God, <u>comes alive</u>. Faith alive now becomes the director of truth in our spirit (inner man).

Our new spirit is designed to receive the word of God as truth, sending it back to our brain through our soul, informing them both that this is the truth from here on out. Our <u>soul</u> yields either to whatever our brain tells it is truth or to whatever our new spirit tells it is truth that has been received from God's word.

This is why our <u>soul</u> needs to be saved! It is helpless in direction and always needs help to process what is truth. This is also why we cannot trust our feelings and emotions, especially during spiritual battles. They too can lie to us and be very contrary to the word of God.

See why it is important for us to find out what God says about our lives in the Bible? Instead of working in our salvation from the outside (everything we see, hear, smell, taste, and touch), we are commanded to work out our salvation with fear (reverence to God) and trembling. These outward things are temporary and will pass away, but the <u>words of faith</u> speaking to our spirit are eternal and will never pass away.

I am convinced that many believers in Christ *do not* know the process of being transformed, living out just the opposite, allowing their minds to tell them what is truth from the world's point of view, when they should be allowing the new man inside them to tell them what is truth from the word of God. This struggle is evident, as I see so many who quit believing.

"Therefore, if anyone is in Christ, he is a new creation; old things have passed away; behold, all things have become new." (2 Cor. 5:17)

THE OPERATIVE

This is why it is pertinent that we have the Holy Spirit's characteristics (power, gifts, and fruit of the Holy Spirit) maturing and operating inside each believer in Christ. Our new spirit recognizes each of them as the substance of Jesus, and as they mature in us, we are more capable to draw from their strength and power, enabling us to respond more like Jesus. But what if I, as a believer, am not aware of this?

Of course, this is a progressive lifestyle common in each believer's life. To date I am unaware of any person on earth who has reached total maturity in Christ. However, this level of maturity will happen to each of us when the rapture of the Church takes place, as we receive our glorified bodies.

"Behold, I tell you a mystery: We shall not all sleep, but we shall all be changed—in a moment, in the twinkling of an eye, at the last trumpet. For the trumpet will sound, and the dead will be raised incorruptible, and we shall be changed. For this corruptible must put on incorruption, and this mortal must put on immortality. So when this corruptible has put on incorruption, and this mortal has put on immortality, then shall be brought to pass the saying that is written: 'Death is swallowed up in victory.' 'O Death, where is your sting? O Hades, where is your victory?'" (1 Cor. 15:51–55)

"For if we believe that Jesus died and rose again, even so God will bring with Him those who sleep in Jesus. For this we say to you by the word of the Lord, that we who are alive and remain until the coming of the Lord will by no means precede those who are asleep. For the Lord Himself will descend from heaven with a shout, with the voice of an archangel, and with the trumpet of God. And the dead in Christ will rise first. Then we who are alive and remain shall be caught up together with them in the clouds to meet the Lord in the air. And thus we shall always be with the Lord. Therefore, comfort one another with these words." (1 Thess. 4:14–18)

The words *transformed* and *changed* are the same Greek word that was used when Jesus was transfigured on the mount. The same original Greek meaning also applies to the transforming of our minds, and we shall be changed—changed from glory to glory. These are actually the same Greek word used as follows:

"*metamorphoo* (met-am-or-fo'-o); to transform (literally or figuratively, "metamorphose"): KJV—change, transfigure, transform."

I do not believe that we just all disappear when the rapture takes place. Nothing within this word implies that we disappear, but it does say that we will be changed, transformed, and even transfigured, just like Jesus was on the mount.

Jesus said that the last days would be as in the days of Noah. In Noah's day, *everyone* who was not on the *ark* when it started to rain and flood realized their mistake of not believing Noah, as he preached righteousness to them. As they witnessed Noah and his family with all the animals safely on the ark, their mistake was made reality to them while they were treading water and drowning. By then, it was too late.

For *now*, it is *not too late*! The same thing will happen when the rapture takes place. I don't want one of you to be late and miss out on the *goodness* of God. Do *not* make the biggest mistake of your life by not believing or by stopping to believe and going back into the world.

Remember the famous painting of planes crashing and cars wrecking that I am sure that most Christians have seen? I am sorry, but this is just not true to the word of God for this reason. We do not disappear.

If a pilot is a believer, when the rapture takes place and he or she is flying a plane, he or she will not disappear, *but* his or her body *will be* changed or transfigured into his glorious body like Jesus's. So I ask you, why would he or she not first safely land the plane? I am sure that there will be plenty of unsaved people with him on the plane. Do you think he would let them die? I *do not* believe that he or she would! This reasoning also applies to believers who are operating trains and cars, etc. I believe the word of God backs me up on this thinking.

It may not be as dramatic, but it certainly will be just as eventful. For those trying to figure out what they are seeing, which are all the glorified bodies with Jesus in the sky, it will be a time like none other this world has ever seen.

THE OPERATIVE

You are now equipped with the scriptures concerning us being changed and <u>not</u> disappearing. Next, scriptures show us that <u>all</u> eyes are going to see Him when He returns! All unbelievers, who <u>will not</u> hear the last trumpet of God and <u>will not</u> be changed will see Jesus and His body of believers. Here are the scriptures to back this up:

"Behold, He is coming with clouds, and every eye will see Him, even they who pierced Him. And all the tribes of the earth will mourn because of Him. Even so, Amen." (Rev. 1:7)

"Now when He had spoken these things, while they watched, He was taken up, and a cloud received Him out of their sight. And while they looked steadfastly toward heaven as He went up, behold, two men stood by them in white apparel, who also said, 'Men of Galilee, why do you stand gazing up into heaven? This same Jesus, who was taken up from you into heaven, will so come in like manner as you saw Him go into heaven." (Acts 1:9-11)

"Then we who are alive and remain shall be caught up together with them in the clouds to meet the Lord in the air. And thus we shall always be with the Lord. Therefore comfort one another with these words." (1 Thess. 4:17, 18)

Revelation 1:7 reveals that during this event, *all* living people at the time of the rapture and all those who previously rejected God (that is, even they who pierced him—speaking of all those who have already died and are in hell, waiting judgement) will see Jesus and us together. For what period of time He allows this to be, only Jesus knows. But we will be seen by those whom we have been witnessing to, working alongside of, or living as neighbors who did not accept Jesus as their Savior.

Our precise location when the trumpet sounds obviously determines who will see us. Once we hear the trumpet, and those in the grave are raised first to receive their glorified bodies, we who are alive will receive our glorified bodies as well.

This happens so fast that it is in a twinkling of an eye. ("If something happens in the twinkling of an eye, it happens very quickly: Microprocessors do the calculations in the twinkling of an eye.")[8]

---

8. *Cambridge Dictionary Online*

Based upon these truths, which are considered facts that are found in the scriptures, we will be changed to look just like Jesus in milliseconds. All who remain will be as those in the days of Noah, realizing their folly and concluding very quickly that they have made the biggest mistake of their life, by not believing in Jesus Christ as their Savior.

There is always time to take care of spiritual matters, many think. However, the time for preparation for their eternal well-being is still available for *now* and has not come and gone. The rapture of the Church will happen; have you made your preparations?

Our focus should be, while we still live here on earth, that we are to be more like Him than ourselves. As we go through trials and tests, it will be the force of His Holy Spirit's fruit or character called *peace* that will bring us on the other side of them!

This is not the false peace the world gives, which is usually the peace we lose so quickly when our adversity comes, but the *peace* of God that passes all human knowledge and comprehension. This is why some feel like a failure when they cannot overcome certain things in their life. They are not applying the *peace* of the Holy Spirit's fruit that is growing within them.

This power, the force of *peace*—God's *peace*—keeps our minds through Christ Jesus, thus guarding our heart (spirit), which, in turn, keeps our bodies healthier without worry or fret. This *peace* keeps us away from the cares of this world, which Jesus said robs our seed of the word, thus not producing any fruit in our lives.

"Now these are the ones sown among thorns; they are the ones who hear the word, and the cares of this world, the deceitfulness of riches, and the desires for other things entering in choke the word, and it becomes unfruitful." (Mark 4:18,19)

THE OPERATIVE

I am reminded here also of the whole armor of God in Ephesians:

"Finally, my brethren, be strong in the Lord and in the POWER of His might. Put on the whole armor of God, that you may be able to stand against the wiles of the devil. For we do not wrestle against flesh and blood, but against principalities, against powers, against the rulers of the darkness of this age, against spiritual hosts of wickedness in the heavenly places. Therefore, take up the whole armor of God, that you may be able to withstand in the evil day, and having done all, to stand.

Stand therefore, having girded your waist with truth, having put on the breastplate of righteousness, and having shod your feet with the preparation of the gospel of peace; above all, taking the shield of faith with which you will be able to quench all the fiery darts of the wicked one. And take the helmet of salvation, and the sword of the Spirit, which is the word of God; praying always with all prayer and supplication in the Spirit, being watchful to this end with all perseverance and supplication for all the saints." (Eph. 6:10–18)

There are three armor parts that I want to point out in this lesson that are very important to put on (or apply) during our daily lives and especially through the trials and tests that come our way. Each of them is given to us because of the wonderful works of God, through Jesus, that were completed at Calvary.

- Armor part number 1. Helmet of Salvation (covers the head, which houses our minds).
- Armor part number 2. Breastplate of Righteousness (this does not come from our good works but from the very righteousness of Jesus Himself as a gift guarding our heart).
- Armor part number 3. This one is usually overlooked the most because it involves praying in tongues (praying always with all prayer and supplication in the Spirit).

Both our *minds* and our *hearts* are protected here with the first two armor parts. However, the third part of our armor, which is praying in the Spirit, provides protection for other people as well as us. Many believers are not using this armor because they do not believe in being filled with the Holy Spirit with the evidence of speaking in tongues. But there it is—proof right there before your eyes. Now, what will you do with it?

Perhaps, Ephesians 6:18 is another scripture that has been discarded as God's inspired word or has passed away with the disciples of Christ. I know that there are many within the Church today that when they read about the whole armor of God, this section is not applied to their life. It only has one meaning with one understanding, and that is those speaking in tongues are praying in the Spirit (Holy Spirit) directly to God, as First Corinthians 14 teaches and the book of Acts reveals.

This then means that there are many Christians who are not fully dressed for battle. Is it any wonder why they are not winning more battles? Always calling upon others to pray for this or pray for that in their lives, they have become dependent upon what others do for them, instead of being totally dependent upon what Jesus has already accomplished for them and applying it to their lives.

I tell you, this is mainly due to poor training or none at all within the Church. This is another example of the Holy Spirit of Jesus being grieved by not allowing Him to perform His responsibilities in a believer's life.

Our feet are also to be shod with the preparation of the gospel (knowing the word, both written and living), loins girded about with truth (Jesus is truth), and sword of the Spirit (Holy Spirit–inspired word of God) in our mouths as confession unto salvation, including tongues.

"For with the heart one believes unto righteousness, and with the mouth confession is made unto salvation." (Rom. 10:10) I submit to you that this also includes tongues, not as a prerequisite of proof of salvation, but included as part of salvation's fruit of righteousness and proof as to whether or not you are filled with Jesus's Holy Spirit.

It is the fruit of the Holy Spirit's *peace*—which is designed by God to guard both our *minds* and *hearts*, the two most important areas of our being—that keeps our faith intact. Is this part of our confession of things that we believe and, therefore, we speak?

All the spiritual armor found in Ephesians work in unison, and as each are put on (applied), you will find that we should also be

THE OPERATIVE

praying always with <u>all prayer and supplication in the Spirit</u>, being watchful to this end with all perseverance and supplication for all the saints.

The Holy Spirit has His own fire triangle as well:

1. Power from baptism.
2. His gifts (including tongues).
3. His fruit. (Remove any one of these three, and you eliminate the Holy Spirit, in part, from the equation of your faith and from the capacity that God and Jesus want Him to be.)

This Holy Spirit's fire triangle is for our protection, as we grow in the grace and knowledge, while renewing our minds from the ways of the world that we were trained in from birth to the ways and words of God since our rebirth.

Praying in the Spirit or being baptized in the Holy Spirit with the evidence of speaking in tongues is where this book *The Operative* was birthed. It is the Holy Spirit praying through me, making intercessions for all the saints, and manifesting the will of God, including for the one doing the praying. The time that I have spent in praying in the Holy Spirit has brought forth the revelations that are contained in here for you to benefit from.

"Likewise the Spirit also helps in our weaknesses. For we do not know what we should pray for as we ought, but the Spirit Himself makes intercession for us with groanings which cannot be uttered. Now He who searches the HEARTS knows what the MIND of the Spirit is, because He makes intercession for the saints according to the will of God." (Rom. 8:26–27)

<u>I do not think we can read or hear this scripture enough!</u> It needs to be read and reread again and again. It needs to be prayed about, meditated upon, and communicated with the Holy Spirit until it becomes so much a part of us that praying in the Spirit is as necessary to each believer as breathing is.

Now, I ask you, who would you prefer praying for you—a person who is lacking in the things of the Holy Spirit or a person full of the Holy Spirit and who knows the things concerning the Holy Spirit?

This is easy for me to answer. I want the one who is full of the Holy Spirit and who knows the things concerning the Holy Spirit and God's will praying for me—the one filled with the Holy Spirit who knows the secrets of the heart and mind, the one who prays directly to God in the Father's language that no man understands, but God Himself! I want the one praying for me in the Spirit, even when they do not even know that they are praying for me.

If I had only one person in the world who is praying for me in the Spirit, I would have all I need, even if that one person, sometimes, is only me. I would rather have *peace* and comfort in knowing that the will of God will be done in my life, instead of having one thousand people praying one thousand different prayers (their wills) of what they think I need from God. Some of them might think I need a good clubbing from the Lord. Be careful for whom you ask to pray for you.

I know, by the scriptures, that one can put a thousand to flight and that two can put ten thousand to flight. This spiritual principle is true. Since I am talking about the spirit realm, I do not trust just anyone to pray for my well-being. Do you?

This is why a spirit-filled husband-and-wife team is so powerful and so dangerous to the devil. You can claim the two, putting ten thousand to flight, and also claim the threefold status by having the third prayer partner, which is the Holy Spirit. <u>It's a win-win situation no matter how you look at it!</u>

When it comes to the Holy Spirit of Jesus and God the Father, there is no disconnection. Being filled with the Holy Spirit with the evidence of tongues, operating in the gifts of the Holy Spirit, being one of the apostles, prophets, evangelists, pastors, and teachers, with each believer having all these and the fruit of the Holy Spirit, the flow of power should be the same. They each are connected by the resurrection power of the Holy Spirit to do whatever task is placed before them by Jesus's Holy Spirit.

What we believe about the Father, Son, and Holy Spirit either releases the miraculous power of the wonderful works of God toward men or not. Being filled, receiving gifts, and allowing the fruit or character of the Holy Spirit growing inside us—all come from the same God, the same Son, and the same Holy Spirit.

Take a good, long, and honest look at the Church today. Do you see the unity and maturity of *Ephesians 4:11–16*, or can you see a lot of dissecting? Verses and paragraphs are actually being ignored as if they were literally torn out of the Bible. One denomination believes this but not that, and another believes that but not this. I tell you, brethren, this should not be so!

When I read the Bible, then compare today's Church, I see two different churches. The first church I see in the Bible is the spiritual church with power and unity. This church is the one we should be simulating.

I see many of today's churches whose operating leans more along the lines of a natural church, each having worldly points of view of what the Bible is saying. By having their own opinions and interpretations, they have created mini churches throughout the world with no unity of faith or power. (As with everything, there are exceptions to the rule.)

Each has its own denominational constitution and bylaws to satisfy governmental standards for a nonprofit organization. In some cases, the constitution and bylaws are held in a higher esteem than the Bible itself. This should not be either!

These traditions, which are no less than private interpretations of the Bible, remove the power from God's word. According to scriptures, there should be no private interpretations when it comes to understanding the Bible.

"Knowing this first, that no prophecy of Scripture [which is all scripture] is of any private interpretation, for prophecy never came by the will of man, but holy men of God spoke as they were moved by the Holy Spirit." (2 Peter 1:20–21)

The Bible is *the* inspired *word* of *God* by the Holy Spirit, and it must be Him who gives the interpretations and understanding of it, according to the scriptures and not according to denominational points of view.

Paul realized this when he was first born again and did not go to men for instructions, but to the Holy Spirit who filled him. The Holy Spirit led him away from the traditions that governed and held him captive as his tutor for his entire life.

"But when it pleased God, who separated me from my mother's womb and called me through His grace, to reveal His Son in me, that I might preach Him among the Gentiles, I did not immediately confer with flesh and blood, nor did I go up to Jerusalem to those who were apostles before me; but I went to Arabia, and returned again to Damascus. Then after three years I went up to Jerusalem to see Peter, and remained with him fifteen days. But I saw none of the other apostles except James, the Lord's brother." (Gal. 1:15–19)

From where did Paul receive all his revelations? The Holy Spirit whom he was filled with, of course! While praying in tongues, God gave him interpretations of the tongues by and from the Holy Spirit (revelation knowledge).

Please do not misunderstand me; I am not against the structured denominations. However, we the Church must get to the point that we no longer care about the tax status with the IRS, as well as each believer regarding their tax deduction for their gifts. What if the tax-exempt status were no longer allowed? Would the Church still operate accordingly? What if each believer could no longer file tax returns, claiming gifts given to the Church as a tax deduction, would they still give?

The worldly system of denominational diversity that the Church finds itself in did not come from God's design of how she is supposed to be operating in the world. By now, I would hope that you have seen the real design of God, concerning the Church's operation and responsibility to Jesus. Someone with all authority once said, *"A house divided cannot stand."* Are we the Church standing firm in the Lord?

Working in the *unity* of *faith* is the key. Unity of faith comes from allowing Jesus's Holy Spirit to reveal His truths to us, enabling us to apply them personally and collectively as the Church. *No* one denomination has total authority over the truth. To the contrary, the *truth* (Jesus) should have total authority over the denominations.

THE OPERATIVE

Revelation knowledge of the Holy Spirit—which Jesus said He would build His Church with and that the gates of hell would not prevail against—still holds true for today. Take a good look around you. Honestly ask yourself, who appears to be prevailing—the Church or the gates of hell? Is the power of *peace* prevalent within the Church today or an illusion of it?

The fruit of *peace* means "peace (literally or figuratively); by implication, prosperity: one, peace, quietness, rest, set at one again, a state of quiet; freedom from disturbance; calm, public quiet, order, and security, harmony between peaceful persons or nations." The question, then, begs to be asked: how are we doing?

Start by asking yourself these questions, and be honest about your answers:

1. Are America's churches filled with believers full of the Holy Spirit, speaking in tongues as the evidence, according to the scriptures found in the Bible?
2. Are Jesus's characteristics coming to the forefront in power, or are we operating within our own strengths and abilities?
3. Are we showing the world our unity among us, regardless of which denominational church we support?
4. Is His Church operating in unity of faith, as one body, the way the Bible teaches and instructs us to be?

If your answers are all yes to all four, then we all are doing and saying the same things. There would no further need for apostles, prophets, evangelists, pastors, or teachers and no further need for the equipping the saints for the work of ministry. We would have a sufficient number of equipped saints to edify the body of Christ to be all she is supposed to be, ready for Christ to come back for His bride.

If this were true, that all believers are in the unity of faith, then wouldn't we have heard the last trump of God for the rapture by now so that all believers can be changed? But I believe that your truthful answers were *no* to each of the four questions above.

So for how long will we need all the Holy Spirit's gifts, His fruit, and the gifts of anointed men and women given by Jesus's Holy Spirit? Only God knows the exact time or hour, but His word reveals enough insight for us to continue His *way* of training the members of the body of Christ. As a matter of fact, we are nowhere near the unity of faith and the knowledge of the Son of God:

"Till we all come to the unity of the faith and of the knowledge of the Son of God, to a perfect [mature] man, to the measure of the stature of the fullness of Christ; that we should no longer be children, tossed to and fro and carried about with every wind of doctrine, by the trickery of men, in the cunning craftiness of deceitful plotting, but, speaking the truth in love, may grow up in all things into Him who is the head—Christ—from whom the whole body, joined and knit together by what every joint supplies, according to the effective working by which every part does its share, causes growth of the body for the edifying of itself in love." (Eph. 4:15-16)

Are we there yet? *Of course not!* But this is in our control, as we allow the Holy Spirit His place in our lives and our Churches. Since the rapture has not taken place, there is still great need for the miraculous, wonderful works of God and still a need for called and anointed men and women to fill positions of accountability directly to Jesus.

There is still need for men and women operating with the Holy Spirit, allowing His gifts to be released through them to prosper them (more than just money) and others <u>for the world to see.</u> There's, definitely, still the need for the fruit of the Holy Spirit, maturing in each of us while we grow up to the measure of the stature of the fullness of Christ in us.

Peace is the fruit that has the power to sustain us through these chains of events and the storms of life. *Peace* gives us calmness like Jesus, so we too can sleep in the back of the boat even though it is filling up with water from the storms and winds of life.

The *peace* of God is able to keep our minds and hearts through Christ Jesus, as we each become more like Him. We need His *peace* in making our decisions. As we follow His peace during His directions and assignments, we know that faith never depends on our understanding. Faith depends on the finished work of Jesus and His *peace* that will always see us through.

THE OPERATIVE

Are you taking advantage of this powerful force called *peace* that is the characteristic of Jesus Christ and His Spirit? If not, you can start today by asking Jesus to baptize or fill you with His Holy Spirit, allowing this *peace* to be brought to the forefront of your life!

Chapter 23 gives us insight into the fruit of *long-suffering*. It's not a popular fruit like love, joy, or peace. It is, however, a needful substance of Jesus's character in us to be able to endure. As you continue reading, you will find some benefits of *long-suffering* and a gauge on whether you have this fruit growing in you or not.

Since help exists for us during trials and tests, then it seems to me that this is why we have them in the first place. When trials and tests come, they apply pressure to the fruit of the Holy Spirit in us. This applied pressure is what causes the fruit to grow stronger and more mature. It's the exact same principle as lifting weights. The lifting and exercising tear muscle tissue, only for it to grow back stronger than before.

The process of the fruit of the Spirit is similar in that when the pressures of life are applied, they press us in such a way that when the trial is over, the fruit is stronger than before, allowing others to see our spiritual growth.

How strong and mature are your love, joy, peace, and *long-suffering*? Let's continue to search deeper and see, shall we?

CHAPTER 23

Fruit of the Holy Spirit
LONG-SUFFERING

"But the fruit of the Spirit is love, joy, peace, LONGSUFFERING, kindness, goodness, faithfulness, gentleness, self-control. Against such there is no law." (Gal. 5:22, 23)

Long-suffering is the one fruit that many people do not want to have operating in their lives, mainly because of a lack of knowledge of what it really means. In reality we cannot get away from it, as it is the very character of God, Jesus, and His Holy Spirit. If Jesus is living in our hearts, it is a must that we partake of His fruit of *long-suffering*.

We sing a song that goes like this:

"To Be Like Jesus" by Ellen Gould Harmon White

> To be like Jesus,
> To be like Jesus,
> All I ask is to be like Him.
> All through life journeys,
> From earth to glory,
> All I ask is to be more like Him.

THE OPERATIVE

Did you know that Jesus is just like His Father God, and His Holy Spirit is too, and they are full of *long-suffering*? It is a characteristic of the Trinity, the Godhead body, that complete being of the Almighty God, Creator of the heavens and the earth.

You would think that the Bible would have this characteristic of God and Jesus and the fruit of the Holy Spirit spoken of many times. But in reality, from cover to cover, *long-suffering* is only mentioned sixteen times. The following are each of the scriptures that mention this character of the Trinity. Let's see how they reveal to us, concerning the fruit of *long-suffering*:

1. *"And the LORD passed before him and proclaimed, 'The LORD, the LORD God, merciful and gracious, longsuffering, and abounding in goodness and truth, keeping mercy for thousands, forgiving iniquity and transgression and sin, by no means clearing the guilty, visiting the iniquity of the fathers upon the children and the children's children to the third and the fourth generation.'" (Ex. 34:6,7)*

2. *"The LORD is longsuffering and abundant in mercy, forgiving iniquity and transgression; but He by no means clears the guilty, visiting the iniquity of the fathers on the children to the third and fourth generation." (Num. 14:18)*

3. *"But You, O Lord, are a God full of compassion, and gracious, Longsuffering and abundant in mercy and truth." (Ps. 86:15)*

4. *"Or do you despise the riches of His goodness, forbearance, and longsuffering, not knowing that the goodness of God leads you to repentance?" (Rom. 2:4)*

5. *"What if God, wanting to show His wrath and to make His power known, endured with much longsuffering the vessels of wrath prepared for destruction, and that He might make known the riches of His glory on the vessels of mercy, which He had prepared beforehand for glory, even us whom He called, not of the Jews only, but also of the Gentiles?" (Rom. 9:22–24)*

6. *"We give no offense in anything, that our ministry may not be blamed. But in all things we commend ourselves as ministers of God: in much patience, in tribulations, in needs, in dis-*

tresses, in stripes, in imprisonments, in tumults, in labors, in sleeplessness, in fastings; by purity, by knowledge, by longsuffering, by kindness, by the Holy Spirit, by sincere love, by the word of truth, by the power of God, by the armor of righteousness on the right hand and on the left, by honor and dishonor, by evil report and good report; as deceivers, and yet true; as unknown, and yet well known; as dying, and behold we live; as chastened, and yet not killed; as sorrowful, yet always rejoicing; as poor, yet making many rich; as having nothing, and yet possessing all things." (2 Cor. 6:3–10)

7. *"But the fruit of the Spirit is love, joy, peace, longsuffering, kindness, goodness, faithfulness, gentleness, self-control. Against such there is no law." (Gal. 5:22–24)*

8. *"I, therefore, the prisoner of the Lord, beseech you to walk worthy of the calling with which you were called, with all lowliness and gentleness, with longsuffering, bearing with one another in love, endeavoring to keep the unity of the Spirit in the bond of peace." (Eph. 4:1–3)*

9. *"For this reason we also, since the day we heard it, do not cease to pray for you, and to ask that you may be filled with the knowledge of His will in all wisdom and spiritual understanding; that you may walk worthy of the Lord, fully pleasing Him, being fruitful in every good work and increasing in the knowledge of God; strengthened with all might, according to His glorious power, for all patience and longsuffering with joy; giving thanks to the Father who has qualified us to be partakers of the inheritance of the saints in the light." (Col. 1:9–12)*

10. *"Therefore, as the elect of God, holy and beloved, put on tender mercies, kindness, humility, meekness, longsuffering; bearing with one another, and forgiving one another, if anyone has a complaint against another; even as Christ forgave you, so you also must do." (Col. 3:12,13)*

11. *"However, for this reason I obtained mercy, that in me first Jesus Christ might show all longsuffering, as a pattern to those*

THE OPERATIVE

who are going to believe on Him for everlasting life." (1 Tim. 1:16)

12. *"But you have carefully followed my doctrine, manner of life, purpose, faith, longsuffering, love, perseverance, persecutions, afflictions, which happened to me at Antioch, at Iconium, at Lystra—what persecutions I endured. And out of them all the Lord delivered me." (2 Tim. 3:10,11)*
13. *"Preach the word! Be ready in season and out of season. Convince, rebuke, exhort, with all longsuffering and teaching." (2 Tim. 4:2)*
14. *"For Christ also suffered once for sins, the just for the unjust, that He might bring us to God, being put to death in the flesh but made alive by the Spirit, by whom also He went and preached to the spirits in prison, who formerly were disobedient, when once the Divine longsuffering waited in the days of Noah, while the ark was being prepared, in which a few, that is, eight souls, were saved through water." (1 Peter 3:18–20)*
15. *"The Lord is not slack concerning His promise, as some count slackness, but is longsuffering toward us, not willing that any should perish but that all should come to repentance." (2 Peter 3:9)*
16. *"Therefore, beloved, looking forward to these things, be diligent to be found by Him in peace, without spot and blameless; and consider that the longsuffering of our Lord is salvation— as also our beloved brother Paul, according to the wisdom given to him, has written to you, as also in all his epistles, speaking in them of these things, in which are some things hard to understand, which untaught and unstable people twist to their own destruction, as they do also the rest of the Scriptures." (2 Peter 3:14–16)*

The Hebrew meaning of what the Old Testament scriptures use in numbers 1–3 for the word *long-suffering* is as follows:

Long-suffering is made from two words—(1) "*'arek* (aw-rake'); long: KJV—long [-suffering, -winged], patient, slow [to anger]" (OT:750) and (2) "*'aph* (af); properly, the nose or nostril; hence, the face, and occasionally a person; also (from the rapid breathing in passion) ire: KJV—anger (-gry), before, countenance, face, forebearing, forehead, [long-] suffering, nose, nostril, snout, worthy, wrath" (OT:639).

The Greek word for *long-suffering* in the New Testament numbers 4–16 are as follow:

> "*makrothumia* (mak-roth-oo-mee'-ah); from the same as NT:3116*; longanimity, i.e. (objectively) forbearance or (subjectively) fortitude" (NT:3115).
> *"*makrothumos* (mak-roth-oo-moce'); adverb of a compound of NT:3117** and NT:2372; with long (enduring) temper, i.e. leniently" (NT:3116).
> **"*makros* (mak-ros'); from NT:2372***; long (in place [distant] or time [neuter plural]): KJV—far, long" (NT:3117).
> ***"*thumos* (thoo-mos'); passion (as if breathing hard): KJV—fierceness, indignation, wrath" (NT:2372).

As you can see, the Greek and Hebrew words are derivatives of other root words. Looking deeper gives us a clearer picture of what's being said by the Holy Spirit and by those inspired by Him. They wrote powerful and meaningful words that were intended for us to learn and to live by.

Based on this information, what definition could *we* assign to the fruit *long-suffering*? Let's start with the Old Testament. When it comes to this characteristic of God, He is "patient and slow to anger as He holds back His wrath as if through His controlled breathing."

Have you ever had something or someone make you angry? Your pulse increased, as you breathed harder, fighting to gain control of your composure to keep from doing what you actually wanted to do at that time, by controlling your anger and temper. Keeping our composure is not always an easy thing to do. However, when accomplished, this is a form of *long-suffering*.

The Old Testament words describe what the *long-suffering* of God is. They reveal that He keeps in check that which He knows one day must come and will come. Until the right age and time period, His grace and mercy are provided to all the whosoevers that call upon Jesus's name to be saved.

THE OPERATIVE

This is what keeps us today from His wrath to come. We have asked for His grace, mercy, and forgiveness, and He has given them to all who have asked. We are spared from His wrath to come. His wrath will be poured out upon nonbelievers who remain after the period of the rapture.

Only those *not* taking the mark of the beast will lose their lives by beheading; by doing so, they will gain God's grace for their eternal salvation. They too will escape His wrath to come.

"And I saw thrones, and they sat on them, and judgment was committed to them. Then I saw the souls of those who had been beheaded for their witness to Jesus and for the word of God, who had not worshiped the beast or his image, and had not received his mark on their foreheads or on their hands. And they lived and reigned with Christ for a thousand years." (Rev. 20:4)

However, I do not advise this course of action of taking a chance to wait till then to obtain your salvation. This period of time may not take place within your lifetime. Even if it does, there is *no* guarantee that you will have the strength not to take the mark of the beast, if the consequences are that you lose your head and life. If you cannot call upon Him now to be saved with a full stomach, how hard will it be when hunger pains are so strong for you and your family, gnawing at your stomach, and you cannot buy or sell anything without that mark of the beast?

Friends, do not put off your eternal well-being, not one moment longer. Can you hear the Holy Spirit saying, "Today is the day of salvation, now is the accepted time"? Call upon Jesus while He may be found!

Let's now take a look at the New Testament meanings for *long-suffering*. Based on the Greek words and a couple of their root words, we can safely say that the New Testament brings out <u>not only the Trinity</u> as having *long-suffering*, but also the fact that we, the believers, are supposed to be living and operating with this fruit as well. Here is my definition of the New Testament *long-suffering*, with a touch of the Old Testament included:

God the Father, through Jesus, His Son, and by His Holy Spirit's power, wisdom, and knowledge, is growing the fruit or character of the Trinity inside His believers, called *long-suffering*. This fruit gives His believers the ability to be slow to anger, forbearing all that is brought to us into a state of fortitude and security in Him, giving us the ability to endure leniently* for whatever time it takes, withholding our temper and anger from exacting revenge by and for ourselves.

*adverb of *lenient*—adjective

1. agreeably tolerant; permissive; indulgent:
(He tended to be lenient toward the children.
More lenient laws encouraged greater freedom of expression.)
2. Archaic. softening, soothing, or alleviative
Dictionary.com

Long-suffering is not that we are always suffering. Suffering can and does happen on occasion. It is not the suffering as much as it is enduring the hardships and the rigors of life with graciousness and mercy instead of anguish and pain. Even waiting until our prayers are answered requires *long-suffering*.

Contained within these original words are the meanings used by the writers so we can understand how connected each of the fruit (singular) is to one another! Do you think that *long-suffering* is connected to the fruit of self-control, which is coming up? You bet it is! Each layer of each fruit morphs into one another, providing us with the continuity of His power!

Long-suffering gives us an insight into the meanings and reasons of having the remaining fruit of the Holy Spirit maturing in us. We will see that this wisdom of the fruit of the Holy Spirit is profound!

Are we allowing *long-suffering* to come to the forefront in our lives? The longer we live, the more opportunities we have to reveal His fruit or character to others, and the stronger and more noticeable it becomes within our spirit.

As others judge the Holy Spirit's fruit of *long-suffering*, they may label it as weakness. But the Bible calls it powerful. Each of His fruit has the same purpose of a power-filled life. Each works in us as a benefit as well as a state of well-being, while showing Jesus to those who do not know Him as their Savior.

As Christians, we should identify one another by the fruit of the Holy Spirit, being revealed through us. Here is a crude example, but here goes. It's like going to a football game, and each side wears their team colors to identify with the side that they are on. We do this, as the fruit of the Holy Spirit reveals to others what side we are on.

The baptism of the Holy Spirit, the gifts of the Holy Spirit, or the fivefold ministry gifts all work together to mature us into a state of being that <u>we think, speak, act, and live</u> more like Jesus than we did the day before.

Personally, this growth process has been working in my life for over thirty-seven years. While it is a gradual work that has not always been visible, I look back to who I used to be and compare myself today; well, let's say, the old Jim is not recognizable anymore.

It's like he was somebody I used to know but lost contact with over the years. Just as it was in the foot-and-half of snow where I dropped to my knees for the first time, I finally saw who I was in the light of who Jesus <u>is,</u> and I still realize that I am becoming more like Jesus with each passing day. It's His power, gifts, and fruit growing stronger in us that mature us into *godly men* and *women* that He expects us to be. We, as parents, expect our children to grow up; why shouldn't God?

Through all my (our) trials, tests, temptations, torments (you know, the things that we do not want to go through in life), like Jesus, our example, in the garden, we pray, "Lord, not my will be done, but yours," knowing every time Jesus does not leave me (us) there. He always brings me (us) through on the other side. Truth is, until I (we) am with Him in heaven with my (our) glorified body, there will always be these garden experiences in my (our) life, giving us, as well as others, the opportunities to respond or react to them.

Jesus responded by saying nothing and doing everything by His actions. Peter reacted by drawing his sword and cutting off the ear of one of the soldiers who came to arrest Jesus. (See the difference?) Then Jesus responded by righting the wrong. He performed a miracle and made the soldier's ear whole again.

I am sure that with the knowledge you acquired as you read the above scriptures containing the word *long-suffering* and their meanings, you will not resist the Holy Spirit when it's time to allow His fruit of *long-suffering* to grow within your spirit and soul. You will embrace it and give Him opportunity for others to partake of His fruit in you.

Long-suffering, coupled with love, joy, and peace, allows us to enjoy the journey, as He leads us in the paths of righteousness. Knowing that He will never leave us alone, neither does He ever leave us where we find ourselves today. <u>That's growth with maturity!</u> Many believers mature physically, but are they maturing spiritually? That is the million-dollar question, is it not?

Chapter 24 gives us insight into the power of the next fruit called *kindness*. It is both refreshing and quite strengthening for one to experience the anointing of the Holy Spirit in this capacity.

Fact being, the teacher always gets taught first, and many times during the presentation, they too learn things not previously seen even by them. This is the process of growing in the grace and knowledge of our Lord and Savior, Jesus Christ.

Battles surely will continue to come to us because our adversary is always trying to get us off the faith and the steadfastness of God. But we have been given so many weapons of warfare that the devil desires to keep us in the dark, concerning them. Why? Because he loses more and more battles when we learn how to operate them against him, with all the weapons that God has made available to us, until he no longer has anything in us.

"I will no longer talk much with you, for the ruler of this world is coming, and he has nothing in Me." (John 14:30) To God be all the glory!

CHAPTER 24

Fruit of the Holy Spirit
KINDNESS

"But the fruit of the Spirit is love, joy, peace, longsuffering, KINDNESS, goodness, faithfulness, gentleness, self-control. Against such there is no law." (Gal. 5:23,33)

The fruit of *kindness* is next in our list of the fruit of the Holy Spirit that grows inside believers. Producing the character of Jesus Christ Himself in us for the world to see and partake of is part of His plan and purpose in allowing us to remain here on earth. Jesus revealed God the Father to mankind. The Holy Spirit now reveals Jesus the Son to each person who will hear His voice and yield to His convictions. Then we believers are supposed to allow the Holy Spirit inside us to personally reveal Jesus to the world through us.

The word *kindness* is mentioned forty-six times in the NKJV of the Bible, eight of which are in the New Testament.

The Old Testament Hebrew word for *kindness* is the following:

"*checed* (kheh'-sed); kindness; by implication (towards God) piety: rarely (by opposition) reproof, or (subject.) beauty: KJV—

favour, good deed (-liness, -ness), kindly, (loving-) kindness, merciful (kindness), mercy, pity, reproach" (OT:2617).

All thirty-eight of the Old Testament scriptures used the word *checed*. Here is a list of the thirty-eight scriptures for you to look up and read in your private study time:

> *Genesis 20:13; 21:23; 24:12; 24:14; 40:14*
> *Joshua 2:12*
> *Judges 8:35*
> *Ruth 2:20; 3:10*
> *First Samuel 15:6; 20:14, 15*
> *Second Samuel 2:5, 6; 9:1, 3, 7; 10:2*
> *First Kings 2:7; 3:6*
> *First Chronicles 19:2*
> *Second Chronicles 24:22*
> *Nehemiah 9:18*
> *Job 6:14*
> *Psalms 31:21; 117:2; 119:76; 141:5*
> *Proverbs 19:22; 31:26*
> *Isaiah 54:8; 54:10*
> *Jeremiah 2:2*
> *Joel 2:13*

The eight New Testament *kindness* scriptures are as follow:

> *Acts 28:2*
> *Second Corinthians 6:6*
> *Galatians 5:22*
> *Ephesians 2:7*
> *Colossians 3:12*
> *Titus 3:4*
> *Second Peter 1:7*

In the New Testament, there are more than one Greek word used to explain *kindness*. The first one is in Acts 28:2. This is where the natives of Malta showed the shipwrecked sailors, along with the prisoners, unusual kindness, meaning the following:

THE OPERATIVE

"philanthropia (fil-an-thro-pee'-ah); from the same as NT:5364; fondness of mankind, i.e. benevolence ("philanthropy"): KJV—kindness, love towards man" (NT:5363).

This is the word we derived *philanthropy* from, meaning the following:

1. Love for mankind; desire and readiness to do good to all men.
2. Philanthropic acts, agency, or like.[9]

It is noteworthy here to point out that the natives unusual kindness afforded to Paul had to have been the Lord going before him, by the Holy Spirit. The Lord spared their lives in this shipwreck after intercession was made by Paul, in the lower deck. I like to believe this shipwreck was His plan and purpose all along, since He is omnipotent, as is the Holy Spirit of Jesus and the Father.

Besides, when you read about this event, the scriptures are clear that Paul *must* go to Rome. Isn't it great how we believers can be used by the Holy Spirit to even spare others lives just by our presence crossing their paths? If Paul had not been on that boat, all prisoners and sailors would have been killed. This is an excellent example of God's *kindness*, wouldn't you agree?

Next we find the second word used to describe *kindness*:

"By purity, by knowledge, by longsuffering, by kindness, by the Holy Spirit, by sincere love." (2 Cor. 6:6) Kindness is defined by another Greek word called *chrestotes*:

> *"chrestotes* (khray-stot'-ace); usefulness, i.e. moral excellence (in character or demeanor): KJV—gentleness, good (-ness), kindness" (NT:5544).

In our text scripture, Galatians 5:22, the word *kindness* in the NKJV is the word *gentleness* in the KJV. It is the very same word *chrestotes* used in Second Corinthians 6:6. The two words are interchangeable.

---

9. *Webster's Dictionary*

All the other scripture references use the word *chrestotes* till we get to the very last one, which is the following:

"But also for this very reason, giving all diligence, add to your faith virtue, to virtue knowledge, to knowledge self-control, to self-control perseverance, to perseverance godliness, to godliness brotherly kindness, and to brotherly kindness love. For if these things are yours and abound, you will be neither barren nor unfruitful in the knowledge of our Lord Jesus Christ. For he who lacks these things is shortsighted, even to blindness, and has forgotten that he was cleansed from his old sins." (2 Peter 1:5–9)

This *kindness* is from the Greek word *philadelphia*. (Anyone heard of the City of Brotherly Love?)

"*philadelphia* (fil-ad-el-fee'-ah); fraternal affection: KJV—brotherly love (kindness), love of the brethren" (NT:5360).

This type of kindness is a strong bond between fellow members of the same group or a private organization. Kindness found in the world usually comes with many stipulations to remain in fellowship of the group or organization. This should not be confused with the real fruit of the Holy Spirit of *kindness* outlined above which means "usefulness, i.e. moral excellence (in character or demeanor): KJV—gentleness, good (-ness), kindness."

Neither is the brotherly kindness used in Second Peter meant to be outside the body of Christ. This brotherly kindness is meant to be between brothers and sisters in the Lord only, as we are never supposed to do for others, *only* if they do for us, right?

Notice the addition in the scriptures in Second Peter 1:5–9: faith + virtue + knowledge + self-control + perseverance + godliness + brotherly kindness + love. If these are in us, <u>we shall not be barren or unfruitful in the knowledge of our Lord Jesus Christ.</u> Those who lack this equation are shortsighted, even to blindness, and have forgotten that they have been cleansed from their old sins. This could *only* be speaking about the Church, who is the body of Christ Jesus, our Lord and Savior.

The fruit of *kindness* is not automatic in our lives. If you do not believe me, watch children play; even well into their teen years, watch how they treat others. This will ultimately carry into their adulthood unless your life is interrupted by God like mine was.

Kindness has to be taught in the natural realm. Within the spiritual realm, as the fruit of the Holy Spirit of *kindness* grows inside us, it is allowed to mature, then others are able to partake of its benefits. Each of the fruit of the Holy Spirit has its counterpart in the natural. The training of each in the natural has degrees of limitations varying by the individual abilities of those being trained and the living examples of others they are fortunate to be around.

In the spirit, growth is governed and watched over by the Holy Spirit and His word. His omnipotence has the perfect timing in and out of every trial and test with victory planned. Knowing exactly what is needed for His fruit to mature inside us allows us to be able to draw from His strength and power. The result reveals more of Jesus, as they come to the forefront in our actions.

However, in the spirit, this growth can and is often stunted or, at least, slowed down, when a believer in Christ does not believe in the fullness of His Spirit. The growth process of the fruit of the Holy Spirit may lie dormant because of doubt and unbelief in His baptism and the working of His gifts. Simply put, their disbelief of them for today produces this action, and their fruit never reaches anywhere near maturity!

"Now hope does not disappoint, because the love of God has been poured out in our hearts by the Holy Spirit who was given to us." (Rom. 5:5)

I would like to say that I can't think of no better act of *kindness* than the death, burial, and resurrection of Jesus for our sins. The second best act is that of the *kindness* of Jesus giving His Holy Spirit as our helper, comforter, and teacher guiding and directing us into all truth.

There is no need to reinvent the wheel here, and I could not have explained the Holy Spirit better myself, so I quote again C. I. Scofield, D.D. footnotes[10] on the summary of the Holy Spirit. (Turn

---

10. *The New Scofield Study Bible KJV* Acts 2:4 footnote number 2 The Holy Spirit, N. T. Summary. 1–9.

to chapter 2 page 26, and read again the footnotes on the summary of the Holy Spirit.)

Who was it that started the accusations that the things of the Holy Spirit have passed away? The devil, of course, is the one who lied about the Holy Spirit not being here as the operative in the Church *today*. Fact is, the Holy Spirit has been here from the beginning of creation, and He has never left, and He certainly did not pass away when the apostles died, taking the things of Jesus with Him and going home, as many believe.

The baptism of the Holy Spirit and His gifts to men anointed or enabled by the Holy Spirit are connected to His fruit or the characteristics of His reality. Jesus actually left Him in charge of the Church and the entire world, including the cosmos. Look around you; He is certainly taking care of business.

Each of us as believers—being members of the body of Christ, regardless of the denomination—must realize these truths. If you do not believe that Jesus is the Son of God, then you fall under the category of what the Bible calls the antichrist spirit.

The phrase "scriptures tell us" should be on the tip of our tongues whenever anyone asks us about God or His word, always ready to give an answer to them who ask, never giving opinions, and always answering by saying, "Scriptures tells us…"

The *kindness* of God is what sent Jesus to earth. It was the *kindness* of Jesus that sent His Holy Spirit. Are we even asking the one who builds the Church what it is that He wants to do in each member, both individually and collectively?

I believe it was Billy Sunday, an evangelist filled with the Holy Spirit, while preaching, the Holy Spirit asked him to go over to the piano and climb up on it and crawl across the top on his hands and knees then climb off the other side. He did it without questioning and even without stopping his message of the word.

After he completed his sermon, he gave an altar call for those who wanted to be born again. A man ran from the back pews and gave his heart to the Lord. After prayer was completed, this charismatic evangelist asked if anyone had a testimony. This man was so excited to tell about his experience. He jumped up and said, "I do!"

THE OPERATIVE

He began to inform everyone that as he sat in the back, listening to yet another Bible-thumper, he said to God, "If you're real, make that preacher climb across the piano." Needless to say, he could hardly wait to get down to the altar. Once he saw the preacher walk over and climb across the piano, without stopping his message and without missing a beat, continuing the whole time, talking about the wonderful works of God, he just had to know this Jesus better. That man might have never been born again if the evangelist was not filled with the Holy Spirit and following His directions. Praise God he was and he did.

I had a similar situation happen to me personally that was detrimental to my being born again, which I would love to share with you now. On Christmas of 1977 my wife and I, along with our son and some of her family, drove down to Florida to spend Christmas and News Year's with her oldest sister and her family.

Little did I know that in the *kindness* of God, I was about to have an encounter that would be a life changer for me. I was still mulling over all the scriptures that I had heard from my friend. Our history was that we played baseball together in our younger years, and after high school, we did some partying together. Our lives went in separate directions for a while when I got married.

He was single, and during our time of not seeing each other, he gave his heart to the Lord. After being born again, the Lord would send him to my house on the weekends. He was sent every Friday and Saturday night for a year and a half. You see the plan, don't you? Faith comes by hearing, and hearing by the word of God. Praise God that he was filled with the Holy Spirit and listened to His directions about witnessing to me for that long and not giving up on me.

While in Florida, we all went shopping at a mall and parked our two vehicles on the very top of the mall parking lot. It was daylight when we went in, but when we came out, it was dark with not one cloud in the sky.

You need to realize now that I was born and raised in West Virginia, and the small town of Enterprise is surrounded by large hills. Most days and nights were cloudy when I was growing up.

When you could see the stars at night, most of the view of the sky was thwarted greatly by the hills and the clouds.

Needless to say, I was literally starstruck when I came out. I had never seen the stars like that before. Something just seemed a little more special that night. Thinking back on it, it was like God saying to me, "Jim, I have something for you to see that I think you will like." By then I knew about the scriptures that said the following:

"But will God indeed dwell on the earth? Behold, heaven and the heaven of heavens cannot contain You." (1 Kings 8:27)

"The heavens declare the glory of God; And the firmament shows His handiwork." (Ps. 19:1)

Arriving at our vehicles, we learned that my sister-in-law had locked her keys in her car. While everybody was scampering around, trying to figure what to do, I was stargazing because the Creator of the universe was now on my mind.

Nobody could get the door open with a coat hanger found in the trunk of the other vehicle. I said, "Let me try." I walked toward the driver's-side door. The coat hanger was already in the window, with part of it hanging out the top due to the failure of the other attempts. As I reached for the hanger, in my mind for the very first time, I talked to the invisible God of the universe.

My thought was, *God, if you are real and hear me, then let me be able to open this door.* This thought was no sooner completed, and my hand grabbed the hanger. With my own eyes, I saw the other end of the hanger in the car attach the hooked end around the door lock knob, and it popped up, without me moving a muscle.

This was all done without one movement of the hanger by my hand. I was astonished! As my eyes opened wide, I took a few steps back away from the car, and everybody was thanking me for opening the door, as they eagerly climbed into the cars, thinking no more about what just happened than if they were thinking of a man in the moon.

I said nothing to anyone until several months later, after I was born again on February 18, 1978. The invisible God of the universe actually heard my thought! Mine? I began to realize then that the Bible was true. Furthermore, I was realizing for the first time that

THE OPERATIVE

God was interested in me. For what and why, I did not know then, but today I sure am glad He revealed His *kindness* to me.

Here are the two spiritual examples of Him hearing our every thought, revealed to me by my friend showing me the scripture. I have seen this for myself and experienced the validity of these two witnesses, concerning this truth contained in the Bible. This was huge for me! God made Himself real to me with that simple connection, because of one thought.

"But Jesus, knowing their thoughts, said, 'Why do you think evil in your hearts?'" (Matt. 9:4)

"Others, testing Him, sought from Him a sign from heaven. But He, knowing their thoughts, said to them: 'Every kingdom divided against itself is brought to desolation, and a house divided against a house falls.'" (Luke 11:16,17)

This may not be exciting to you, but for me, it was a game changer. It started me on a journey of revelation after revelation and a life filled with His presence and power, keeping my family while giving us directions on which way to turn and what to do next.

It took a snowstorm and being secluded in the house for three days and a touch of cabin fever for me to begin reading a book about how God had delivered another man who was in a worse condition than I was in. A real story of a man delivered by God from being in a maximum-security prison for dealing cocaine gave me such hope for my own life.

It would not be until after the third day of this February snowstorm that we would be able to travel. After coming back from the store with my wife and son, I left the house on foot, never intending on returning alive. Little did I know, I would experience God's *kindness* in full measure once more.

In a foot-and-half of snow at the top of a mountain in West Virginia, I knelt down and gave my heart and life to Jesus, seeing, for the first time, the person I was, in the light of who He is, only to realize later that it was all because of the operations of the Holy Spirit drawing me unto Jesus, using a spirit-filled man of God to plant and water the seed of faith that He activated within my spirit and soul.

You see, the Holy Spirit is alive, and He certainly is real. This fruit we are now talking about is His character growing in us—Christian character exactly like Jesus's character, because the Holy Spirit is the Spirit of Jesus Christ! Why would His Spirit be any different from Jesus Himself?

My prayer is that you run to Him and ask Jesus to baptize you in His Holy Spirit, with the evidence of speaking in tongues, so you too can experience the fullness of God through His Son and His Holy Spirit. Ask the Holy Spirit to use you in His gifts and anoint you for His service, realizing that His fruit or His character will grow in you.

We also love to sing this song, and it goes like this:

> "Everywhere He Went" by Norman & Mac Luna
> Everywhere He went, He was doing good!
> He's the mighty Healer! He cleansed the lepers.
> When the cripples saw Him, they started walking like they should.
> Everywhere He went, my Lord was doing good.

Sounds like Jesus, right? Recently, while singing this song, the Holy Spirit added this part to bring it up-to-date. I sing the above words first, then I go to this next stanza, which follows:

> Everywhere I go, Jesus in me is doing good.
> He's the mighty Healer! He cleanses the lepers.
> When the cripples see Him in me, they start walking like they should.
> Everywhere I go, Jesus in me is doing good, He is doing good.

Take the time to ask yourself, is the fruit of *kindness* growing and maturing inside me? If not, ask the Holy Spirit to bring it forth so that others may partake of His fruit in you, not only of love, joy, peace, and long-suffering, but now God's *kindness* as well. So that everywhere you go, Jesus will be doing good through you too.

In chapter 25, we will be examining the fruit of *goodness*. The continuity of the fruit of the Holy Spirit is amazing! His fruit draws power from the same source that raised Christ from the dead. His fruit is alive and vibrant and allows us to draw from its resource of the resurrection power of Jesus's Holy Spirit.

Each characteristic reveals another layer of the sweetness of the Holy Spirit. As He grows the character of Jesus in us, His fruit will reveal through us for others to see the goodness and *kindness* of God through Jesus Christ, His Son.

There is no better example of an act of *kindness* than that of God the Father sending Jesus, His Son, for each of us so we can become His family throughout eternity.

Continue with me on this spiritual journey to find out more about the Holy Spirit and the part His continual presence and His filling our spirit plays in the spiritual growth, both individually and collectively as the body of Christ today!

* * *

Are you up for a challenge? On a shelf in our bedroom, my wife has a plaque that reads, "No act of kindness, no matter how small, is ever wasted."

Find someone to be kind to today! Better yet, reconnect with someone who showed you an act of kindness, and with a grateful heart, thank them for their thoughtfulness toward you, and let them know what a difference they made in your life!

CHAPTER 25

Fruit of the Holy Spirit
GOODNESS

"But the fruit of the Spirit is love, joy, peace, longsuffering, kindness, GOODNESS, faithfulness, gentleness, self-control. Against such there is no law." (Gal. 5:22–23)

This time we focus on the fruit of *goodness*. If you recall, the previous fruit of *kindness* included goodness within its definition. Why would the Holy Spirit use two fruit, meaning similar things? I too asked that same question. So let's find out. I have placed a capital letter *A* or *B* by each of these, in hopes of removing any confusion.

The word *A—goodness—*in this scripture means the following:

"*agathosune* (ag-ath-o-soo'-nay); from [NT:18]; goodness, i.e. virtue or beneficence: KJV—goodness" (NT:19).

"*agathos* (ag-ath-os'); a primary word; "good" (in any sense, often as noun): KJV—benefit, good (-s, things), well" (NT:18).

The word *B—kindness—*is the NKJV word, while the KJV word used is actually *gentleness*, and it's meaning is as follows:

THE OPERATIVE

"*chrestotes* (khray-stot'-ace); usefulness, i.e. moral excellence (in character or demeanor): KJV—gentleness, good (-ness), kindness" (NT:5544).

A—Goodness deals more with virtue and benevolence of our goods, things, and blessings that the Lord gives us, so we can be a blessing to others, starting with our families and working out as far as the Lord expands the boarders of our territory.

"And Jabez called on the God of Israel saying, 'Oh, that You would bless me indeed, and enlarge my territory, that Your hand would be with me, and that You would keep me from evil, that I may not cause pain!' So God granted him what he requested." (1 Chron. 4:10)

B—Kindness/gentleness deals with our demeanor, which means our conduct, our behavior, or even our facial expressions. This fruit deals with how we handle things in life (respond or react) that come to us through tests, trials, or blessings.

A and *B* are closely related because the *act* of philanthropy is found in both definitions. Philanthropy is the sharing of our blessings with less fortunate others, instead of spending it on ourselves only. How can one be a blessing to others, if they are not blessed by God themselves?

There are many ways the Bible talks about the act of philanthropy. Included, but not limited to, are alms, beneficence, charitableness, liberality, helping neighbors, and helping the poor. Here are a few examples of this type of giving to others, according to the scriptures:

"And when Jesus came to the place, He looked up and saw him, and said to him, "Zacchaeus, make haste and come down, for today I must stay at your house." So he made haste and came down, and received Him joyfully. But when they saw it, they all complained, saying, "He has gone to be a guest with a man who is a sinner."

Then Zacchaeus stood and said to the Lord, "Look, Lord, I give half of my goods to the poor; and if I have taken anything from anyone by false accusation, I restore fourfold." And Jesus said to him, "Today salvation has come to this house, because he also is a son of Abraham; for the Son of Man has come to seek and to save that which was lost." (Luke 19:5–10)

Notice how Jesus considers Zacchaeus's words to be closely connected to salvation. Zacchaeus recognized Jesus for who He was, and he was willing to give up half of his goods to the poor. Also, if he had taken anything from anyone by false accusation, he would restore four times that amount. This is the fruit of *goodness* in operation, for sure.

The act of giving our resources and goods to those less fortunate than ourselves is not limited to Christians alone. There are many in this world who have generous hearts when it comes to helping others who truly need it. But rarely have I ever heard of even the richest folks of today giving half of their goods to the poor.

Of course, I do not know everybody in the world. I would like to think that there are those who have very large sums of wealth who are willing to give like this. After all, how much does one man or woman actually need?

My next example of a person having this kind of fruit of the Spirit operating in them is found in the book of Acts. A philanthropist named Dorcas died. Those close to her sent two men to get Peter, as he was close by. He came and the result was that through Peter, Dorcas was brought back to life.

This is God's favor and His *goodness*. I believe it is because of her lifestyle of giving that the Holy Spirit allowed Peter to raise her from the dead and recorded it in the Bible.

"At Joppa there was a certain disciple named Tabitha, which is translated Dorcas. This woman was full of good works and charitable deeds which she did. But it happened in those days that she became sick and died. When they had washed her, they laid her in an upper room. And since Lydda was near Joppa, and the disciples had heard that Peter was there, they sent two men to him, imploring him not to delay in coming to them. Then Peter arose and went with them. When he had come, they brought him to the upper room. And all the widows stood by him weeping, showing the tunics and garments which Dorcas had made while she was with them. But Peter put them all out, and knelt down and prayed. And turning to the body he said, "Tabitha, arise." And she opened her eyes, and when she saw Peter she sat up. Then he gave her his hand and lifted her up; and when he had called the saints and widows,

THE OPERATIVE

he presented her alive. And it became known throughout all Joppa, and many believed on the Lord. So it was that he stayed many days in Joppa with Simon, a tanner." (Acts 9:36–43)

We also have the account of Cornelius in the book of Acts, which we have covered in a previous chapter. His fruit of generosity allowed him and his whole household to receive the baptism of the Holy Spirit and speak in tongues, which agrees with Acts 2:4 and the other examples found in the book of Acts.

There were many groups of people, plus local churches throughout the countries, that gave and joined their resources to give to the poor *(Acts 11:29–30, 24:17; Rom. 15:25–28; 1 Cor. 16:1–4; 2 Cor. 8:1–4, 9:1–5; and Heb. 6:10)*—all acts of *goodness*!

So we can say that with the fruit of kindness and goodness, giving is connected, as they both go hand in hand. As this fruit grows inside each born-again believer, it makes the believer prosperous in the many ways that Jesus teaches us in Luke 8, Matthew 13, and Mark 4. These accounts show us that the word of God, once sown in the good ground of the heart, brings forth fruit even unto a hundredfold.

So you see, it's all connected together through the Holy Spirit, who is the operative in the Church and world today, because of the *goodness* of God for sending us Jesus Christ. When Jesus left, He sent the other helper, comforter, and teacher—the one who raised Him from the dead with His resurrection power. He sent us His Holy Spirit. All fruit grows in us from His existence dwelling in His believers and by His power flowing through each of us.

The fruit of *goodness* is just as important in our lives as love, joy, peace, long-suffering, kindness, faithfulness, gentleness, and self-control.

Against such there is no law, known to man or from God, that can take away the results of His fruit maturing inside each believer. We benefit from the results of their maturity, as well as others do, as we each share their produce with them by our works or actions in our lives.

Since Jesus has redeemed us from the curse of the law, like Zacchaeus, salvation is inclusive of sins being forgiven, receiving healing, receiving financial prosperity, and receiving deliverance and all things that pertain to life and godliness.

"Christ has redeemed us from the curse of the law, having become a curse for us [for it is written, "Cursed is everyone who hangs on a tree"], that the blessing of Abraham might come upon the Gentiles in Christ Jesus, that we might receive the promise of the Spirit through faith." (Gal. 3:13–14)

"Beloved, I pray that you may prosper in all things and be in health, just as your soul prospers." (3 John 2)

"For all the promises of God in Him are Yes, and in Him Amen, to the glory of God through us." (2 Cor. 1:20)

The curse of the law is that no person alive can keep all of them, and when one person breaks just one law, according to the law, they are guilty of them all. This is what Christ has redeemed us from. Legalism has the curse of the law, and its penalty for breaking one law is death.

For we are saved by grace (receiving that which we do not deserve and not obtaining that which we do deserve) through faith. Works alone never save anyone, no matter how good they are. Good works are a derivative of the fruit of *kindness* and *goodness* and are realized because of the fruit that grows within our spirit, enabling us to be generous in ways that we never participated in prior to our salvation.

Those not born again who display these good works of kindness and goodness are close to salvation, like Zacchaeus. Unlike Zacchaeus who acted upon salvation that was offered to Him by Christ, it is not until any unsaved philanthropist takes heed to the Holy Spirit's calling that they are able to receive the gift of eternal salvation by calling upon the name of Jesus to be saved.

"For by grace you have been saved through faith, and that not of yourselves; it is the gift of God, not of works, lest anyone should boast." (Eph. 2:8–9)

"For the Scripture says, 'Whoever believes on Him will not be put to shame.' For there is no distinction between Jew and Greek, for the same Lord over all is rich to all who call upon Him. For 'whoever calls on the name of the LORD shall be saved.'" (Rom. 10:11–13)

THE OPERATIVE

Praise God for Jesus and His obedience unto fulfilling the law! He, being the only person who was able to live His entire life without breaking one law, redeemed all those who call upon His name to be saved—saved from the curse of law because of His resurrection. This is implemented to all the <u>whosoevers</u> at the time we call upon Jesus to be saved.

How does our souls prosper as in Third John 2? By the word of God, which includes the gift of the Holy Spirit for all those who believe and ask the Lord Jesus to baptize them, which, in turn, brings His resurrection power, gifts of the Holy Spirit, and the fruit of the Holy Spirit to maturity, and through patience, we receive the promises.

The chains of events that follow are worthy of reviewing God's goodness toward man. Sharing them with others would be both acts of kindness and goodness.

Line upon line, line upon line, precept upon precept, precept upon precept, here a little, there a little, and finally, the full picture comes into focus. The beauty of the plan is in the sharing of God's truth with others. Always enjoy the journey!

<u>Event # 1.</u> At conception every child receives a measure of faith.

"For I say, through the grace given to me, to everyone who is among you, not to think of himself more highly than he ought to think, but to think soberly, as God has dealt to each one a measure of faith." (Rom. 12:3)

<u>Event # 2.</u> Then faith comes and is activated by hearing the word of God.

"So then faith comes by hearing, and hearing by the word of God." (Rom. 10:17)

<u>Event # 3.</u> Once a person hears then believes the word of God in their heart, they call upon Jesus to be saved.

"For with the heart one believes unto righteousness, and with the mouth confession is made unto salvation. For the Scripture says, 'Whoever believes on Him will not be put to shame.' For there is no distinction between Jew and Greek, for the same Lord over all is rich to all who call upon Him.

For 'whoever calls on the name of the LORD shall be saved.'" (Rom. 10:10-13)

Event # 4. Being born again, and because sin is forgiven, each person has a choice to believe in the gift of the Holy Spirit from Jesus or not. If believers take God's word as truth, they will ask to receive the promise of the Spirit of God. Because of their faith in believing the word of God, Jesus is allowed to baptize them in the Holy Spirit with the evidence of speaking in tongues with boldness.

"If you then, being evil, know how to give good gifts to your children, how much more will your heavenly Father give the Holy Spirit to those who ask Him!" (Luke 11:13)

"And being assembled together with them, He commanded them not to depart from Jerusalem, but to wait for the Promise of the Father, 'which,' He said, 'you have heard from Me; for John truly baptized with water, but you shall be baptized with the Holy Spirit not many days from now.' Therefore, when they had come together, they asked Him, saying, 'Lord, will You at this time restore the kingdom to Israel?' And He said to them, 'It is not for you to know times or seasons which the Father has put in His own authority. But you shall receive power when the Holy Spirit has come upon you; and you shall be witnesses to Me in Jerusalem, and in all Judea and Samaria, and to the end of the earth.'" (Acts 1:4–8)

"Then Peter said to them, 'Repent, and let every one of you be baptized in the name of Jesus Christ for the remission of sins [water baptism]; and you shall receive the gift of the Holy Spirit [baptism of the Holy Spirit]. For the promise is to you and to your children, and to all who are afar off, as many as the Lord our God will call.'" (Acts 2:38–39)

Event # 5. Once a person is filled with the Holy Spirit, each time they pray in tongues, which only God knows and understands, that person builds themselves upon their most holy faith by praying in the Spirit.

THE OPERATIVE

"And they were all filled with the Holy Spirit and began to speak with other tongues, as the Spirit gave them utterance." (Acts 2:4)

"Pursue love, and desire spiritual gifts, but especially that you may prophesy. For he who speaks in a tongue does not speak to men but to God, for no one understands him; however, in the spirit he speaks mysteries. But he who prophesies speaks edification and exhortation and comfort to men. He who speaks in a tongue edifies himself, but he who prophesies edifies the church. I wish you all spoke with tongues, but even more that you prophesied; for he who prophesies is greater than he who speaks with tongues, unless indeed he interprets, that the church may receive edification." (1 Cor. 14:1–5)

"But you, beloved, building yourselves up on your most holy faith, praying in the Holy Spirit." (Jude 20)

Event # 6. As people build themselves up on their most holy faith by praying in the Holy Spirit with tongues, the Holy Spirit picks and chooses from those people who are yielding to Him to operate in whatever gift(s) to meet the need(s) at hand.

"But one and the same Spirit works all these things, distributing to each one individually as He wills." (1 Cor. 12:11)

Event # 7. Meanwhile, the fruit of love, joy, peace, long-suffering, kindness, goodness, faithfulness, gentleness, and self-control is growing inside, making a mature believer more prosperous in all ways that pertain to life and godliness than we were, as Jude 20 previously revealed.

"Grace and peace be multiplied to you in the knowledge of God and of Jesus our Lord, as His divine power [Holy Ghost] has given to us all things that pertain to life and godliness, through the knowledge of Him who called us by glory and virtue, by which have been given to us exceedingly great and precious promises, that through these you may be partakers of the divine nature, having escaped the corruption that is in the world through lust." (2 Peter 1:2–4)

"But you, beloved, building yourselves up on your most holy faith, praying in the Holy Spirit, keep yourselves in the love of God, looking for the mercy of our Lord Jesus Christ unto eternal life." (Jude 20,21)
"Now hope does not disappoint, because the love of God has been poured out in our hearts by the Holy Spirit who was given to us." (Rom. 5:5)
"Now godliness with contentment is great gain." (1 Tim. 6:6)
<u>It's all connected together,</u> and removing any part of these gifts short-circuits the process of growing in the grace and knowledge of our Lord and Savior, Jesus Christ.

We believers dare not remove Jesus from our lives. Why, then, is it that we so easily remove His Holy Spirit from our lives and our Church services?

"You therefore, beloved, since you know this beforehand, beware lest you also fall from your own steadfastness, being led away with the error of the wicked; "but grow in the grace and knowledge of our Lord and Savior Jesus Christ. To Him be the glory both now and forever. Amen." (2 Peter 3:17,18)

After all, isn't this our goal—to be more like Jesus?
"Brethren, I do not count myself to have apprehended; but one thing I do, forgetting those things which are behind and reaching forward to those things which are ahead, I press toward the goal for the prize of the upward call of God in Christ Jesus." (Phil. 3:13–14)
Realizing that each fruit of the Holy Spirit is <u>not</u> separate from the others helps us to gain the understanding that each fruit depends upon the other fruit to flow in the continuity of the power of the Holy Spirit. Just as we all are members of the same body of Christ, we should <u>never</u> consider ourselves separated from one another, no matter what the denomination we are attending. Each of us members supplies that which is needed to the other members for the edification of the body.

"But, speaking the truth in love, may grow up in all things into Him who is the head—Christ—from whom the whole body, joined and knit together by what every joint supplies, according to the effective work-

ing by which every part does its share, causes growth of the body for the edifying of itself in love." (Eph. 4:15, 16)

The fruit of *love* cannot be effective without the fruit of *goodness*, nor can *goodness* be effective without the fruit of *faith*, no more than the Baptist can be fully effective without the Pentecostals, which cannot be fully effective without the Methodist or any other denomination that believes in Jesus Christ as the Son of God and Savior of all men, inclusive. We must become aware that the unbelievers take notice of these man-made divisions that dominate within the church organizations today.

This trickery of the devil, pertaining to these divisions that are being used to try and keep this last-day Holy Ghost revival harvest from happening, must be thwarted. It's just a matter of time till the Church catches the vision of these powerful revelations by beginning the <u>fellowship of necessity</u> with each member realizing that they need each of the other members of the body of Christ to remain vital. Right now the body of Christ has a lot of tourniquets upon it, stopping the flow of the Holy Ghost power to His whole body.

Do we really understand the body of Christ? In our partaking of communion, are we correctly discerning His body that is made up of every member, or are we just considering the members of our local church only? I submit to you that the latter is more dominant within the thinking of many local churches.

Here it is, 2016, have we figured out what *First Corinthians 11:17–34* is actually saying to us? Each time we partake of communion, we are instructed by others in the service to judge ourselves as to whether or not we are worthy to partake of communion (that is, if I have not sin, I am worthy, and if I am not born again and have sin, I am not worthy). The traditions of men, along with not rightly dividing the word of truth, have given unto us a false interpretation of what is actually being said here.

The key to understanding what Paul was dealing with here lies within the true context and the setting of that which he was addressing and the problem that he had concerning the Corinthians and the way they were conducting the Lord's table. The topic changes at *First Corinthians 11:17*, from the Christian order of God's chain of command to the disorders at the Lord's table. Paul actually was rebuking them, for they were wrongly practicing the Lord's table or what we call communion today.

Verses 17–22 and the end of verses 33 and 34 actually bring the context of the disorder of the Corinthians, as they partook of the Lord's table or communion. He begins by stating, *"Now this I declare unto you I praise you NOT, that ye come together, NOT for the better but for the WORSE."*

The wrongful practice of communion was that they were bringing actual meals from home. He was instructing them that when they came together for communion services, it was not to eat their suppers at the Lord's table. They were actually bringing meals, and some were even drunk. Verse 22 says the following:

"What! Do you not have houses to eat and drink in? Or do you despise the church of God and shame those who have nothing? What shall I say to you? Shall I praise you in this? I do not praise you." (1 Cor. 11:22)

They were bringing complete meals from their houses to the church and did not even share with those who had nothing to bring and were hungry. As mentioned before, some even came drunk, thinking that *This is remembering what Jesus did for us* each time they partook of communion.

Paul was rebuking them for these actions. In verse 29 these actions brought judgment to each believer who was practicing the Lord's table this wrong way of remembering what Christ had done for them. He was, in essence, saying, "Judge yourselves to see if you are partaking correctly of the bread (that represents the body of Christ) and the wine (that represents the blood shed for all). Not by bringing meals from home to the Lord's table—not whether or not each individual was worthy (which, by the way, was inserted and not in the original text—some of these work, and some do not, this one does not work.) to partake of communion.

Let me ask you this: While partaking of communion, aren't we supposed to remember what Jesus did for mankind? Absolutely, we are to remember Jesus and all that He has done for us. After Paul rebukes them, he gives them these instructions:

THE OPERATIVE

"For I received from the Lord that which I also delivered to you: that the Lord Jesus on the same night in which He was betrayed took bread; and when He had given thanks, He broke it and said, 'Take, eat; this is My body which is broken for you; do this in remembrance of Me.' In the same manner He also took the cup after supper, saying, 'This cup is the new covenant in My blood. This do, as often as you drink it, in remembrance of Me.'" (1 Cor. 11:23–25)

Since the word <u>unworthy</u> was added in verse 29, we know by the context of Paul's rebuke that they were bringing judgment upon themselves by wrongly partaking in the Lord's table, by bringing complete meals from home that they did not even share with the hungry or those who even came in drunk. This wrongful action was what brought judgment upon them, *not* whether or not individuals were worthy or not worthy. We teach "Come as you are," don't we?

The question then begs to be asked: is it correct to say that if someone comes into our services who does not know Jesus as their Savior, are they unworthy to partake of communion? Based upon the scriptures and the character of Jesus, I *do not* think that Jesus would turn anybody away from communion. Remember Judas partaking of communion with Jesus and the other disciples in the upper room?

Communion should bring sinners to think about what Jesus did for them. In no way does them partaking in communion make them unworthy or bring judgment upon them, by joining others in remembering what Christ has done. It's like saying in a service, "Now everyone bow their heads and remember what Jesus's body and His blood did for us. And oh, by the way, if you are here and you have not asked Jesus to forgive you of your sins, then DO NOT THINK ABOUT what His body and blood did for you, because you will bring judgment upon yourself and maybe even death." Now what do you think?

These symbolic emblems of Christ's body and His blood speak of the good news of the death, burial, and resurrection of Jesus Christ. If this act of partaking of communion makes them unworthy with judgment, then why doesn't the preaching of the gospel do the same? It makes no sense and is completely out of context with Paul's teaching to the Corinthian church.

This is why we are not discerning the body of Christ with all His members. We cannot even get the sacrament of communion rightly divided within our own understandings.

If our message is to be about what Jesus has done for mankind through His body and blood that were given at Calvary's cross, how is this so different? Are we not remembering all that Jesus did for us at communion when we partake of the emblems? Have we wrongly divided the word of truth, making nonbelievers think that they are not worthy to remember what Jesus has done for them, even telling them that if they partake of communion without being born again, they would bring judgment upon them, even possible death? Oh, Lord Jesus, I ask for forgiveness for not seeing and understanding your body.

If we are teaching the word of truth wrong, are we not just as guilty as those who taught in the Corinthian church to bring meals to the meeting and to celebrate Jesus even while being intoxicated? I think yes—we are as guilty. Paul even brought it to their attention that many were weak and sickly, and some had died because of this type of wrongful judgment, and he was talking to the church folks, not the unsaved.

"For he who eats and drinks in an 'wrongfully' manner eats and drinks judgment to himself, not discerning the Lord's body. For this reason, many are weak and sick among you, and many sleep." (1 Cor. 11:29–30)

Each member of Jesus's body is no more disconnected from Christ's literal body than each of us is disconnected from one another. We must rightly divide the word of truth with the help of the Holy Spirit, for without Him, we fall prey to traditional thinking and understanding. We remove the power from God's words.

Can you see how everything is connected to the Holy Spirit of Jesus? Do you see the devil's plan of eliminating His presence from our lives, if he possibly can? The Holy Spirit raising Christ from the dead was the reason the devil lost, for the devil thought that he had won at Calvary. Also, what better way to keep Jesus's Church without His power than by convincing the believers that He is not relevant for today?

THE OPERATIVE

God shows the world that the living Church of the Most High God is bonded together in His love and the unity of His faith, and this is one of our missions while we are still here on earth. We are to live together according to the scriptures and not our preferences to justify our lifestyle and worship of God. Each believer must be worshipping the Lord in spirit and in truth. This means believing everything Jesus *is*, including His Holy Spirit's operations in our lives while understanding His word, as He originally intended it to be.

With the fruit of *goodness* maturing abundantly within each of us, empowered by all other fruit of the Holy Spirit and the presence of His anointing, we become more productive when it comes to making a difference in other people's lives, as we share Jesus with them.

It is God's *goodness* that reveals His true character of a loving, eternal Father. By sending Jesus, we owe everything to Him, because He gave everything of value for us. For Jesus to live would have been gain for Him, but for Him to die, then live again, was gain for us.

Before moving on to the next fruit of *faith* in chapter 27, I would like to break from teaching about the fruit of the Holy Spirit to share a few points about rightly dividing the word of truth. After seeing the example concerning our communion services, I believe you will agree that rightly dividing the word of truth deserves further revelation in our lives.

"Remind them of these things, charging them before the Lord not to strive about words to no profit, to the ruin of the hearers. Be diligent to present yourself approved to God, a worker who does not need to be ashamed, rightly dividing the word of truth." (2 Tim. 2:14–15)

Being able to have the right understanding of God's word is a very important part of every believer's life, wouldn't you agree? Every believer must receive proper training and teaching from *His* ministry gifts. Then when it is time for each believer to be sent out by the Holy Spirit, they will teach others the correct way. As they instruct other believers, like will produce after its kind. By correctly understanding the Holy Spirit's view and interpretation of the Bible, <u>we all will be teaching and preaching the same things</u>, which leads us to the unity of faith that is our goal.

The importance of this topic demands, at least, a complete chapter and not just a couple of paragraphs. By rightly dividing the word of truth, our lifestyles will be conducive to the word of God.

False teachings because of not rightly dividing the word of truth, which often is repeated from generation to generation, have even spilled outside the Church into many people's thinking, especially about communion. If you don't believe me, start asking those you know are unsaved about it, and see what their answer to you will be. This has kept people away from the things of God long enough, especially from Jesus and His Holy Spirit.

This is a perfect example, concerning communion, of not rightly dividing the word of truth. Let us, as the body of Christ, not pass this lie on one more day. Let's ask the Holy Spirit to take the emblem of the body of Christ, along with the blood of Christ that was shed and given for *all* and to make them a reality within every heart and mind, as He convinces them of sin, righteousness, and judgment.

Long before I was born again, the Holy Ghost was using the play *Jesus Christ Superstar* that I watched. I just could not get the cross out of my mind. It was embedded within my mind in such a capacity that I took my son's G.I. Joe figure (full-size) and made a model out of it of Jesus nailed to the cross. This was, at least, three years before I gave my heart to the Lord.

If He can use something like this, then how much more can He be using the communion services to bring in the lost? Just some food for thought.

Join me in chapter 26, as we discover how important and necessary, the topic of rightly dividing the word of truth is, and demanding it for ourselves and our Church leadership.

CHAPTER 26

Fruit of the Spirit
Rightly Dividing the Word of Truth

My observation for thirty-seven years now is that there are reasons to be concerned over the lack of spiritual maturity in the Church or body of Christ. Many appear to act and think the same as when they were born again—ten, twenty, and even thirty or more years ago.

Multiplying physically has not been a problem. Multiplying spiritually, on the other hand, is where the problem comes in for the Church. I believe that one of the reasons for this is because there are many who have been placed in leadership of churches who simply are not rightly dividing the word of truth. I do not mean to be disrespectful to anyone in particular, but leadership is where the buck stops, isn't it?

With so many different denominational beliefs regarding the Bible today, this tells me, and it should tell you too, that <u>somebody</u> is *not* rightly dividing the word of truth.

We are instructed to worship Him in spirit and truth, are we not? Then if we were all worshipping Him in spirit and truth, there would be unity of faith, correct? Is unity of faith found within the

Church today? I believe we answered this already in a previous chapter, but it bears repeating—no, it is *not*!

Each member of the body of Christ would be preaching and teaching the same things if the unity of faith were within the Church today. The word of the Lord, which is forever settled in heaven, must not be changed by man, denominational thinking, or—for that fact, we could add to the list—governmental thinking. God's word should never be changed to what man thinks it says but should remain as the infallible word of the Lord forever!

"Forever, O LORD, Your word is settled in heaven. Your faithfulness endures to all generations; You establish the earth, and it abides." (Psalms 119:89,90)

"Jesus Christ is the same yesterday, today, and forever." (Heb. 13:8)

True revival, which is the coming alive unto the things of God (especially the word of the Lord), will only happen when emphasis is placed upon the *word* of the *Lord* and His power of Spirit and life, which it is supposed to be presented with.

"For our gospel did not come to you in word only, but also in power, and in the Holy Spirit and in much assurance, as you know what kind of men we were among you for your sake." (1 Thess. 1:5)

Is Church leadership presenting the word of God in power and in the Holy Spirit with much assurance? The results of this kind of presentation is the responsibility of the Holy Spirit. You only have to take the time to read Psalms 119 to realize the importance that is placed upon the word concerning revival. Faith comes by hearing, and hearing by the word of God. The more we hear it, the more we can hear what it is saying to us.

<u>Jesus,</u> who is known as the word of God, became <u>the actual living word of God</u> in the flesh upon His conception by the Holy Spirit. He was born into this world as the only begotten Son of the Father God, full of grace and truth.

Emphasis must be placed upon the written word of God (as the written word reveals the living word of God). Furthermore, it is Jesus's Holy Spirit who brings life and power unto the words of those who are proclaiming and teaching it as truth.

THE OPERATIVE

"It is the Spirit who gives life; the flesh profits nothing. The words that I speak to you are spirit, and they are life." (John 6:63)

"However, when He, the Spirit of truth, has come, He will guide you into all truth; for He will not speak on His own authority, but whatever He hears He will speak; and He will tell you things to come. He will glorify Me, for He will take of what is Mine and declare it to you."—Jesus Christ (John 16:13–14)

One device the devil uses is to remove the emphasis from the word of God. Do you think he has been successful, to any degree, of doing this within the Church you are attending today, both individually and collectively? I believe that he has been successful to a large degree, as I fellowship with many believers who do not know or understand the word of God the way that one would think they should, given the amount of years they claim to be a believer.

For this very reason, men and women must make up the difference by supplying something, and that something is usually intellect and/or the traditions of men. According to Jesus, these traditions remove the power of God from His word, making it no longer effective as He originally intended it to be and still intends it to be—effective or powerful.

"He answered and said to them, 'Why do you also transgress the commandment of God because of your tradition?'" (Matt. 15:3)

"Making the word of God of no effect through your tradition which you have handed down. And many such things you do." (Mark 7:13)

"(Making of none effect) *akuroo* (ak-oo-ro'-o); (as a negative particle) and; to invalidate: KJV—disannul, make of none effect" (NT:208)

Traditions of men take the validity out of God's word. In essence, they remove the Spirit, life, and truth from it, thus removing the resurrection power of the Holy Spirit, which is the same as removing Jesus from God's word. Is it any wonder why the Church is filled with so many programs, skits, plays, and traditional ways of worshipping the Lord year after year? Every Christmas season, we place Jesus back in the manger as a baby. Folks, let me let you in on a big secret—He is way, way past this image.

We hear more and more Christians saying that if they wanted entertainment, they would stay at home and watch another TV program. What does this say about the leadership in our churches? Have they replaced the anointing of the Holy Spirit with the entertainment of the mind?

Timothy was instructed by Paul to present this to his congregation.

"Remind them of these things, charging them before the Lord not to strive about words to no profit, to the ruin of the hearers. Be diligent to present yourself approved to God, a worker who does not need to be ashamed, rightly dividing the word of truth." (2 Tim 2:14–15)

Here we have Paul instructing Timothy to bring these things to the believer's memories, charging them before the Lord "not to strive about words to no profit, to the ruin of the hearers." He informed Timothy that the only way this could be done was by rightly dividing the word of truth.

(Rightly dividing) *orthotomeo* (or-thot-om-eh'-o); to make a straight cut, i.e. (figuratively) to dissect (expound) correctly (the divine message): KJV—rightly divide (NT:3718).

There is only one way this rightly dividing the word of truth can be accomplished successfully, and that is with the personal guidance and instructions of Jesus's Holy Spirit. Before Paul gave these instructions to Timothy in chapter 2:15, contained within his introduction, Paul gave these words of encouragement to Timothy to overcome his fear of what he knew that he should be doing:

"Therefore I remind you to stir up the gift of God which is in you through the laying on of my hands. For God has not given us a spirit of fear, but of power and of love and of a sound mind." (2 Tim. 1:6–7)

Timothy was a young minister when Paul encouraged him to "stir up the gift of God, which is in you through the laying on of my hands." What gift of God have we learned about, so far, that has been and is to be given to believers by the laying on of hands? You guessed it—the baptism of the Holy Spirit with the evidence of speaking in tongues. We have already covered all this information, and if you need to go back and review it, by all means, please do so.

THE OPERATIVE

Paul reminded Timothy that he was already equipped with all that he needed to accomplish the task ahead of him of bringing to the people's memories the truth contained within God's word—"charging them before the Lord not to strive about words to no profit, to the ruin of the hearers."

Notice what the fruits or results of "words to no profit" are to those who listen. It is to their ruin. I never want to be known for the words that I speak to be the ruin of others! Jesus and Paul are saying the same things here. If the traditions of men invalidate the word of God, don't you think they would fall within the class of "words to no profit"?

I certainly do! Because of these two very important reasons—traditions of men and words to no profit—there has never been a greater time in the Church history than now that <u>we must rightly divide the word of truth.</u>

As the Holy Spirit gives us the revelation knowledge needed to understand the word of God correctly, the believers will grow in the grace and knowledge of our Lord and Savior, Jesus Christ, with sound faith within each of them. As He confirms these revelations by other scriptures teaching the same things or same principles, before we preach or teach the message(s), we can have the confidence and assurance that they are the truth, as the Holy Spirit expects us to believe them to be.

By now I pray that you are seeing the *importance* of learning how to do this with the Holy Spirit. For us who are already filled and pray in tongues, we need just to continue praying in tongues, and as we read the Bible with the Holy Spirit, the revelations that appear, along with the understanding of them, are deepened. Once confirmed, we then are able to share with others their spiritual contents and applications.

For those of you who are not filled with the Holy Spirit and not praying in tongues, ask Jesus to give this miraculous gift of God to you, for He has given so many believers this gift since His resurrection. <u>You must ask Him, though</u>, because being filled with His Spirit is not automatic once you're born again, as we have previously realized this truth.

For whatever reason, if you choose to remain the same as the day you were born again, your spiritual growth will continue to be stunted. You may even be fooled into believing some Christian lingo or phrases, whose principles <u>are not</u> found in the Bible, like "God helps those who help themselves."

<u>If this were true, then why, in this world, would we ever need a Savior?</u> Yes, we are to work, as the Bible is clear that those who do not work should not eat.

"For even when we were with you, we commanded you this: If anyone will not work, neither shall he eat. For we hear that there are some who walk among you in a disorderly manner, not working at all, but are busybodies." (2 Thess. 3:10,11)

How far from this have we come because of feelings and emotions? Now do not get me wrong here. I am not opposed to helping those who legitimately need help. If you have ever found yourself where you tried to get to work but couldn't buy a job, then you will understand what I am saying.

Free lunches, so to say, to masses of people who will never work at a job even if one is offered to them are wrong. I know in this day and age we live in, I never would have thought that so many people here in the United States would be out of work and couldn't find a job. For them help is justifiable; however, long-term welfare and food stamps as occupations and benefits are not the solution. <u>The word of God is!</u>

For this reason, <u>continual</u> government handouts to people are wrong. Temporary assistance is acceptable. This handout and "you owe me" mentality is contrary to God's word. There are many factors that are to be taken into account by each case, but in every case, those accepting the assistance should be making plans somehow, someway, not to rely on it as their life occupation.

Jesus only fed the masses a couple of times because it was too late and too long of a journey for them to go and purchase food. He took advantage of this opportunity to reveal to them His Holy Spirit's gift of working of miracles and also to prove that He was the Son of God. Many believed Him because of these miracles. But nowhere in the Bible does it teach an ongoing supply of food for the masses. Otherwise, this teaching would be found contrary to the word of God when the Holy Spirit wrote, "If a man does not work, he does not eat."

This is where the living Church should get involved and not the government. Trusting God and His promises that are yes and amen in Christ Jesus is their answer. Until those requiring help are able to hear the word of God, which activates the faith for salvation that is given to them at conception, some assistance may be required but for a short period of time. And we need our pantries open to the hungry, to feed them with both spiritual food and natural food until they learn to walk the walk of faith with Jesus and His Holy Spirit.

If they choose not to do things God's way, then there is nothing further at that time to do except to pray for them and be there for them when they realize their mistake and come back to the truth. But how will they know the truth if we are <u>not</u> teaching it to them?

As heartless as this may sound to you now, nothing changes a man or woman's mind faster than an empty stomach. Does the word of God not mean what it says that if a man will not work, he should not eat? Hunger is a great motivator, I know, because I have been there before and had to do whatever I had to do to supply food for my family.

I remember taking work with a brother in the church when we first moved to Virginia twenty-seven years ago, cleaning out sewage lines in a trailer park for $5.00 per hour, maybe three hours a day for a couple of days a week. It wasn't much, but I did it. One sister in the church brought us a box of food once, but for the remainder of the several months we lived in this particular place, we applied God's word, and He honored His principles.

But God did not leave us there, as we continued to follow His word and believed Him that His promises were yes and amen in Christ Jesus. My first-year income in Virginia was a little over $4,000.00 for the four of us, a far cry from the $50,000.00 per year I was making in the coal mines in West Virginia, not to mention what my wife was making at the time we moved. This is why I am able to say these things that I have said, because my family and I have lived through them firsthand, and God was always faithful to His word, as we put Him first and continued in His faith.

At the time this was happening, I just could not bring myself to file for unemployment and receive food stamps or welfare, not because of pride—no—it was because we knew the God we served was bigger than these programs, and at the same time, knowing Him to be faithful, we decided that His ways would last longer than any government-made plan that existed. And it has!

Would it be wrong for us to sign up for these programs? Of course *not*! I am just stating the facts of where we were in faith in Him, and He proved us to be right by not leaving us there. Was it easy? *No*, but it was really satisfying seeing Him open doors and closing others, pertaining to His will in our lives instead of ours. It was a lesson we had to learn in His plan and purpose for us so that we can be who we are today.

This type of teaching, I believe, should be done by those who are filled with the Holy Spirit because of the revelation knowledge that accompanies their study and fellowship with the Lord. Their life experiences of fellowshipping with Him bring them far more solid reference points to hang on to His faith when other trials and tests come, and they do come. Sharing those trials and victories with others who are learning is a valuable asset to give.

His power, gifts, and fruit sustain us every day of our lives. It is our experience that once a person knows Him personally, <u>instead of knowing of Him</u>, they will trust Him no matter what road or path He leads them through. As mentioned before, these are two different viewpoints of walking with God, knowing *of* God, or knowing Him through personal fellowship through His Son Jesus's Holy Spirit.

Men and women of God who are rightly dividing the word of truth have the many answers available to man's problems in this life. It is not that we know it all, but we know the one who does and have a close relationship with Him so that we can go boldly before His throne of grace to obtain help in our times of need <u>in all matters.</u>

It is my belief that if a believer in Christ does not believe in the baptism of the Holy Spirit with the evidence of speaking in tongues, then they have already demonstrated that they *are not* rightly dividing the word of truth. With all the evidence in the Bible, how can you not see and understand? It's because the Holy Spirit is lacking in your spiritual fire triangle. (See page 141 to review.)

There are too many scriptural references, as you now know, to this truth, and if not adhered to, then there is no way possible that it could be considered, even remotely, to be rightly dividing the word of truth.

I believe that if we the Church (*all* believers) were doing all we can do to help those less fortunate than us, then there would be no need for government welfare programs draining the coffers of our tax dollars. There can be no legitimate war on poverty, as Jesus said, "The poor you have with you always." The following are three witnesses to back this up:

"For you have the poor with you always, but Me you do not have always." (Matt. 26:11)

"For you have the poor with you always, and whenever you wish you may do them good; but Me you do not have always". (Mark 14:7)

"For the poor you have with you always, but Me you do not have always." (John 12:8)

Based upon the witness of these three writers, how must we divide or understand them in what they are saying? Are all three of them saying the same thing? If so, what is the truth that needs to be imparted here to us and to others? The truth of the matter is that there will always be poor people in the world. Therefore, there will always be opportunities of benevolence while we live here on earth.

Now, when we hear a man or woman stand before a camera or read in a newspaper or magazine their strong comments, making them look like they are more than they really are, as they say something like, "We are declaring war of poverty. We can eliminate hunger in the world by having this program or that program," are they actually calling Jesus Christ a liar? Yes, they are!

Are you seeing the importance of rightly dividing the word of truth? This is why we need to know the word of God and the God of the word and have correct understanding of what the word of God is saying. I know that there are many in the world who couldn't care less what the Bible says. That is their choice. But for believers to side with those who do not believe what the Bible says, because it sounds good, well, this will not do, and it is certainly <u>not</u> rightly dividing the word of truth now, is it?

God the Father, with His contract or new covenant with His *only* Son Jesus, along with the power of His Holy Spirit, is the only one who gives help freely to all who come boldly before His throne of grace and ask for it. Instead of pointing people to government programs, why not point them to the throne of grace? Maybe we don't point them to the throne of grace because our experiences are our hands doing it for us instead of allowing the Lord's Holy Spirit to lead us in these manners.

When I worked in the coal mines, I was witnessing to a group of men one day about the goodness of God. A particular man became very upset and used some choice words I would rather not repeat here, but he was saying, "I work for everything I have, God never gave me nothing." And with that he got up and walked out of the crosscut dinner hole. I continued to inform the others about how God had given us life, health, job opportunities, etc.

You see, he did not want to give this credit to the Lord, because of his pride in supplying for his family. To be proud of following the directions of the Lord is one thing; to have so much pride that you do not recognize the goodness of God is completely another thing and could lead to a man's downfall. Who can rightfully say that they gave to God first? Does He not give unto all things that pertain to life and godliness?

"Let us therefore come boldly to the throne of grace, that we may obtain mercy and find grace to HELP in time of need." (Heb. 4:16)

My point being, I see nothing in this scripture, or any other scripture for that fact, that teaches the principle that God will *not* help others until they help themselves. How backward is that thinking? If I can always help myself, then why would I be commanded to go boldly before the throne of grace for mercy and grace to help me in my time of need? Aren't we humans a needy people? Can you see how this statement negates itself? God helps those who help themselves—where did this come from? I will tell you. It is one of the devil's devices that <u>does not</u> rightly divide the word of truth.

THE OPERATIVE

> Rightly dividing the word of truth cannot successfully be done without the continual help of the Holy Spirit!

As biblical principles are taught properly by those who are rightly dividing the word of truth, the Church body would be informed of the biblical reason we are supposed to work in the first place. Do you know what that is? First there is *"If a man does not work, he should not eat."* Let's see if the word of God has anything further to say about this, shall we?

"Let him who stole steal no longer, but rather let him labor, working with his hands what is good, that he may have something to give him who has need." (Eph. 4:28)

What I read and what I am seeing within the Church are two different things completely. The pride of life, the lust of the flesh, and the deceitfulness of riches have crept into the members of the Church body so subtly that many no longer recognize that they are there. Do we actually think the unbelievers of the world do not see this as well? Then we wonder why more people are <u>not</u> attending our church services, and those who are have probably been there for several years and maybe even decades without the knowledge and anointing to teach others the word of truth correctly.

Rightly divided word of truth is what we should be proclaiming from the housetops because it is part of the good news of Jesus, and surely, at least, it should be coming from the pulpits and our Sunday schools—explaining God's principles in our Sunday-school classes, if they are still offered, and not teaching and reinforcing false or half-truths that are easy to remember. Attempting to make others think that you are more spiritually than you are, by repeating these phrases is wrong. Only the Holy Spirit can truly make a believer a spiritual person.

Many can be discouraged in their life when it seems like absolutely nothing they try seems to work for them. To them it may seem like Jesus has left them. I have good news for all of you who find yourselves in need of help. Jesus never went anywhere! How do I know this? Because He promised that He would never leave us or forsake us.

"Let your conduct be without covetousness; be content with such things as you have. For He Himself has said, 'I will never leave you nor forsake you.' So we may boldly say: 'The LORD is my helper; I will not fear. What can man do to me?'" (Heb. 13:5–6)

I have not found in word or principle anything that speaks as fact that God helps those who help themselves. If you have, please share it with us so I can stand corrected. To the contrary, He longs to help each of us. He has even designed it to be that we *need* His help in everything. Then, when trials and tests of life come, God makes them to become our employees.

"And we know that all things work together for good to those who love God, to those who are the called according to His purpose." (Rom. 8:28)

Do you love God and believe that you are called according to His purpose? If so, then let every circumstance, good or bad, become your employee, and let them work it out for your good. That which the devil sends to destroy us works for us and brings us nothing but good, because of God's goodness toward us, His children.

Here is one more example of a partial truth that I fell prey to in the beginning years of my ministry: "For God has chosen the foolishness of the message preached to save them that are lost." Have you ever quoted First Corinthians 1:21 this way? If not, good for you. If you have, please read on to find out your mistake.

I was preaching in a revival service, and I quoted, "God has chosen the foolishness of preaching to save them which are lost." This was how it was quoted in our church. The Holy Spirit stopped me right in the middle of the message and said, <u>"That's not completely correct."</u>

I asked the folks to excuse me for one moment, as I went back to the pulpit where my Bible was lying. As I read First Corinthians 1:21, inside my spirit I said, *That is what is says.* The Holy Spirit said, "Read it again," which I did, and I still did not see it. "Read it again," He said.

After the third time, He evidently opened my spiritual eye, and finally, I saw it. There it was all along. I couldn't believe my eyes.

THE OPERATIVE

"For since, in the wisdom of God, the world through wisdom did not know God, it pleased God through the foolishness of the message preached to save those who believe." (1 Cor. 1:21)

See it? It says that God chose the foolishness of the message preached to save those who <u>believe</u>—those who <u>believe</u>, not the lost. God has actually chosen that which the world thinks is foolishness, which is the message of the preached word of God to save those who believe or those who are already born again in the Church.

We are born again once but saved continually from ourselves, our habits, our enemies, etc. It's the <u>preached word of God</u> that we hear continually that God has chosen to <u>keep us saved,</u> reminding us of who we were and who we should be consistently. Otherwise we humans have a tendency to forget, don't we?

By misquoting this verse, it was actually blinding me to its true content each time I quoted it. How crazy was that? I began to think, *Were there other scriptures that I was guilty of doing this with?* I repented and moved forward.

My point is, in rightly dividing the word of truth, as we are commanded to do, we each must be sure the things that we are saying are the truth according to the Holy Spirit's interpretation of the Bible, because we speak that which we believe, and if we are speaking something wrong, then our believing is wrong as well. If what we are speaking does not match what we should believe according to the scriptures, then what do we call that? It certainly is *not* rightly dividing the word of truth!

I cannot begin to tell you how many churches we have visited over the years <u>that, for some strange reason, have removed the foolishness of the preached word from the pulpit</u> and are replacing it with teaching the word of God only or with programs, plays, dancing, etc.—pure entertainment instead of soul-piercing truths in a message from God's word containing the resurrection power of His Holy Spirit, which discerns the truth about the thoughts and intents of a man or woman's heart.

Whether proclamation or explanation, the message from the one whose life has been changed and called to preach and teach the word of God should come through them in word and the power of the Spirit that he or she has experienced.

Now do not get me wrong. These things (programs, plays, dancing, etc.) have their place in outreach, but <u>only</u> if there is the <u>preaching</u> or the proclamation of the message of the word of God and when the correct teachings, by rightly dividing the word of truth, are being accomplished on a continual basis and the majority of the time.

This is God's chosen way of keeping His people saved and believing the correct way. Are we seeing this within the Church today? Not in all of them, and more and more are falling by the wayside in this manner. There is only one way to do things, and that is the Holy Spirit's way of understanding, along with His directions from the word of God.

We dare not leave His chosen way and practice another gospel. This will save nobody, let alone convince others they need a Savior, nor does it properly maintain our walk with the Lord. We believers *must* maintain the preached word of God. Has your church removed the proclamation of the word of God?

These two categories of preaching (proclamation) and teaching (explanation) the message of the mystery once hidden from man, but now has been made available unto all who hear, are detrimental to our spiritual health and well-being. This mystery is Christ Jesus, the hope of glory! Something continues to come alive and remain healthy within us when the word is proclaimed. That something, or should I say someone, is Jesus Christ, the hope of glory, living inside each believer.

From chapter 1 of this book and to the end, I am *teaching* or instructing in the word of God. When invited to a church to minister, I *proclaim* the word of God, along with teaching occasionally as the Holy Spirit directs. Sometimes, it's loud, sometimes soft, sometimes long, and sometimes short. I will be proclaiming or heralding the word of God out to the believers within the Church, which God has chosen for His believers to hear His anointed and everlasting word to help build our faith stronger.

One-on-one evangelism in my daily life—as I come in contact with those around me where I work, get gas, go to the grocery store, fellowship, etc.—is of utmost importance to me. Unless there are special meetings in the church—specifically, for outreach, like revival meetings, or my favorite tent meetings—then evangelism takes on a whole new life of its own during that time frame.

These meetings are designed to reach the needs not only of the believers, but the unbelievers as well. Trust me, when the power of Jesus's Holy Spirit manifests, there will be no lack of believers or unbelievers filling the seats. It will be standing room only, overflowing into the parking lot.

If there is any who is not born again in the meeting, it's the word of God that is responsible to activate the measure of faith already within them and the Holy Spirit's power to convince them of sin, righteousness, and judgment.

The Holy Spirit is faithful to bring them to a place of godly sorrow that brings forth repentance, not to be repented from. The Holy Spirit of Jesus in others and myself must have free reign to manifest the operations of His gifts revealing the wonderful works of God.

"For godly sorrow produces repentance leading to salvation, not to be regretted; but the sorrow of the world produces death." (2 Cor. 7:10)

Technically, before each of us was born again, we were lost. I believe the reason the Holy Spirit inspired the words "to save those who believe" is because, first, He knows who will believe and who will not (even though it is God's will that none shall perish, but all come to repentance).

Secondly, He has designed the foolishness of the message preached to confound the world, while keeping those who are believers saved by hearing it proclaimed and taught over and over. A constant feeding upon the living word keeps us spiritually healthy.

Ministers, I encourage you to maintain a healthy spiritual congregation! *Preach* the word of God as per His design to feed His believers. There is something that happens that turns on a believer's spirit, when the word of God is proclaimed. Nothing stirs the spirit quite like preaching the word does. The fires of the Holy Spirit burn strongest when men and women proclaim His truth!

Believers doing the work of the ministry are also the vehicles, tools, and instruments in the hand of God. He works with us presenting His word to as many as He sends us to, either by preaching, teaching, or both. Sometimes it is simply by being an example to others. But most certainly, His word will and should be presented in His power and might, which takes His Holy Spirit to present the word of God in this manner.

While attending a well-known denominational church, the assistant pastor was teaching the congregation that Jesus never preached. He was teaching that Jesus only was a teacher of the word of God to the people and that Jesus was a great teacher!

(Have you ever heard this from any other false doctrines of other religions?) Practically all of them recognize Jesus as a great teacher. But that is all the due credit they give Him. They never acknowledge Him as the Son of God, let alone as the Savior of the world. If they do not, the scriptures declare that they have the antichrist spirit.

"Beloved, believe not every spirit, but try the spirits whether they are of God: because many false prophets are gone out into the world. Hereby know ye the Spirit of God: Every spirit that confesseth that Jesus Christ is come in the flesh is of God: And every spirit that confesseth not that Jesus Christ is come in the flesh is not of God: and this is that spirit of antichrist, whereof ye have heard that it should come; and even now already is it in the world." (1 John 4:1–3, KJV)

"Who is a liar but he who denies that Jesus is the Christ? He is antichrist who denies the Father and the Son. Whoever denies the Son does not have the Father either; he who acknowledges the Son has the Father also." (1 John 2:22–23)

"For many deceivers have gone out into the world who do not confess Jesus Christ as coming in the flesh. This is a deceiver and an antichrist." (2 John 7)

Red flags started waving, as we listened to his message. This same assistant pastor was allowed later on to teach the adult class during the weekday service on the topic of the occult. Needless to say, I wanted no part of learning what all other religions believed, and it certainly was not relevant for my family and me.

You can trust me when I tell you that <u>all we need to know</u> is <u>what the Bible says</u>. This way we will recognize truth when we see it, as well as a lie. All that shows up contrary to the Bible will stick out like a sore thumb and for the lie that it is. These sore thumbs and red flags waving are informing us that something is not quite right.

How will you know a false teaching when it shows up? By previously studying your Bible, which contains the truth—something you, as a Christian, need to practice on a daily or regular basis, not just receive the word in your Sunday-school class (if it's still being offered), Sunday's messages, and/or during the midweek service, if there is one.

By knowing the word of God with the Holy Spirit as your teacher, you will be rightly dividing the word of truth. Yet there are many believers who are only being spoon-fed the word of God by those who are in leadership within the Church. Does this mentality sound familiar in any way? If it does, run from it, and run to the Holy Spirit of truth and life.

The practice of placing your eternal belief and well-being solely in the hands of someone else is a risky business. How do you know if they are speaking the truth if you do not know the truth yourself? This is a poor way to handle a personal relationship with Jesus Christ and His Holy Spirit.

This warning is not given so that you will not listen to those in authority at your church, but for you to be sure that what they are preaching and teaching are from the word of God and that they too are rightly dividing the word of truth. And the only way that you will ever know this is if you are rightly dividing the word of truth yourself.

Always remember the "two or more witness" litmus test, which always establishes a truth. Scriptures are designed by the Holy Spirit to interpret one another. If they do not, do not receive it as a truth until you find the other witness(es) that is revealing the same principles.

My wife and I received some words of wisdom from an evangelist friend of ours. He said, "Studying and hearing the word of God are like eating fish. Eat the meat, but spit out the bones." For example, you're born-again and you attend your church service on Sunday or in the middle of the week, and there is an altar call for salvation. The bone of the message is, just because an altar call is given, you do not have to go forward and ask for forgiveness again, because you are already born-again. The altar call is valid, but only for those who are not born-again. That is the meat of the message.

By no means am I trying to keep you from the altar. Let the Holy Spirit be your guide as to when you need to be there. Sometimes the pastor will open up the altar for anyone to come down and pray. This is very healthy for a church to have this available to them on a frequent basis.

However, if you have committed an act of sin, then ask the Lord to forgive you, and do not wait until another service, then move on with Him. He is faithful and just to forgive us and cleanse us of all unrighteousness by His blood. Do not be condemned over it one second longer. Remember, the devil and men condemn (no hope) and the Holy Spirit convicts (convinces of the truth, which always has hope in Christ).

"If we confess our sins, He is faithful and just to forgive us our sins and to cleanse us from all unrighteousness." (1 John 1:9)

"There is therefore now no condemnation to those who are in Christ Jesus, who do not walk according to the flesh, but according to the Spirit." (Rom. 8:1)

These were written to the Church. So as the Holy Spirit is able to convince you of any sin in your life, confess it to Jesus, and ask Him to forgive you, which He is faithful and just to do so, thereby keeping you cleansed from all unrighteousness with His blood.

Getting back to Jesus preaching and teaching and rightly dividing the word of truth, let's take a closer look at some other important scriptures in the New Testament:

"And Jesus went about all Galilee, teaching in their synagogues, preaching the gospel of the kingdom, and healing all kinds of sickness and all kinds of disease among the people." (Matt. 4:23)

As a direct result of His preaching and teaching, many people were healed of all kinds of sickness and disease. So we must ask, are we seeing this happening in the modern-day churches or in our own lives? *See also Matthew 9:35 and Acts 5:42; 15:35; 28:30, 31.*

There, the truth has been established by the mouth of two or more witnesses that Jesus preached as well as taught the words of the Father. He both proclaimed and explained His words. To confirm, here is what the Greek word meaning is for both *preaching* and *teaching* used in these scriptures:

> "preaching—*kerusso* (kay-roos'-so); of uncertain affinity; to herald (as a public crier), especially divine truth (the gospel): KJV—preacher (-er), proclaim, publish" (NT:2784).
> "teaching—*didasko* (did-as'-ko); a prolonged (causative) form of a primary verb *dao* (to learn); to teach (in the same broad application): KJV—teach" (NT:1321).

What if I did not know the truth and my wife and family sat in these kinds of teachings and just accepted them as truth without searching the truth out for us? Then as we see today, other religions are demanding equal recognition, with each saying that Jesus was a great teacher, but never the Son of God, and the only Savior of mankind, nor do they say that He is the only *way* to heaven.

We might believe them, and our faith would be diminished because now we believe that Jesus is only a great teacher instead of as the only begotten of the Father, full of grace and truth as the Son of God and Savior of our soul. Do you see the danger?

The fivefold ministry gifts—apostles, prophets, evangelists, pastors, and teachers—are those who are responsible in proclaiming and teaching what thus says the Lord. And to those who say Jesus was a teacher only, this is not only half a truth, as we have seen above, but a lie as well. While He was a great teacher, He was, and is, so much more than that!

All believers can proclaim the word of God, and all can teach. Many teachers usually only teach, as they give instructions, which differs from those who are heralding the message proclaimed from the housetops, if necessary. This rooftop scenario is, of course, an example of how important it is to proclaim the good news of Jesus Christ.

Having said this, I have been teaching before, when the anointing of the Holy Spirit would change the message to proclamation for a period of time. So there are no absolutes here, because it's the Holy Spirit who chooses, just like with His gifts, deciding who does what or says what and how to present it, either by teaching, preaching, or both. However, this truly only happens when those speaking are being led by His Holy Spirit. Otherwise, your personality will be guiding you and not the Holy Spirit.

You may be asking by now, what does rightly dividing the word of truth have to do with the fruit of the Spirit? I am glad you finally asked. Let me explain.

What if I were not filled with the Holy Spirit of Jesus, and I treated what He said to me as a passing thought? Perhaps, I would be too embarrassed of having to reread the scripture I misquoted above? I stood corrected by the Holy Spirit, who took the opportunity to teach the lesson not only to me, but also to those attending the meeting. All were instructed, all were edified, and the Church was built up.

Can you now see how wrong our messages can be if we are *not* rightly dividing the word of truth? Even though they may sound very spiritual, the content could not be farther from the truth.

I wanted to point out one of my mistakes so that everyone else could learn from it as well. After all, aren't we supposed to be examples—epistles read by all men?

"You are our epistle written in our hearts, known and read by all men; clearly you are an epistle of Christ, ministered by us, written not with ink but by the Spirit of the living God, not on tablets of stone but on tablets of flesh, that is, of the heart." (2 Cor. 3:2–3)

What does it say about us ministers if we write the wrong message on your heart from ours that are being read by others? Leaders, the importance of rightly dividing the word of truth cannot be repeated enough. It, truly, is a life-or-death situation, spiritually and naturally for believers and for those who may be kept away from their eternal salvation by a lie, because somebody *did not* rightly divide the word of truth!

I can guarantee that if I were not filled with the Holy Spirit and not following His lead, my pride would have hidden this misquoting from me and the rest of the people in that service. I would have finished the message without bringing attention to it unless someone had challenged me in this quote. I would not have addressed it, even if I noticed my mistake. But that was the old Jim, and the new man that I've become is not afraid to show my humanity and admit to my mistake, because, after all, I am human.

If I were not willing to allow the Holy Spirit's fruit to grow inside me, and I remained the same man I was when I was born again several years ago, how can I expect others to change when I have not? What if I were not learning how to listen to that "still small voice" inside me while learning to hear what His instructions were for me?

What if I were ministering to you personally? Who would you prefer I be listening to—the Holy Spirit who has the truth, power, and gift to meet your need, or myself who is limited in my knowledge, power, and experience, which every man and woman are? You decide, and the next time you ask somebody to pray or minister to you, remember to ask yourself this question: who would I prefer to minister to me—the man or the Holy Spirit in the man?

For those that make this choice of not believing that the baptism of the Holy Spirit is not for today, must realize that this course of action will have them remaining on the milk of the word longer that they should. Which in turn, keeps them dependent upon others to telling them what truth is, instead of learning to eat the meat of the word with the Holy Spirit teaching them what truth is.

The devil never has feared a new convert, because there is always the possibility of him or her being convinced to go back into the world or just go no further with the Lord. Going to church once a week is enough, and praying only when you're in trouble is more than adequate, isn't it? I have found it <u>not</u> to be so.

However, the devil trembles when believers are filled with the Holy Spirit and the fire of God. Believers who mature and are skillful in the use of this double-edged sword of the Spirit defeat their attackers at every turn, uncovering his traps that he thinks he has set for our destruction, only to find out that they work for our good.

"And I, brethren, could not speak to you as to spiritual people but as to carnal, as to babes in Christ. I fed you with milk and not with solid food; for until now you were not able to receive it, and even now you are still not able; for you are still carnal. For where there are envy, strife, and divisions among you, are you not carnal and behaving like mere men?

For when one says, 'I am of Paul [or to say Baptist],' and another, 'I am of Apollos [or to say Pentecostal]', are you not carnal?" (1 Cor. 3:1–4)

Based on this scripture alone, where would you say that you are in Christ? Where would you say that the Church you're attending is in Christ? By *not* believing these gifts are of God and for today, you are choosing the side that is allowing a division within the body of Christ. What should we consider ourselves, according to *First Corinthians 3:4?*

It has taken twenty-six chapters in this book just to get to where we are now. What does it say about us believers if we do not have the unity of faith, according to the scriptures that we say we believe? What happens to us as believers if we are teaching half-truths or, maybe, principles that are not even found within the Bible? Are we rightly dividing the word of truth?

Paul wrote to the church of Galatians and informed them of this.

"But even if we, or an angel from heaven, preach any other gospel to you than what we have preached to you, let him be accursed. As we have said before, so now I say again, if anyone preaches any other gospel to you than what you have received, let him be accursed." (Gal. 1:8–9)

Which Gospel (good news) are you listening to? Which Gospel are you practicing? Which Gospel are you preaching and teaching? Experience God's *goodness* by believing the whole word of God, every scripture, every page, every chapter, and every book within the context that the Holy Spirit inspired it.

The one who knows the depth of its true meaning is the one who should be revealing them to each of our understanding so that we can be rightly dividing the word of truth. Receiving the substance that Jesus said would build His Church and against which the gates of hell could not prevail brings fortitude individually and collectively. That substance is revelation knowledge!

"And I also say to you that you are Peter, and on this rock I will build My church, and the gates of Hades [hell] shall not prevail against it." (Matt. 16:18)

Peter answered, *"Thou art the Christ, the son of God,"* and Jesus said, *"Flesh and blood has not revealed this to you."*

THE OPERATIVE

I know this may be foreign to some of you, but it is yours as well as my responsibility to rightly divide or understand the word of God, whether or not we are to be preaching and teaching the correct Gospel, not a Gospel that is a watered-down version that tickles the ears of the hearers—giving them just enough information to sound spiritual and having a form of godliness but denying the power thereof.

"Be diligent to present yourself approved to God, a worker who does not need to be ashamed, rightly dividing the word of truth." (2 Tim. 2:15)

"Having a form of godliness but denying its power. And from such people turn away!" (2 Tim. 3:5)

"Beloved, do not believe every spirit, but test the spirits, whether they are of God; because many false prophets have gone out into the world. By this you know the Spirit of God: Every spirit that confesses that Jesus Christ has come in the flesh is of God, and every spirit that does not confess that Jesus Christ has come in the flesh is not of God. And this is the spirit of the antichrist, which you have heard was coming, and is now already in the world." (1 John 4:1–3)

If we are <u>rightly dividing the word of truth,</u> we can only come to the correct conclusion—that the <u>baptism</u> of the Holy Spirit, the <u>gifts</u> of the Holy Spirit, and the <u>fruit</u> of the Holy Spirit are available for each of us individually in the body of Christ in the modern Church for *today*!

The choice is yours. If you are convinced that the Holy Spirit is the operative in today's body of Christ, then I pray that you have already asked Jesus to baptize you with the Holy Spirit and have received the evidence of speaking in tongues. Also, I pray that you are yielding yourself to Him to be used in the operation of His gifts and realizing that His fruit is growing stronger within you each time you pray in the Spirit or tongues.

In chapter 27 we will explore the next fruit of *faithfulness*. Not only will we find God's faithfulness to us, but we will also learn how faith helps us to be faithful to Him by rightly dividing the word of truth.

CHAPTER 27

Fruit of the Holy Spirit
FAITH

"But the fruit of the Spirit is love, joy, peace, longsuffering, gentleness, goodness, FAITH, meekness, temperance: against such there is no law." (Gal. 5:22–23, KJV)

We now take a look at the fruit of *faith*. The word used in the NKJV for *faith* is *faithfulness*. The original definition of the word is the same as *faith* in the KJV, and for this reason, I have used the KJV scripture for this fruit.

> "faith—*pistis* (pis'-tis); from NT:3982; persuasion, i.e. credence; moral conviction (of religious truth, or the truthfulness of God or a religious teacher), especially reliance upon Christ for salvation; abstractly, constancy in such profession; by extension, the system of religious (Gospel) truth itself" (NT:4102).
>
> "*peitho* (pi'-tho); a primary verb; to convince (by argument, true or false); by analogy, to pacify or conciliate (by other fair means); reflexively or passively, to assent (to evidence or authority), to rely (by inward certainty): KJV—agree,

assure, believe, have confidence, be (wax) confient, make friend, obey, persuade, trust, yield" (NT:3982).

Based on these two definitions, we can say that the fruit of *faith* is being convinced of religious and moral truths as a conviction and not a preference, fully persuaded by acting upon and aligning oneself to those convictions, especially salvation through Jesus Christ, and having the utmost confidence in these truths, agreeing with their teachings, by trust and obedience producing *faith*, by the evidence of the authority by which they came from.

If you will recall from previous chapters, the traditions of men invalidate the word of God. Traditions remove validation of the last sentence of the definition of *faith* above that states, "Having the utmost confidence in these truths as to agreeing with their teachings, by trust and obedience producing FAITH, by the evidence of the authority by which they came from."

This fruit of *faith* is the characteristic of Jesus revealed to us and through us by His Holy Spirit and is the substance that pleases God. It is not that we please God by our faith, but the *faith* that pleases Him is found in the *faith* of Jesus in whom He is well pleased. Since Jesus is living His life inside each believer, we must learn how to trust in Jesus's *faith* to please the Father.

"Trust in the LORD with all your heart, And lean not on your own understanding; In all your ways acknowledge Him, And He shall direct your paths." (Prov. 3:5–6)

"Trust—*batach* (baw-takh'); a primitive root; properly, to hie for refuge [but not so precipitately as OT:2620]; figuratively, to trust, be confident or sure: KJV—be bold (confident, secure, sure), careless (one, woman), put confidence, (make to) hope, (put, make to) trust" (OT:982).

"*chacah* (khaw-saw'); a primitive root; to flee for protection [compare OT:982]; figuratively, to confide in" (OT:2620)

We must learn to make Him our refuge and our hiding place and have the confidence that His *faith* will be released in our lives in the capacity that is pleasing to God. This can only be realized, as we believe that He *is*, and as we continue to hide in Him and seek His presence, God does the rewarding.

"But without faith it is impossible to please Him, for he who comes to God must believe that He is, and that He is a rewarder of those who diligently seek Him." (Heb. 11:6)

Our commitment to God's word, as we are faithful to maintain the correct relationship toward His word, should be enhanced tremendously by rightly dividing the word of truth.

Faith has substance! This substance is the evidence of what we are trusting God to bring into existence that is not within our life or possession. This enables us to enjoy the benefits of it before it manifests. Why? Because it is just as real in the spirit realm as it will be in the natural realm once it is manifested in our lives as a possession.

"Be anxious for nothing, but in everything by prayer and supplication, with thanksgiving, let your requests be made known to God; and the peace of God, which surpasses all understanding, will guard your hearts and minds through Christ Jesus." (Phil. 4:6–7)

Notice the presence of the fruit of *peace* in thanking Him for answering our prayers and supplications, because His answer is already yes and amen. His *faith* sees the thing hoped for long before it is materialized in the natural realm in our lives or as our possession.

We must learn to use our spiritual eye to do the same, with the aid of our seeing eye and our hearing ear that God created within us. The evidence of the thing hoped for, that faith sees, is the substance, of the thing hoped for, that all things that have been created and given by God, are made with. From this spiritual substance, all things were created by Him and for Him.

"Now faith is the substance of things hoped for, the evidence of things not seen. For by it the elders obtained a good testimony. By faith we understand that the worlds were framed by the word of God, so that the things which are seen were not made of things which are visible." (Heb. 11:1–3)

"He [Jesus] is the image of the invisible God, the firstborn over all creation. For by Him all things were created that are in heaven and that are on earth, visible and invisible, whether thrones or dominions or principalities or powers. All things were created through Him and for Him.

And He is before all things, and in Him all things consist. And He is the head of the body, the church, who is the beginning, the firstborn from the dead, that in all things He may have the preeminence." (Col. 1:15–18)

For example, how do we know that we have a glorified body available that will make us look and act exactly like Jesus at the time of the rapture? *Faith* sees our glorified body, as we believe and accept the word of God as truth that reveals His will, concerning His promise of us receiving our glorified body.

Faith views the image of it within our spirit and informs our transformed mind of its truth. We see it long before we receive it. This process provides our possessions that we are made a steward over or they are answers to prayers for others. This is the reason we do not have to settle for a fixed income after retiring. He supplies all our needs, according to His riches in glory, not our riches on earth.

"And my God shall supply all your need according to His riches in glory by Christ Jesus." (Phil. 4:19)

In Hebrews 11:1–3, we just found out that the tangible substance of all things known in the natural realm of the cosmos was made from the spiritual substance found within the spirit realm, which is also very tangible. For the sake of time, I will not go into detail here. However, in my second book entitled *The Original Thought*, I explain what the Bible has to say about what this substance of faith is and where it comes from.

Briefly, I believe the Bible teaches clearly that the substance of *faith* are Jesus and His Holy Spirit. *"Faith comes by hearing, and hearing by the word of God."* It is Jesus with His Holy Spirit who shows up each time the word is spoken and heard.

"For where two or three are gathered together in My name, I am there in the midst of them." (Matt. 18:20)

As you are reading right now, faith came because your spirit, soul, and body are hearing the word of God. Jesus, you, and I are gathered together via these words. In the realm of eternity, things like time, space, or distance are not barriers, as they are here on earth. You are experiencing His presence and anointing right now through His Holy Spirit, as I write and you read.

According to Hebrews, everything around us, even the very air we breathe, came from this substance found in the spiritual realm. Jesus came to give life, and life more abundantly.

The cosmos and its hosts are all facsimiles of the real substance found in the spirit realm. Scriptures declare this in Hebrews and Colossians that we just read, which confirms it by showing us that all things were made by and for Jesus, and nothing was made without Him.

God has given the answer to the age-old question for which modern-day scientists have continued to search for the answer for centuries, concerning, "how is matter held together?" May I have the pleasure of answering this question for you and them?

"God, who at various times and in various ways spoke in time past to the fathers by the prophets, has in these last days spoken to us by His Son, whom He has appointed heir of all things, through whom also He made the worlds; who being the brightness of His glory and the express image of His person, and upholding all things by the word of His power, when He had by Himself purged our sins, sat down at the right hand of the Majesty on high." (Heb. 1:1–3)

See the answer? God is speaking to us in these last days through His Son, Jesus ("Son language"), and He (the Son) upholds all things created by and for Him by the word of His power.

This word of his power differs from the power of His word in this manner. The power of His word speaks of life and Spirit that His word contains. The word of His power speaks of <u>Him giving His word</u> as a promise that it will do this or that until He changes it.

His faithfulness over His promised word is to see to it that it also does that which He sent it to do. His word never returns to Him empty, as it always produces that which it is intended to produce, whether salvation to men or holding all things together; His *faithfulness* is quite clear. I believe this is why the cosmos is still expanding. It has a life of its own because He made it so.

All things being equal, every law of quantum physics and all other governing laws of the universe will remain operational until He is finished with them. This is the word of His power because He promised this before the foundations of the world, and the Holy Spirit inspired the words "upholding all things by the word of His power."

During the initial creation of all things, every law of physics and, probably, many laws of the cosmos that we are presently unaware of were created. They each were placed in existence by His promise that they each would work accordingly until He either interrupts them to perform a miracle, as in the working of a miracle, or until He is finished with them.

It is Jesus keeping His promises that are yes and amen, like God the Father did with the rainbow in the sky, promising us that the world would <u>never</u> be flooded again, no matter with how many doomsday global warming or climate changing people try to say otherwise.

"For all the promises of God in Him are Yes, and in Him Amen, to the glory of God through us." (2 Cor. 1:20)

Take a few moments and meditate on this; you'll come to one conclusion. The word of God is correct in all that it says! Taking *faith* one step further, I briefly mentioned this above that I believe *faith's* substance to be the very person of Jesus, and "When two or more are gathered in my name, in the midst of them I will be," He said.

"Again I say to you that if two of you agree on earth concerning anything that they ask, it will be done for them by My Father in heaven. For where two or three are gathered together in My name, I am there in the midst of them." (Matt. 18:19–20)

Remember what Jude said was needed to build up yourself on your most holy faith—by praying in the Spirit? The fruit of *faith* is the foundation that we are building ourselves upon, each time we pray in the Holy Spirit in tongues. We are made stronger and stronger upon what? Our most holy faith! What *faith* is holier than Jesus's *faith*? What better foundation can a believer build upon than the foundation of Jesus Christ?

"For no other foundation can anyone lay than that which is laid, which is Jesus Christ." (1 Cor. 3:11)

As we found out that faith makes us stronger, *faith's* growth in a believer can be stunted and weakened by not believing correctly or by not praying in the Spirit. Praying in the Holy Spirit matures and strengthens the faith of Jesus in us. According to the scriptures, the faith that we believers are supposed to be living our lives <u>by</u> is actually the *faith* of Jesus and not our own faith.

"I am crucified with Christ: nevertheless I live; yet not I, but Christ liveth in me: and the life which I now live in the flesh I live BY the faith of the Son of God, who loved me, and gave himself for me." (Gal. 2:20, KJV)

We know that we are to be more like Jesus. We know that He lives His life in us once we are born again. How is this accomplished? By *His faith* living and growing inside us that we accept as truth, and He is full of grace and truth.

Whose faith, then, is it that we should be living our lives by? Is it our faith or His *faith*? It is <u>by the faith of the Son of God,</u> who loved us and gave Himself for us. It's the substance that the measure of faith given to us at conception originated from. It grows stronger and stronger in each of us, as we hear the word of God and pray in tongues.

Why does *faith* come when we hear the written word of God proclaimed? Because the foolishness of preaching exchanges the written word of God into the living word of God—Jesus in our ears, minds, and spirits. He literally comes alive within us each time He hears somebody talking about who He is and what He has accomplished for us.

The word *faith*, a fruit of the Holy Spirit found in *Galatians 5:22, 23*, is the same word used for the *faith* of the Son of God in *Galatians 2:20*. As much as many believers like reading the NKJV of the Bible, we still have to be aware of certain words in it that loses the original inspired thought from the Holy Spirit.

Galatians 2:20 is one of those scriptures. For this reason, I will also show you the NKJV for you to compare for yourselves:

"I have been crucified with Christ; it is no longer I who live, but Christ lives in me; and the life which I now live in the flesh I live by faith IN the Son of God, who loved me and gave Himself for me." (Gal. 2:20, NKJV)

According to the KJV of *Galatians 2:20*, it's Jesus's faith we are to be living our lives by. The NKJV says that we are supposed to *"live by the faith in the Son of God."* These are two distinct and different methods of faith. See the problem?

The NKJV version has us using our faith in Jesus, and the KJV has us using the faith of Jesus. Faith in Jesus is completely different from the faith of Jesus.

However, since it is Jesus's faith that we are supposed to live by, then we should realize that it is His faith and not ours that is actually living and maturing inside us. Our faith has doubts and unbelief where <u>His faith does not</u>.

Be very careful with different versions of the Bible. There are scriptures that are found in some versions of the Bible that the "Holy Spirit originally inspired" message is not what is given, compared to the KJV. (I will give further evidence of this and how misleading the other versions can be with some scriptures later in chapter 29.)

If a version of the Bible gives a different meaning or interpretation other than that of the original intent of the Holy Spirit, is this preaching another gospel? We must not take the things of the Holy Spirit lightly, as they are eternal. By keeping as close to the original message as possible, we receive the true revelation knowledge needed to be part of the Church that the gates of hell will not prevail against. With the Holy Spirit's help, we can stay true to the inspired message He intends us to have.

To live by the faith of the Son of God is to be using the faith of Jesus. You have heard it said—Jesus said it, I believe it, and that settles it. I submit to you that <u>Jesus said it, and that settles it!</u> Whether we believe or not, Jesus's *faith* remains intact. He cannot and will never deny His existence. His faith remains the same yesterday, today, and forever!

Here is another quick example of this being lost in a different version. The NKJV says in Second Timothy 2:13, "If we are faithless, He remains faithful; He cannot deny Himself."

The KJV says, "If we believe not, yet he abideth faithful: he cannot deny himself."

At first glance they both appear to be saying the same thing. However, they both tell the reader a different message. Many people say they have faith but do not believe in God or His word. According to this scripture, God remains faithful to His word because He cannot deny Himself. So one can have faith and still not believe, because they simply do not have the faith of Jesus Christ activated within them yet.

So the bottom line is that God cannot deny Himself, whether we believe His word or not. However, we know by other scriptures that *nobody* is <u>faithless</u>. We have read scripture that has proven that everyone is given a measure of faith.

I believe that the KJV has a better interpretation than the NKJV in this comparison as well. This is why I study the KJV with the original Hebrew and Greek words more than the NKJV. I use both throughout this book just for a comparison model.

If you are using something other than one of these two versions, you will be interested in my comparisons in chapter 29 of the one scripture in the Bible that I judge every version by. If a version misses the mark of the original inspired truth on this one scripture, I do not trust it to give me insight on any other unless I research for myself to see if they align with the original inspiration by the Holy Spirit.

As mentioned, to live by the faith in the Son of God implies that I now have to have a faith of my own and believe <u>in</u> Jesus, instead of using the faith <u>of</u> Jesus, knowing that He *is*. His *faith* moves mountains, heals the sick, raises the dead, and casts out demons, to name a few. Our faith falls short of the glory of God. This is why His *faith* keeps coming!

Remember, as we studied the gifts of the Holy Spirit, one of those gifts was the gift of *faith*? Whose *faith* is this when the Holy Spirit uses the gift of *faith* supernaturally? Is it our faith that is supercharged or Jesus's *faith* that is already filled with resurrection power of His Holy Spirit? Of course, it is His *faith*. This is why it is considered a gift, given at special times to accomplish specific tasks and meet specific needs that man's abilities and resources cannot.

During our daily walking by faith and not physical sight alone, we need to recognize that it is the faith of the Son of God, living in us that keeps nourishing the measure of faith that is growing and maturing inside us with His life-giving substance. Because of this connection of life through His faith, we are able to continue to trust

Him with all our hearts and know that He is working all things for our good.

This faith of His transforms us from (our) glory to (His) glory, and by living our lives by His faith, we are enabled to look past that which is trying to get us away from God by doubt and unbelief, keeping us headed toward our mark and toward our goal of the high calling of God.

"But we all, with unveiled face, beholding as in a mirror the glory of the Lord, are being transformed into the same image from glory to glory, just as by the Spirit of the Lord." (2 Cor. 3:18)

Both are from the same substance, which is Jesus. The fruit of faith we live by, according to *Galatians 2:20*, is a growth process of maturing in the grace and knowledge of our Lord Jesus, by allowing His faith in us to be strengthened and to mature us spiritually by hearing His word and praying in tongues. We can and do eventually mature into the person He wants us to become.

However, it would be too much for our earthly body to receive Him in His fullness all the time, as we are still in this earthly body of flesh. For this reason, we grow in this grace and knowledge of Him because of the faith of the Son of God in us, until we receive our glorified bodies—line upon line, precept upon precept, here a little, there a little.

This will take place, and we will be just as He is. The last trumpet of God will sound, and He gives the order to change the governing laws of the cosmos, pertaining to our bodies, and we each receive our glorified bodies that will now be able to house Him in His *fullness*!

The gift of His faith, through His Holy Spirit, is as if it were Jesus doing it through us (fully matured faith, lacking nothing in any way.) Isn't this actually what happens when we minister Jesus to people, and they get born again or healed and even delivered? This is the gift of *faith* that helps us to act like God. Is it any wonder that this pleases Him? Aren't you pleased when you see your children acting like you?

The other two gifts that help us to act like God are the gifts of healing and working of miracles. These are parts of the wonderful works of God, as they are the results of Jesus being who He is. "This is my beloved Son in whom I am well pleased." See why Jesus's faith <u>in us</u> pleases God, and without His faith, we cannot please God?

He did the works of the Father while here on earth, giving us examples so that we can yield to His Holy Spirit, allowing Him now to do the works of the Father through us. Because of the operation of these gifts of His Holy Spirit that are given to us by promise, we too can be—as Peter, Paul, and others were—vessels of honor and channels of His power, by showing the world the wonderful works of God.

I am convinced that many good men, women, and children have been discouraged because they desired an abundant life in Christ and fell short because they tried or are trying to muster up enough faith to walk a walk of faith. The devil and circumstances can shake our faith on its best day. Our faith is just not good enough to get the job done. <u>We should be aware of this very important truth!</u> If it were good enough to get the job done, then why would we need Jesus at all after we are born again?

Hopefully, we can now see this truth, and we correct the way we believe accordingly. Have some of our spiritual leaders in the Church failed to see this crucial point? The Holy Spirit revealed this answer when He revealed that <u>a measure of faith</u> is given to every man. Let's read it one more time and see what else this scripture is offering us:

"For I say, through the grace given to me, to everyone who is among you, not to think of himself more highly than he ought to think, but to think soberly, as God has dealt to each one a measure of faith." (Rom. 12:3)

Did you notice, prior to informing us, that we *all* were given a measure of faith and, as I mentioned before that I believe this measure is at the time of conception, that the Lord informs us of how men would think of themselves?

God knew that there would be no lack of men who would think more highly of themselves than they should, so in order to think soberly, <u>God dealt</u> to <u>each</u> one a (same) measure of faith upon conception. This is a benefit from God. The reality of this truth is that not all men and women allow this measure of faith to be activated, because they think more highly of themselves than they should. How sad this is that many are throwing away not only their abundant life here on earth, but their eternal lives as well. Then some who are born again seem to be able to use their faith more than others do, perhaps because of enticing words of man's wisdom.

If we use *our* faith, some men would think more highly of themselves than they should. Faith comes and grows, and individual faith is not all on the same level of strength. But what if all believers start using the faith of Jesus?

For this reason, it is very important to rightly divide the word of truth as a normal practice for all believers, as we just found out in the previous chapter, is it not?

(Let's follow God's design here.) The word was with God. This is God the Father speaking to the angels, cherubim, and seraphim after creating them first. This was so He could have fellowship and communication with someone other than Himself. Before the creation of the cosmos, His way of communicating had already been established by <u>His Word</u>.

Upon establishing the stars, planets, solar systems, etc. in order, the Word of God was the agent of communication until the Word became flesh—"The Word of the Lord came to me" with an occasional visitation of angels. In the course of time, the Word miraculously became flesh, then it was Jesus from there on out. This is why all things are considered made by Him and for Him—Jesus, that is, because He was the spoken Word of God the Father, who created all things.

Becoming flesh, the Word dwelled among us and became known to us as Jesus, Emmanuel—"God with us." He lived and walked among us until He was crucified then raised from the dead. The faith of God found in Jesus is the creative force, substance, and power of God the Father used to raise Jesus from the dead, which is His Spirit's resurrection power.

When Jesus was crucified, the power contained within His *faith*, which made it possible for Him to be raised from the dead, filled His being with the resurrection power of the Holy Spirit. We now know Him as the Spirit of Jesus Christ, or the Holy Ghost (Spirit).

The only time that there was any kind of separation was for that brief moment in time that the fleshly body of Jesus contained all sin of all men, women, and children, which was placed upon and within His flesh. This, of course, was seen in the spiritual realm only, not looked upon by God until His fleshly body died as Jesus, through His Holy Spirit, gave it permission to do so once the last sin was contained, which legally destroyed the power of sin with it.

But Jesus's Holy Spirit was intact and never disconnected from God the Father for a moment and still remains connected to both Jesus the Son and His glorified body, along with God the Father.

"Then Jesus, being filled with the Holy Spirit, returned from the Jordan and was led by the Spirit into the wilderness, being tempted for forty days by the devil." (Luke 4:1)

"For He [Jesus] whom God has sent speaks the words of God, for God does not give the Spirit by measure." (John 3:34, NKJV)

"For he whom God hath sent speaketh the words of God: for God giveth not the Spirit by measure unto him." (John 3:34, KJV)

Compare the KJV above with the NKJV, and see the difference once again. The NKJV would have us believe that God does not give the Spirit by measure, which He actually does, to men. Then the KJV clearly says that God gives not, meaning He did not give the Spirit by measure unto Him, meaning Jesus. This really can give the reader the wrong impression, which changes the understanding completely if we do not dig deeper for the true revelation and inspired word of the Holy Spirit.

Jesus died so that we might live—not just exist, but live! The design of God for our spirit and soul is that the Holy Spirit plants the seed of Jesus's *faith* in each of our spirit and soul at conception. I believe that at conception, this is the light of life that lights all men.

"In Him was life, and the life was the light of men." (John 1:4)

The Holy Spirit works to activate His seed of *faith* planted, giving it life each time we hear the word of God, which has the creative power of the Holy Spirit of Jesus Christ to do so.

One main hindrance to this process, besides the opposition from the devil, is the will of man. Since the Holy Spirit never forces

THE OPERATIVE

Himself upon man, He patiently moves and speaks in lawful ways that He knows will be more conducive for a person to receive.

It is men and women's rejection or acceptance of this power that determines how their outcome will be—eternal damnation and torment or eternal life with God the Father, Jesus the Son, and His Holy Spirit. God doesn't send *anyone* to hell!

"The Lord is not slack concerning His promise, as some count slackness, but is longsuffering toward us, not willing that any should perish but that all should come to repentance." (2 Peter 3:9)

Notice the fruit of *long-suffering?* The harsh reality is that man's will is a factor that prolongs the time that it takes for a man, a woman, or a child to come to the Lord or <u>not</u> at all. It is <u>not</u> God who sends mankind to hell. It is his or her choices.

As I mentioned before, and it bears repeating, I used to believe in reincarnation very strongly. My attitude was, *If I blow it in this life, I will get another chance to change things for the better in another life.* Many others believed this in the sixties and seventies and still do believe it today. But the hard truth is quite different.

"And as it is appointed for men to die once, but after this the judgment, so Christ was offered once to bear the sins of many. To those who eagerly wait for Him He will appear a second time, apart from sin, for salvation." (Heb. 9:27–28)

Once that truth hit my eyes and ears, my mind, then my heart (spirit), *faith* came to me even though I did not yield unto salvation at that time. But my belief system was challenged and shaken as the lie of reincarnation crumbled before my very eyes.

What hope did I have then? It was His *faith* (Jesus) that actually came to me and changed my mind and what I believed. The power of truth overcame the lie of reincarnation. Thank God I was smart enough to act upon it when I met Him face-to-face, seeing who I was in the light of who He is.

For me, the turning point in my life was during that Christmas trip to Florida in 1977. It triggered my thinking about the invisible God of the universe, which ultimately led me face-to-face with the truth of seeing who I really was. After I repented of my sin, I now belonged to Him. The only way I could have a close relationship with Him was to fellowship and to worship Him in spirit and truth. I knew that if I did not worship the Creator, I would continue to worship the creation.

The seed of faith given to me at my conception was activated by hearing, and hearing by the word of God, each time it was presented to me by another believer. *Faith* came, and He changed my life. For me, it took twenty-seven-and-a-half years to hear and for salvation to manifest into a reality. It does not have to take that long for you. Now is the accepted time; today is the day of salvation!

I had tapped into something bigger than I was, and it was His *faith* that came alive, which He planted within me long ago, enabling me to see the truth and to act upon it. This is what happened to you or will happen to you, depending upon your circumstances at the time of reading this book. You too will hear and see the truth that will set you free as well as bring forth your salvation even if you do not realize that it is happening.

The best biblical example of Jesus's *faith* in operation—I must repeat myself by telling it—and that was when Peter said, "Lord, bid me to come to you." What did Jesus's *faith* say? "No, Peter, you better stay in the boat. You know humans cannot walk on water"? No, Jesus's *faith* said, <u>"Come,"</u> and Peter stepped onto the water and walked.

It was not till Peter began to use his faith, which saw the wind and the waves in the natural realm instead of Jesus's faith that he originally trusted in, and his mind began reasoning, *You can't walk on water* when down he went. Even when we use our faith, Jesus is still there to lift us back up again. Our faith always sees the details of the circumstances; Jesus's faith always looks past them and sees the finished product of His will.

"Trust in the LORD with all thine heart; and lean not unto thine own understanding. In all thy ways acknowledge him, and he shall direct thy paths." (Prov. 3:5–6, KJV)

We draw from the strength of His *faith* giving us the ability to press on toward the mark of the high calling of the Lord.

"Now the just shall live BY faith; But if anyone draws back, My soul has no pleasure in him." (Heb. 10:38)

It is His *faith* then and today that we live and walk in the Spirit by faith and not by sight. We see by His *faith*, concerning matters, instead of what we see or feel in the natural. Whose report are you going to believe?

"Who hath believed our report? and to whom is the arm of the LORD revealed?" (Isa. 53:1, KJV)

It's like signing for a package that you did not order. Once you sign for it, you get what's in that package. <u>Stop signing for the wrong packages</u>, especially those you did not order. Make sure that your packages contain what you need from God and not something the devil is trying to pawn off on you.

Has this ever happened to you—the contents of the package signed for were contrary to the word of God and His promises? If so, take a stand now, and use the pressure of the *faith* of the Son of God to change the circumstances. Ask, seek, and knock until you have the results that will line up with the promises of God, which are yes and amen.

"For all the promises of God in Him are Yes, and in Him Amen, to the glory of God through us." (2 Cor. 1:20)

To see His mighty hand upon my family and me throughout these thirty-seven years has been a wonderful thing to experience. Decades of walking by faith, realizing that He is the *faith* that is in me (us) and is still growing and becoming stronger with each day I trust in Him, is such great comfort to me (us).

This chapter would not be complete without us taking a look at *faithfulness*, so let's do so now, shall we?

faithfulness
Also found in Medical, Legal, Encyclopedia, Wikipedia.
faith·ful (fāth′fəl)
adj.

1. Adhering firmly and devotedly, as to a person, cause, or idea; loyal.
2. Engaging in sex only with one's spouse or only with one's partner in a sexual relationship.

3. a. Responsible; conscientious: the faithful discharge of his duties.
   b. Dependable; reliable: The faithful engine started right up.
4. Consistent with truth or actuality: a faithful reproduction of the portrait.
5. Having or full of faith.

pl.n.

1. The practicing members of a religious faith, especially of Christianity or Islam: a pilgrimage to Mecca made by the faithful.
2. The steadfast adherents of a faith or cause: a meeting of the party faithful.

faith′ful·ly adv.
faith′ful·ness n.
Synonyms: faithful, loyal, true, constant, fast1, steadfast, staunch[11]

It's important that we realize that faithfulness is a character trait that is derived from *faith* and not the other way around. Understanding the original inspiration of the Holy Spirit's fruit of *faith* is what allows us to be faithful.

We become faithful because of His *faith* in us. We do not have *faith* because of being faithful. I trust that you can see this for what it is. *Faith* comes to us as we hear the word of God, and *faith* is not a product of being faithful. However, faithfulness is a product of His *faith* alive within each believer! Faithfulness, then, is our good works because of Jesus's *faith* in us.

If we have a wrong understanding concerning the fruit of the Holy Spirit, whichever fruit it may be, but especially *faith/faithfulness*, it places undue burden upon our performances. Faith in our lives is not produced because of our works, but our works are pro-

---

11. The Free Dictionary by FARLEX

duced because of *faith*. Many people are faithful over many things, but all of them do not believe in Jesus just because they are faithful.

This is another reason it is so important to rightly divide the word of truth and with the inspired content of the Holy Spirit's original meaning. This can only be realized by Him helping us and showing us the truths that He intended for us to see and understand. Jesus knew this, and this is why He sent His Holy Spirit to us as that promised gift as our helper, teacher, comforter, and counselor.

Whose *faith* are you living your Christian walk by? Is it your faith—full of frustrations and disappointments, doubt and unbelief? Or is it His *faith*—full of the power of God bringing the blessings and divine appointments your way, showing you that He loves you and cares for you like nobody else could? Live each day as if God created it just for you, because He did!

The measure, gift, and fruit of *faith* contain the very same substance of Jesus. That substance is the evidence that Jesus Christ Himself is living inside each believer. As we choose to allow His Holy Spirit preeminence in our lives, things that are impossible for us to do are made possible for Him to do through us by the power of His Holy Spirit.

"Verily, verily, I say unto you, He that believeth on me, the works that I do shall he do also; and greater works than these shall he do; because I go unto my Father." (John 14:12, KJV)

By allowing the Lord to do the work through us via His Son and His Holy Spirit, all things become possible. This is what the statement "Let go and let God" means!

Have you let go of your faith and let God's *faith* of His Son come alive inside you, giving positive proof that Jesus is alive and living His life in your heart (spirit)? If not, please do so today, and enjoy the freedom that comes with His *faith*.

There are only two more fruit of the Spirit, remaining, which are gentleness and self-control. In chapter 28, we will take a closer look at the fruit of *gentleness*. Stay with me, and find out how the power of gentleness enhances our walk of *faith*!

Let Go and let God!

CHAPTER 28

Fruit of the Holy Spirit
GENTLENESS

"But the fruit of the Spirit is love, joy, peace, longsuffering, kindness, goodness, faithfulness, GENTLENESS, self-control. Against such there is no law." (Gal. 5:22–23)

We have traveled a great distance together to get to where we are today with this information. After we learn about *gentleness* contained in this chapter, there is only one other fruit of the Spirit to research, and that is the fruit of self-control, which is covered in chapters 29 and 30.

Let's get started by taking a look into the original meaning of the word used by the Holy Spirit for *gentleness* in *Galatians 5:22–23*.

"Gentleness—*prautes* (prah-oo'-tace); from [NT:4239]; mildness, i.e. (by implication) humility: KJV—meekness" (NT:4240).

"*praus* (prah-ooce'); apparently a primary word; mild, i.e. (by implication) humble: KJV—meek" (NT:4239).

This fruit brings into our lives the character of Jesus and His Holy Spirit, which is *gentleness*. From the information above, we derive a definition of *gentleness* as "one whose character reveals mildness with humility, without having a high or lofty thinking of themselves."

That is simple enough, is it not? We can sum this fruit up with one word—*humility*!

The word *gentleness* is found only seven (7) times in the New Testament. Each scripture has the same word found in 4240 or 4239 above. Let's take a look at each of them and see how this word *gentleness* is being used in context to the various New Testament scriptures.

"What do you want? Shall I come to you with a rod, or in love and a spirit of gentleness?" (1 Cor. 4:21)

"Now I, Paul, myself am pleading with you by the meekness and gentleness of Christ—who in presence am lowly among you, but being absent am bold toward you." (2 Cor. 10:1)

"But the fruit of the Spirit is love, joy, peace, longsuffering, kindness, goodness, faithfulness, gentleness, self-control. Against such there is no law." (Gal. 5:22–23)

"Brethren, if a man is overtaken in any trespass, you who are spiritual restore such a one in a spirit of gentleness, considering yourself lest you also be tempted." (Gal. 6:1)

"I, therefore, the prisoner of the Lord, beseech you to walk worthy of the calling with which you were called, with all lowliness and gentleness, with longsuffering, bearing with one another in love, endeavoring to keep the unity of the Spirit in the bond of peace." (Eph. 4:1–3)

"Let your gentleness be known to all men. The Lord is at hand." (Phil. 4:5)

"But you, O man of God, flee these things and pursue righteousness, godliness, faith, love, patience, gentleness." (1 Tim. 6:11)

More than one scripture above allude to the fact that the fruit of *gentleness*, like all the other fruit, is something we attain instead of having. Some of the above scriptures point to *gentleness* as belonging to Jesus and His Holy Spirit and is acquired as a gift that we should, at a minimum, be seeking for.

Other scriptures use the words *spirit of gentleness* or *spirit of meekness*. I believe a spirit of gentleness or meekness is a product of the other fruit growing in our spirits—again, making us more like Jesus today than we were yesterday.

Coming to terms with the fact that the fruit of the Holy Spirit is growing within our spirit makes it easier for us to understand that it is something we can't learn but rather someone that we become.

As previously mentioned, we have knowledge of each of these fruit characteristics to a degree, but because of our flesh, they are limited in use, and knowledge alone cannot increase them to the point of making us more like Jesus. (We may be stronger in the natural, in love, and weak in all the others or stronger in self-control and faith but have no love.)

God's way is higher than our learned levels of what we think as to how His fruit should be presented in our lives. What we learn through intellect always falls short of the glory of God. The Holy Spirit's fruit growing in us draws from the glory of God, which is found in Jesus Christ living His life in each of His believers.

The produce of His fruit is realized by the planting of the seed inside the spirit of all who call upon the name of the Lord to be saved. Planted there by His Holy Spirit, Jesus's active presence in our lives is nurturing us through our trials and tests as He waters us with His word, thus harvesting Christian maturity within each of His believers.

"Husbands, love your wives, just as Christ also loved the church and gave Himself for her, that He might sanctify and cleanse her with the washing of water by the word, that He might present her to Himself a glorious church, not having spot or wrinkle or any such thing, but that she should be holy and without blemish." (Eph. 5:25–27)

After planting His fruit, the Holy Spirit waters His field with the water by the word to cleanse and mature each of us individually and collectively at the same time as only He can. His fruit produces in each believer the visible character of Christ, without spot or wrinkle or any such thing because of His blood cleansing us from all unrighteousness. (This process is His, and there are no shortcuts that the flesh can take in maturing His fruit into the likeness of Jesus Christ.)

"This is the message which we have heard from Him and declare to you, that God is light and in Him is no darkness at all. If we say that

we have fellowship with Him, and walk in darkness, we lie and do not practice the truth. But if we walk in the light as He is in the light, we have fellowship with one another, and the blood of Jesus Christ His Son cleanses us from all sin.

If we say that we have no sin, we deceive ourselves, and the truth is not in us. If we confess our sins, He is faithful and just to forgive us our sins and to cleanse us from all unrighteousness. If we say that we have not sinned, we make Him a liar, and His word is not in us." (1 John 1:5–10)

It is the Holy Spirit's resurrection power contained in His fruit growing in us that changes us from our glory to His glory. The produce of the fruit is the proof that Jesus lives in our hearts by His resurrection power. It is His fruit (character) that begins this transformation in us and sees it through to the end. This process of being transformed continues until we are changed into the exact image (likeness) of Jesus Christ (Savior of our souls).

This was why I was able to previously make the statement, "I look at who I am today, and I do not recognize the person I used to be." That old man has died. The new man, my new spirit man, has grown more like Christ than I was thirty-seven years ago.

"Therefore, if anyone is in Christ, he is a new creation; old things have passed away; behold, all things have become new." (2 Cor. 5:17)

Our growth rate depends upon time spent with Jesus and His Holy Spirit in His word, studying, hearing, and applying what we freely receive into our lives, only to give it to others. This is the Holy Spirit watering His fruit in us.

"Study to shew thyself approved unto God, a workman that needeth not to be ashamed, rightly dividing the word of truth." (2 Tim. 2:15, KJV)

Prayer and meditation (thinking about) on the word of God are practices that should be done continually in a believer's life. Our fellowshipping with Him in the light of His presence brings the increase of His fruit, allowing our transformation to be realized step-by-step.

"That which we have seen and heard we declare to you, that you also may have fellowship with us; and truly our fellowship is with the

Father and with His Son Jesus Christ. And these things we write to you that your joy may be full." (1 John 1:3–4)

I do not believe this is talking about fellowshipping with each other individually or as a Church, as John wrote that, truly, our fellowship is with the Father and with His Son, Jesus Christ. The fruit of *gentleness* maintains the humility needed while becoming like Jesus. It keeps us from being puffed up and thinking we are somebody when we really are not. As these truths resonate loud and clear within our spirits, we are constantly reminded of where we came from and the course directions needed to keep us on track to where we are headed.

We're still in our body that is capable of performing acts of sin at any moment. Evil comes easy to us humans because sin is in our flesh. The acts of doing and being good have to be worked at and watched over by somebody who knows what makes us tick. This is where growing in the grace and knowledge of our Lord and Savior, Jesus, steps up. It is His Holy Spirit filling us who maintains the goodness in our lives as He watches over Christ maturing inside our spirits.

Our fellowship with one another is important too. But it is not the fellowship that increases the fruit of our righteousness. The fellowship that does this is the time we spend with the Father and His Son, Jesus Christ, through His Holy Spirit. How do we do this? Again, by prayer and meditation on His word. Hearing His word brings faith (Jesus) every time it is presented in any forum. Reading and studying His word water the fruit planted and help us to remain God conscious.

This allows the fruit of the Holy Spirit to continue to grow and mature in our spirits, revealing to others how much of the character of Jesus is operating in us. John the Baptist said, "I must decrease, and He must increase." This was what he was talking about—each of us becoming less of who we were and allowing Christ to become the center of attention instead of us.

Our spirit man is the eternal us. The fleshly man is whom we see in the mirror every morning. This flesh wars against the spirit and is always trying to get us from the true things of God.

THE OPERATIVE

"Where do wars and fights come from among you? Do they not come from your desires for pleasure that war in your members?" (James 4:1)

"There is therefore now no condemnation to those who are in Christ Jesus, who do not walk according to the flesh, but according to the Spirit. For the law of the Spirit of life in Christ Jesus has made me free from the law of sin and death. For what the law could not do in that it was weak through the flesh, God did by sending His own Son in the likeness of sinful flesh, on account of sin: He condemned sin in the flesh, that the righteous requirement of the law might be fulfilled in us who do not walk according to the flesh but according to the Spirit.

For those who live according to the flesh set their minds on the things of the flesh, but those who live according to the Spirit, the things of the Spirit. For to be carnally minded is death, but to be spiritually minded is life and peace. Because the carnal mind is enmity against God; for it is not subject to the law of God, nor indeed can be. So then, those who are in the flesh cannot please God.

But you are not in the flesh but in the Spirit, if indeed the Spirit of God dwells in you. Now if anyone does not have the Spirit of Christ, he is not His. And if Christ is in you, the body is dead because of sin, but the Spirit is life because of righteousness. But if the Spirit of Him who raised Jesus from the dead dwells in you, He who raised Christ from the dead will also give life to your mortal bodies through His Spirit who dwells in you." (Rom. 8:1–11)

These scriptures are certainly worth a day or two of meditation and study. This time spent in doing so is well worth the benefits of refreshing our inner man.

I have explained this before, but I feel the need to repeat it. The fruit of gentleness brings humbleness into our lives so that we will not think too highly of ourselves, but think about ourselves as we ought to think, reminding ourselves of where we came from and that God's grace is sufficient to finish the work that He began within each of us as His children. This is certainly something to sing about. Take a moment, and praise His Holy name!

"For I say, through the grace given to me, to everyone who is among you, not to think of himself more highly than he ought to think, but to

think soberly, as God has dealt to each one a measure of faith." (Rom. 12:3)

"Being confident of this very thing, that He who has begun a good work in you will complete it until the day of Jesus Christ." (Phil. 1:6)

We have established that man is a spirit that has a soul, and both are housed in a fleshly body, connected through the battleground of the mind. It is there in our minds that we either win or lose during the trials and tests of life.

"For the weapons of our warfare are not carnal but mighty in God for pulling down strongholds, casting down arguments and every high thing that exalts itself against the knowledge of God, bringing every thought into captivity to the obedience of Christ, and being ready to punish all disobedience when your obedience is fulfilled." (2 Cor. 10:4,5)

"But I fear, lest somehow, as the serpent deceived Eve by his craftiness, so your minds may be corrupted from the simplicity that is in Christ." (2 Cor. 11:3)

There are fifty-five scripture references to our mind in the New Testament. Here is a collection of a few of them with a brief part of that scripture. Take the time, and read them <u>all</u> at your leisure for the context.

> *"With all your mind." (Matt. 22:37)*
> *"He is out of His mind." (Mark 3:21)*
> *"God gave them over to a debased mind." (Rom. 1:28)*
> *"Law of my mind." (Rom. 7:23)*
> *"Carnal mind is enmity against God." (Rom. 8:7)*
> *"Same mind." (1 Cor. 1:10)*
> *"But we have the mind of Christ." (1 Cor. 2:16)*
> *"Sound mind." (2 Cor. 5:13)*
> *"Lowliness of mind." (Phil. 2:3)*
> *"To mind your own business." (1 Thess. 4:11)*
> *"Shaken in mind or troubled." (2 Thess 2:2)*
> *"But of power and of love and of a sound mind." (2 Tim. 1:7)*

With these many references regarding our mind, it is obvious that it is important not only having knowledge concerning what the scriptures have to say, but also understanding with the wisdom to apply them to our lives.

A victorious life is realized when our mind knows the truth from God's word before any test arrives. Gaining knowledge and the understanding of it and applying wisdom in our lives make for a victorious and abundant life.

"I beseech you therefore, brethren, by the mercies of God, that you present your bodies a living sacrifice, holy, acceptable to God, which is your reasonable service. And do not be conformed to this world, but be transformed by the renewing of your mind, that you may prove what is that good and acceptable and perfect will of God." (Rom. 12:1–2)

Staying in the spirit of gentleness enables us to process the knowledge acquired to win battles and all future warfare with the devil as he tries to devour us as he roams this earth. Worldly men may call *gentleness* a weakness while God's use of the spirit of gentleness is the ability to allow His power and presence to flow through us, thus always giving us the victory and making us more than a conqueror through Jesus Christ.

"Yet in all these things we are more than conquerors through Him who loved us." (Rom. 8:37)

"But thanks be to God, who gives us the victory through our Lord Jesus Christ." (1 Cor. 15:57)

"Therefore I take pleasure in infirmities, in reproaches, in needs, in persecutions, in distresses, for Christ's sake. For when I am weak, then I am strong." (2 Cor. 12:10)

It's the fruit of gentleness that's producing the humility needed to realize that though <u>a child</u> of God, we can still be overcome by evil, especially if we have not been trained properly to guard against it.

Yes, our soul needs saving because it is full of feelings and emotions, which can lie to us. We can find ourselves falling prey to their whims, and the devil counts on it. This is why we cannot trust them and must not be moved by them at all. Faith looks past all feelings and emotions and sees the end result of standing upon God's word as truth.

Now, I am not saying here to discard your feelings and emotions, because they are designed and given to us by God. However, they should not be allowed to rule us. They are one of the two things that separate us from all animals.

First is our ability to reason and communicate with others with words, and second is our ability to have feelings and emotions and the knowledge of why we have them and how they apply to our circumstances.

Animal's acts of caring and nurturing are built into them by God as instinct, which is designed by Him so that they can continue to reproduce while being able to care for their young as they grow. Once a lion cub grows to maturity, it must follow all the rules of the wild or be killed, even by its own parents in some cases. They cannot explain why they do the nurturing or why they do what they do. They just do it.

Humans, on the other hand, know why they have feelings for others. Maybe we like the way a person looks, acts, laughs, etc. We cry with them and laugh with them because they're vital parts of our lives, either by birth or chosen as friends. We know and understand life as animals do not. For them it is constant survival of the fittest.

How does all this tie in to *gentleness*? If you'll notice, all the fruit of the Spirit of Jesus are housed within our soul where all our feelings and emotions reside. We all have a degree of love, joy, peace, long-suffering, kindness, goodness, faith, gentleness, and self-control. However, these characteristics have limitations, while the fruit of the Spirit is limitless in growth and capabilities.

The soul is connected to the mind in such a way that only the Lord knows the details, and He created it to be so. Our mind processes feelings and emotions, and based upon our knowledge of things is whether we respond or react or a mix of both at times. This is known as life management.

Whether a joyous occasion or the worst thing that has ever happened to us, along with everything in between, every life event should be considered as a trial or test of faith. They each affect our spirit, soul, and body. We need to study to know what God's word says then apply it to all our circumstances. This is another way that we can say, "Not my will, Father, but yours be done."

As mentioned before, the fleshly man (inclusive) viewed in the mirror is not the sum of who we really are. The flesh, being where sin came into the picture long ago, is the problem. The flesh can get used to being treated special through our feelings and emotions. This is where many believers are living their Christian lives. They allow the flesh to control what the spirit and soul do. <u>God's plan is that</u> the believer's spirit should be controlling what the soul and the flesh do. The spirit is the one that knows the truth.

"Therefore, just as through one man sin entered the world, and death through sin, and thus death spread to all men, because all sinned." (Rom. 5:12)

"For as in Adam all die, even so in Christ all shall be made alive." (1 Cor. 15:22)

"There is a natural body, and there is a spiritual body. And so it is written, 'The first man Adam became a living being. The last Adam became a life-giving spirit.'" (1 Cor. 15:44–45)

<u>Let's review the state of man prior to salvation.</u> Our fleshly man is directly touched by outer influences through our five senses. Knowing this truth, it stands to reason that we are touched in the flesh first. Then, our minds process the various events as they trigger our feelings and emotions within our soul. This is as far as it usually goes inside a person who is not born again.

Our spirit has to take what the flesh and the soul give. We have tendencies to base our belief system upon that which we experience in the world only. This process always falls short of the glory of God as well because of the limitations in the world and the fact that like us, it too was created.

However, <u>once a person becomes born again,</u> this process is changed. Let me explain.

Once a person is born again, we now have ability to circumvent the process of outer influences from the fleshly man to the inner man, <u>to</u> the inner man influencing the outer fleshly man. New converts, especially, need to be trained in this truth as we make them disciples.

Stress that instead of the fleshly man making all the rules of what to believe or what not to believe based upon experiences of life, there is now a more excellent way of living. The believer's inner man acquires the knowledge of God through His word, thus reversing the process whereby a man can make decisions based on eternal things instead of the temporal things of the flesh.

This reversal process of becoming is what Romans 12:1, 2 explains. Instead of man being molded, shaped in iniquity by sin in the flesh that he was born with, and reinforced by the things of creation from the outside inward, he is now influenced with the word of God and is changed from the inside out. This changes everything!

Once a man or woman is born again, they start to be remolded and reshaped by the eternal things of God's Spirit found in His word, giving him a new eternal reference point and compass to change the course of his or her life in their born-again spirit.

"Therefore, my beloved, as you have always obeyed, not as in my presence only, but now much more in my absence, 'WORK OUT' your own salvation with fear and trembling; for it is God who works in you both to will and to do for His good pleasure." (Phil. 2:12–13)

All that happens to us, good or bad, according to God's word, becomes our employee and goes to work for us to make the end results good instead of bad—security for us realizing as we apply gentleness and the other fruit of the Holy Spirit in our words and actions, then the power of the Holy Spirit does the rest.

"And we know that all things work together for good to those who love God, to those who are the called according to His purpose." (Rom. 8:28)

This is why we can have the peace and confidence in Jesus that no matter what happens, we are more than conquerors and that we always have the victory! We now can keep our feelings and emotions in check and live accordingly to the truth of the word of God instead of every wind of doctrine of men telling us how to live our lives according to our feelings and emotions! God be true and every man a liar!

God being faithful to His word by watching over it, as well as having His angels to do the same and to perform the doing of His word, brings His word to pass because of Jesus's *faith* operating in *us* and released upon our circumstances.

THE OPERATIVE

Once His word is accepted by our spirit man as truth, our feelings and emotions no longer control how we respond or react to events happening in our life, especially through the two big ones—worry and fear.

As we grow in the grace and knowledge of our Lord and Savior, Jesus Christ, His fruit matures. This, in return, helps our spirit to take control of our thoughts, feelings, and emotions because we now see through our spiritual eye and hear through our spiritual ear, because they are focused upon Him and tuned in to Him because of His *faith*.

Seeing those things that are not, and calling them as though they were—isn't this what God does? Isn't this what He wants for us? Of course, it is—speaking and calling those things that are not (things hoped for and asked from God) as though they already existed in our lives as another possession of gifts given to us by God.

How long do we continue this? Until what we see and hear shows up, and becomes a reality in our lives. Your healing comes, desires and needs are met, salvation of your loved ones happen, deliverances become reality, and the list goes on and on.

"For I consider that the sufferings of this present time are not worthy to be compared with the glory which shall be revealed in us. For the earnest expectation of the creation eagerly waits for the revealing of the sons of God. For the creation was subjected to futility, not willingly, but because of Him who subjected it in hope; because the creation itself also will be delivered from the bondage of corruption into the glorious liberty of the children of God. For we know that the whole creation groans and labors with birth pangs together until now.

Not only that, but we also who have the firstfruits of the Spirit, even we ourselves groan within ourselves, eagerly waiting for the adoption, the redemption of our body. For we were saved in this hope, but hope that is seen is not hope; for why does one still hope for what he sees? But if we hope for what we do not see, we eagerly wait for it with perseverance.

Likewise, the Spirit also helps in our weaknesses. For we do not know what we should pray for as we ought, but the Spirit Himself makes intercession for us with groanings which cannot be uttered. Now He who searches the hearts knows what the mind of the Spirit is, because He makes intercession for the saints according to the will of God.

And we know that all things work together for good to those who love God, to those who are the called according to His purpose. For whom He foreknew, He also predestined to be conformed to the image of His Son, that He might be the firstborn among many brethren. Moreover, whom He predestined, these He also called; whom He called, these He also justified; and whom He justified, these He also glorified." (Rom. 8:18–30)

This is when it is so beneficial to be filled with the Holy Spirit of Jesus with the evidence of speaking in tongues, speaking directly to God the Father. Because when you do not know what to pray for, He does, and He asks for exactly that which we have need of and that which lines up with the plan, purpose, and will of God in our lives.

The fruit of gentleness has a big part in us obtaining the results we are looking for as we live the abundant life promised by Jesus. Like the rest of the fruit, they are each connected directly to the tangible presence of the Holy Spirit of Jesus Christ.

What would you think will happen when we, the Church, realize that the very resurrection power that raised Christ from the dead is available to us through the presence and the anointing of the Holy Spirit of Jesus filling us and that being filled with the Holy Spirit, according to the scriptures, brings His power to reality through us by His presence working in us by the operating of His gifts as He chooses us to do so?

Recognizing the fruit of the Spirit growing in us brings Jesus's character in our spirits, not us learning how to mimic them, with the hope that something—maybe, sometime—could possibly happen if only we believe hard and long enough.

Then, and only then, will we look more like the early church!

I submit to you that we, and the miracles performed through us, would once again be the calling card of God because of His Son, through His Holy Spirit. Seeing these miracles, the Creator of the heavens and the earth and the possessor of the deeds thereof would once again reveal His goodness to men. Men and women everywhere will begin to thirst and hunger after true righteousness, which is Christ Himself.

These last days of the Church here on earth, I believe, will not be filled with gloom and doom as some preach and teach. The time will come when the wrath of God is poured upon those who are the children of disobedience or the unbelievers, but it is not now!

Let the fruit of *gentleness* release the power of Jesus's character in all that you do so that others can see Him and cry out, "What must I do to be saved?"

We are saved by grace and cleansed by Jesus's blood. We've been purchased with a price, and that price was the life of Jesus, allowing us to be the Church of today if we so choose! Your opportunity is *now*! We must redeem the time while it is still day and while He can be found.

In chapters 29 and 30 we will look at the last fruit of the Holy Spirit, which is self-control or temperance in the KJV. I believe it was no coincidence that this fruit was listed last in the progression of Jesus's Holy Spirit's fruit taking us from the old man to the new, all the while maturing each of us into the unity of faith according to the scriptures.

The strength and power of self-control will keep us from being tossed here and there with every wind of doctrine. It helps us to continue forward toward that goal of being more like Jesus today than we were yesterday.

The fruit of self-control is the fruit that gels all the other fruit, allowing each one to be strengthened, stabilized, and reinforced by one another's substance. Wait, isn't this what we, the members of the body of Christ, are supposed to be doing?

"From whom the whole body, joined and knit together by what every joint supplies, according to the effective working by which every part does its share, causes growth of the body for the edifying of itself in love." (Eph. 4:16)

"But now God has set the members, each one of them, in the body just as He pleased. And if they were all one member, where would the body be?

But now indeed there are many members, yet one body. And the eye cannot say to the hand, 'I have no need of you;' nor again the head to the feet, 'I have no need of you.' No, much rather, those members of the body which seem to be weaker are necessary.

And those members of the body which we think to be less honorable, on these we bestow greater honor; and our unpresentable parts have greater modesty, but our presentable parts have no need.

But God composed the body, having given greater honor to that part which lacks it, that there should be no schism [divisions] in the body, but that the members should have the same care for one another.

And if one member suffers, all the members suffer with it; or if one member is honored, all the members rejoice with it. Now you are the body of Christ, and members individually." (1 Cor. 12:18–27)

Hmm! Do you think any of this is somehow connected?

I hope you will continue to join me on this journey of finding out more about the promises of God through His Son, Jesus, and His Holy Spirit's fruit. As we look at the last fruit of self-control, it will wrap everything up in a neat package with a beautiful bow as it pulls everything together with the Holy Spirit dwelling in us, with the power of God that is manifested in our lives.

CHAPTER 29

Fruit of the Holy Spirit
SELF-CONTROL
Part 1

"But the fruit of the Spirit is love, joy, peace, longsuffering, kindness, goodness, faithfulness, gentleness, SELF-CONTROL. Against such there is no law." (Gal. 5:22–23)

Our journey has brought us to the final fruit of the Holy Spirit, but not to our final destination—last but by no means least, the fruit of *self-control*. As previously mentioned, this is the gel that keeps all the fruit of the Holy Spirit as one powerful unit within our spirit and soul, as the character of Jesus Christ our Savior.

It's possibly the one fruit that many struggle with most and, yes, even the unsaved as well in the natural. Christians, however, must realize that like the other fruit growing in us, the Holy Spirit has planted in us the fruit of *self-control* to mature, not learn.

Self-control, like the other fruit of the Holy Spirit, can be learned and managed to a certain degree in the natural realm. *Self-control*, on the other hand, is a little bit harder to mask than all the other fruit.

It's in the forefront of our actions, and this fruit is the sum of all the other fruit combined.

It was Jesus's *self-control* that saw Him through in the wilderness. Hungry and thirsty, the devil pulled out all that he had to offer, and the power of His *self-control* dug deep and pulled out the living words of God to defeat the devil with all three temptations. Jesus did not settle for anything less than what He already had, which was everything, including all that the devil offered.

Jesus's *self-control* was so powerful that it enabled Him *not* to retaliate toward those who beat Him, spat upon Him, whipped Him, and ultimately, hung Him on a cross to die. This characteristic of Jesus also kept Him humble when all others were praising Him for the wonderful works of God that He did even though He was the key to them all.

Today is Good Friday at the time of writing this first draft of this chapter, and I must say that nobody killed Jesus. He gave up the Ghost (Spirit that kept His body alive) and His life in the flesh at the precise moment that all of mankind's sins were transferred onto His body, taking from noon to 3:00 p.m. He <u>gave up</u> His life, and as His fleshly body died, with it died also all the power that sin had over men. This is the *good news* of the Bible.

It was the power of His *self-control* within Him from His Holy Spirit that enabled Him to accomplish all that He did for us! It is this same character or fruit of *self-control* from Jesus's Holy Spirit that we need to tap into, by being aware of its growth inside our spirit.

It is doable as the Holy Spirit gives us each the insight mixed with His wisdom regarding this power of God in us. The word used in the KJV is *temperance*. In the NKJV the word used is *self-control*, meaning "temperance."

"Now as he reasoned about righteousness, self-control, and the judgment to come, Felix was afraid and answered, 'Go away for now; when I have a convenient time I will call for you.'" (Acts 24:25)

> "*egkrateia* (eng-krat'-i-ah); from NT:1468 self-control (especially continence): KJV—self-control/temperance" (NT:1466).

> "*egkrates* (eng-krat-ace'); strong in a thing (masterful), i.e. (figuratively and reflexively) self-controlled (in appetite, etc.): KJV—temperate" (NT:1468).

"Do not deprive one another except with consent for a time, that you may give yourselves to fasting and prayer; and come together again so that satan does not tempt you because of your lack of <u>self-control</u>." (1 Cor. 7:5)

In this scripture of First Corinthians, the original KJV Greek word used is *incontinency* (NT:192), which means "the want of self-control."

> "*akrasia* (ak-ras-ee'-a); from NT:193; want of self-restraint: KJV—excess, incontinency" (NT:192).
>
> "*akrates* (ak-rat'-ace); powerless, i.e. without self-control: KJV—incontinent" (NT:193).

"But I say to the unmarried and to the widows: It is good for them if they remain even as I am; but if they cannot exercise self-control, let them marry. For it is better to marry than to burn with passion." (1 Cor. 7:8–9)

Here the phrase <u>"cannot exercise self-control"</u> found in the NKJV is "if they cannot contain" in the KJV. The meaning is as follows:

> "*egkrateuomai* (eng-krat-yoo'-om-ahee); to exercise self-restraint (in diet and chastity): KJV—can ([-not]) contain, be temperate" (NT:1467).

This is a very good example of the translators getting it right from the KJV to the NKJV. The integrity of the verse's context is not compromised. This is why it is always wise to study other translations with the original Greek and Hebrew words because there are times when I think the KJV word would have been better served if left alone.

"But the fruit of the Spirit is love, joy, peace, longsuffering, kindness, goodness, faithfulness, gentleness, SELF-CONTROL. Against such there is no law." (Gal. 5:22–23)

> "*egkrateia* (eng-krat'-i-ah); from NT:1468; self-control (especially continence): KJV—temperance" (NT:1466).
>
> "*egkrates* (eng-krat-ace'); strong in a thing (masterful), i.e. (figuratively and reflexively) self-controlled (in appetite, etc.): KJV—temperate" (NT:1468).

"Nevertheless she will be saved in childbearing if they continue in faith, love, and holiness, with <u>self-control</u>." (1 Tim. 2:15)

Here in First Timothy we find yet another word used in the KJV for *self-control*, which is *sobriety*.

> "*sophrosune* (so-fros-oo'-nay); soundness of mind, i.e. (literally) sanity or (figuratively) self-control: KJV—soberness, sobriety" (NT:4997).

"But know this, that in the last days perilous times will come: For men will be lovers of themselves, lovers of money, boasters, proud, blasphemers, disobedient to parents, unthankful, unholy, unloving, unforgiving, slanderers <u>without self-control</u>, brutal, despisers of good, traitors, headstrong, haughty, lovers of pleasure rather than lovers of God, having a form of godliness but denying its power. And from such people turn away!" (2 Tim. 3:1–5)

The word <u>self-control</u> in the NKJV is the word *incontinent*, meaning the following:

> "*akrates* (ak-rat'-ace); powerless, i.e. without self-control: KJV—incontinent" (NT:193).

In Second Timothy, the same meaning of the word is used for *First Corinthians 7:5* above. The emphasis is placed on the <u>lack of self-control instead of having self-control.</u>

"But also for this very reason, giving all diligence, add to your faith virtue, to virtue knowledge, to knowledge self-control, to self-control perseverance, to perseverance godliness, to godliness brotherly kindness, and to brotherly kindness love. For if these things are yours and abound, you will be neither barren nor unfruitful in the knowledge of our Lord Jesus Christ." (2 Peter 1:5–8)

THE OPERATIVE

In this scripture we are back to the word meaning <u>"temperance"</u> above for *self-control*. It can be a little confusing, but when you realize that the *Strong's Concordance* is based on the original Hebrew and Greek words used, then check to see what word(s) the translators used in its place (like in this case, *self-control* in the NKJV for the KJV word of *temperance*), it all becomes clearer.

(Some words are interchangeable. Other words used can mislead the reader as to the original inspired meaning and content. It's always best not to take anything for granted by studying the deeper meaning and understanding of the original revelations.)

As we study the original meanings of what the Holy Spirit is saying, it becomes clearer to all that *self-control* plays a huge part even in studying the Bible. We think of *self-control* mostly in terms of quitting a bad habit or not doing things that we were told not to do. It takes *self-control* to maintain a level of study so that you can realize the truth of God's word for yourself and not have to rely on others to feed you.

There are many different versions of the Bible, like *The Living Bible*, the *New International Version*, or the *New American Standard Bible*, to name a few. If there is a danger of a possible misinterpretation between the KJV and the NKJV, you can rest assured that other versions have this same danger too.

Hearing from those who use other versions of the Bible, they say that they are easier to understand. *However*, when reading and studying the Bible, understanding with our minds only is not our first priority. <u>Understanding the original content and revelation of its meaning in our spirit is our first priority and should remain so!</u>

We have previously seen the differences that can be found just between the King James Version (KJV) of the Bible and the New King James Version (NKJV). Some words lose their original meaning when used improperly. This can change the complete context of the verse, which changes everything from our understanding to how we believe. So be mindful of the different versions of the Bible that are available today.

What if we are requesting direction from the Holy Spirit, regarding a very serious matter in our life? He inspired the original writings and contents, giving this direction for us to find. If the version of the Bible we are relying on uses a word(s) that means one thing today, but the original inspired word means something completely different, how can we receive the correct guidance and direction from the Holy Spirit?

When I read versions of the Bible other than the KJV or the NKJV, there is one section of the Bible I turn to and read to see if this version is a reliable version to trust or not. It's found in Genesis 6:1–6, and depending upon what a particular version says about this section of the Bible is whether or not I will give it any credence at all.

I am giving several examples of different versions of this section to help you determine what they are actually saying, which is actually what those who are using these versions of the Bible are believing. Remember, that which we believe, we speak or, in this case, write. By doing this, it reveals to us what they actually want you to believe is truth as well. We will find out otherwise. We begin with the KJV:

> *1. And it came to pass, when men began to multiply on the face of the earth, and daughters were born unto them, 2. That the sons of God saw the daughters of men that they were fair; and they took them wives of all which they chose. 3. And the LORD said, My spirit shall not always strive with man, for that he also is flesh: yet his days shall be an hundred and twenty years. 4. There were giants in the earth in those days; and also after that, when the sons of God came in unto the daughters of men, and they bare children to them, the same became mighty men which were of old, men of renown. 5. And GOD saw that the wickedness of man was great in the earth, and that every imagination of the thoughts of his heart was only evil continually. 6. And it repented the LORD that he had made man on the earth, and it grieved him at his heart. (Gen. 6:1–6, KJV)*

THE OPERATIVE

Now let me show the same verses in *The Living Bible*, and see what you think. Then we will take a look at some original words that are underlined above to tell the true story. I will leave the verse numbers in each version to make it easier to compare.

> *1. Now a population explosion took place upon the earth. 2. It was at this time that beings from the spirit world looked upon the beautiful earth women and took any they desired to be their wives. 3 Then Jehovah said, "My Spirit must not forever be disgraced in man, wholly evil as he is. I will give him 120 years to mend his ways." 4. In those days, and even afterwards, when the evil beings from the spirit world were sexually involved with human women, their children became giants, of whom so many legends are told. 5. When the Lord God saw the extent of human wickedness, and that the trend and direction of men's lives were only towards evil, 6. he was sorry he had made them. It broke his heart. (Gen. 6:1–6, The Living Bible)*

Let's get to dissecting the original words used in the KJV to find out the original definitions, seeing if their meanings line up with the interpretation of *The Living Bible* version, shall we?

We will start with the word <u>men</u> found in verse 1, in the KJV.

"*adam* (aw-dawm'); from [OT:119]; ruddy i.e. a human being (an individual or the species, mankind, etc.)" (OT:120)

"*dam* (aw-dam'); to show blood (in the face), i.e. flush or turn rosy: KJV—be (dyed, made) red (ruddy)" (OT:119).

We can safely say that the *men* in verse 1 are human. Now let's look at the word *daughters* also found in verse 1.

"*bath* (bath); from [OT:1129] (as feminine of [OT:1121]); a daughter (used in the same wide sense as other terms of relationship, literally and figuratively)" (OT:1323).

> "*banah* (baw-naw'); a primitive root; to build (literally and figuratively): KJV—(begin to) build (-er), obtain children, make, repair, set (up), surely" (OT:1129).
>
> "*ben* (bane); from OT:1129 (see above); a son (as a builder of the family name), in the widest sense (of literal and figurative relationship, including grandson, subject, nation, quality or condition, etc." (OT:1121).

Based upon these original meanings, we can safely conclude that the *daughters* who were born of men were *human* as well and considered vital to the building of a family name as the men (human) had sexual relationships with the daughters being born to build their families. Sounds pretty normal to me, right?

Go back and read again what *The Living Bible* version says in verses 1 and 2. Now let's see what the "sons of God" meant within the originally inspired words used in the KJV. In finding out this original definition, it will begin to reveal the true facts and unveil the lies:

> "'sons of' OT:1121 *ben* (bane); from [OT:1129] (see above); a son (as a builder of the family name), in the widest sense (of literal and figurative relationship, including grandson, subject, nation, quality or condition, etc."

Isn't this interesting? It's the very same word that is used for a human son (the builder of a family name, including a grandson).

Who does *The Living Bible* say they are? 2. "It was at this time that beings from the spirit world looked upon the beautiful earth women and took any they desired to be their wives."

I believe we can once again safely conclude that the sons of God are considered human men who are the family-name builders. They definitely are *not* beings from the spirit world who had sex with the beautiful earth women.

<u>Oops! This must be debunking number 1.</u>

Next let's see what the KJV has to say about the giants found in the land at this time, which is spoken of in verse number 4:

> "(the giants) *nephiyl* (nef-eel'); or nephil (nef-eel'); from OT:5307; properly, a feller, i.e. a bully or tyrant: KJV—giant" (OT:5303).
>
> "*naphal* (naw-fal'); a primitive root; to fall, in a great variety of applications (intransitive or causative, literal or figurative): KJV—be accepted, cast (downself, [lots], out), cease, die, divide (by lot), (let) fail, (cause to, let, make, ready to) fall (away, down, -en, -ing)" (OT:5307).

I believe that we can also come to the conclusion that these were men of great accomplishments in the land, and some were even tyrants. The Holy Spirit taught me this truth while I was preparing one day to answer this very question about these giants. The prisoners whom I used to minister at Camp 24 in Virginia asked me to prove what I was telling them about this section of the Bible.

As I was preparing my notes to give them a copy of the outline concerning the words, like I have above, the TV was turned on low in the background. On the evening news, a report came on regarding the death of Roy Rogers. Everybody my age knows who he was. The reporter, who was telling about Roy's great accomplishments, said and I quote, "He was a giant of a man."

I about fell out of my chair. The light of this revelation turned on so brightly and profoundly that I will never forget it. I finished what I am about to reveal to you, which is the rest of the story, like another giant of a man would say. His name was Paul Harvey. If you are not familiar with either of these two men, please google them as this will be well worth your time to read about both of them and their accomplishments in their lives.

Let's see now what *The Living Bible* calls these giants in verse number 4 (*"In those days, and even afterwards, when the evil beings from the spirit world were sexually involved with human women, their children became giants, of whom so many legends are told."*).

I think it is also safe to say that, based upon the original meanings of the Hebrew words that these giants were accomplished men, don't you? They are *not* the evil beings from the spirit world who were sexually involved with human women, then their children became giants, of whom so many legends are told.

<u>Oops! This is debunking number 2.</u>

Now we will take a closer look at the meaning of <u>"the same became mighty men"</u> also found in verse number 4. The words *the same* mean exactly the same men we have been talking about in the previous verses—you know, the *humans*.

The word *became* was added to make the verse read better. Here is the note on it:

"NOTE: inserted word (x); This word was added by the translators for better readability in the English. There is no actual word in the Hebrew text. The word may be displayed in italics, or in parentheses or other brackets, to indicate that it is not in the original text" (OT:9999).

We now come to the words *mighty men*. Let's see what original Hebrew word is used to describe these mighty men:

> "*gibbowr* (ghib-bore'); or (shortened) *gibbor* (ghib-bore'); intensive from the same as OT:1397; powerful; by implication, warrior, tyrant: KJV—champion, chief, excel, giant, man, mighty (man, one), strong (man), valiant man" (OT:1368).

Now let's take a look at what *The Living Bible* has to say about these mighty men in verse number 4 (*"In those days, and even afterwards, when the evil beings from the spirit world were sexually involved with human women, their children became giants, of whom so many legends are told"*).

Here again, "their children became giants, of whom so many legends are told"? Oh, please!

<u>Oops! This is debunking number 3.</u>

THE OPERATIVE

My last debunking concerning *The Living Bible* is about the phrase "<u>men of renown.</u>"

The words *men of* is "*'iysh* (eesh); [or perhaps rather from an unused root meaning to be extant]; a man as an individual or a male person; often used as an adjunct to a more definite term (and in such cases frequently not expressed in translation): KJV—also, another, any (man), a certain, champion, consent, each, every (one), fellow, [foot-, husband-] man, [good-, great, mighty) man (OT:376).

And the word for *renown* is "*shem* (shame); a primitive word [perhaps rather from OT:7760 through the idea of definite and conspicuous position; an appellation, as a mark or memorial of individuality; by implication honor, authority, character: KJV—base, [in-] fame [-ous], named (-d), renown, report" (OT:8034).

I think again we can safely conclude that the men of renown were individual males who excelled to great positions of honor among the people. We already know what *The Living Bible* says about them, and that is "of whom so many legends are told."

<u>Oops! This is debunking number 4.</u>

Are you seeing these lies, tales, and falsehoods in this version of the Bible? If you are one of those using *The Living Bible*, I would immediately recommend that you begin using a KJV, and study the original words. I even double-check the NKJV and "eat the fish and throw the bones away" as well. These two are the closest interpretations to the original meanings of the Hebrew and Greek that contain the original inspired words of the Holy Spirit. Don't let anyone tell you any different.

A person may not like how the KJV reads, but since we are entrusting the state of our eternal spirit, soul, and body to what our Bible contains, then I believe we should understand what it is that the Holy Spirit is really saying to us, don't you? We must not take stock in and give credence to something that reads like a science-fiction movie, calling it truth.

Now that you know the true meanings, I will place a couple more versions here so you can make up your own mind about them as well. At a minimum, read the KJV with your favorite version, and check to be sure what they are saying is parallel to the inspired message of the Holy Spirit.

The *New International Version*—this one does not sound too bad. But what if you did not know the original meanings of the KJV, and you were using this version, and you were in a Bible Study with those using *The Living Bible,* and they might begin telling the class what their version said and what they were believing?

By not knowing the truth for yourself, you could still fall prey to the lies about evil spirits or giant offsprings as their children, and the legends are told to be true because of them. This confusion, which certainly does not come from God, can foster doubt and unbelief or just plain wrong believing because of the version of the Bible you may be using.

You may still be asking yourself, *what does all this have to do with self-control?* Everything! What if you do not have the *self-control* to study the original definitions and meanings of the Greek and Hebrew words? It takes a lot of self-control to seek the truth with correct revelation by rightly dividing the word of truth.

How would you combat these kinds of questions that will come to you sometime or another in your walk with Jesus? We must be ready to give account to every man who asks about our hope. Knowing the truth sets us free, and the only way you're going to know the truth is for others to tell you, or you seek it out for yourself. Don't be deceived by words that sound good or spiritual.

Here is <u>The New International Version</u>. You judge for yourself:

> *1 When men began to increase in number on the earth and daughters were born to them, 2 the sons of God saw that the daughters of men were beautiful, and they married any of them they chose. 3 Then the LORD said, "My Spirit will not contend with man forever, for he is mortal; his days will be a hundred and twenty years."*
>
> *4 The Nephilim were on the earth in those days—and also afterward—when the sons of God*

> *went to the daughters of men and had children by them. They were the heroes of old, men of renown.*
>
> *5 The LORD saw how great man's wickedness on the earth had become, and that every inclination of the thoughts of his heart was only evil all the time. 6 The LORD was grieved that he had made man on the earth, and his heart was filled with pain. (Gen. 6:1–6, NIV)*

Here we have the <u>New American Standard Bible.</u> Let's see how well those translators did:

> *1 Now it came about, when men began to multiply on the face of the land, and daughters were born to them, 2 that the sons of God saw that the daughters of men were beautiful; and they took wives for themselves, whomever they chose. 3 Then the LORD said, "My Spirit shall not strive with man forever, because he also is flesh; nevertheless his days shall be one hundred and twenty years." 4 The Nephilim were on the earth in those days, and also afterward, when the sons of God came in to the daughters of men, and they bore children to them. Those were the mighty men who were of old, men of renown.*
>
> *5 Then the LORD saw that the wickedness of man was great on the earth, and that every intent of the thoughts of his heart was only evil continually. 6 The LORD was sorry that He had made man on the earth, and He was grieved in His heart. (Gen. 6:1–6, NASB)*

Remember, how are you going to answer the one using these versions, if they too question the Nephilim, and neither of you have studied the KJV original meaning? The same thing could happen.

Let's look at the <u>American Standard Version</u> and see how it reads:

6:1 And it came to pass, when men began to multiply on the face of the ground, and daughters were born unto them,

2 that the sons of God saw the daughters of men that they were fair; and they took them wives of all that they chose.

3 And Jehovah said, My spirit shall not strive with man for ever, for that he also is flesh: yet shall his days be a hundred and twenty years.

4 The Nephilim were in the earth in those days, and also after that, when the sons of God came unto the daughters of men, and they bare children to them: the same were the mighty men that were of old, the men of renown.

5 And Jehovah saw that the wickedness of man was great in the earth, and that every imagination of the thoughts of his heart was only evil continually.

6 And it repented Jehovah that he had made man on the earth, and it grieved him at his heart. (Gen. 6:1–6, ASV)

The problem is still with the word *Nephilim* being in there. Some Christians believe in the spiritual side of the Bible the way that Hollywood does, with some kind of mystical, freaky, out-of-this-world thing. This seems to follow the path of "evil spirit having sex with women, creating a different species." Give me a break, please!

There are many people, even Christians, who point to these versions of the Bible and say, "Explain the Nephilim, then." Well, I just did, thank you very much. Now how will you take action? Will you react to this teaching by getting upset as your anger increases, or will you respond accordingly and follow the directions of the Holy Spirit? There can be only one word of God with one interpretation, *not* many interpretations!

Let's explore one more version. Today's English Version sounds promising, doesn't it? I probably could understand it easier, right? Let's check it out with Genesis 6:1–6 and find out:

1 When mankind had spread all over the world, and girls were being born, 2 some of the heavenly beings saw that these girls were beautiful, so they took the ones they liked. 3 Then the LORD said, "I will not allow people to live forever; they are mortal. From now on they will live no longer than 120 years." 4 In those days, and even later, there were giants on the earth who were descendants of human women and the heavenly beings. They were the great heroes and famous men of long ago.

5 When the LORD saw how wicked everyone on earth was and how evil their thoughts were all the time, 6 he was sorry that he had ever made them and put them on the earth. He was so filled with regret. (Gen. 6:1–6, TEV)

Can you believe this—*"Descendants of human women and the heavenly beings"*? How far are these versions of the Bible removed from the truth that is contained within the original inspired word of God? Each of them rants about other beings from either the spirit world or heavenly beings. Even Jesus saying that the angels neither marry nor are taken in marriage reveals to us that angels do not have sexual relationships in any manner.

As I mentioned before, it takes *self-control* to study in this fashion and manner that we need to give the appropriate attention to the word of God. The Holy Spirit and I wanted to take the time and space here to prove our point. And this is why it takes *self-control* to study the word of God—simply because it will cost us our time, and if done properly, it will cost us a lot of time. However, the time spent in fellowship with the word (Jesus) of God and His Holy Spirit by no means is ever wasted.

What does all this have to do with the fruit of *self-control*? Repeating myself, it has everything to do with *self-control* and every fruit of the Holy Spirit! He is the Spirit of truth—the Spirit of truth beloved, <u>not</u> the spirit of lies and fairy tales.

"If you love Me, keep My commandments. And I will pray the Father, and He will give you another Helper, that He may abide with

you forever—the Spirit of truth, whom the world cannot receive, because it neither sees Him nor knows Him; but you know Him [Do we, Lord?], for He dwells with you and will be in you. I will not leave you orphans; I will come to you." (John 14:15–18)

"But when the Helper comes, whom I shall send to you from the Father, the Spirit of truth who proceeds from the Father, He will testify of Me. And you also will bear witness, because you have been with Me from the beginning." (John 15:26–27)

"I still have many things to say to you, but you cannot bear them now. However, when He, the Spirit of truth, has come, He will guide you into all truth; for He will not speak on His own authority, but whatever He hears He will speak; and He will tell you things to come. He will glorify Me, for He will take of what is Mine and declare it to you. All things that the Father has are Mine. Therefore I said that He will take of Mine and declare it to you." (John 16:12–15)

"You are of God, little children, and have overcome them, because He who is in you is greater than he who is in the world. They are of the world. Therefore they speak as of the world, and the world hears them. We are of God. He who knows God hears us; he who is not of God does not hear us. By this we know the spirit of truth and the spirit of error." (1 John 4:4–6)

If you are one of the many who prefer using one of these versions of the Bible that I have mentioned, you may be feeling a little unsettled and confused, and we know who the author of confusion is, right? So it is up to you to confirm the truth within the version of the Bible that you are relying upon, which may or may not be following the Spirit of truth!

"For God is not the author of confusion but of peace, as in all the churches of the saints." (1 Cor. 14:33)

If God is not the author of confusion, then who is? <u>The devil—that's who!</u> I hope you can see the eternal importance of finding out what the original words of the Bible mean. You do not have to learn the Hebrew and Greek languages to do this. At the least, you can buy a *Strong's Concordance*, and you will have access to every original Hebrew and Greek word used in the Old and New Testaments and their definitions.

The hard copy was what I used for the first twenty-five years as a believer. It's labor-intensive but worth every penny spent on the *Concordance*. Fortunately, we live in a day and age of technology, and there are many research materials available online. Word of caution—make sure the creator of the product keeps the integrity of the scriptures.

I currently use the *PC Study Bible* program. I highly recommend that you get the latest version of it. Having access to a wealth of information at the click of your mouse saves hours of study time. But if the hard copy is all you have, study with the Holy Spirit, and let Him reveal the truth of His word. Whatever tools you choose, remember to always study them with the Holy Spirit of truth, who wrote the original book.

CHAPTER 30

Fruit of the Holy Spirit
SELF-CONTROL
Part 2

"But the fruit of the Spirit is love, joy, peace, longsuffering, kindness, goodness, faithfulness, gentleness, SELF-CONTROL. Against such there is no law." (Gal. 5:22–23)

Self-control, in our English language, is self-explanatory, and the word used for the lack of self-control is *incontinence*, meaning "a want of self-restraint" or "the lack of self-restraint."

The fruit of *self-control*, or temperance, is the one fruit that I believe most struggle with, to one degree or another. One may have the fruit of self-control in areas like eating while others do not. Those having self-control in their eating may not have self-control in other areas, such as spending money, losing their temper with others, and sexual behaviors just as a few examples.

As we look at one another, we are all too quick to (do what Jesus said <u>not to do</u>)judge with an unrighteous judgment.

THE OPERATIVE

"Do not judge according to appearance, but judge with righteous judgment." (John 7:24)

But what is a righteous judgment? A righteous judgment is judging by knowing all the facts about that which is being judged. Only God has given this privilege to His Son, Jesus, and He said that His judgment was from God, His Father, and not of Himself.

"I can of Myself do nothing. As I hear, I judge; and My judgment is righteous, because I do not seek My own will but the will of the Father who sent Me." (John 5:30)

Since we know that a righteous judgment is based upon our heavenly Father's will (His word) and His knowledge of everything, then what is an unrighteous judgment?

I can sum it up in one short sentence: <u>an unrighteous judgment is making judgments without knowing all the facts.</u>

Have you ever made an unrighteous judgment? I have to add my name to the list because I never know <u>all</u> the facts about anything or anyone. We live our lives in a public forum. We deal with circumstances to either let go of them, get rid of them, start doing them, or just stop them altogether. This is a lifetime process as the Holy Spirit works in the facts of our life!

We must be careful with our judgments as we are only supposed to be "fruit inspectors." Why fruit inspectors? Looking at or judging other's fruit, based upon the <u>scriptures,</u> including all the information that we have covered, we are able to judge where the person(s) is in their spiritual growth. This gives us information regarding them, allowing us to be as accurate as we can be within interacting with them. Let me give you two examples that will explain.

A man or woman who is claiming to be a Christian has their lifestyle viewed by others. As others watch their lives, they can see where they are in their spiritual growth, based upon their actions of either operating out of love or not, peace or not, gentleness or not, meekness or not, long-suffering or not, self-control or not. Others observing them know whether or not they have to share either the milk of the word or the solid meat of the word. This makes the witness of the ones viewing the man or woman in this example more effective for God when they are ministered to.

Dealing with an unsaved person, we believers should have enough knowledge and understanding of God's word and the wisdom to apply it. We should be able to see where they are spiritually coming from and deal with each accordingly. This in no way removes the benefits of the gifts of the Holy Spirit. Remember, He chooses the when, where, and who uses them, making us capable vessels of honor for God's outstretched hands.

"Behold, I have put My words in your mouth. See, I have this day set you over the nations and over the kingdoms, To root out and to pull down, To destroy and to throw down, To build and to plant." (Jer. 1:9–10)

As we learn through the fruit of *self-control* when and what words to speak to both the saved and the unsaved, we will be more effective in our witnessing to others. With the power and discipline of His Spirit's fruit of *self-control*, we <u>will know</u> when to speak words to root out, pull down, or destroy lies by throwing them down by the power of His truth. We <u>will know</u> those who need more planting or building up. Perhaps, our words will provide the water needed or give the sunshine to what has already been planted in the heart by somebody else.

Through the maturing of the fruit of *self-control*, we learn to be less grievous to others and more productive for the kingdom of God. The skill of being led by the Holy Spirit plus listening to His directions through the power of His fruit produced in our life, help us to make a difference in other people's lives.

The last thing that Jabez prayed for was that he would cause no pain. When we use the word of God to minister to others, we do not want to cause any harm or pain. Our goal is to be as productive as we can be as a believer, causing the least amount of trouble possible at any given time to others.

However, in saying this, we shouldn't think we can control what other people believe or think. It is up to them as to whether they respond or react. I enjoy incorporating the prayer of Jabez in my prayer time. Just in case you forget, here it is again:

"And Jabez called on the God of Israel saying, 'Oh, that You would bless me indeed, and enlarge my territory, that Your hand would be with

me, and that You would keep me from evil, that I may not cause pain!' So God granted him what he requested." (1 Chron. 4:10)

One more thought is needed regarding the judgment given to us as fruit inspectors and is the fact that <u>it is the only judgment that is given to us Christians</u>. It *does not* determine whether or not the person's fruit that is being viewed is going to make it to heaven or end up in hell. That judgment is for Jesus alone! We have nothing to do with that judgment. Can you now see how important the fruit of *self-control* is?

Sometimes during this fruit-inspecting endeavor, our eyes can deceive us. For this reason, it's always best to have more than one method to ensure that others are not wrongly labeled, keeping in mind the definition of an unrighteous judgment ("making a judgment not knowing all the facts"). Since we can never know all the facts as Jesus does, we must have other means to verify or confirm what we thought we saw with what was actually really happening.

I have found a way to know where an individual is in life, regardless of whether they are born again or not. While teaching a class, the Holy Spirit gave me some insight into this matter of inspecting fruit. There is <u>no</u> better way for the fruit of the Spirit to come to the forefront of one's life than by direct revelation.

"Either make the tree good and its fruit good, or else make the tree bad and its fruit bad; for a tree is known by its fruit. Brood of vipers! How can you, being evil, speak good things? For out of the abundance of the heart the mouth speaks. A good man out of the good treasure of his heart brings forth good things, and an evil man out of the evil treasure brings forth evil things." (Matt. 12:33–35)

Did you see it? It's been right there in front of us all the time.

<u>"Out of the abundance of the heart, the mouth speaks."</u>

Jesus is not talking about just what is in a man's heart, but what is in his heart in *abundance*. He said that this abundance in the heart always comes out through the mouth through the words that we speak. Funny thing about the words we speak—they are tied directly to each of our destinies as well.

"For by your words you will be justified, and by your words you will be condemned." (Matt. 12:37)

Are you ready for a big dose of *self-control*? We just need to be still and know that He is God. What is in your heart (spirit) in abundance—truth from God's word or misconceptions from the devil? To reveal the abundance of your own heart to yourself, just start paying attention to the words that are coming out of your mouth, especially when you are talking about the things of God and His word.

I would hope that you would see the importance of having the right substance in abundance in your heart. The words you speak tell others more about you than you think, especially if those listening know what to listen and look for. Looking into the following scriptures gives us further insight into the abundance of the heart spoken out of our mouths.

"And since we have the same spirit of faith, according to what is written, 'I believed and therefore I spoke, we also believe and therefore speak.'" (2 Cor. 4:13)

"I believed, therefore I spoke, I am greatly afflicted. I said in my haste, All men are liars." (Ps. 116:10–11)

"For with the heart one believes unto righteousness, and with the mouth confession is made unto salvation." (Romans 10:10)

According to these scriptures, <u>what we believe, we speak.</u> Couple that with what Jesus said, *"For out of the abundance of the heart the mouth speaks,"* what conclusions can we make?

1. What we believe is in our heart (spirit—the part of us that we actually are).
2. What is in our heart in abundance, our mouth speaks.
3. Therefore, when we speak, we are telling others what is in our hearts, not only in abundance, but also the very things that we believe.

As previously mentioned, during a period of time in my life, I ministered at a local prison. I taught this principle to the inmates who attended our weekly meetings. I often told them, "Tell me about yourselves, go ahead and take five minutes, and I will tell you who you are, and that is two minutes too long."

Within the first three minutes after meeting someone for the first time, you can know the type of person they are and where they are coming from, the exceptions being the crafting ones who either know about this principle and lie to throw you off or just fill their conversations with deceits because this is what is in their hearts in abundance. Either way, we can still know what is in their hearts in abundance.

Even if this happens, we believers filled with the Holy Spirit can rely on His gifts, like a word of knowledge or discerning of spirits, to know if they are lying to us or not. There literally is nowhere a person can hide what they believe or who they really are from God, and the believers filled with the Holy Spirit if He chooses a believer to reveal something in another's life.

I encourage you, the next time you meet somebody for the first time or have a conversation with a friend, <u>listen carefully</u>. That which they speak is what is in their hearts in abundance. Listen closely to their words as they tell you what they believe and who they really are.

This method is a precise way of checking the fruit in a person's life. If the Holy Spirit's fruit is growing in there, you will hear it in their words. They will talk more about Jesus and matters about His kingdom than anything else, including themselves.

What we see with our natural eyes might not be what actually is happening in the lives of others either, so we cannot rely totally on what we see. This is why Jesus wants us to check and see if there is any fruit of the Holy Spirit. If there is, their actions and words will reveal it.

I believe there are half-truths that have infiltrated the Church, one of them being "What we do speaks louder than words." While there is some validity to this statement, I believe that Jesus would have us listening to spoken words more than looking at actions. He always placed an emphasis on words. They are seeds to our destiny!

The method of comparing ourselves among one another as the gauge of right and wrong can be unstable, to say the least. Since a righteous judgment is making a judgment knowing *all* the facts about any one particular person or thing, the Holy Spirit reveals his wisdom through the apostle Paul.

"For we dare not class ourselves or compare ourselves with those who commend themselves. But they, measuring themselves by themselves, and comparing themselves among themselves, are not wise." (2 Cor. 10:12)

Isn't this what most people use as a gauge—comparing others by their abilities, accomplishments, positions, wealth, etc? Ask yourself, why is this not considered wise with the Lord? Because as we compare ourselves with others, we are using an unrighteous judgment, and we forget not only where we came from but also how individual we are. This is also when men and women begin to think more highly of themselves than they should. The truth being that our actions are by-products of what we think and speak.

Men and women ultimately end up in heaven or hell because that which they believe, they speak, and therefore, they act upon them as being truth within his or her own eyes.

"For with the heart one believes unto righteousness, and with the mouth confession is made unto salvation." (Rom. 10:10)

This principle, be it in the spiritual or the natural realm, of that which we believe fills our hearts (spirits) in abundance, and we will speak this substance through our mouths, and our words, as Jesus says, will determine our destiny in this life and even our eternity.

The precise way to <u>observe</u> the fruit of the Holy Spirit is to <u>listen</u>—something we must be trained to do, and this takes the fruit of *self-control*. Can you now see the importance of the fruit of *self-control*? It is our supernatural helper for when we open our own mouths too, as the Holy Spirit gives us what to say.

Those of us who love the word of God, study it continually, to the point that the substance contained within our hearts in abundance is Jesus. We can never receive enough of Him. For He will always be that friend who sticks closer than a brother.

"A man that hath friends must shew himself friendly: and there is a friend that sticketh closer than a brother. (Prov. 18:24, KJV)

When these folks begin to speak, the word of God flows like a well of spring water gushing from the pressure of containment from within their hearts, across their tongues, and landing on the ears of those listening. It is a time of refreshing!

We are not called to receive the word of God then shut it up inside us. The word of God cannot be contained. It always goes out and performs that which God sends it to and will never return unto Him void.

"For as the rain comes down, and the snow from heaven, And do not return there, But water the earth, And make it bring forth and bud, That it may give seed to the sower And bread to the eater, So shall My word be that goes forth from My mouth; It shall not return to Me void, But it shall accomplish what I please, And it shall prosper in the thing for which I sent it." (Isa. 55:10–11)

His word always reproduces His Son, Jesus, to all He sends it to, to reach everyone born on the face of the earth, because it is His will that none should perish, but *all* come to repentance.

"But, beloved, do not forget this one thing, that with the Lord one day is as a thousand years, and a thousand years as one day. The Lord is not slack concerning His promise, as some count slackness, but is longsuffering toward us, not willing that any should perish but that all should come to repentance." (2 Peter 3:8–9)

We must always keep in mind that the fruit of the Holy Spirit is the character of Jesus, who is made in the exact image as the Father. When it comes to salvation of man, God is full of love, joy, peace, long-suffering, kindness, goodness, faithfulness, gentleness, and *self-control*.

We should be thankful that He is and that this is His character for the dispensation that we are currently living. Being His child, He keeps us from His wrath that will come upon all unbelievers once His Church is removed from the earth.

His fruit of *self-control* is what currently helps to hold back His wrath until the appointed time. We are in the greatest dispensation or time of mankind. This dispensation of God's grace and mercy are fresh and new every morning, revealing the true character and love of the Father. Great is His faithfulness!

His message today to all who will hear is, "Alley, alley in free."

His grace is sufficient to save everyone who will believe that He sent His only begotten Son, Jesus, full of grace and truth. And for all who call upon His name, they shall be saved—no exceptions!

Are you saved or born again? If not, do you desire to be made a new creature today? Now is the accepted time; today is the day of salvation. While there is still time to hear and while He still may be found, call upon His name, which is above all other names. The only name under the heavens and the earth whereby men might be saved.

Jesus!

That's right—Jesus—call upon Him, and you will find that He is right where you are, waiting for you to decide about the truth that He is Lord of all. Jesus will receive you just as you are even if men will not. Jesus will forgive all your sins and wash you in His eternal blood, blotting out the handwriting of the law, placing your name in the book of life!

Why have the fruit of the Spirit of Jesus growing in you? Because against such, <u>there is no law</u> that negates love, joy, peace, long-suffering, kindness, goodness, faithfulness, gentleness, and *self-control*. And you certainly do not want to live by the law, do you?

"Therefore, just as through one man sin entered the world, and death through sin, and thus death spread to all men, because all sinned—(For until the law sin was in the world, but sin is not imputed when there is no law. Nevertheless death reigned from Adam to Moses, even over those who had not sinned according to the likeness of the transgression of Adam, who is a type of Him who was to come. But the free gift is not like the offense. For if by the one man's offense many died, much more the grace of God and the gift by the grace of the one Man, Jesus Christ, abounded to many. And the gift is not like that which came through the one who sinned. For the judgment which came from one offense resulted in condemnation, but the free gift which came from many offenses resulted in justification. For if by the one man's offense death reigned through the one, much more those who receive abundance of grace and of the gift of

righteousness will reign in life through the One, Jesus Christ.)" (Rom. 5:12–17)

"Christ has redeemed us from the curse of the law, having become a curse for us for it is written, 'Cursed is everyone who hangs on a tree,' that the blessing of Abraham might come upon the Gentiles in Christ Jesus, that we might receive the promise of the Spirit through faith." (Gal. 3:13–14)

Believers who are asking the Lord for the blessing of Abraham to come upon you, Jew or Gentile, guess what is part of that blessing?

The promise of the (Holy) Spirit through faith.

Now, we have come full circle. We are now back where we started, and that is the book of Acts.

"And being assembled together with them, He commanded them not to depart from Jerusalem, but to wait for the Promise of the Father, 'which,' He said, 'you have heard from Me; for John truly baptized with water, but you shall be baptized with the Holy Spirit not many days from now.' Therefore, when they had come together, they asked Him, saying, 'Lord, will You at this time restore the kingdom to Israel?' And He said to them, 'It is not for you to know times or seasons which the Father has put in His own authority. But you shall receive power when the Holy Spirit has come upon you; and you shall be witnesses to Me in Jerusalem, and in all Judea and Samaria, and to the end of the earth.'" (Acts 1:4–8)

Now I ask you, do you think that it took the fruit of *self-control* for the disciples to tarry in the upper room in Jerusalem for ten days? Of course, it did, and it will take *self-control* for you and me to study the word of God, to wait upon His promises, and to live a life pleasing unto God with the faith of Jesus. Everything we do as a believer takes *self-control*. Let this fruit of the Holy Spirit mature within you today!

Salvation, full and free by the grace of God through Jesus, His Son, to all who call upon His name to be saved. The power of the Holy Spirit of the resurrected Christ brings His gifts by promise, which are yes and amen in Christ Jesus, our Lord and Savior.

I truly hope you have been blessed by this teaching as much as I have been blessed in presenting it to you. I pray that Jesus's Holy Spirit will give unto you the substance of His revelation knowledge with understanding and wisdom to apply their contents in your life, in Jesus's name. I further pray that Jesus will baptize each of you with His Holy Spirit of promise as you speak in tongues the wonderful works of God.

"The End is only the Beginning."[12]

---

12. Printed by permission from *Destiny in Time, Observations in the Light* by James J. Hamrick, 2001.

CLOSING THOUGHTS AND SUMMARY

It's been quite an exciting journey, has it not, covering this topic of the baptism of the Holy Spirit, His gifts, and His fruit? If there is only one thing that you, the reader, could take from this book, I pray that it would be this—that the Holy Spirit and His presence, gifts, and fruit are real and are for every believer to experience *today* and to live by His power with the evidence that you are filled with the Holy Spirit as you're speaking in tongues.

This evidence has been presented from the book of Acts, regarding the knowledge and actions of the Holy Spirit. The only reason I can think of concerning why a believer would not accept the baptism of the Holy Spirit and speaking in tongues is because of a lack of knowledge and/or they have been taught wrong and are believing a lie taught as truth—therefore, not really having a need to research past what the church they are attending currently believes and what is being taught by their leadership.

Since you no longer have a lack of knowledge and should be able to see the truth in this matter, what would hinder you from asking Jesus to baptize you with His Holy Spirit as He gives you the evidence of tongues? I know of nothing; do you?

In the Gospels, Jesus sent His disciples out two by two, then on another occasion, a larger number was sent out in His name. They performed miracles to the point that even the demons obeyed them in Jesus's name. Nothing was recorded in the Bible of any of these kinds of miraculous events happening again by them until Acts 2:4 took place when the Holy Spirit came upon them all in the upper room.

The reason being, once Christ was arrested, they ran and hid, and one even denied knowing Him or having anything to do with Him. This reminds me of the peer pressure of today, hindering many from witnessing as their conviction goes right out the door or remains hidden.

Jesus instructed the disciples to wait in Jerusalem. After His resurrection and ascension, He spent forty days with them. However, along the way and during their time of waiting, many turned back. How do I know this? Because in the upper room, out of the five hundred people whom He spent time with and witnessed Jesus's return to heaven, only one hundred and twenty of them remained in the upper room.

While waiting and praying in Jerusalem, the disciples had no clue as to what they would be waiting for. As an act of obedience, they were still terrified that they might be killed next. They did find comfort in gathering in an upper room, behind closed doors, praying for and with one another.

One day turned into two, two into three, and with each day their friends were abandoning them in this spiritual endeavor. The disciples knew the feast of Pentecost was upon them. (This feast of Pentecost occurred exactly fifty days after Jesus's resurrection, which included the forty days Jesus walked with over five hundred believers, teaching them about the wonderful works of God toward man, plus the ten days they tarried and prayed.)

As the time approached for this feast, they were preparing for it as they had done many times before, not realizing the time was at hand for Joel's prophecy to come to pass in their generation.

Pentecost—that is, "fiftieth," found only in the New Testament (Acts 2:1; 20:16; 1 Cor. 16:8). The festival so named is first spoken of in Exodus 23:16 as the feast of harvest and again in Exodus 34:22 as the day of the firstfruits (Num. 28:26). From the sixteenth of the month of Nisan (the second day of the Passover), seven complete weeks—that is, forty-nine days—were to be reckoned, and this feast was held on the fiftieth day.

The manner in which it was to be kept was described in Leviticus 23:15–19 and Numbers 28:27–29. Besides the sacrifices prescribed for the occasion, everyone was to bring to the Lord his "tribute of a free-will offering" (Deut. 16:9–11). The purpose of this feast was to commemorate the completion of the grain harvest. Its distinguishing feature was the offering of two leavened loaves made from the new corn of the completed harvest, which, with two lambs, were waved before the Lord as a thank-you offering.

> *The day of Pentecost is noted in the Christian Church as the day on which the Spirit descended upon the apostles, and on which, under Peter's preaching, so many thousands were converted in Jerusalem (Acts 2).*[13]

However, this feast brought a new experience into their world that was unexpected—a prophecy fulfilled.

This feast took on a whole new dimension. Instead of outwardly celebrating that which was coming, they ended up celebrating inwardly with the *one who came*—Jesus, the resurrected Christ, and His Holy Spirit of truth.

Let's travel back and review with some word pictures, shall we? They gathered in the upper room as they had many days previously and began to pray. Their minds and hearts might have been troubled, fighting fear and all the while trying to focus on the feast. Little did they know, their lives were about to be known not only during their time, but also throughout biblical times and world history as those who turned the world upside down!

The room's atmosphere began to change—lively with a rushing mighty wind. The disciples welcomed this wind without fear as they experienced this before. Perhaps, it was Peter who would proclaim,

---

13. From *Easton's Bible Dictionary*, *PC Study Bible* formatted electronic database. Copyright 2003. Biblesoft Inc. All rights reserved.

"This is the same breath I felt when Jesus breathed upon us and said, 'Receive ye the Holy Spirit.'" As fear and doubt disappeared, the other disciples remembered how it felt to them as well. "You're right, Peter," another proclaimed, "I remember it well."

One hundred and twenty believers were obedient to Jesus's instructions to tarry as the peace of God flooded their hearts and minds through the presence of Jesus's Spirit. All fear, doubt, and unbelief were removed. They yielded themselves to Him while tongues of fire were divided among them.

Jesus entered that room (behind closed doors before), showing them that they were not dreaming or just seeing a vision. During the days that followed, they walked with Him after His resurrection. The reality that He was glorified was now a fact to them. This time, however, He entered the room by the power of His Holy Spirit's wind, not being visible to their natural eyes, but they recognized Him all the same.

The result of His presence in this capacity was a new experience to each of them. God was doing a new thing that had never been experienced to date. This new experience was Jesus keeping His promise to baptize them in the Holy Spirit and fire as well as a prophecy being fulfilled.

"Then I will give them one heart, and I will put a new spirit within them, and take the stony heart out of their flesh, and give them a heart of flesh, that they may walk in My statutes and keep My judgments and do them; and they shall be My people, and I will be their God." (Ezek. 11:19, 20)

They all began to speak for the first time the heavenly language of tongues, speaking directly to their heavenly Father.

Tongues became known that day to the disciples as the evidence given by the Holy Spirit indicating as to when others were filled with the same Holy Spirit—<u>proof of those being filled with the Holy Spirit and fire then and now!</u>

Those living in Jerusalem and entering for the feast of Pentecost filled the city streets with people from every region of the land, celebrating the same way they had done so many times before. However, this feast was different in that they were hearing and experiencing the wonderful works of God for the very first time.

As prophecy was being fulfilled, they heard the words of life, falling upon their ears and piercing deep into their spirit and soul as never before. They were experiencing that which before they had only read about.

Each person representing a language that day was given understanding as to what was being spoken in tongues. Paul later revealed that this was one of the nine gifts of the Holy Spirit, called the interpretation of tongues while the disciples were operating in one of the other gifts known as tongues. These gifts of tongues and interpretation of tongues were now being introduced to the disciples as the Holy Spirit distributed them to those chosen by Him to operate through.

Never before had anyone experienced such boldness and felt so much joy in the presence of God as they did on that day. Some asked, "What does this all mean?" Others were saying, "These men are mad!" Then there were those who said, "They had been drinking wine all night and were all drunk." (This is a good example of tares in the Church, always having an answer as to what they think instead of what the Bible says and always trying to explain away the things of God.)

Peter—who, just fifty-three days earlier, denied knowing Jesus three times before the rooster crowed—now having been filled with the Holy Spirit, had become a different person. He never again would be that cowardly man he displayed earlier. He stood up and boldly answered the crowd—that very same crowd that cried out earlier before to "crucify him, crucify him."

(The scripture says that if they had known about the wonderful works of God through Jesus and what He was about to accomplish for man's salvation, they would not have crucified Him. But it was hidden from them to fulfill the plan and purpose of God to bring salvation to His creation through His Son, Jesus.)[14]

---

14. First Corinthians 2:7, 8.

Peter, a man now without the spirit of fear,[15] proclaimed, "These are not drunk as you suspect but <u>this is that</u> which the Prophet Joel spoke of." Revelation of the Holy Spirit pierced their spirit and soul. The secrets of their hearts were being revealed to them as only God could do. Leading them to repentance, they were baptized not only in water, but also with the Holy Spirit. (The same as the disciples were filled with the Holy Spirit and spoke in tongues in the upper room.)

Over three thousand souls were added to the Church that glorious day. Unlike any other day that Pentecost was celebrated, this one changed the known world, turning it upside down! Those filled with the Holy Spirit and speaking in tongues were proof that day that God Himself, through the works of His Son, made available His presence and power to all who believed and asked for it. The birth of His Church, the bride of His Son, united by God, now became His extended dwelling place.

They would find out later that many times after this original experience, the joy was too much to contain, forcing them to share the goodness of God with all they came in contact with. They would pray often in tongues again and again. Each time they did, they knew and felt that their faith was becoming stronger with boldness.

This experience was happening to others as well as they too were filled with the Holy Spirit and, for the first time, received this baptism by the laying on of hands by others who had already been filled with the Holy Spirit.

In nine different occasions in the book of Acts, believers were filled either for the first time or along with the disciples being filled again and again. This building-up process fulfilled yet another prophet's words, named Jude.[16]

Miracles began to happen by the hands of the apostles after that feast of Pentecost. Many sick people were laid on the streets with just the hope that Peter would walk by, and the shadow of this Spirit-filled man would heal them. Later the act of sending out prayer

---

15. Second Timothy 1:7.
16. Jude 20.

clothes, with which Paul wiped the sweat off his brow, healed many who received them.

Now, not only had salvation come to man, but also deliverance and every other blessing of the abundant life promised by Jesus were attached to this wonderful work of God. Salvation was full and free to all who called upon the name of Jesus to be saved.

Saul, who later became Paul, wrote a large portion of the New Testament. He too was born again and filled with the Holy Spirit. Paul's teachings, though sometimes hard to understand, came to him by revelations from the Holy Spirit. Paul revealed that the scriptures were spiritually discerned, and understanding them took the revelations from the Holy Spirit who inspired them.

Natural man, one that is not born again, cannot receive the spiritual understanding needed for the correct interpretation of God's word. This is why those who do not know God and His Son, Jesus, as Savior should not be giving the Church any kind of instructions or advice. Let me give you an example that many of you will recognize.

Our country was founded upon godly or Christian principles. It was George Washington who was to have said, "It is impossible to rightly govern a nation without God and the Bible." It is disputed as to whether or not George was the person who said these words. But that doesn't matter to me as I agree with the content of the message of the statement, and here is why:

"God reigns over the nations; God sits on His holy throne." (Ps. 47:8)

"Blessed is the nation whose God is the LORD, The people He has chosen as His own inheritance." (Ps. 33:12)

"Happy are the people who are in such a state; Happy are the people whose God is the LORD!" (Ps. 144:15)

George Washington was a wise individual giving us insight into this biblical truth that when adhered to would bring a nation much blessings and happiness. This was what God had in mind when He created this land that we call America, a nation founded on God's word in principles and in deeds.

Israel, in the Old Testament, is considered the earthly example of the Church. Believers in the New Testament are considered the spiritual Church. I see America as the earthly example of heaven—full of blessings and happiness to be pursued. Designed by the Holy Spirit, our government gives each man and woman the right of the pursuit of happiness and to acquire blessings along the way to every right and freedom given to us by God.

A biblical truth is that the earthly example always comes first.[17] America is the light shining bright upon the hill for the world to see. Why else do you think so many foreigners want to come here, and why do so many dictators want to destroy it?

Having said this, let's take a look at a portion of our Constitution of the United States of America. What does it say about a controversial topic of the so-called separation of Church and state? The Constitution reads as follows:

Amendment 1—Freedom of Religion, Press, Expression. Ratified 12/15/1791.

> *Congress shall make no law respecting an establishment of religion, or prohibiting the free exercise thereof; or abridging the freedom of speech, or of the press; or the right of the people peaceably to assemble, and to petition the Government for a redress of grievances.*[18]

We the people are capable of understanding the meaning of these words. They are very clear. Nowhere in any of these words do they imply a separation of Church and state (government).

They do, however, say that the state cannot pass any laws respecting an establishment of religion—that is, to prefer, say, Catholics over Protestants, Baptists over Pentecostals, Methodists over Lutherans, and so on. Including using tax payer dollars to fund any programs within the structure of any of these Churches.

It continues to say that the state cannot prohibit the *free* exercise of religion or do away with the freedom of speech or the right of the press or to publish. It also says we have the right to assemble

---

17. First Corinthians 15:46.
18. The Constitution of the United States of America.

peaceably. The state cannot stop American citizens from petitioning the government for a redress to remedy or set right the things that are wrong through a grievance process.

The <u>only</u> separation outlined in the first amendment of the Constitution of the United States is that of the <u>state staying out of the Church's business.</u> The state <u>cannot</u> tell the Church how to operate or when and where to operate, according to our Constitution. Instead of saying there is a separation of Church and state, the <u>better way</u> to express the contents of our first amendment would be to say there is a <u>separation of state and Church.</u>

The first statement, "separation between Church and state,"—the way it is always quoted today—has the connotation that the Church has no business in the affairs of the government—that is, "Ten Commandments" in courthouses, prayer in our schools, etc. This too is so far from the truth I do not know where to begin.

On the contrary, men and women of faith should be the ones holding public offices. (A quick side note here—I am convinced that if every Christian citizen of the United States of America, of legal age and registered to vote, voted according to biblical principles and morals they believed in the Bible, Christians would always control the outcome of every election. This is what many of those holding offices within the state today, no matter the level of government, fear the most.)

For all of you crying out that you want a godly nation again, this is how it will happen. Sadly, many believers in the Church have bought into the <u>lie</u> that their one little vote does not make any difference. <u>If one vote did not make a difference, then why are hundreds of millions of dollars being spent by the candidates to get elected?</u> They target specific groups, and if one person's vote did not count, then they wouldn't be going after them.

Every vote counts! Based on these scriptures above, found in *Psalms 33, 47, and 144*, do you think that God the Father, Jesus, His Son, or their Holy Spirit are staying away from politics? Politics and politicians are two of the many hosts that Jesus is Lord over.

As the Holy Spirit of truth brought it to the disciple's attention, in the midst of sects and religion steeped deep with the traditions of men and many with lies, He is bringing the truth back to us today, starting with the Church, where judgment must first begin. We need more men and women filled with the Holy Spirit of truth, taking a stand for truth the way the early Church did. God's word still be true and every man a liar!

Also perpetrating upon the people of this world is that there are two things that should never be spoken about with friends or in the public—politics and religion. How conveniently and eloquently packaged is this lie? What better way to cut the feet out from under the majority and to control the minority than this? What better way to keep people from the truth than convincing them not to talk about it in public? <u>We are smarter than this, aren't we?</u>

Again for clarity's sake, separation of state and Church, being the better viewpoint of the first amendment, is actually stating that the state (as well as the federal government) has no right to favor any religion, or start their own religion, like secularism. It further is stating that the state, being a natural governmental structure, has nothing to do with spiritual matters of the Church. God's word agrees and confirms this truth.

You may be wondering, what does all this have to do with the topic of the Holy Spirit? Bear with me as we follow this revelation, and you will see. <u>You will be glad you did.</u>

Separation of the state and Church means that those making the laws (government) cannot and should not stick their noses in the business affairs of the Church. Why? The answer is twofold.

First, our form of government was not designed and established to pick sides. Its design is brilliant and should be giving equal opportunity for every man, woman, and child. But there are those who will always abuse this, unless we the people stop them.

Second, and this is the very reason this topic was brought into this summary and closing thoughts, remember I said, <u>"This is why those who do not know God and His Son, Jesus, as Savior should not be giving the Church any kind of instructions or advice"</u>?

Originally, wisdom and direction by the Holy Spirit were given to our founding fathers. The omnipotent Holy Spirit knew that there was always a chance that this could be reversed from keeping the state out of the affairs of the Church to the state governing and telling the Church what they could and could not do according to the laws that had been passed. Because the affairs of the Church are spiritually discerned, those who are not born again by Spirit and water should not be passing laws that govern the Church in any way! They use a term called *discrimination* to get by with it. God applies His word equally to all, as He is no respecter of persons, and neither should we be.

The Holy Spirit knew there would come a time that there would be many men and women in the American society that would not believe in God. They do not believe in God for various reasons that need not be discussed here. My question to you is, how did this small group of unbelievers convince the whole nation that there is a separation of Church and state?

I will tell you how. We, the Church, allowed it to happen! We did not enforce the word of God upon those who were elected to office. The Church—with the Holy Spirit and His gifts and their operations giving power and boldness—need to take a stand, saying, "This is wrong according to God's word." Many unbelievers have enjoyed free reign to do whatever they believed to be right in their own eyes.

However, we should see a new trend happening due to recent events in America's political arena. Many Americans are wakened for the first time, saved and unsaved, and they are seeing the dangers of not speaking out the truth, according to the Bible, or fair and good morals in a person, respectively. I see Spirit-filled Christian politicians taking office and once again guiding us in paths of righteousness for Jesus's name's sake.

Spiritually speaking, *natural men's* words are shallow when it comes to spiritual matters. When deep calls to deep, there is no understanding, and their knowledge is void of the substance being conveyed to them. The wisdom of the first amendment is to *keep those in government out of the business of the Church*, not the other way around.

Jesus Christ, God's only Son, died on the cross for each American (as well as every person in the world). He rose from the dead and is now seated at the right hand of the Father, sending us another comforter, helper, teacher, and counselor for our benefit. Is the Church taking advantage of His assistance?

The devil is counting on us not knowing about His assistance's availability. Together we can make a difference, causing the devil to lose his hold over this great and mighty country of ours called the United States of America. Once again we can be that light shining on a hill, giving direction and hope to all who see her.

As for such a time as this, men and women filled with the Holy Spirit according to the scriptures, see and hear what the Spirit of the Lord is saying and doing. Not only did the Holy Spirit make it plain and clear for us to understand our Constitution, but He also made provision for it to remain so. What is this provision? The second amendment, of course, which reads as follows:

> *Amendment 2—Right to Bear Arms. Ratified 12/15/1791.*
>
> *A well regulated Militia, being necessary to the security of a free State, the right of the people to keep and bear Arms, shall not be infringed.*

This is self-explanatory as far as I am concerned. This wisdom also came from the Holy Spirit. God forbid that it ever has to be used. This amendment has kept others from invading America since her birth over two hundred and thirty-nine years ago. This speaks nothing about hunting, but everything about our security as a free state, giving the right of (*all*) the people to keep and bear arms (no restrictions on what kind or how many), which shall not be infringed.

We ministers are quick to preach the message on providing for our own, found in the following verse:

"But if anyone does not provide for his own, and especially for those of his household, he has denied the faith and is worse than an unbeliever." (1 Tim. 5:8)

We present our list of provisions that include housing, clothing, and food. What many do not include are the security and well-being of those in our own household from physical harm. Self-defense is excluded in most sermons on this scripture. I believe this verse contains the wisdom of the Holy Spirit used to give us the second amendment to our Constitution of the United States of America.

The Bible, understood by the Holy Spirit who inspired it, should only be handled and regulated by those able and qualified to operate by faith. Those who understand spiritual matters and compare them with spiritual things according to the scriptures found in the Bible are the only leaders who should have the privilege to say the who, what, when, and where of the Church.

These believers who are filled with the Holy Spirit of Jesus are the ones who also need to be running for offices of our government to return this great country on the correct course. The Holy Spirit knows this, and the founding fathers knew it, and now today, because of the Holy Spirit giving us spiritual understanding and revelation to this truth, we, the people, know it.

God bless America!

Relevant for today are the operations of the gifts of the Holy Spirit found in *First Corinthians chapters 12, 13, and 14* and the book of Acts. Paul and Dr. Luke clarified the many questions that the early Church had concerning their operations and the recording of the truths that they lived by as they saw them with their own eyes and gave witness to the same. These mighty and wonderful works of God were normal then and should be normal within the Church today. If they were, we too would be turning the known world of today upside down!

Why are we not seeing and hearing of more miracles like the early Church experienced on a daily basis? Because it's easier to justify that they do not exist than to yield ourselves to something we don't believe is for today. You see, when men are used to perform miracles by the power of Jesus's Holy Spirit, the miracle actually has to take place.

Many behind our pulpits are without the power of the Holy Spirit backing them, simply because they do not believe that He is who Jesus said He was in the Bible. Their intellect and learned mannerism have taken them far in their own endeavors of ministry, but they will find that over the course of time, it will take them only so far.

Also, believers not filled with the Holy Spirit have received salvation brought to them by the Holy Spirit giving them a new spirit and placing Jesus to grow in their hearts. Unless there is a sovereign move of the Lord, there will be no experiences to match what is being read in the scriptures and covered in this book.

The common ground every believer in Christ has today is salvation in Jesus's name according to the scriptures. His death, burial, and resurrection are the common-ground foundation that all Christians have and should, by all means, build upon.[19] But this is only a portion of what is needed to turn the world upside down. This common ground should be considered the definition of "Religion" in our Constitution, Bill of Rights, and our Laws.

Salvation is the foundation we are to build upon; however, we, the Church, must choose <u>not</u> to remain a foundation body only, but let Jesus build His Church with the truths and revelations of the Holy Spirit.[20] It must be a Church like Jesus envisioned, with the gates of hell not prevailing over her.

By allowing the Holy Spirit to mature the Church, we will not remain babes in Christ. If we do, then the members who remain babes will not reach their fullest potentials.

"Till we all come to the unity of the faith and of the knowledge of the Son of God, to a perfect man, to the measure of the stature of the fullness of Christ; that we should no longer be children, tossed to and fro and carried about with every wind of doctrine, by the trickery of men, in the cunning craftiness of deceitful plotting, but, speaking the truth in love<u>, may grow up in all things into Him who is the head</u>—Christ from whom the whole body, joined and knit together by what every joint supplies, according to the <u>effective working</u>* by which every part does its share, causes growth of the body for the edifying of itself in love."[21]

---

19. First Corinthians 3:11.
20. First Corinthians 3:2; Hebrews 5:12–14.
21. Ephesians 4:13–16.

THE OPERATIVE

> *"energeia* (en-erg'-i-ah); from NT:1756; efficiency ("energy"): KJV—operation, strong, (effectual) working" (NT:1753).
> "*energes* (en-er-gace'); active, operative: KJV—effectual, powerful" (NT:1756).

Remember the image of the fire triangle used in explaining the Trinity. Remove any one of these, and the fire of God goes out. Is the Church trying to operate in the spiritual matters without the fire or Spirit of God? In order to have the Holy Spirit fire of God, you must have the following:

1. God the Father
2. Jesus the Son
3. The Holy Spirit

Remove the operations of any one of these and their responsibilities, and the fire of God goes out. I would dare to say, a large portion of the Church is trying to operate in the spiritual realm by removing the Holy Spirit from the equation. <u>This will not work.</u>

Paul believed and spoke that which he believed to be the will of God in this matter.

> *"I wish that you all spoke in tongues."*[22]

I am convinced that Church members being filled with the Holy Spirit as in Acts 2:4 in the beginning is <u>the unity of the faith</u> that pulled both Jew and Gentile together, which Paul referenced when he wrote to the Ephesians.[23] The operation of the Holy Spirit is what is lacking within the Church today and has been lacking for quite some time now.

His operation, or the lack thereof, is the biggest thing that divides the body of Christ along the denominational lines. We agree on the death, burial, and resurrection, with salvation to all who call upon the name of Jesus and His blood cleansing us from our sins. But

---

22. First Corinthians 14:5; 37, 38.
23. Ephesians 4:11–16.

the upper-room experience of the Holy Spirit and tongues is where the severing begins, and the power of God is removed. How long will you and I, believers in Christ, stand for this? Or will we once again stand by sheepishly like the Church has with America? If it does not stop with the Church, there will be no gaining ground whatsoever. So many lives depend on what we do; give us the strength, dear Lord, to go on with *You*!

The natural man *cannot* fully understand the spiritual content of the Bible. They remove the fire and power of God when they try, because of the traditions of men.[24]

It is the unity of the faith in the filling, presence, and operation of the Holy Spirit that will bring forth this last-day Holy Ghost revival. It is built upon the foundational truth of salvation for all men and will show a house unified by the power of the Holy Spirit of the living God and eternal Father, Jesus Christ.

The unbelievers then will see the Church as a single entity—people from all over the world united by the Holy Spirit as the mature body of Christ, speaking the wonderful works of God in the heavenly language that only God the Father understands, which will be a sign unto all those who do not believe.

<u>Oh, what a glorious day and hour to be alive,</u> with the things that are upon our horizon, ready to burst forth like the new-day sun peeking over the trees and mountains, staring at us face-to-face as we see God's amazing grace.

As with those devout men on the day of Pentecost, having a spiritual ear to hear and eye to see what the Spirit of the Lord is saying and doing regarding this coming last-day revival, we who are filled with His Spirit see this event clearly—these last days where many, many souls will come to the truth and call upon Jesus to be saved and to be filled with His Holy Spirit and all that implies according to the scriptures.

As with each powerful move of God, the devil will try to stop it and counterfeit Him by bringing many more tares into the Church with false authority. As time goes on, those who grow and mature

---

24. Mark 7:13.

remain while those who don't begin to fall away, then look up as our redemption draws near unto all who remain on earth as the last trumpet of God will be heard by those having ears to hear what the Spirit is saying and doing, which will bring Jesus back once again.

Jesus is coming back for His living Church. He's not coming back for a Church that is unfamiliar with His presence, but for a Church with each member filled with the presence of Jesus's Holy Spirit. Like the breath of Jesus upon the disciples, revealing the Holy Spirit's wind, we are experiencing the very presence of Jesus Himself through His Holy Spirit filling us and working with us as our helper, comforter, councilor, and teacher. The *wind* of the Holy Spirit is blowing now! Can you hear the rustling within your spirit as He blows the breath of Holy Ghost revival?

His Church is without spot or blemish because of the wonderful works of God provided to her by His Blood. The Spirit, life, and truth contained within the word of God, flows through individuals filled with the Holy Spirit of Jesus as wells of living water poured out upon the earth for its inhabitants to drink from as salvation comes for those who will receive Jesus as their Savior.

As we live and walk in the Spirit of Christ, by being filled with His Holy Spirit and all that this implies, we do this as the representative of God, while releasing His miraculous gifts, producing power flowing through the Church members to a lost and dying world of hurting people.

With the bride of Christ matured, and knowing who she is in Him, both becoming one through the work and operation of His Holy Spirit, a bride prepared and adorned for her husband, ready for Jesus's return, stands strong in the power of His might.

Can you see this vision, or does denominational thinking blind you? Don't continue in a superficial walk, being frustrated and disappointed. Rather, walk in the supernatural power of His Holy Spirit.

Your superficial walk with the Lord will cause you to feel less a child of God than you really are—trying to have self-control when you don't, losing your temper and saying and doing things that are regretted later, and always frustrated by falling short of what you know self-control really is. You continue to try to start your car without a battery. And no matter how many times you try to start it, the car just will not turn over to start!

Seed(s) that lie dormant in some cases and in others may grow slower while in those who are filled with the Holy Spirit mature in a manner not indicative to other believers. This immaturity is why many Christians remain more carnal or fleshly. They walk more in the flesh than they walk in the Spirit. These two are constantly warring against each other, but the Holy Spirit gives power to overcome.

Choose to be led by the Holy Spirit and Him filling you. He started the process in you to become more like Jesus when you became born again. Now, let Him finish it by allowing Jesus to fill you with His Holy Spirit according to the scriptures.

Being filled with the Holy Spirit and speaking in tongues were how He started His Church.

<u>Why would He want us to finish with anything less?</u>

You have already been shown that being filled with the Holy Spirit and speaking in tongues help us to act like God, speak like God, and think like God. The fruit of the Spirit helps us to live like God. This is the ultimate goal that each Christian should be aiming for. Now, knowing all this has been made available to you in this life, and by applying it to your walk of faith, you can be fully equipped and able to be all that you are created to be!

Once a believer realizes these truths of the Holy Spirit growing His fruit inside them and the power they contain, they can release this power as He gives them full access to His fruit.

Instead of trying to produce love, joy, peace, long-suffering, kindness, goodness, faithfulness, gentleness, and self-control, which cannot be produced through the flesh except to certain levels of accomplishments, they find that the Holy Spirit has matured His fruit within them, helping each believer to work it out from the inside to the outside.

"For this reason I bow my knees to the Father of our Lord Jesus Christ, from whom the whole family in heaven and earth is named, that He would grant you, according to the riches of His glory, to be strength-

ened with might through His Spirit in the inner man, that Christ may dwell in your hearts through faith; that you, being rooted and grounded in love, may be able to comprehend with all the saints what is the width and length and depth and height to know the love of Christ which passes knowledge; that you may be filled with all the fullness of God." (Eph. 3:14–19)

After all you have read in this book, is this not what the Holy Spirit is doing by filling us, giving us His supernatural gifts to operate in, and growing His fruit within us? It's all connected together and should never be separated. If separation occurs, it's like the spiritual fire triangle—the fire of God goes out when one or more of the three characteristics of God the Father, Jesus the Son, or His Holy Spirit are removed. It takes the Holy Spirit's fullness, not just part of Him, to mature the Church and each member.

Maturing in the Bible does not mean being in a sinless state of being. We still live in a fleshly body where sin came through, and as long as we do, we will battle it with its lusts and desires until the day that we receive our glorified bodies.

The same tests are true for those who are filled with the Holy Spirit. The battles of the flesh are the same with all its lusts and desires. The difference is, our helper does it from the inside out, and those <u>not</u> filled with the Holy Spirit are attempting to do this from the outside in. You're actually setting yourself up for failure, more often than not, because it just does not work like that.

Our intellect allows us to lean more toward the flesh that is warring constantly with our spirit, trying to keep us in the ways of the flesh. This is the natural man who must die daily! This process is strengthened when you are filled with the Holy Spirit by His presence. I can only imagine the struggle of trying to live a spiritual life without being filled with the Holy Spirit.

We who are filled with the Holy Spirit rely on the continual building ourselves up on our most holy faith each time we pray in the Spirit. Walking and living in the Spirit are not automatic for any of us.

Why does God allow our fleshly bodies to constantly war against our new spirit man? *I believe the reason is that as we mature in the grace and knowledge of Jesus, the changes we go through are examples for others to see. We are "epistles read of men" as Paul explained it.*[25] Our lives allow others to see that we, like them, are still human, but we live with the hope of glory in our hearts, which is Christ Jesus. The more we become like Jesus, the more they will be able to see Him in us.

Believers who are not filled with the Holy Spirit, according to the scriptures, rely mostly on acquired knowledge of how they are supposed to be and act. Some have enough self-control to display restraint in many areas of their lives, giving the essence of a counterfeit fruit of the Holy Spirit.

This, in turn, creates different levels of men's (inclusive) eligibilities that are sought through individual intellect and not individual spirituality and anointing. This has created another problem with the Church today, opening the door for more tares to acquire status and positions like never before in the history of the Church, relying upon their own understanding when spiritual matters are involved.

Notice any similarities with what is happening to the Church and our country at the same time? It's because the two are connected and run parallel to each other. The Lord intends for His Church to be the guiding force that steers our country in the right direction. The infiltration of counterfeit Americans and counterfeit believers is uncanny, is it not? What if the two are related? I believe that they are.

In Proverbs the writer wrote, *"Trust in the LORD with all your heart, And lean not on your own understanding; In all your ways acknowledge Him, And He shall direct your paths. Do not be wise in your own eyes; Fear the LORD and depart from evil. It will be health to your flesh, And strength to your bones."*[26]

Paul wrote to the Church in Corinth by saying the following:

"But God has chosen the foolish things of the world to put to shame the wise, and God has chosen the weak things of the world to put to shame the things which are mighty; and the base things of the world and the things which are despised God has chosen, and the things which are

---

25. Second Corinthians 3:2.
26. Proverbs 3:5–8.

not, to bring to nothing the things that are, that no flesh should glory in His presence.

But of Him you are in Christ Jesus, who became for us wisdom from God—and righteousness and sanctification and redemption—that, as it is written, 'He who glories, let him glory in the LORD.'"[27]

Peter and the other disciples realized these truths, and because of them, those who allowed the Holy Spirit to perform miracles by their hands and with their words answered the questions of those in authority, and those in authority had no choice but to respond by these words.

"Now when they saw the boldness of Peter and John, and perceived that they were uneducated and untrained men, they marveled. And they realized that they had been with Jesus."[28]

Continue reading, and you will find out that those in authority could not deny the notable miracle that was done through the hands of the disciples. So that this would spread no further, <u>they</u> commanded the disciples that they should not speak to anyone again in Jesus's name.

Just as the leaders missed Jesus actually coming as the Messiah, many leaders in today's Church are missing Jesus's Holy Spirit whom He sent to be our helper, comforter, counselor, and teacher of the things of Jesus and the things to come. Because of this blindness, the body is suffering and lacking by not being whole. Jesus's earthly body, the Church whom we believers are, needs to be healed, and I ask this Jesus, in your name. Amen!

Since many of the leaders are missing Jesus's Holy Spirit, all who follow them are also missing out on His power, counsel, help, and comfort and all other benefits of being filled with the Holy Spirit, such as His gifts and the power of His mature fruit.

It was said of these men who were not educated and were untrained that they actually were the ones who turned the world upside down.[29] If educated and trained men and women would get

---

27. First Corinthians 1:27–31.
28. Acts 4:13.
29. Acts 17:6.

the job done, then these questions beg to be asked: Why is this job not done? Why are these miracles not happening today within the modern Church?

The answer is very simple. The Church is not in harmony, believing and saying the same things, as it was back when the early Church started in the upper room, according to Acts 2:4 and all other scriptures that reference to the baptism or filling of the Holy Spirit, which are recorded in the Bible.

As the early Church was experiencing the baptism of the Holy Spirit, every believer was filled with the Holy Spirit and spoke in tongues. This became the evidence, the validity of being filled with the Holy Spirit throughout that time, as it was on the day of Pentecost.

Today, comparatively speaking, there is only a small percentage in the Church who are filled with the Holy Spirit. It seems that instead of being comfortable with the unity of faith, the Church is more comfortable with the disunity of faith.

Differences cause you to stay in your church building and those who do not believe the way you do to stay in their church building—*isolation*! Is this what is taught in the Bible? I think not. <u>We need one another more than we think!</u>

Believers filled with the Holy Spirit need all the believers who currently are not filled with the Holy Spirit just as much as they need us. We are members in particular as the Bible says about the body of Christ Jesus.[30] I, for one, believe it's time that we all start operating like this is truth! <u>Time for personal agenda in ministry is over!</u>

I believe this book has been written for every believer, whether you are currently filled with the Holy Spirit or not—written for the saved and the unsaved alike and giving you instructions or confirmations that you are either rightly dividing the word of truth, or you are not. There is <u>no</u> middle ground or position when it comes to this. Truth about the Holy Spirit could not be clearer and more precise than we understand it to be today even as they did back in the early Church.

---

30. First Corinthians 12:12–31.

THE OPERATIVE

With scripture interpretations aligned with other scriptures pertaining to the gifts of the Holy Spirit and their operations, along with the divine fruit of the Holy Spirit, there should be no confusion in the matter. If there is still confusion, it must be by choice because God is not the author of confusion.

What does everything that I have covered in this book have to do with being filled with the Holy Spirit and speaking in tongues? What do these things shared here have to do with the Holy Spirit's gifts and fruit? Let me answer both questions with one word:

Everything!

By now we have seen His fingerprint on everything that has to do with mankind. From the very first creature God created, the entire cosmos, and everything within it, the fingerprint of Jesus can be found through His Holy Spirit's presence and actions. Throughout man's history, He has gently kept the will of God intact and is moving it forward.

Within God's will, all the different government structures, all the planets in the entire cosmos, along with the beauty of nature, from the largest mountain to the smallest atom of everything, <u>God is!</u>

Yes, His Son's Holy Spirit created this magnificent planet for us to live in. It contains all the right conditions and plenty of substance for all, throughout man's history, with no lack (removing greed out of the equation, that is.). But there remains only one creation of His that He has planned nothing but <u>GOOD</u> for—His most important creation, <u>man and woman.</u>

"What is man that you should exalt him and place your mind upon him? What is man that he is born of a woman and could be pure and righteous? What is man that you are mindful of him and the son of man that you visited him? What is man Lord that you take notice of him and are mindful of the son of man?"[31]

---

31. Job 7:17; Job 15:14; Psalms 8:4; Psalms 144:3.

You see, my friends, it has everything to do with the Holy Spirit, from the air we breathe to the food we eat. The Holy Spirit is involved in it all. He knows our every thought, and His word is that which discerns the true thoughts and intents of our hearts.

From the establishment of the family structure to the highest level of government, he has molded and shaped each one as easily as He possibly could, with man's will within the equations of life.

There are times in each of our lives that the master's hands are molding and shaping new and afresh the pliable clay of men. Even when one is weary and broken, there is no way He turns away a broken and contrite spirit. He has living water that will turn your hardened dry clay back to a pliable substance, bringing you back to His plan and purpose for your life.

When we reach the point of weariness in well doing and find ourselves brittle and broken from the battles of life, we will find that it is the precious hands of Jesus's Holy Spirit that reaches out to us, saying, "I can do something with this!" With the water of His word, He makes us once again pliable in the master's hands to mold and shape us toward the impressionable image of His Son, Jesus.

Today, with joy and a song ringing in my heart, I believe the Holy Spirit sums things up for this book as He reminded me of this song by having it play within my spirit as I awakened on this good day. I believe that it does just that, and I would like to share it with you now. It goes like this:

> Something beautiful, something good,
> All my confusion, He understood.
> All I had to offer Him was brokenness and strife,
> But He made something beautiful of my life.[32]

After reading this book, all confusion, doubt, and unbelief should disappear concerning the Holy Spirit's baptism. We know where the confusion comes from, and it surely is not coming from Jesus or His Holy Spirit.[33]

---

32. Something Beautiful by Bill Gaither 1971
33. First Corinthians 14:33.

THE OPERATIVE

Confusion comes to the mind because of a lack of knowledge of the truth, giving way to the trickery of the devil, from where all confusion is derived, and he loves to add on to it with fear and doubt.

You now have all the knowledge you need to make an intelligent decision for yourself as to whether or not you are going to believe Jesus, concerning Him sending His Holy Spirit back as the comforter, counselor, helper, and teacher. Do not be unaware of the devil's devices one moment longer. The Holy Spirit is right there with you, right where you are. He is patiently waiting for your permission to place the master's hands upon your spirit, soul, and body to mold you into the sweet image of God's only Son, Jesus Christ, from the inside out.

<u>Now, what do you believe—is it the end or your beginning?</u>
The end?

No—a thousand times *no*! This is just the beginning of the rest of your life with the Holy Spirit of God and Jesus filling you, helping you, comforting you, teaching you, and directing you in the paths that you should go.

"May God Bless You With The Presence Of His Glory, For Jesus Is His Glory!"

WHAT MUST I DO TO BE SAVED?

In the book of Acts chapter 16:30, Paul and Silas found themselves in prison for preaching the *good news* of Jesus Christ. At midnight, Paul and Silas were praying and singing hymns to God, and their fellow prisoners were listening.

Suddenly there was a great earthquake that shook the whole prison, down to the foundation. (The truth always goes to the foundation or the root of the problem.) The head guard woke from his sleep and found the doors wide open. Knowing that he would be killed for this, he took out his sword and was going to kill himself when Paul cried out, *"Do yourself no harm, we are all still here."*

The guard took a light and went into the cell of Paul and Silas. Falling at their feet, he said, *"What must I do to be saved?"* So they said unto him, *"Believe on the Lord Jesus Christ, and you will be saved, you and your household."* The guard took them out of prison and brought them to his house that night.

He took them the same hour of the night and washed their stripes. Then they spoke the word of the Lord to him and to all who were in his house. Immediately he and all his family were baptized. Now when he had brought them to his house, he set food before them, and he rejoiced, having believed in God, along with all those in his house.

1. The first step toward receiving the salvation that Jesus has given to every man, woman, and child is to believe that God sent His only Son, Jesus, to die for our sins.[34]
2. Once you believe in your heart that He did this, then you will call upon the name of Jesus to be saved.[35]
3. You now must recognize that you are born again and have a new spirit that is compatible to house Jesus Christ, our Savior.[36]
4. Since the Holy Spirit was able to convince you of sin, righteousness, and judgment, he has also given you a godly sorrow that brings this repentance or turning away from where you were headed to go in the direction that He now shows unto you. You will never regret this day of your eternal salvation.[37]
5. Recognize that your name is now written in the lamb's book of life.[38]

Please allow me to be the first to congratulate you on becoming a child of God. That's it—you are now born again, qualified to be filled with the Holy Spirit and power according to the scriptures outlined in this book and the Bible. The choice is yours to make yourself.

You now can enjoy the presence of the Holy Spirit of Jesus Christ as He grows inside you. As He works His way to the outside of you, in the many ways available to Him through His Holy Spirit, I am sure that many others will see Him living His life in you as well. As you walk in the Spirit (Spirit in spirit, not hand in hand) with the Holy Spirit of Jesus, you will find more power than you have ever dreamed of—a power for the *goodness* of God and not evil.

---

34. John 3:16, 17.
35. Romans 10:8, 9, and 13.
36. Second Corinthians 5:17.
37. Second Corinthians 7:10.
38. Revelation 3:5; 20:15.

THE OPERATIVE

Enjoy your new birth in Christ, and press on toward the mark of the high calling of our Lord and Savior, Jesus Christ, and eternal heavenly Father.[39]

Can you hear the angels full of joy
in heaven, rejoicing over you coming
to the Lord Jesus today?[40]
They are rejoicing, and so are we!

---

39. Philippians 3:14.
40. Luke 15:7.

ABOUT THE AUTHOR

James J. Hamrick has been a student of God's word for the last thirty-seven years, since his born-again experience and being filled with the Holy Spirit of Jesus. He has had the privilege of being taught by some of the world's leading preachers and evangelists. However, the teacher he relies most upon is the Holy Spirit of Jesus Christ.

As an international guest speaker, he has ministered in several countries, like Brazil, Cuba, Mexico, and Thailand, to name a few. Conducting revival meetings throughout the USA, he has ministered within many denominational churches, which includes but not limited to Assemblies of God, Baptist, Foursquare, and United Methodist. True Holy Ghost revival in the Church and the world has always been his greatest desire and prayer.

He was educated at Fairmont State College, currently Fairmont State University, and Berean Bible College and, in 1996, became an ordained minister with the United Christian Church and Ministerial Association. In 1991, James founded Catch the Vision Ministries, whose vision is contained in *Ephesians 4:11–16*.

He is married to his wife, Rosalyn, of forty-four years, having three sons and five grandchildren. The Operative is his third book, and his deepest desire is that the readers come away with a greater understanding of Jesus's Holy Spirit, sent back to His body, the Church, which each believer is a member of. He believes that there is no better teacher, comforter, counselor, or helper available to mankind than the Spirit of Jesus Christ.